BECOMING A WOMAN OF LETTERS

BECOMING
A WOMAN OF LETTERS

※ Myths of Authorship and Facts of the Victorian Market ※

LINDA H. PETERSON

PRINCETON UNIVERSITY PRESS

Princeton and Oxford

COPYRIGHT 2009 © BY PRINCETON UNIVERSITY
PRESS

Published by Princeton University Press, 41 William Street,
Princeton, New Jersey 08540

In the United Kingdom: Princeton University Press, 6 Oxford Street,
Woodstock, Oxfordshire OX20 1TW

Library of Congress Cataloging-in-Publication Data

Peterson, Linda H.
   Becoming a woman of letters : myths of authorship and facts
of the Victorian market / Linda H. Peterson.
   p. cm.
   Includes bibliographical references and index.
   ISBN 978-0-691-14017-9 (cl : alk. paper)   1. English literature—
Women authors—History and criticism.   2. Women and
literature—Great Britain—History—19th century.   3. Authors and
publishers—Great Britain—History—19th century.   4. Literature
publishing—Economic aspects—Great Britain—History—19th
century.   5. English literature—19th century—History and
criticism.   6. Authorship—Economic aspects—Great Britain.
7. Books and reading—Great Britain—History—19th century.
8. Literature and society—Great Britain—History—19th century.
9. Printing—Great Britain—History—19th century.   I. Title.

   PR468.W6P46 2009
   820.9'928709034—dc22   2008036302

British Library Cataloging-in-Publication Data is available

This book has been composed in Adobe Caslon

Printed on acid-free paper. ∞

press.princeton.edu

Printed in the United States of America

1 3 5 7 9 10 8 6 4 2

For my sisters

Deborah, Carla, and Kristy

❧ CONTENTS ❧

Contents

❧ LIST OF ILLUSTRATIONS ❧

❧ ACKNOWLEDGMENTS ❧

During the decade in which this book was written, I have relied on the expert knowledge, advice, and encouragement of many friends and fellow scholars. Among those who got me started are Linda Hughes and Janice Carlisle, who recommended me for a month-long fellowship at the Harry Ransom Humanities Research Center at the University of Texas, and Shelley Fisher Fishkin, who insisted that I leave New Haven for a term fellowship at Clare Hall, Cambridge. I thank these friends and academic institutions for their early support, as well as my home institution, Yale University, for granting me sabbatical leaves to begin and complete this book.

Among colleagues in New Haven who responded to early versions, partial chapters, and imperfect arguments are Ruth Bernard Yeazell, Alexander Welsh, Claude Rawson, Stefanie Markovits, Jill Campbell, and Leslie Brisman. Fellow Victorianists in the United States, United Kingdom, and Canada helped me shape this project, and though they are too numerous to list and some lost to memory, I wish especially to thank Isobel Armstrong, Alison Booth, Deirdre d'Albertis, Alexis Easley, Maria Frawley, Lis Jay, Mark Samuels Lasner, Deborah Logan, Andrew Maunder, Sally Mitchell, Valerie Sanders, Joanne Shattock, Margaret Stetz, Don Ulin, and the two anonymous readers of my book manuscript.

The research for this project took me to many libraries and archives. I happily testify to the fact that there is nothing like an able librarian to help a scholar find essential materials. In this category are Kate Perry at Girton College, Cambridge; Caroline Kelly, assistant keeper, Manuscripts and Special Collections, at the University of Nottingham; Lori Misura, reference librarian, and curators Angus Trumble, Gillian Forrester, and Elizabeth Fairman at the Yale Center for British Art; in the Yale University Library Larry Martins at Seeley Mudd, Todd Gilman and Susanne Roberts at Sterling Memorial, and Stephen Jones and the entire team at the Beinecke

Rare Book and Manuscript Library. Not a librarian, but a knowledgeable literary executor and generous host, Oliver Hawkins gave invaluable assistance in the Meynell family library, Greatham, West Sussex. For permission to quote from letters and manuscripts, I thank Oliver Hawkins and the Meynell family; the Mistress and Fellows of Girton College, Cambridge; the Harry Ransom Humanities Research Center, the University of Texas; and Manuscripts and Special Collections, the University of Nottingham.

Without the response of listeners and like-minded scholars, this book would have lacked a sense of audience. For invitations to present papers at scholarly conferences, I thank the many organizers of RSVP (Research Society for Victorian Periodicals), BWWC (eighteenth- and nineteenth-century British Women Writers Conference), and NAVSA (North American Victorian Studies Association). In the United Kingdom, especially important were Marian Thain and Ana Vadillo, organizers of the "Women's Poetry and the Fin de Siècle" conference at the University of London; Margaret Beetham and Ann Heilmann, organizers of the "Feminist Forerunners" conference at Manchester Metropolitan University; Margaret Beetham and Alan Shelston, hosts of a conference titled "Elizabeth Gaskell and Manchester" at Manchester Metropolitan University; and Cora Kaplan and Ella Dzelzainis, organizers of the "Harriet Martineau: Subjects and Subjectivities" conference at the University of London.

For permission to reprint revised segments of articles that emerged from these conferences—ranging from several sentences to several pages—I thank the following journals: *Nineteenth Century Literature* for "From French Revolution to English Reform: Hannah More, Harriet Martineau, and the 'Little Book,'" 60, no. 4 (March 2006), 409–50; *Media History* for "The Role of Periodicals in the (Re)Making of Mary Cholmondeley as New Woman Writer," 7 (2001), 37–44; *Prose Studies* for "Collaborative Life Writing as Ideology: The Auto/biographies of Mary Howitt and Her Family," 26 (2003), 176–95; *Victorian Literature and Culture* for "Alice Meynell's *Preludes*, or Preludes to What Future Poetry?" 34, no. 2 (2006), 405–26; *Victorian Periodicals Review* for "Mother-Daughter Productions: Mary and Anna Mary Howitt in *Howitt's Journal, Household Words*, and other Mid-Victorian Periodicals," 31, no. 1 (Spring 1998), 31–54; and *Women's Writing* for "(Re)-Inventing Authorship: Harriet Martineau in the Literary Marketplace of the 1820's," 9 (2002), 237–50 and "Charlotte Riddell's *A Struggle for Fame*: Myths of Authorship, Facts of the Market," 11 (2004), 99–115. Thanks are also due to Cambridge University Press for permission to include a brief discussion of women's professionalism first published in *The Cambridge Companion to Elizabeth Gaskell*, edited by Jill Matus, and to Pickering and Chatto for reuse of both ideas and expression from my introduction to *The Life of Charlotte Brontë* in *The Works of Elizabeth Gaskell*, edited by Joanne Shattock.

Special thanks to Hanne Winarsky, my editor at Princeton University Press, for encouraging this project and providing valuable suggestions about its shape; to Ellen Foos and Beth Clevenger, my production editors, for smooth sailing between submission and publication; and to Jenn Backer for excellent copyediting.

Spouses and partners tend to be placed at the end of the acknowledgments—perhaps on the principle of saving the best for last. My spouse, Fred Strebeigh, is unquestionably the best. It has been a secret pleasure to write a book on nineteenth-century women's entry into the profession of letters while he has been writing a book, *Equal: Women Reshape American Law*, on twentieth-century women's breakthroughs in the profession of law. Both of our histories testify, I hope, to the achievements of women before us and around us.

※ BECOMING A WOMAN OF LETTERS ※

INTRODUCTION

It has become common to refer to eighteenth- and nineteenth-century women writers as "professional" in their literary lives—whether Aphra Behn supporting herself solely by her pen, Fanny Burney identifying with the professional Streatham circle rather than the more amateur Bluestockings, Jane Austen negotiating the publication terms of her novels with John Murray, or Charlotte Brontë buying *The Author's Printing and Publishing Assistant* (1839) to inform herself on matters of paper, typeface, and layout before publishing the *Poems* (1847) of Acton, Currer, and Ellis Bell.[1] These women were professional in a modern sense: they show an interest in making money, dealing with publishers in a business-like way, actively pursuing a literary career, and achieving both profit and popularity in the literary marketplace. Yet whether authorship was or, indeed, should be considered a profession—equal to that of law or medicine, the military or the clergy—was a hotly debated question in the nineteenth century. In the early decades, the profession of authorship, for both men and women writers, was neither assumed nor assured. Looking back in 1888 on the previous fifty years, Walter Besant may have declared, in celebration of the progress of the profession of letters, "There has been a great upward movement of the professional class,"[2] but his was a retrospective glance.

For one thing, early in the century it was not clear that financial remuneration for literary work was substantial or stable enough to warrant the claim that authorship qualified as a "profession." As Lee Erickson has argued in *The Economy of Literary Form*, only with the rise of periodicals in the 1820s and 1830s could authors count on substantial fees for their literary work: 20, 30, and even 40 guineas per sheet (a guinea being a professional fee of a pound plus a shilling, a sheet equaling 16 pages), with payments of £100 or more per article to famous authors and annual salaries of £500, £600, or more for editors. With these payments, "young men seeking their fortune in

London and Edinburgh soon could afford to become professional journalists and could make enough money to live as gentlemen"[3]—and this financial basis propelled the development of authorship as a profession. Yet being able to "live as gentlemen" (or gentlewomen) did not assure the *status* of a middle-class professional: beyond economics lay linguistic, social, and intellectual distinctions.

Nineteenth-century linguistic usage distinguished between a profession and a trade, the former "a vocation in which a professed knowledge of some department of learning or science" is applied "to the affairs of others," the latter a business that manufactures or sells some object or commodity.[4] Many nineteenth-century writers, men and women alike, feared the taint of trade because they sold manuscripts to publishers and thus, perhaps, dealt in commodities: books, pamphlets, articles. Most handled this nicety of usage by referring to authorship as a "profession" and to publishing or bookselling as "the trade."[5] During the campaign for a reformed copyright act in the 1830s and 1840s, as Catherine Seville has shown, authors instigated a parallel distinction between the "work" and the "book"—the work itself being the subject of copyright, the book in which it was contained being the "commodity" that the printer produced and the publisher sold.[6] But the ambiguity of literary work—whether authors were offering knowledge to their readership or selling commodities to publishers—often gave authors pause. Their insistent distinction between the "profession" and the "trade" had less to do with money per se (for publishers were often fabulously wealthy, while authors earned little more than modest middle-class incomes) than with a conception of the author as, in Wordsworth's phrase, "a man speaking to men."[7] Among themselves, writers made further distinctions by separating "authors" from "hacks," the former writing out of superior knowledge, native genius, or achieved literary talent, the latter merely producing copy for the press. In "The Hero as Man of Letters," Carlyle went even further when, quoting Fichte, he labeled the false literary man a "Bungler, *Stümper*."[8] As the *OED* more soberly notes, a professional designates someone "engaged in one of the learned or skilled professions, or in a calling considered socially superior to a trade or handicraft."[9]

Underlying such distinctions was an uncertainty about whether authors might legitimately claim membership in a "profession of letters." This phrase, which increasingly came into use as authors gained confidence in their chosen work and found they could earn sufficient income to maintain a middle-class life, typically cited as £300 per year, implied a social achievement that was debatable even at mid-century. Male writers we today would call "professional," without giving the label a second thought, came down on both sides of the question—with G. H. Lewes asserting in *Fraser's Magazine* (1847) that "literature has become a profession," offering "a means of subsistence almost as certain as the bar or the church," and William Jerdan, for many years editor of the *Literary Gazette* and a man who had garnered an income well in excess of Lewes's requisite £300 per annum, countering in his *Autobiography* (1852–53) that such was not the case.[10] For Jerdan, literature lacked the structure of rewards, prizes, and public recognition that marked the learned professions—an insight anticipating criteria that modern sociologists use to distinguish professions from other working groups: the existence of entrance requirements, an organization to represent members' interests and set standards for their work, a hierarchy or developmental sequence that includes awards and prizes for high achievement, an economic monopoly in the field, and the ability of members to set their own fees.[11]

In considering these questions, authors debated whether writing should be pursued in the leisure hours after fulfilling the obligations of a traditional, learned profession (or, in the case of women, domestic duties) or whether it should be a full-time occupation. The phrase "man of letters" looks back to an earlier era when a gentleman could pursue his study, reading, and writing in leisure hours. In the eighteenth century and at the start of the nineteenth, a man of letters was simply a scholar, a man of learning—as Walter Scott suggested when he called Lord Minto "a man of letters, a poet and a native of Teviotdale."[12] For Scott, the designation "man of letters" was distinct from that of "professional author." Indeed, it was Scott who determined to rely on his legal training for his livelihood and quipped that literature should be a staff and not a crutch.[13] Not until late in the nineteenth century, with the instigation in 1878 of John Morley's series, *English Men of Letters*, did the phrase become nearly synonymous with the concept of a professional author (what we now call a "public intellectual") and widely used as an honorific for a writer who had achieved literary distinction as well as financial success. Even Morley wondered, in his *Recollections* (1917), whether literary pursuits might be better achieved "in two hours after a busy day" rather than by working full-time as a writer.[14]

Professional women of letters emerged, as a group, simultaneously with their male counterparts during the nineteenth century. Although Norma Clarke has argued, in *The Rise and Fall of the Woman of Letters*, that the woman of letters is an eighteenth-century phenomenon, made possible by the firm status of patrician culture and the formation of elite social circles like the Bluestockings, she is in fact aligning the woman of letters with an older usage: the humanist sense of "letters" as polite "literature and scholarship."[15] The "fall" in Clarke's title reflects her view that, by the nineteenth century, with "improved educational facilities, a vastly expanded commercial press, and the reading and buying public that sustained it," the older, patrician culture of letters had declined and the status of women writers fell with it.[16] This book challenges the historical arc of "rise and fall." I argue that the "vastly expanded commercial press" made possible the modern man and woman of letters, and trace the ongoing, if not always smooth, development of women's professional authorship during the nineteenth century. I explore the question of status not only in terms of women as a group but as a recurring concern that all authors, male and female alike, faced in the Victorian literary field and that women authors negotiated individually—sometimes successfully, sometimes not. In emphasizing the differences among literary careers, my project extends the work of Betty A. Schellenberg in *The Professionalization of Women Writers in Eighteenth-Century Britain*, who argues that women constructed their authorial identities self-consciously and diversely, from Sarah Scott's steadfast refusal to acknowledge a literary career, to Sarah Fielding's "republic of letters" model of authorship, to Charlotte Lennox's wholly professional approach, "more prescient of the future of authorship."[17] That "future of authorship," the flowering of literary professionalism, lay in the nineteenth century with the burgeoning of print culture and the opening of new genres for women writers: the essay, the literary review, the periodical column, the biographical portrait and historical sketch, the travelogue, and the serialized tale.[18] Women writers were no longer confined to fiction and drama, the authors (and subjects) of "nobody's story," as Catherine Gallagher has titled her study of eighteenth-century women in the literary marketplace.[19] With these new periodical genres emerged the modern woman of letters and her new self-constructions.

The phrase "woman of letters" is, tellingly, a Victorian invention. It first appears on the title page of Julia Kavanagh's *English Women of Letters: Biographical Sketches* (1863), a work that creates a genealogy for Victorian women authors by tracing an eighteenth-century heritage in Aphra Behn, Sarah Fielding, Fanny Burney, Charlotte Smith, Ann Radcliff, Jane Austen, Amelia Opie, and Lady Morgan—that is, by referring to the writers we highlight today in the history of women's literary professionalism.[20] But the phrase "woman of letters" does not surface regularly in book or periodical writing until the 1880s when James Payn, a journalist, essayist, and editor for the *Fortnightly Review* and the *Cornhill Magazine*, uses it offhandedly in a humorous sketch titled "Fraudulent Guests" (1883). Payn refers to seeking "an introduction to a well-known woman of letters in London" as a "very young man," and being told by a mutual friend, "she will have nothing to do with you. She says she knows a great deal too many people already."[21] Payn's reference to his youth dates this incident to the 1850s (born in 1830, he was contributing to *Household Words* by the mid-1850s and editing *Chamber's Journal* by 1859), so perhaps the phrase was in play as early as the 1850s. It appears regularly, however, only after Morley initiated the *Men of Letters* series in the late 1870s. No doubt, the honorific concept of a "woman of letters" was present when Morley commissioned Margaret Oliphant early in the 1880s to write a volume on Richard Sheridan (on the principle that it takes one to know one).[22] The woman of letters was fully established when George Meredith designated Alice Meynell as a great "Englishwoman of letters" in an 1896 article in the *National Review* and when the *Men of Letters* series added volumes on George Eliot, Fanny Burney, and Maria Edgeworth after the turn of the century.[23] But whether or not in common usage, as this book argues, women of letters flourished throughout the century, as women increasingly conceived of their literary careers and constructed their public personae in a professional mode.[24]

The debates of nineteenth-century authors over the status of the literary life they had chosen reveal the terms, trials, and (sometimes) triumphs of authorship as a profession. Women figured significantly in these debates—occasionally (alas, all too predictably) as amateur counterparts against which male authors defined their professional careers, more often as participants in public discourses aiding the cause of professionalization, always as co-laborers in an emerging field of artistic and cultural endeavor. It has been common, following in the wake of Mary Poovey's "The Man-of-Letters as Hero: *David Copperfield* and the Professional Writer," to assume that women in the domestic sphere provided a "stabilizing and mobilizing" function in legitimating the professional male author.[25] While this may be an accurate account of Dickens's strategy, it represents only one perspective on the professionalization of authorship, one moment in a process that unfurled during the long nineteenth century. A full history of authorship in Victorian England, one that takes into account women writers and their work, has yet to be written.[26] As a contribution to this much-needed history, chapter 1 examines the discourses of professional authorship—whether authorship was or was not a profession, what aspects of literary work made it a profession, what lacks or drawbacks authors needed to remedy—at three pivotal moments: at its emergence in the 1830s, a decade associated with the rise of periodicals and adequate payment for writers' work; at mid-century, when the claims for professional status were forcefully articulated in the drive for copyright and when men and women authors sought to define their contributions to the nation; and in the 1880s and 1890s, when Walter Besant (re)asserted in the *Author*, the journal he edited for the newly established Society of Authors, and in his guidebook for aspiring writers, *The Pen and the Book*, the claim that Lewes had made fifty years earlier: "that a respectable man [or woman] of letters may command an income and a position quite equal to those of the average lawyer or doctor."[27] In this historical survey, my emphasis falls on periodicals, for that is where the debates about authorship were aired, where the discourses evolved, and where writers established their literary reputations. It was in periodicals that the modern conception of the man and woman of letters emerged: the writer whose critical thinking about culture and society rose above the commonplace and offered what Coventry Patmore (in a review of Alice Meynell's essays) called "classical" achievement, writing that embodied "new thought of general and permanent significance in perfect language, and bearing, in every sentence, the hall-mark of genius."[28]

The multifaceted question of how Victorian women entered the profession of letters—how they articulated their role as authors, negotiated the material conditions of authorship, and constructed myths of the woman author, often against the material realities—is pursued in the six case studies of this book. I focus on issues that women writers considered privately and debated publicly with their female contemporaries: whether they should adopt masculine patterns of work or formulate feminine (or feminist) models of maternal, familial, or collaborative literary production; whether they should participate in debates over copyright, royalties, and other material aspects of authorship or restrict their public statements to intellectual and imaginative concerns that reflected a more high-minded, idealistic view of literary labor; and how they might achieve economic success without sacrificing the equally important need for critical esteem and lasting literary status. In the nineteenth-century literary field, the final cluster—economic success, critical esteem, and lasting reputation—determined whether a woman writer might be designated a "woman of letters." The myths of authorship she presented publicly and her savvy negotiations in the literary market were essential to winning that honorific designation.

For the case studies, I have chosen six women of letters whose careers reveal new possibilities for the professional woman author and whose commentaries on their literary lives reveal the obstacles they faced and the strategies by which they succeeded (partially, if not wholly). All professionally innovative, these women took different approaches to authorship—approaches determined in part by their historical moment, in part thrust upon them by the demands of the marketplace, in part adopted as expressions of highly personal values and contingencies. The case studies do not, as one of my readers noted, "round up the usual suspects" (though canonical figures appear frequently in this book); rather, I have focused on women whose literary innovations and public self-constructions are pivotal in the history of authorship. I alternate women whose lives were marked by professional success and literary esteem with lesser-known writers, famous in their day, uncanonical now, but nonetheless representative of important models of nineteenth-century authorship. It might be tempting to divide these women into "winners" and "losers," but I wish to resist the "great woman" approach to literary history (except when the writer herself invokes it). The case studies are arranged in pairs to suggest the different choices made by women authors of roughly the same generation and to explore the effects of their choices in the formation of literary careers, their own and those of their successors.

I begin with Harriet Martineau, the most prominent woman of letters of the 1830s, perhaps of the century. Martineau viewed herself as a "professional son" and "citizen of the world," entering the literary field with the same career aspirations and work practices as her male counterparts. In her *Autobiography* and letters, Martineau presents herself as a "solitary young authoress" with "no pioneer in her literary path," and constructs her life story along the lines of the heroic man of letters popularized by Thomas Carlyle in

On Heroes, Hero-Worship, and the Heroic in History (1841). Yet, paradoxically, Martineau began her career in a recognizably feminine mode: writing devotional literature, producing tales for a publisher of didactic tracts, and contributing essays on religious and moral subjects to the Unitarian *Monthly Repository*. Martineau's (re)invention of her career as public commentator on the great political and social issues of her day, from these apparently feminine origins, is the focus of chapter 2, as I analyze the means and motives for this transformation from her early career in the 1820s to the publication of her wildly successful *Illustrations of Political Economy* (1832–34), which made her name and fame as a woman of letters and established a model adopted by many subsequent women of letters, most notably George Eliot, Frances Power Cobbe, and Eliza Lynn Linton.

In contrast, Mary Howitt, another seminal figure of the 1830s, embraced a model of literary production as an extension of a woman's domestic duties and social responsibilities. Howitt collaborated with family members—her husband, William, her sisters, Anna and Emma, and her daughter Anna Mary—in a distinctive early Victorian form of a "family business," treating her work as part of a domestic economy and advocating communal labor and achievement. Yet Howitt often registers a tension between domestic collaboration and individual aspiration. Chapter 3 explores that tension, arguing that she was in fact most successful (financially, aesthetically, and professionally) when working in a collaborative mode. Howitt transmitted her ideology of collaborative work to the first generation of British feminists, the writers, painters, and social reformers of the Langham Place Group who envisioned an artistic "sisterhood," adapted her ideology of work, and argued for the superior achievement of collaborative artistic production. I trace Howitt's legacy in the work of Barbara Leigh Smith, Bessie Rayner Parkes, and especially her daughter Anna Mary Howitt, whose *Sisters in Art* (1852) articulates and transforms her mother's collaborative poetics.

At mid-century many women writers embraced the "parallel streams" model that Elizabeth Gaskell promulgated in *The Life of Charlotte Brontë* (1857), one that separated the woman from the author, the private, domestic self from the public persona and literary creator. One motive in writing the *Life* was to preserve the category of artistic genius for women's authorship, even while demonstrating that literary women could fulfill (and would not abandon) the duties of domestic life. Later women authors found this model powerful and enabling in that *The Life of Charlotte Brontë* locates the origin of literary genius in an ordinary parsonage in an isolated Yorkshire village; shows its subject as an avid reader and scribbling adolescent who, with her sisters, writes romantic tales and secretly publishes a book of poems, even as she labors as a schoolteacher; and traces a meteoric rise to fame with a pseudonymous novel, *Jane Eyre*, and its successors, *Shirley* and *Villette*. This myth of the woman author was far more appealing than the story of a long literary apprenticeship told in Martineau's *Autobiography* (1877) or of hard study, editorial drudgery, and a late novelistic career mapped by John Cross in *George Eliot's Life* (1885). Yet it also proved untenable after mid-century. As Charlotte Riddell demonstrates in her *kunstlerroman A Struggle for Fame* (1883), the Brontëan model was useful for expressing the high aspirations of women authors and countering the common perception that men's literary efforts superseded theirs. But as Riddell's life and work also show, in the commercialized literary market of the 1860s and 1870s, with an ever-increasing split between popular fiction and high art and with the increasing pressure of literary celebrity, the "parallel streams" model proved ineffective for achieving distinction—not to mention impossible to enact. Chapters 4 and 5 discuss this debate over *The Life of Charlotte Brontë* and its myths of female authorship.

Finally, chapters 6 and 7, on Alice Meynell and Mary Cholmondeley, suggest various models of authorship available to the fin-de-siècle woman of letters—some inherited from female predecessors, others suggested by male authors' careers, still others constructed to address specific literary, cultural, and material contexts of the 1880s and 1890s. In large part because of the volatility of the periodical and book market, none could fully assure lasting distinction as a woman of letters. Meynell represents a remarkable case of critical esteem leading to financial reward and secure reputation, whereas Cholmondeley reveals a case of critical success failing to sustain a career. Meynell began as a nature poet and Sapphic poetess, but recognized the limitations of these poetic modes in fin-de-siècle literary culture. Forced by financial necessity to undertake periodical journalism, she served a decade-long apprenticeship in which she mastered the forms of art and book reviewing, critical biography, and the belletristic essay. Chapter 6 analyzes the contexts in which, paradoxically and quite contrarily to common accounts of the nineteenth-century literary field, the essay replaced the poem as the prestigious genre, and Meynell's serial publication, in regular columns written for the *Scots Observer* and *Pall Mall Gazette*, became a means of achieving literary "distinction." De facto, periodical writing led to Meynell's *succès d'estime*. The literary field of the 1890s in which she worked did not operate by the conventional rules—in part because of its new fascination with the essay, in part because of an appetite for small, aesthetically pleasing books, in part because of the opening of the American periodical market—and Meynell's career reveals her careful negotiation of its various demands.

Cholmondeley, in contrast, was unable to achieve lasting distinction as a woman of letters. Her early career reveals a disjunction between aspiration and achievement, between her popular success as a sensational novelist and her desire for critical esteem. Yet, for a moment in the late 1890s, Cholmondeley was able to join popular success with artistic achievement and critical acclaim in *Red Pottage* (1899), her New Woman novel and *kunstlerroman*. In creating Hester Gresley, a "woman of genius" with no trace of the Grub Street hack, Cholmondeley protests against her devaluation in the market after the collapse of the triple-decker novel and reinvents herself as an "advanced" writer in an emerging modern(ist) field of elite art—to great critical acclaim. The loss of regular outlets for her work in fin-de-siècle periodicals and book publishing made it difficult for Cholmondeley to capitalize on her success, as her surviving letters reveal. In this chapter I underscore the new publishing trends and market pressures that made it difficult for late Victorian women of letters to sustain their careers—and that were so different from the conditions that had sustained the work and reputations of their early and mid-Victorian counterparts.

Some readers may miss, in this preview of chapters, the names of notable nineteenth-century women of letters—George Eliot and Margaret Oliphant, Anna Jameson and Vernon Lee, Caroline Norton and Francis Power Cobbe, to cite half a dozen. This is one consequence of a case study approach and a decision to focus on women authors who forged new career patterns at pivotal moments in the history of authorship. But many of these women of letters do in fact appear—whether as collaborators with, inheritors of, or commentators on the authorial innovations of the featured subjects. Anna Jameson, for instance, collaborated with Martineau and Howitt on women's legal rights and contributed a major statement on women's work that influenced Howitt and her circle. George Eliot (then Mary Anne Evans) followed a professional model that Martineau had forged a generation prior, moving from provincial beginnings to periodical apprenticeship to a full-fledged London literary career; indeed, Eliot, who worked as subeditor on the *Westminster Review* when Martineau was a frequent contributor, acknowledged her predecessor as "a trump—the only Englishwoman that possesses thoroughly the art of writing."[29] Oliphant, Eliot's contemporary, adopted the "family business" model of Mary Howitt, moving to London in the 1840s with her new husband, a painter and stained-glass artist, and entering literary circles that included the Howitts, the Halls, and other dual-career couples. An astute observer of the London literary scene and principle reviewer for *Blackwood's Magazine* for nearly fifty years, Oliphant provides important contemporary analyses of women's professional literary careers—as do others like Jameson, Norton, and Parkes, whose contributions figure more briefly in this study.

I have titled this book *Becoming a Woman of Letters* with at least two senses of *becoming* in mind: the entries of individual women into authorship as revealed in the beginning moments of their literary careers, and the development of the woman of letters as a conceptual category during the nineteenth century. Perhaps the present participle suggests a third meaning: the state of always being in process, of always seeking yet never quite achieving secure professional status—a predicament that faces men and women of letters even today.

I have subtitled the book "Myths of Authorship and Facts of the Victorian Market" to suggest a distinction between the models of authorship that writers project in their prose, poetry, or fiction and the material conditions in which women writers produced their work. By "myths," I mean the accounts that "embody and provide an explanation, aetiology, or justification for something" (*OED*)—in this instance, for authorship. In using this term, I do not mean to deflate the self-constructions that Victorian authors, both men and women, articulated for themselves and their reading public. If, as Pierre Bourdieu has suggested, the literary field is "a site of struggles,"[30] its boundaries in particular revealing the terms of the disputes, then authorial self-constructions—models and myths of the author—are as important for understanding the struggles as are the market pressures and possibilities in which they worked.

As this study will reveal, I believe that nineteenth-century women's myths were more enabling than disabling, and that they allowed women writers to claim new territories of endeavor and high achievement for their work. My approach is thus more varied in emphasis than earlier studies of nineteenth-century women's authorship, which tend to stress the limitations and lack of opportunities that women faced or the social norms they transgressed in the act of publishing. Dorothy Mermin's seminal study, *Godiva's Ride: Women of Letters in England, 1830–1880*, emphasizes such transgression, especially the sense of exposure that women writers felt in producing socially useful literature.[31] Yet Lady Godiva was only one of many myths that nineteenth-century women of letters invoked, and not the dominant one. Even in a more balanced account, Mary Poovey's *The Proper Lady and the Woman Writer*, the emphasis falls on the dual consciousness of eighteenth- and early nineteenth-century women who published: "nearly every woman who wrote was able to internalize a self-conception at least temporarily at odds with the norm, . . . and the legacy of this period is a repertoire of the strategies that enabled women either to conceive of themselves in two apparently incompatible ways or to express themselves in a code capable of being read in two ways."[32] It may be that a dual consciousness continued to inform some early Victorian conceptions of the woman author, as in the "parallel streams" model of Gaskell's *Life of Charlotte Brontë* or in Martineau's comment that it was the loss of family fortune and "gentility" that freed her from writing privately and gave her the "liberty to do my own work in my own way."[33] But it is also the case that many women writers—from Mary Howitt in the 1820s to Alice Meynell in the 1870s—suffered from no apparent psychological duality as they embarked on literary careers. Indeed, the archives on which I draw show these women to be astute participants in what Robert Darnton has called the "communications circuit."[34]

As social norms for women changed during the nineteenth century, so too did attitudes toward women's writing, yielding a greater range of possibilities in the profession of letters. Recent biographies of individual women of letters—Elisabeth Jay's *Margaret Oliphant: A Fiction to Herself* (1995), Rosemary Ashton's *George Eliot: A Life* (1996), Judith Johnston's *Anna*

Jameson: Victorian, Feminist, Woman of Letters (1997), Vineta Colby's *Vernon Lee: A Literary Biography* (2003), Sally Mitchell's *Frances Power Cobbe: Victorian Feminist, Journalist, Reformer* (2004), and Linda K. Hughes's *Graham R.: Rosamund Marriott Watson, Woman of Letters* (2005), among others—suggest a steady progress in the professionalization of literary women and a diminishment, if not complete disappearance, of the duality that Poovey and other scholars note for the early decades of the century. By the end of the nineteenth century, a duality—if, indeed, it is legitimate to reduce complexities to binaries—splits not the "proper lady" from the "woman writer" (a socially gendered distinction) but the popular writer from the high-art woman of letters (economic and aesthetic distinctions). But whatever the historically based conceptions of women's authorship might be, it is the interaction of the myths (the articulated desires about what it means to be an author) and the material conditions (the complexities of the marketplace in which authors must labor) that interests me and gives focus to this book.

THE NINETEENTH-CENTURY
PROFESSION OF LETTERS AND
THE WOMAN AUTHOR

The Rise of the Professional Author:
Periodicals and the Literary Field of the 1830s

The early nineteenth century saw the founding of new periodicals and their increasing circulation and cultural importance—the *Edinburgh Review* (founded 1802), *Quarterly Review* (1809), *New Monthly Magazine* (1814), *Literary Gazette* (1817), *Blackwood's Edinburgh Magazine* (1817), *London Magazine* (1820), *London and Westminster Review* (1824), *Athenaeum* (1828), and *Fraser's Magazine* (1830), to name the most prominent. With the rise of periodicals, writers found it possible to support themselves solely by the pen and thus to consider themselves professional authors. As Lee Erickson explains in *The Economy of Literary Form*, "writers were best paid by periodicals between 1815 and 1835, when the reviews and magazines had not yet attracted the competition of a large number of other magazines and had not yet had their circulation undermined by the literary weeklies and newspapers. Young men seeking their fortune in London and Edinburgh soon could afford to become professional journalists and could make enough money to live as gentlemen."[1] Payments of £100 per article to famous writers like Walter Scott and Robert Southey, smaller but still substantial fees to lesser writers, and salaries of £500, £600, or more per annum for editorships of leading periodicals became common—thus providing incomes substantial enough to support the claim that by the 1830s an essayist could "make a gentleman's living" by writing for the periodicals, or by editing one of them.[2]

What of women? Did they seek entry into the literary marketplace in the 1820s and 1830s, take advantage of expanding venues for reviews and essays, and become "authors by profession," to adopt Isaac Disraeli's phrase, or "women of letters," to use a designation that emerged later in the century?[3] Most studies of professional authorship have omitted women from consideration, especially at its inception, assuming that women did not move to the metropolis to pursue literary careers, or that they were largely excluded from periodical writing because of their sex, or that they did not seek (or publicly acknowledge) professional status as it would undermine social respectability.[4] In this discussion of the 1830s I challenge these assumptions by examining the "Gallery of Illustrious Literary Characters" published in *Fraser's Magazine* during this decade. Usually considered the first important attempt to represent the professional author, the *Fraserian* sketches of literary figures introduce contemporary writers to the reading public, show them in exemplary or deflating scenes, and project the ideals and anxieties of the profession of letters. As I shall suggest in analyzing these sketches, it was neither a foregone conclusion that male authors wished to be considered "professional" in the 1830s, when the literary market offered great financial incentives, nor a certainty that women could not, if they wished, join the ranks of their male colleagues and work as professionals. The 1830s show us a "fault line in conceptions of what constitutes a literary life,"[5] to borrow Patrick Leary's metaphor—and the fault line was not drawn simply in terms of gender. Both men and women had access to a literary field that, perhaps for the first time, acknowledged the professional author.

Fraser's Magazine, the "most daringly outspoken organ of the London press,"[6] marks the pivotal moment. In January 1835, *Fraser's* featured an article, with two-plate illustration, on "The Fraserians"—a group of twenty-seven writers it wished to associate with the magazine and celebrate as distinguished or up-and-coming literary figures (see figure 1).[7] Some were active contributors (Thomas Carlyle, Robert Gleig, Francis Mahony, a.k.a. Father Prout, Bryan Procter, a.k.a. Barry Cornwall, and William Maginn, the editor). Others were elderly or dead "patron saints" (Robert Southey, Samuel Taylor Coleridge).[8] Still others were assimilated into the group because their political views were compatible with the magazine's pro-Tory stance, even though they contributed infrequently (John Gibson Lockhart and David Moir of *Blackwood's*; Theodore Hook of the *Quarterly Review*; the antiquarian Sir Egerton Brydges; the scientist Sir David Brewster; and William Jerdan of the *Literary Gazette*). All "Fraserians" were male. This group portrait, along with the sketches of individual authors that *Fraser's* published between 1830 and 1838, heralds the advent of literary professionalism; it provides an early Victorian representation of literary celebrity, exemplary authorship, and the literary professional at work and at his ease. As Judith Fisher has argued, *Fraser's Magazine* intended its "Gallery of Literary Portraits" to do battle with effeminate Regency-style authors and Byronic dandies, and to provide models of "appropriate and inappropriate professionalism." In the 1830s, an era of transition from an aristocratic Regency past, with Byromania still in play, to a Victorian middle-class future, *Fraser's* promulgated a version of the literary professional "as a manly male of the middle classes."[9]

FIGURE I. "The Fraserians," *Fraser's Magazine* II (January 1835), 2–3.
Courtesy of the Yale University Library.

A year later, in its January 1836 issue, *Fraser's Magazine* followed with a one-plate illustration and brief verbal sketch of "Regina's Maids of Honour"—eight leading women authors of the day, worthy also of celebration by *Fraser's* (which referred to itself in print as *Regina's*). (See figure 2.) The ladies are gathered around a table, "every one a lovely she, very busy taking tea, or coffee, as the chance may be," to quote the text that accompanies the illustration.[10] None of these women authors was particularly associated with *Fraser's*, perhaps unsurprisingly given the masculine model of authorship that the magazine projected. Laetitia Landon (L.E.L.) had contributed a poem to the first volume but was identified with the *Literary Gazette*, the *New Monthly Magazine*, and popular annuals; Caroline Norton, also a poet, edited *La Belle Assemblée*; Lady Blessington edited *The Book of Beauty*; Mary Russell Mitford had published her famous sketches, "Our Village," in the *Lady's Magazine* a decade earlier and in the 1830s was editing *Fisher's Drawing Room Scrapbook*; and Mrs. S. C. Hall, Lady Morgan, and Miss Jane Porter were popular novelists identified with Irish and Scottish fiction. That is, these literary women were known for their poetry, fiction,

REGINA'S MAIDS OF HONOUR.

FIGURE 2. "Regina's Maids of Honour," *Fraser's Magazine* 13
(January 1836), 80. Courtesy of the Yale University Library.

and light essays and for editing literary annuals and women's magazines. Like the popular almond-flavored tarts called "maids of honour," they represent dessert, an after-course appreciated for its sweet, light taste.[11] In *Fraser's* view "Regina's maids" occupy positions of honor in the English literary world and serve as a foil to its ideal male author.[12] Only Harriet Martineau, newly famous for her *Illustrations of Political Economy* (1832–34), diverges from the model of the properly feminine woman writer, happy in her domesticity and happy to produce light work appropriate to her gender and sphere. (But note that she is included.) By suggesting a binary between male and female models of literary production, *Fraser's* portrait of "Regina's maids" helps stabilize the identity of literary men who were entering a career that included too many men who modeled themselves on the effeminate dandy or assumed otherwise unmanly public personae.

Or so the standard interpretation suggests. Yet, for all the evident binarism of the *Fraser's* portraits, the professionalism of the male authors in the group portrait, even in many individual portraits, is less than evident. Much has been made of the fact that the women authors sit at tea in a domestic space—some holding teacups, one reading to another from a book, all engaged in conversation, "with volant tongue and chatty cheer, welcoming in, by prattle good, or witty phrase, or comment shrewd, the opening of the gay new year."[13] If we look again, however, we will see that the male authors are similarly depicted at their ease "at a round table," drinking wine, toasting the New Year, sharing tales or literary intelligence, and listening to a eulogy by their leader, William Maginn, for the recently deceased Edward Irving. The only book visible is in the hands of James Fraser, the publisher, and it is held behind his back.[14] The "literature" incorporated into the article, offered by various members of the circle, consists of tributes to absent colleagues or, more frequently, drinking songs that entertain the group and satirize its enemies. A manuscript presented in absentia by Sir David Brewster, "On the Universality of Goethe's Genius," is, in fact, a debunking of the great German poet—to which Maginn responds with the comment, "We are wasting time sadly. . . . I say, give me a squib or a Saying and Doing of [Theodore] Hook's, in preference to any thing old Johann Wolfgang ever daubed paper with."[15] Overall, the group portrait of the male authors valorizes the clubability of the Fraserians, just as its counterpart does the sociability of the women, and minimizes any depiction of literary labor. What is at stake in this portrait of the author is his gentlemanly status, genial wit, and camaraderie.

As a representation of the modern man of letters, moreover, the Fraserian portrait is ambiguous as to whether literature is in fact a profession—or should be treated as such. Patrick Leary has demonstrated that well over half of the contributors to *Fraser's* "derived their living from nonliterary sources," including the traditional professions of law, medicine, the military, and the clergy; these writers represent one early nineteenth-century model of a literary life, "that of a professional or bureaucrat whose duties leave sufficient time for writing and whose position has at least the potential of preserving him from the tangible consequences of literary failure."[16] Notably, in the verbal sketch that accompanies the portrait, the learned professions receive a place of prominence. The author Oliver Yorke (the pseudonym under which Maginn edited and contributed) first identifies the "three reverend divines" who sit to his left: Robert Gleig, Francis Mahony (Father Prout), and Edward Irving. Maginn frequently engages in conversation with the barrister Bryan Procter (the poet "Barry Cornwall"), mentions the absent Sir David Brewster (trained as a clergyman but knighted for his scientific discoveries), refers to the Scottish surgeons David Moir and Robert Macnish, and includes a military man with minimal literary credentials, Sergeant Francis Murphy. Given the prominence of the traditional professions, we might read the Fraserian portrait either as a representation of literary men joining their ranks or, paradoxically, as an acknowledgment that literature had not quite attained the status of a profession able to sustain a man of middle-class or higher rank. Crofton Croker, a contributor who supported himself through an appointment in the Admiralty Office, voices a doubt when he observes, "We literary folks are always thinking that we are the finest fellows in the world, and have therefore the right to look down upon the rest of mankind; whereas, if the truth was known, all the rest of mankind look down most damnably upon us."[17]

Indeed, the fact that active Fraserians are missing from the portrait—its subeditor John Abraham Heraud, the newspaperman George Henry Francis, the writer Thomas Powell who later moved to America to edit *Frank Leslie's Weekly*, among others[18]—suggests that Maginn, the editor, or Maclise, the illustrator, excluded men whose careers were solely dependent upon literature and whose achievements made doubtful the claim of middle-class professional. (The genius of James Hogg, the Ettrick Shepherd, rather than the hackwork of John Heraud wins a place at the table.) We know that *Fraser's* excluded its two most important female contributors from the portraits: Selina Bunbury, whose tales appeared in fifty issues of the magazine between 1836 and 1850, and Harriet Downing, whose popular "Remembrances of a Monthly Nurse" ran for over a year.[19] All traces of the "trade," the "hack," and the female "drudge" have been effaced—evidence that if the Fraserians aspired to professional recognition, they were uncertain about it and took care to distinguish themselves as professional authors from those of lower ranks.

To this ambiguity about professionalism, the article itself adds its own complexities. When the word *professional* surfaces in the conversation, its meaning is uncertain. Maginn asks Gleig for a contribution "in a professional way," and the clergyman responds with a humorous "Epistle to the Hebrews"—a poem about contemporary Jewish politics, not the Pauline epistle of the New Testament. Is Gleig's professionalism in his poetry, its ecclesiastical reference, or its attention to contemporary political events? Then, when Oliver Yorke describes the celebration of the Fraserians, he harks back to bygone eras and associates authorship with venerable institutions of former days. He links *"la table round"* at which they sit with King Arthur—an allusion that recalls the service Arthur's knights performed for the kingdom and reinforces the newly coined term "free-lance writer" to designate periodical writers. Yorke prophesies that the "old inscription"— "HIC JACET ARTHURUS, REX QUONDAM REXQUE FUTURUS"—will "come in a measure to pass" within the following four years when the Whigs are routed and Arthur Wellesley, Duke of Wellington, returns as prime minister (a Tory prophesy that failed). Later, Yorke refers to the gathering as a "symposium" and a "convivium," both references to classical Greek gatherings of philosophers and poets, both drinking parties with lively conversation and intellectual entertainment. The representation of authorship in *Fraser's* is, as these instances suggest, less clear about the meaning of modern professionalism than it has seemed, more likely to look back nostalgically to pre-professional gatherings of intellectuals and to exclude the modern writer who relies solely on literature for his income and social status. The *Fraser's* portraits—of both male and female groups—project idealized constructions of authorship from a socially conservative point of view; they cannot be read as historically accurate representations.

In the context of this mid-1830s uncertainty about literary professionalism, it is worth reexamining the portraits of female writers to ask what they reveal about the state of women's authorship. Like the round-table gathering of the Fraserians, the women's group portrait gives readers a private view of contemporary authors, here with close attention to matters of dress, hairstyle, and deportment. (A later commentator on this portrait would acknowledge its essentially imaginary nature, for "dire pains and penalties have been deservedly incurred by those rash individuals of the inferior sex who have dared to intrude upon the sacred rites and mysteries of the ladies in secret conclave assembled.")[20] Like the men's portrait, the women's is nostalgic, harking back to the Bluestocking circle.[21] As in Hannah More's poem "The Bas Bleu," this mid-1830s literary circle comprises "persons distinguished, in general, for their rank, talents, or respectable character," who meet for conversation and tea drinking.[22] To quote More:

> Hail, CONVERSATION, soothing Power,
> Sweet Goddess of the social hour!
> . . . .
> Long may thy polish'd altars blaze
> With wax-lights' undiminish'd rays!
> Still be thy nightly offerings paid,
> Libations large of lemonade!
> On silver vases, loaded, rise
> The biscuits' ample sacrifice.
> Nor be the milk-white streams forgot
> Of thirst-assuaging, cool orgeat;
> Rise, incense pure from fragrant tea,
> Delicious incense, worthy thee![23]

This link to the earlier Bluestockings (a group more amateur, as Betty Schellenberg notes, than the professionalized Streatham circle)[24] is underscored—in the tea drinking, the witty conversation, and the figure of the Countess of Blessington, whose individual portrait, published in *Fraser's* issue of March 1833, refers slyly to her age and wonders if it "entitle[s] her to be ranked among the *bas bleus*."[25] Yet whereas the earlier *bas bleu* circle had included men, this modern group allows women only: by the 1830s, women have been segregated by the "gender panic" that cultural historian Dror Wahrmann locates in the late eighteenth century.[26] *Fraser's* portraits of women authors are thus retrospective as well as representational, backward looking as well as contemporary, full of nostalgia about earlier modes of literary life and anxieties about status of authorship in the early Victorian period.

That is to say, the *Fraser's* portraits—of both individuals and groups, men and women—project a particular social ideology, not a transparent representation of authorship. They are uncertain about whether the author, male or female, is or should be professional and, if professional, how he or she should construct public identity. For all their uncertainty, however, the portraits willingly acknowledge women writers and editors as active participants in the London literary scene. They document the social respectability of literary women and attest to their rising public prominence. And by sketching women authors visually and describing them verbally, *Fraser's* makes their participation in the literary field of the 1830s visible to its readership.

We might further note that the *Fraser's* portraits reject three models of contemporary authorship, two involving gender ambiguity, a third involving class, all involving politics. In the first instance, as Judith Fisher has argued, the *Fraser's* portraits satirize male writers who express Whiggish sentiments and style themselves in a dandaical or Byronic mode; they valorize male authors who share pro-Tory views and show a capacity for manly, businesslike work. For example, the portrait of Thomas Campbell (No. 2), editor of the *New Monthly Magazine* published by the rival Colburn and Bentley, appears in a reclining posture, smoking a long pipe and languidly holding his cravat—a negative model of the modern author (see figure 3). In contrast, William Jerdan (No. 1), editor of the pro-Tory *Literary Gazette*, sits upright in a chair, properly dressed, reading a manuscript and surrounded by books; he is praised as "employed in that profession by whose labours the opinions, or at least the declarations, of our statesmen are conveyed to the world"—a rare use of the term *profession* and a notable choice of the commendable term *labour* (see figure 4). It is not only that Campbell is languid; it is also that *Fraser's* satirizes him for "arbitrating the wrangles of the Refuse, agitating in the turmoils of the College of all the Cockneys [the University of London], . . . and dropping in amid the various coteries of whiggery"—all the wrong political activities and evidence of his "puerile dandyism of the mind." Jerdan, in contrast, represents the author as statesman and contributor to the national weal, as in his editorship of the *Sun* newspaper, where "his well-meant endeavours for the public good" rooted out "vice . . . in this metropolis."[27]

Other negative examples of male authorship appear in the portraits of Robert Montgomery (No. 20), author of the popular poem *The Omnipresence of the Deity and of Satan*, who stares narcissistically at a picture of himself, admiring his Byronic hairdo; of Edward Bulwer Lytton (No. 27), whose portrait depicts him as a Byronic dandy looking into a large mirror and trimming facial hair; and of Benjamin Disraeli (No. 36), shown with girlish ringlets, large eyes, and a slender waist (see figures 5 and 6).[28] As Fisher explains, these satirical portraits chastise male writers who operate in an enervated mode; they help contain the "sexual-social anxieties" that dandaical

Yours truly
T. Campbell

THE EDITOR OF THE NEW MONTHLY

FIGURE 3. Thomas Campbell, *Fraser's Magazine* 1 (July 1830), 714.
Courtesy of the Yale University Library.

authors aroused with their languid poses, effeminate dress, and sexually ambiguous facial features. Yet these male authors were, in fact, popular, productive, and professional—arguably as much involved in the professionalization of literature as the Fraserians. (Indeed, Bulwer Lytton actively promoted the Dramatic Copyright Act of 1833, which sought to secure for the author of "any tragedy, comedy, play, opera, farce or other piece of

THE EDITOR OF THE LITERARY GAZETTE.

FIGURE 4. William Jerdan, *Fraser's Magazine* 1 (June 1830), 605.
Courtesy of the Yale University Library.

dramatic entertainment" the sole liberty of representing it; from 1837 to 1842,
he campaigned for the reform of domestic copyright, considered by most
authors as essential to establishing their profession on a firm basis.)[29]

If the *Fraser's* portraits attack social and political affiliations it dislikes,
they also satirize writers from humble backgrounds, especially those who
espouse radical causes or aspire too obviously to raise their social status.

AUTHOR OF THE SIAMESE TWINS.

FIGURE 5. E. L. Bulwer, *Fraser's Magazine* 6 (August 1832), 112.
Courtesy of the Yale University Library.

Francis Place (No. 66), author of *The Principle of Population*, is scurrilously abused as illegitimate: "This hero was found, we believe, in a dustpan, upon the steps of a house in St. James's Place, about sixty years back, by an honest Charlie, who forthwith conveyed him to the next workhouse, where (for these were unenlightened times) the little stranger was kindly taken care of"—the parenthetical comment containing an attack on his Malthusian

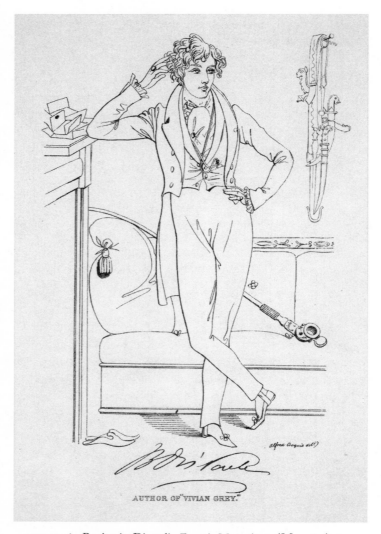

AUTHOR OF "VIVIAN GREY."

FIGURE 6. Benjamin Disraeli, *Fraser's Magazine* 7 (May 1833), 602.
Courtesy of the Yale University Library.

principles and Radical, pro-Reform politics that championed the New Poor
Law.[30] Alaric A. Watts, a minor poet and editor of literary annuals, becomes
"No. 60—Mr. Alaric Attila Watts," in a renaming that identifies him as a
northern barbarian despoiling a civilization. Maclise's portrait shows Watts
"flying down stairs with a picture under either arm"—that is, feloniously
taking goods from an aristocratic house, stealing "culture" from its rightful

THE EDITOR OF 'THE LITERARY SOUVENIR'.

FIGURE 7. Alaric Atilla Watts, *Fraser's Magazine* 11 (June 1835), 652.
Courtesy of the Yale University Library.

owners. (See figure 7.) Maginn's biography calls him "the lawfully begotten
son of a respectable nightman of the name of Joseph Watts, on the New
Road"—that is, the son of a refuse collector, too low-born to merit professional status. Watts is a re-packager and imitator of high literary culture, a
key Fraserian vice (or, worse, he's a purveyor of drek). Yet writers from such
lower-middle-class or working-class backgrounds were also part of the

professionalization of authorship in the 1830s (and beyond, as the well-documented case of Charles Dickens attests). The burgeoning periodical market allowed men of talent, energy, and rhetorical ability to enter a profession that required no university degree, independent income, or social pedigree.

Unsurprisingly in the third case, the *Fraser's* portraits of women authors valorize beauty, femininity, and domesticity; they praise women who work in appropriate genres and satirize those who are, in Andrew Dowling's useful phrase, "hegemonic deviants."[31] In the group portrait Maclise depicts the women in the fashionable dress of the 1830s or the style of their famous youth. Maginn compliments them as much on their good looks as on their "mournful" verses or "pleasant tales": Mrs. Hall, "so fair and fine"; the "lovely L.E.L." with "swan-like neck"; Caroline Norton with "sunny eyes" and "locks of jet"; the "gorgeous" Countess of Blessington; and "dear, darling" Mary Russell Mitford, "the jolliest of them all, soft-seated on a well-filled bustle." So, too, in the individual portraits, Maclise shows the women authors in characteristic domestic settings—pouring or drinking tea, fondling dogs, writing at dainty tables, or (in the case of the semi-deflating portrait of Sydney Owenson, Lady Morgan) looking in a mirror to adjust a hat. These portraits initiate the cult of the author's home, underscore the importance of public personae even at this early stage of professionalism, and foreshadow the celebrity journalism that will dominate the fin-de-siècle literary field, allowing readers to peep into the private lives of authors.[32] Within *Fraser's* literary mythmaking, the portraits create acceptable versions of the female author—women contained within the domestic sphere and the "cultural space" of "feminine poetry" that Marlon Ross suggests, in *The Contours of Masculine Desire*, characterized "the relatively smooth ideological field" of the "generation of feminine writers like Baillie, Hemans, and L.E.L."[33]

Yet we might question whether the ideological field of the 1830s was, in fact, all that smooth. If we look only at *Fraser's* portraits of the novelists and poetesses, this characterization holds. The portraits endorse a femininity of persona and production—beginning with the first sketch of "No. 10.—Mrs. Norton" (figure 8), who is depicted as "the modest matron making tea in the morning for the comfort and convenience of her husband," praised for the absence of "unfeminine display about her which can supply matter for the anecdote-monger," and urged to continue writing either poetry or fiction, so long as she does not venture into politics, "an enormity equal to wearing breeches."[34] (This sketch was published in March 1831, before Caroline Norton's official separation from her husband, George, and before she began writing articles in advocacy of the legal rights of wives and mothers.) Other women in *Fraser's* "Gallery" fall into similar patterns of feminine persona and production: Mary Russell Mitford (No. 12) garners praise for her sketches of village life, "so pretty a basket of good-looking and sweet-smelling natural flowers"; the Countess of Blessington (No. 34) for "the feminine faculty of

THE AUTHOR OF "THE UNDYING ONE."

FIGURE 8. Caroline Norton, *Fraser's Magazine* 3 (March 1831), 222.
Courtesy of the Yale University Library.

discerning the peculiarities of character"; Laetitia Landon (No. 41) for
writing of love and not "of politics, or political economy, or pugilism, or
punch"; and the elderly Miss Jane Porter (No. 58) for being "a quiet and
good-humoured lady, rather pious" (see figures 9 and 10). In the final portrait of a woman writer (No. 71—Mrs. S. C. Hall), Maginn begins,

FIGURE 9. Mary Russell Mitford, *Fraser's Magazine* 3 (May 1831), 410.
Courtesy of the Yale University Library.

"Honour to Woman!" is our standing toast. For are not the maids, wives, and widows of these sea-girt isles our pride and heart's delight? Long may they continue, as their mothers were before them, essentially and mentally feminine![35]

So overtly are these portraits idealized constructions of the woman writer that we might question their nostalgic motive and the apparent smoothness

FIGURE 10. Letitia Elizabeth Landon (L.E.L.), *Fraser's Magazine* 8 (October 1833), 433. Courtesy of the Yale University Library.

of the literary field they wish to depict. What was at stake for Maginn, Maclise, and *Fraser's Magazine*? If *Fraser's* satirical portraits of men suggest anxiety about "effeminate" male authors, the feminine portraits suggest a parallel anxiety about "masculine" women authors. They encourage women to "continue as their mothers were before them"—as if such admonition were needed in the face of modern countertrends.

In a study of print media from 1830 to 1870, Alexis Easley argues that the 1830s are precisely the historical moment at which to locate "the instability of the female author as a critical construct." In contrast to Marlon Ross, who focuses on Romantic poetry, Easley examines periodical journalism and the essay, and finds not a "smooth ideological field" but one with disruptions and crosscurrents. "By imposing notions of masculinity and femininity on literary works" and their authors, she argues, periodicals like *Fraser's* "attempted to formulate a distinctly middle-class cultural identity." This was the intended cultural work of its portraits. Even so, "the anonymity of the periodical press also enabled many writers—especially women—to subvert gender hierarchies in their literary practice."[36] This was a material condition of the marketplace, and its effect was to disrupt the ideology of the *Fraser's* portraits. Women could write, publish, and earn money and even fame for periodical writing—perhaps not yet enough to establish themselves as independent women of letters, but enough to unsettle the claims of men who, on the same terms, called themselves professional authors.

Fraser's admits a disruption in the literary field. Among its portraits of women authors, Harriet Martineau is a notable exception to femininity of persona and production. In the group portrait Maginn describes her as "meditating, grimly" (despite the fact that Maclise depicts her drinking tea and listening attentively). In the individual portrait (No. 42) Maginn expresses disgust that "any lady, old or young," would use her pen to write "on the effects of a fish diet upon population" or on the "preventive check" of Thomas Malthus—that is, on themes of political economy and birth control (see figure 11).[37] Martineau stands out as deviating from the dominant model of women's authorship: she writes on topics traditionally disallowed; enters the arena of politics dominated by men; and thus represents a new style of woman writer whom *Fraser's* deplores (and fears). By 1835, after the financial and critical success of her *Illustrations of Political Economy* (1832–34), she very much appears to be (what she was) a professional woman of letters.

Martineau's *Illustrations*, discussed in chapter 2, would have aroused Maginn's ire whether its author had been male or female. As Miriam Thrall documents in her study of *Fraser's Magazine*, from its inception this periodical included "numerous articles and burlesques voicing its protest against the materialism of the political economists."[38] Such protest occupies the longest paragraph of Maginn's verbal sketch, with its attack on Martineau as the "idol of the *Westminster Review*" (the periodical of the Utilitarians) and its expression of disgust that Malthusian doctrines should "be disseminated into all hands, to lie on the breakfast tables of the young and the fair, and to afford them matter of meditation." Even so, I suggest that *Fraser's* is irate about more than Malthusian doctrines, Utilitarian magazines, and party politics. Maclise's visual portrait shows Martineau not in a domestic setting but in London lodgings—boiling water for her tea and warming her feet on

FIGURE 11. Harriet Martineau, *Fraser's Magazine* 8 (November 1833), 576.
Courtesy of the Yale University Library.

the fender. Maginn refers to "her tea things, her ink-bottle, her skillet, her scuttle, her chair . . . all of the Utilitarian model." "There she sits," he adds, "cooking—

> __'rows
> Of chubby duodecimos,'

certain of applause from those whose praise is ruin, and of the regret of all who feel respect for the female sex, and sorrow for perverted talent, or, at least, industry."[39] Martineau's implements, deftly sketched by Maclise, may or may not be Utilitarian; but, tellingly, the chair she occupies is in the same style as those occupied by the male Fraserians at the round table. Implicitly, she belongs with them, not with "Regina's maids of honour," whose more ornate chairs suggest the decorative cultural work of poetesses and female novelists. Martineau has moved from domestic to political work, exchanging her place within a family setting for a place in the public realm of literary production. (Quite literally, she had moved from the provincial town of Norwich to London in November 1832 to live in lodgings in Conduit Street to be nearer to the sources of her work on the *Illustrations*. By the time this sketch was published, she had set up her own house, with her mother and aunt as companions, in Fludyer Street—a domestic detail that *Fraser's* conveniently ignores.)[40]

In this move Martineau made visible a possibility that was emerging in periodical writing specifically and literary life generally: the professionalization of the woman author, the career of the woman of letters. The process of professionalization occurred during the long nineteenth century but surfaced—visibly in *Fraser's*—in the 1830s. As early as 1815, *La Belle Assemblée*, a magazine with aristocratic pretensions, had featured Hannah More in its "Biographical Sketches of Illustrious and Distinguished Characters" as a member of the literary profession. The article praised More's writing for its "elegant simplicity," "virtuous and pious sentiments," and "peculiar grace from a female pen," noting that More "tended much to increase the respectability and general importance of that profession of which she has been so bright an ornament."[41] Despite its conventional judgments, this is an early, remarkable use of the word *profession* to designate women's authorship, appearing in a women's magazine consumed with fashion and the concept of "the lady."[42] By the early 1820s other articles on More, Anna Laetitia Barbauld, and their peers began appearing in general periodicals, not just women's magazines. Martineau anonymously contributed "Female Writers on Practical Divinity" to the Unitarian *Monthly Repository*, in which she surveyed the contributions of More and Barbauld to applied ("practical") religion. Although her article emphasizes women's duties and the "warmth of feeling" that makes them gravitate to devotional matters, Martineau argues that the application of biblical principles to everyday life and morality is among women authors' best achievements,[43] thus authorizing women's writing in the realm of religion and creating a distinguished literary history for their work. In the 1820s and 1830s the *Monthly Repository* opened its pages to other women authors, including Sarah Flower Adams, Mary Leman Grimstone, Letitia Kinder, Emily Taylor, and Harriet Taylor, who published articles on subjects as diverse as "The Protective System of Morals," "Charade Drama," and "The Mysticism of Plato."[44] In the 1830s and 1840s the *Westminster Review* began commissioning articles from women writers, most notably Harriet Grote, Mary Shelley, and Harriet Martineau (though none of their work was signed, given the policy of anonymity that held until the 1860s).[45]

In her construction of a literary career and self-construction as a professional author—a "professional son" and "citizen of the world," as she would phrase it in an 1833 letter to her mother—Martineau was at the forefront of a new phase of women's authorship, as we shall see in the next chapter. What I want to emphasize here is that it was Martineau's *public* assumption of a professional persona—not writing for the periodical market or making money or even winning literary fame—that unsettled the field. Women writers before her had successfully published in periodicals (including Mary Russell Mitford, the Countess of Blessington, and Laetitia Landon, all depicted in the individual and group portraits), yet *Fraser's* did not subject them to censure. Mitford had earned substantial profits from her "Our Village" series and its successors, but *Fraser's* disguises this moneymaking aspect of her literary work by using the metaphor of "hopping" to market with "her basket," "so neat, so nice, so trim, so comely"; later Maginn acknowledges "the profits of her business," but adds that they were used in a way that, were it known, "would redound to her praise and honour."[46] As fellow writers understood, Mitford had used her earnings to support her family after their improvident father brought them to virtual poverty. But Mitford trumpets neither her earnings nor her father's faults—and hence earns *Fraser's* praise for acting sub rosa: "we have always looked at the subject before us *only as it comes before the public*" (my italics).[47] On a similar principle, Laetitia Landon's earnings from periodical reviewing and other literary drudgery fall beneath public notice, and her professional life in London lodgings—22 Hans Place, where fellow writer Emma Roberts also resided—escapes representation. Instead, Maclise and Father Prout (who wrote the verbal sketch of L.E.L.) present her as a poetess, holding a violet in acknowledgment of her most famous volume of verse, *The Golden Violet* (figure 10).[48] This sketch reinforces Landon's public persona, which she privately acknowledged was a "professional" tactic when an admirer tried to console her for the broken heart she so frequently lyricized. Maginn knew the material aspects of Landon's literary life, including her penury and sexual impropriety; but *Fraser's* evades or suppresses the dubious features of a woman's professional life because Landon remains feminine in her public persona and literary productions. For women in the 1830s, as for men, the key aspects of professional authorship were respectable social status, genius or genial wit, and silence about earnings.

Indeed, social status is the issue that provokes the most anxiety in the *Fraser's* portraits. In modern sociological terms, this signals that *Fraser's* represents a phase of "status professionalism," where "style and manners" are "co-determinants of prestige, and prestige [is] more important than career."[49] (The phase of "occupational professional" would develop in the mid-Victorian period.) Given the concern with social status, it is no coincidence that Maclise, the illustrator, and Maginn, the editor, populate the women's portrait with titled ladies: the Countess of Blessington, Lady Caroline Norton, and Sydney Owenson, Lady Morgan (who added the title when her husband, a surgeon, was knighted). The presence of titled women adds luster to "Regina's maids of honour," as (alas) does the status symbol of the black servant who pours tea. Neither is it a coincidence that *Fraser's* depicts Sir Walter Scott (No. 6) as a baronet, owner of Abbotsford, "sauntering about his grounds, with his Lowland bonnet in his hand, dressed in his old green shooting jacket, telling old stories of every stone and bush, and tree and stream."[50] For all authors, the baronetcy bestowed on Scott in 1820, after the publication of the Waverley novels, raised the status of the literary profession. And the *Fraserian* portraits were in the business of maintaining status, excluding the unworthy, and projecting a conception of authorship that merged Romantic literary genius with a new Victorian middle-class ideal of business success.

The Professional Author at Mid-Century:
Literary Property, Public Service, and
the Development of a Literary Career

In a seminal article in the history of authorship, "The Condition of Authors in England, Germany, and France," published in *Fraser's Magazine* in 1847, G. H. Lewes begins with an assertion: "Literature has become a profession. It is a means of subsistence almost as certain as the bar or the church." Given the silence about money in the *Fraser's* portraits of the 1830s, this overt linking of professional status to income reflects a new turn in the discourse of authorship. Lewes gives a figure of £300 per year as a baseline for a professional literary income (later suggesting a range of "1000 down to two hundred a-year"). Much of his essay—de facto, a state-of-the-profession analysis—details the relative payments to English and European writers for different kinds of work—for example, 20 guineas per sheet for English periodicals versus 250 francs (£10) for French, £200 for an average novel in England versus one-tenth that fee (£20) for a novel in Germany, despite lower production costs on the continent. Lewes also discusses the relative status of genres in the three countries—for example, the popular status and hence high payment for drama in France, the high status but low payment for scholarly books in Germany, and the high payment for articles, reviews, and novels in England. In his analysis of national differences, he attributes the success of the professional author in England to the rise of periodicals: "The real cause we take to be the excellence and abundance of periodical literature. It is by our reviews, magazines, and journals, that the vast majority of professional authors earn their bread; and the astonishing mass of talent and energy which is thus thrown into periodical literature is not only quite unexampled abroad, but is, of course, owing to the certainty of moderate yet, on the whole, sufficient income."[51] For Lewes the English literary field is the best playing field on the globe.

Lewes's frankness about money matters emerges from a wider debate about emergent professions and appropriate income. As Clare Pettitt has shown, inventors and scientists campaigned vigorously in the 1830s and 1840s to secure new patent laws to protect their intellectual property and secure adequate middle-class incomes.[52] As Frank Turner has similarly shown in *Contesting Cultural Authority*, young lay scientists conducted an extensive drive toward professionalization in order to wrest power from clergyman-naturalists at Oxbridge and secure instead permanent positions for "real" scientists within the university.[53] In the 1840s, moreover, a movement for the reform of university education, particularly at Oxford, produced a debate in the periodical press about the academic profession, including estimates of tutors' and fellows' income, that closely parallel the authors' discussion. Proposed academic reforms were hotly debated, with articles appearing in the *British Quarterly Review* and *Tait's Edinburgh Magazine* in 1846, just before Lewes published his 1847 "Condition of Authors." One proposal urged the conversion of all 557 Oxford college fellowships into 200 professorships of £400 per annum. Another, advanced by Bonamy Price, a Rugby master, advocated a hierarchical system in which tutors could work their way up to professorships, eventually reaching an annual income of £1,000. As A. J. Engel observes in *From Clergyman to Don: The Rise of the Academic Profession in Nineteenth-Century Oxford*, these reforms intended (and eventually managed) "to make the position of university teacher a permanent career," separate from but socially equal to that of the clergyman.[54] Of necessity, the reforms required specifying a professional income sufficient for a "gentleman." The figures proposed—from £400 to £1,000—strikingly resemble those Lewes cites in his 1847 article on the literary profession and most likely influenced his argument.

Although Lewes emphasizes annual income, he might have emphasized instead literary property and newly secured copyright protection of it—as modern historians like Catherine Seville do: "The nineteenth century sees the birth of the profession of authorship, and copyright is the first issue around which the new profession coalesces."[55] Authors' public discussions of professional income in this period often focus on, and emerge from, the introduction of domestic and international copyright bills in Parliament from 1837 onward. With Thomas Noon Talfourd's domestic copyright bill of 1837 and the campaign for international copyright that began simultaneously, English authors became vocal about their ownership of literary property, their need for perpetual copyright, and the loss of income resulting from American piracy. On the domestic front, Wordsworth, Southey, and Carlyle testified to the difficulties of laboring in a profession unprotected by adequate laws, with Southey declaring that "he had been prevented by the existing copyright law from undertaking works of weight, research, and permanent value" and urging perpetual copyright not only for the sake of the author and his heirs but also for the greater distinction of English literature.[56] Most famously on the international front, Dickens, during his 1842 North American tour, made speeches in Boston and Hartford on behalf of an American copyright law, using the impoverishment of the dying Walter Scott to illustrate the injustices suffered by British authors.

> [I]f there had existed any law in this respect, Scott might not have sunk beneath the mighty pressure on his brain, but might have lived to add new creatures of his fancy to the crowd which swarm about you in your summer walks, and gather round your winter evening hearths. . . . I [have] pictured him to myself, faint, wan, dying, crushed both in mind and body by his honourable struggle, and hovering round him the phantoms of his own imagination—. . . not one friendly hand to help raise him from that sad, sad bed. No, nor brought him from that land in which his own language was spoken, and in every house and hut of which his own books were read in his own tongue, one grateful dollar-piece to buy a garland for his grave.[57]

Less rhetorically and more practically, Dickens presented to Senator Henry Clay a petition signed by leading American authors that urged passage of a copyright act (not by any means the first such petition, as Carlyle noted to Dickens when asked to sign: "Several years ago, if memory err not, I was one of the many English Writers who, under the auspices of Miss Martineau, did already sign a petition to Congress, praying for an International Copyright between the Two Nations").[58] After the U.S. Congress failed (yet again) to enact legislation, Dickens took the matter public, publishing letters in the *Literary Gazette*, the *Examiner*, and other British periodicals to express his disgust with the "existing system of piracy and plunder,"[59] and following in 1843 with a lawsuit against Peter Parley's *Illuminated Library* pirating of his Christmas story, reproduced as *A Christmas Ghost Story: Reoriginated from the Original by Charles Dickens*. Dickens's actions encouraged other authors to speak up about money and agitate for legal protection.

In the public debates of the 1840s about professional income, women are mostly silent about money, though in their private correspondence they reveal a lively interest in it. In an autobiographical letter written to Richard H. Horne in 1844, for instance, Martineau notes that she has "been reckoning up my earnings (still flowing in, however) & I find them between £5000 & £6000";[60] during the 1840s also, perhaps because she feared that her invalidism would strain her resources, she toted up her income from books, articles, and reviews—a document she showed to John Chapman and continued to keep throughout the 1850s. In the 1840s, too, Mary Howitt explicitly writes about royalties and professional fees in letters to her sister Anna Harrison, referring to a contract for £1,000, mentioning payments for poems, translations, and articles, and explaining that she is "bent on A.M. [her daughter Anna Mary] making £300 next year by translating."[61] And Elizabeth Gaskell, visiting the home of the Howitts, remarks on authors' income, describing to Elizabeth Holland the splendid engravings and plaster casts that the family owns and commenting, "My word! Authorship brings them in a pretty penny!"[62]

If women authors tended to discuss financial matters privately, they nonetheless took active roles in the copyright campaigns. Martineau, because of her active political involvement in Westminster and the many acquaintances she had made during her North American tour of 1834–35, organized the authors' petitions for the international copyright bill, using her house in Fludyer Street, Westminster, as headquarters for signing. As early as 1 November 1836 she wrote to Mary Somerville, the respected Scottish savant and science writer, to ask for her signature on a document, "Memorials from the Living Authors of England to both Houses of Congress," adding that she was also requesting the signatures of Maria Edgeworth, Joanna Baillie, and Lucy Aikin.[63] The "Memorials," as Martineau describes them, included "a plain statement of our want of protection, as to both the property & integrity of our works; the injury to American authors; & an appeal for a law."[64] A week later, on 9 November 1836, she wrote to other women authors, including Mary Russell Mitford, urging, "Everybody is signing; and the case is so clear that I think you cannot hesitate."[65] At the same time Martineau sent letters to influential political and literary men on both sides of the Atlantic, asking author-MPs like Lord Brougham to sign the "Author's Petition" and literary figures like William Cullen Bryant to "petition Congress, to the same effect, & at the same time as ourselves."[66] Once Senator Clay had submitted the petition and his report to Congress, she wrote to thank him for his "exertions on the Copyright business."[67]

Martineau similarly helped with petitions in support of the domestic copyright bill and became one of four notable women authors to sign Talfourd's 1839 petition on its behalf. (The others were Joanna Baillie, Marguerite, Countess of Blessington, and Mary Russell Mitford. Prominent male authors included Robert Browning, Thomas Carlyle, Charles Dickens, Leigh Hunt, Thomas Hood, and Samuel Rogers.)[68] Before her physical collapse in 1839, Martineau labored actively for both international and domestic copyright, prodding her peers to petition, make their views known, and thus secure their literary property.

Most women authors, however, focused less on "materialistic" matters and more on "idealistic" aspects of the writer's public service—an aspect of professional authorship that Lewes engages in the second half of "The Condition of Authors" and that goes to the heart of mid-century debates over what constitutes professionalism. As Susan E. Colón has recently argued, we can only fully understand mid-Victorian authorship by considering its ideals, "the overlapping religious, ethical, and transcendentalist convictions that structured much of Victorian life."[69] As a thirty-year-old journalist, Lewes writes as a young man staking a claim to middle-class status and hoping to raise his chosen "vocation" (his term) in the estimate of his readers. He credits authors by figurative association with clergymen, as "the lay teachers of the people." He argues, by association with the military, that authors provide as much service to the state "as the man who has marched at the head of a regiment." And he calls for an improvement in their ranks using classical allusions, as he laments the "innumerable host of angry pretenders" who are "like the army of Xerxes" when authors should instead be "a Macedonian phalanx, chosen, compact, and irresistible."[70] In these associations Lewes does verbally what the 1835 *Fraser's* portrait of male authors did visually: he sets authorship among the learned professions, arguing that "the man who has devoted his talents and energies to the laborious task of improving and amusing mankind, has done the State as much service as the man who has marched at the head of a regiment." Authors, he claims in a series of metaphors that draw on services rendered by the traditional professions, have "battled worthily for our intellectual liberty"; "helped to make us wise, moderate, and humane"; and "charmed many a weary hour, and peopled many listless days with 'fond, familiar thoughts.'"[71]

Despite the continuing association of authorship with the learned professions, *Fraser's* in 1847 was not the *Fraser's* of 1835—as we can see from the anxieties Lewes expresses as well as the arguments he makes. As Lewes surveys the "condition of authors," a "host of angry pretenders" ruffles his confidence—despite the improvement in English authors' incomes that he so painstakingly details. Among the "pretenders" Lewes names barristers, physicians, and clergymen—writers whom *Fraser's* had happily included among its ranks in the 1830s. These men comprised the majority of contributors to the magazine, writers who "derived their living from nonliterary sources" and represented a common early nineteenth-century model of literary life, "that of a professional or bureaucrat whose duties leave sufficient time for writing."[72] Walter Scott embodied this model at its best; as expressed in the preface to "The Lay of the Last Minstrel," Scott determined

> that literature should be my staff, but not my crutch, and that the profits of my literary labour, however convenient otherwise, should not, if I could help it, become necessary to my ordinary expenses. Upon such a post [the clerkship of the Supreme Court, which he sought and obtained] an author might hope to retreat, without any perceptible alteration of circumstances, whenever the time should arrive that the public grew weary of his endeavors to please, or he himself should tire of the pen.[73]

By 1847, such dual-career writers—and the model of literary life they represented—have become the target of Lewes's scorn: "barristers with scarce briefs, physicians with few patients, clergymen on small livings, idle women, rich men, and a large crop of aspiring noodles." All these become, in Lewes's analysis, non-professionals or failed professionals poaching in another man's territory.[74]

The reference to "idle women" raises the question of women authors—whether Lewes considers them professional or whether he continues in 1847 to treat them, as *Fraser's* did in the 1830s, as amateur counterparts to men of letters. By "idle," does Lewes merely target aristocratic women writers like Lady Morgan, whose "absurd exaggeration and empty pretense" *Fraser's Magazine* regularly lampooned, or Catherine Gore, whose silver fork novels it abused,[75] or does he include all women who stray into the realm of literature?

In some periodical writing of the 1840s, Lewes admits able women into the field of fiction, citing Fielding and Austen as "the greatest novelists in our language." So, too, Lewes was copious in his praise of contemporary women novelists, notably Charlotte Brontë and Elizabeth Gaskell.[76] In 1847, for instance, when he read *Jane Eyre* by "Currer Bell," he was intoxicated; he recalled later in an 1855 letter to Gaskell: "The enthusiasm with which I read it, made me go down to Mr. Parker [the editor], and propose to write a review of it for 'Frazer's Magazine.'"[77] In an omnibus review that Lewes published in the December 1847 issue, he praised the "remarkable power" of the novel, calling it "a book after our own heart" and writing privately to the author (in a letter sent via Smith, Elder, Brontë's publisher) to offer his praise and advice for future work.[78] Throughout her brief career as a novelist, Currer Bell's work elicited public and private praise from Lewes's pen.

Yet Lewes offended Brontë (and other women of letters) by his review of *Shirley* (1849) in *Blackwood's Magazine*, with its opening speculations about the "organic" differences between the sexes, his pronouncement that the "grand function of woman . . . is, and ever must be, *Maternity*," and the "bitter humour about the possibility of women being equal to men in various walks of life, including authorship"—wounding comments in an essay ostensibly in praise of a great woman novelist and one he knew to be unmarried.[79] Lewes also wrote, at the end of the 1840s, a column for the *Leader* under the pseudonym Vivian titled "A Flight of Authoresses," in which he begins: "There! I knew it . . . those women! Not content with invading our manly domain of literature and lowering the price of articles, they have now assaulted us in our last stronghold—the London season."[80] While Lewes grants Currer Bell (Charlotte Brontë) and Zoë (Geraldine) Jewsbury their place of honor as "women [who] have claims," he satirizes other "pretenders"—the poetess Miss Bunion, the authoress Mrs. Buony Jones—who invade London from the provinces, write silly poems or pretentious treatises like *Triune Development of the Spirit*, and generally bring down the profession of letters. The anxiety about competition from women authors and their "lowering" effect is palpable in the *Leader* column, but the essentialism of Lewes's 1850 *Blackwood's* review posed a greater challenge to women authors—a challenge they would take up in their own statements about their "function."

In the 1847 "Conditions of Authors," however, Lewes worries less about female competitors than about the general lack of respect for authors shown by the public. His article ends with a call for "justice" and a telling personal anecdote in which he reveals his own ambiguous social status. Lewes recounts a trip to the registrar's office to record the birth of his child (most likely Herbert, born 10 July 1846). The registrar asks,

> "I believe, sir, you are an author?"
> Assent was signified by a bow.
> "Humph!" said the registrar, deliberating. "We'll say, *Gent.* . . . I suppose, sir, *authors rank as gents?*"

For Lewes this exchange testifies to the still uncertain social status of the literary profession: Is the author, or is he not, a gentleman? It also gives urgency to his call for public acknowledgment of authorship as a profession. Authors, he argues, ought not to acquiesce in the common "unwillingness of literary men to own themselves professional authors."[81] They should espouse their calling, agitate for government-sponsored "professorships," and disown unworthy rivals, the "host of interlopers" who are "willing and able to work for lower wages."[82] Authors should, in effect, publicly construct themselves—as well as conduct themselves—as professionals as a crucial step toward achieving middle-class, gentlemanly status.

Lewes's approach—public self-construction matched by public conduct—is a seminal tactic that other Victorians, including painters and actors, adopted in seeking middle-class respectability, and it was fundamental as well to the success of the professional woman of letters. As Julie Codell has demonstrated in *The Victorian Artist: Artists' Life Writing in Britain, 1870–1910*, the "family biographies" of male painters, written by widows or children, knowingly constructed the painter "as a professional artist and solid family man—right down to the 'normative' images and photographs [that] countered degenerate stereotypes."[83] Mary Jean Corbett similarly observes, in her study of Victorian actresses, that achieving middle-class respectability was dependent on projecting "bourgeois subjectivity" both on and off the stage—and a necessary tactic for meeting "real economic goals."[84] As a literary man, Lewes understood the importance of persona. His call for public ownership of authorship as a profession articulates, in a periodical context, a strategy that his contemporaries implicitly employed in fiction (Dickens's *David Copperfield*, Thackeray's *Pendennis*) and poetry (Elizabeth Barrett Browning's *Aurora Leigh*, Tennyson's "The Epic"). In this historical context, it should come as no surprise that in the "Dignity of Literature" debate of 1850, most literary critics praised Dickens for his representation of authorship in *David Copperfield*, whereas Thackeray was abused for the denigration of literature in *Pendennis*.[85]

In its call for authors to acknowledge their vocation and exclude the unfit and unworthy, "The Condition of Authors" is precise on difficulties but weak on remedies. Lewes pinpoints the individual efforts that authors must make as they present themselves and their work to the public, but he lacks an agenda for collective, institutional, or governmental action. (Fifty years later, Walter Besant, writing the history of the first attempt to found the Society of British Authors while initiating his own successful organization, would chastise Lewes for his lack of collaboration and "intellect . . . too lofty to stoop to things practical.")[86] In his penultimate paragraph, Lewes merely urges the abolition of the ineffective governmental practice of bestowing civil pensions on writers stricken by illness or literary widows faced with penury. Yet, while he proposes that the government better deploy its funds to institute "professorships" and "open public offices to authors," he gives no account of how such professorships might work or who might qualify. Nor does he define those who are "unfit" to receive governmental support (beyond citing the widow of Colonel Gurwood, editor of Wellington's *Dispatches*, as unworthy of a civil list pension bestowed in "consideration of the *literary* merits of her husband).[87] Lewes nonetheless brings to the fore problems that mid-century authors recognized in making literature a viable profession: the lack of entry requirements, the difficulty of developing a career, and an inadequate system of public rewards.

These are institutional deficits that William Jerdan, veteran Fraserian from the prior generation, raises in spades in his *Autobiography* (1852–53)—a professional life history that provoked much periodical debate. Jerdan had been the poster boy of *Fraser's Magazine*: the first literary man chosen for a solo portrait, shown seated in an upright, business-like posture with manuscript in hand; among the few authors meriting the label "in the profession" in Maginn's verbal sketch; and identified in Maclise's portrait as "editor of *The Literary Gazette*," a pioneering journal in its concern for authors' rights and an early champion of an international copyright law.[88] In the opening pages of his memoir, however, Jerdan speaks against literature as a profession, claiming that it cannot be called so. As he recalls his youthful ambition and surveys the current achievements of his adolescent friends, he regrets that he did not, as they did, enter an established profession. As a young man he had been sent to London to pursue a commercial career and later to Edinburgh to read law, but had succumbed to his inclination to write poetry—a grievous error, in his view.

> I unsteadily forsook the choice of a profession, and, within a few years, found myself leaning for life on the fragile crutch of literature for my

support. And here again would I earnestly advise every enthusiastic thinker, every fair scholar, every ambitious author, every inspired poet, without independent fortune, to fortify themselves also with a something more worldly to do. . . . Let no man be bred to literature alone, for, as has been far less truly said of another occupation, it will not be bread to him.[89]

Jerdan's allusion to the "fragile crutch of literature" acknowledges his failure to heed the advice of Walter Scott. Consequently, his pursuit of literature as a profession resulted in "fallacious hopes, bitter disappointments, uncertain rewards, vile impositions, and censure and slander"—all of which he demonstrates with his own experience and with reference to Isaac Disraeli's *Calamities of Authors*. Literature, Jerdan concludes, is compatible with the practice of law, medicine, or the church, and that is how it should be pursued: "the chinking of fees in the law is almost in tuning with the harmony of the poet's verse."[90]

In Jerdan's mid-century assessment the key problems that prevent professionalism are not annual income or lack of international copyright but that the "profession of letters" (a phrase he questions) does not allow for the development of a career nor entail a recognizable reward system that confers status on the practitioner. Jerdan associates the professions with a recognizable hierarchy of posts and the possibility of social reward, especially the attaining of an aristocratic title—the "Sir" that his youthful friends David and Frederick Pollock achieve or the title "Lord Truro" that the humble Thomas Wilde is granted. He denies literature to be a profession on these terms—recognizing, though with less clarity of expression, a problem parallel to one that mid-nineteenth-century analysts of the English university system identified when they saw that most tutors had nowhere to go after ten years, except into country livings held by their colleges, often ill suited to men of learning. Jerdan also anticipates the studies of such twentieth-century social historians as Burton J. Bledstein who, in *The Culture of Professionalism*, emphasizes the acquisition of "cultivated talent," the "vertical" development of a career, and the necessity of professional institutions to support and recognize the achievement of members[91]—social and institutional underpinnings that nineteenth-century literature lacked.

For his comments denigrating the profession of letters, Jerdan found himself chastised by contemporary reviewers, especially in the *Westminster Review* and the *Literary Gazette*, the periodical he had edited for two decades. On 15 May 1852 the *Gazette* reviewed the first volume of his *Autobiography*, leading with this ominous comment: "It is with unaffected pain that we proceed to the notice of the work before us." The *Gazette* justified its stern review because of the false "theory" that Jerdan advances—"a theory which is not simply unsound, but most mischievous, and calculated in the highest degree to degrade the literary profession and to defraud the literary character—properly so called." Whereas Jerdan argued that "the profession of letters is a curse to the man vain, weak, or frantic enough to adopt it," in the *Gazette*'s view the facts prove that "the only thing worth mourning over has been [Jerdan's] own willful and wicked flinging away of the finest opportunities." The reviewer describes the many professional opportunities, high remuneration, and significant social recognition that Jerdan enjoyed during his working career as an editor. It also describes the flaws in his character, "the social failings" that would have been "his stumbling-block in every profession and in any trade": "Has he ever taken the trouble to calculate the self-denial, the steady perseverance, the patient self-devotion, which enabled Sir Frederick Pollock [Jerdan's adolescent friend] to make his upward way?"[92] Implicitly, the answer is "no"; explicitly, the reviewer blames Jerdan for extravagance and recklessness. The *Westminster Review* draws the same conclusion in its 1852 review, "The Profession of Literature": "The secret of all the disasters that have befallen him is unconsciously betrayed in a picture he gives us of his mental idleness and incapacity for work."[93]

The debate between Jerdan and his reviewers may seem merely personal— and no doubt the new editor of the *Literary Gazette* was annoyed by the poor financial condition in which his predecessor had left the magazine. But its ramifications extend far beyond the individual case. Indeed, as part of the "Dignity of Literature" debate that erupted at mid-century, it was about the profession of letters itself: not just its social status and financial rewards, but more fundamentally about its aims, ambitions, and contributions to the public good.[94] In the commentary that continued in reviews of subsequent volumes of Jerdan's *Autobiography*,[95] the important mid-Victorian questions about authorship got aired: Could authors earn an adequate, middle-class income that would sustain them and their families during a lifetime? Could authors advance during their careers, as lawyers and physicians did, or were they likely to decline into poverty and unemployment late in life? What kind of service did authors offer to the public? Did the reading public acknowledge and respect this service, whether by the conferral of social status (a title), government remuneration (a pension or professorship), or adequate copyright laws? And the debate revealed a dilemma that remains unresolved in virtually all Victorian discussions of literary professionalism: Do we recognize authors as professionals because they possess some quality or knowledge that they offer to the public or because they are established members of professional institutions that affirm their status, control their fees, and protect their labor?

Mid-Victorians tended to emphasize the man himself, following in the train of Thomas Carlyle's "Hero as Man of Letters" (1841) and the lesser examples of success in Samuel Smiles's *Self Help* (1859). J. W. Kaye, in a contemporary review of Thackeray's *Pendennis*, shows this emphasis when he observes: "there is no protection for [the literary man] to claim; no exclusiveness to defend him from an over-whelming array of rivals," and it is thus "all the more honourable to succeed."[96] Lewes shows the same emphasis in his dismissal of literary failures as either "very unlucky or very 'impracticable.'" Yet both Lewes and Jerdan understood also that without supporting institutions and governmental protections, a professional author could not sustain himself and his career.

For women authors, the most pressing question seemed to lie not in institutional or governmental support but in the matter of service: what kind of service the woman author renders and how the public understands that service. This is not to say that women did not participate in institutional and legal efforts. Some, notably Harriet Martineau, worked to establish the Society of British Authors in the 1840s; in his retrospective history of this short-lived institution, Walter Besant praises her as the "most interesting," "most clear-sighted," and "most far-seeing" of all authors involved.[97] Other women, notably Caroline Norton, recognized the importance of governmental reform and campaigned for legal changes that would enable married women writers to control their professional earnings and escape the official nonexistence of coverture. In her *Plain Letter to the Lord Chancellor* (1839), Norton pointed out that husbands had the legal right to seize their wives' literary profits and that "a good wife's property might be at the disposal of a bad husband: that even her laborious earnings might be squandered by him on selfish and guilty pleasures, and that there is nothing in the law to prevent the husband spending his wife's money on his kept mistress, or in any other way that pleases him."[98] In the 1850s Norton would repeat this point in *English Laws for Women in the Nineteenth Century* (1854), using her own divorce case as evidence in support of the Married Women's Property Bill: "The law does not countenance the idea of separate property. All that belongs to the wife is the husband's—even her clothes and trinkets: that is the law of England. Her earnings are his. The copyrights of my works are his, by law."[99] This parliamentary campaign would galvanize women's collective efforts to change English law, lead them to petition for the passage of the Married Women's Property Bill in 1856, and eventually found feminist institutions of their own (including the informal Langham Place Group and the official Society of Female Artists). But, whether lacking Martineau's business acumen or wishing to avoid the public scandal of Norton's case, in the 1840s many women authors tended not to publish on, or actively campaign for, professional, institutional, or legal matters.

Instead, in what may have been a shrewd tactic rather than an enforced silence, they focused on the personal qualities and literary abilities that affirmed women's literary work. As we shall see in chapter 4, an analysis of authorial myths in *The Life of Charlotte Brontë*, the possession of "talent" or "genius" was a secure basis for affirmation—a long-established Romantic criterion, still held as a requisite for genuine literary achievement. Even so, Brontë's was an exceptional case. As Christine Battersby has argued in *Gender and Genius*, Victorian constructions of femininity tended to preclude women from the rank of "genius" and cast them in supporting roles: "women—seen primarily as sensitive, emotional, passive, intuitive, and imitative—were believed capable only of transmitting or nurturing genius in males as wives, mothers, daughters, and sisters."[100] Thus, more frequently at mid-century, as we shall see in chapter 3 with the career of Mary Howitt, the extension of feminine duties authorized women's entry into literature, with service to the reader and the nation underpinning professional labor.

It was the mid- to late 1850s that proved a pivotal moment in defining the professional woman of letters, and in this (re)definition the intellectual work of Anna Jameson proved crucial. Jameson, an author known for her *Diary of an Ennuyée* (1826), *Characteristics of Women* (1832), and *Sacred and Legendary Art* (1848), articulated the case for women's work in terms that partially repeated feminine self-constructions of the 1840s but also offered new terms for women's professional labor that were taken up by younger women writers of the 1850s and 1860s. In two influential lectures, *Sisters of Charity* (1855) and *The Communion of Labour* (1856), Jameson advanced three points about all work: that the world needs a "communion of labour" to which both men and women contribute, that men and women contribute differently to the world's work, and that women's normal (normative) contributions in the domestic realm should be extended into the world at large. Using a Shakespearean phrase, Jameson argues that the current age is a *"working-day world"*: "it is a place where work is to be done,—work which *must* be done,—work which it is *good* to do;—a place in which labour of one kind or another is at once the condition of existence and the condition of happiness."[101] Adapting and extending this Carlylean notion of work, she adds that "the harmony and happiness of life in man or woman consists in finding our vocation" and in doing "works of necessity" as well as "works of mercy"—the first phrase referring to paid, professional work, the second to charitable.[102]

In these lectures Jameson acknowledges the gendered difference of this work, arguing

> The man governs, sustains, and defends the family; the woman cherishes, regulates, and purifies it; but though distinct, the relative work is inseparable,—sometimes exchanged, sometimes shared; so that from the beginning, we have, even in the primitive household, not the *division*, but the *communion* of labour.[103]

As her reference to the "household" implies, her model for women's work depends on the extension of "domestic life" into the "social community." She views this as a means of social progress: "As civilization advances, as the social interests and occupations become more and more complicated, the family duties and influences diverge from the central home,—in a manner, radiate from it,—though it is always there in reality. The man becomes on a larger scale, father and brother, sustainer and defender; the woman becomes on a larger scale, mother and sister, nurse and help."[104] Summing up, Jameson calls her points "truisms such as no man in his senses [ever] thinks of disputing."[105]

Delivered privately in the home of the Unitarian philanthropist Elisabeth Reid, then published in book form, Jameson's lectures participate in a wider debate about women's work that erupted in the 1850s and that implicitly challenge Lewes's notion that the "grand function" of woman is maternity. Social historian Ellen Jordan has suggested that *The Communion of Labour* initiates a new discourse of women's work, one with a slippage between an aristocratic discourse of work (work as philanthropy and public service) and an entrepreneurial discourse (work as self-dependence, self-realization, and self-help).[106] This slippage was, I suggest, an enabling one for women of letters. It allowed Jameson and her colleagues to disrupt the conventional binary of the early nineteenth century, which placed women in the home (doing domestic and moral service) and men in the public sphere (doing business and politics) by arguing instead that the duties of both men and women emerge from the home and radiate out into the public sphere. In Jameson's scheme, both sexes have duties relevant to both spheres; in the progress of history, these expand "on a larger scale" for both men and women. Instead of an *either/or*, the model becomes a *both/and*.

A close friend of leading women of letters of her own generation, including Mary Howitt, Margaret Oliphant, and Elizabeth Gaskell, Jameson—and the philosophy of work she advanced—made it possible for women to articulate models of professional authorship based on their domestic roles without raising hackles about gender transgression. This strategy was common in the 1840s and continued into the 1850s.[107] As late as the 1870s, in a review of Jameson's *Memoirs* and Fanny Kemble's *Records of a Girlhood*, Oliphant dismisses the notion that "the employment of women" is a new phenomenon: "from the beginning of history, . . . whenever it has been necessary, women *have* toiled, have earned money, have got their living and the living of those dependent upon them, in total indifference to all theory." As examples Oliphant cites Jameson, daughter of a miniature painter, and Kemble, daughter of a famous acting family, as women who "stepp[ed] into the busy current of active life when necessity made it desirable to do so—finding work that suited them, and doing it."[108] Oliphant argues that women undertake professional work when family circumstances require it and as their abilities allow it; in the professional "artist-classes" the "loyal and dutiful daughter" becomes, as in Kemble's acting debut, "the mainstay and saviour of the house": "it is art alone which (more or less) equalizes the value of labour without respect of sex or circumstance."[109]

Yet, despite Oliphant's familial interpretation of Jameson's career, it is also the case that Jameson mentored women artists and authors of the next generation whose conceptions of work were more thoroughly professionalized: Anna Mary Howitt, Bessie Rayner Parkes, Barbara Leigh Smith, and

Adelaide Procter, founding members of the Langland Place Group, the first English feminists. Jameson's arguments enabled these younger women to emphasize the entrepreneurial discourse of work—without, as Ellen Jordan puts it, "totally rejecting the domestic ideology"—and to advance an argument for women's entry into suitable professions. Their more daring arguments moved women out of the home and into the professional fields of art, literature, publishing, medicine, and business. We can see this effect in Leigh Smith's *Women and Work* (1857), the first section of which is titled "Women Want Professions." The opening remarks ground women's work in divine command: "God sent all human beings into the world for the purpose of forwarding, to the utmost of their power, the progress of the world."[110] Leigh Smith adapts the Carlylean position that "no human being has a right to be idle" and paraphrases Jameson when she observes, "Let women take their place as citizens in the Commonwealth, and we shall find they will fulfil all their home duties better."[111] Then, however, she shifts to material facts that necessitate women's work and initiates her argument for their entry into various professions and trades. "Of women at the age of twenty and upwards," she asserts, "43 out of the 100 in England and Wales are unmarried"; the existing trades of needlewoman and governess are already overcrowded; working- and middle-class women need "more ways of gaining livelihoods," that is, other trades and professions suitable to their natures and abilities. Thus she suggests:

> Apprentice 10,000 to watchmakers; train 10,000 for teachers of the young; make 10,000 good accountants; put 10,000 more to be nurses under deaconesses trained by Florence Nightingale; put some thousands in the electric telegraph offices over all the country; educate 1000 lecturers for mechanics' institutions; 1000 readers to read the best books to the working people; train up 10,000 to manage washing-machines, sewing-machines, &c.[112]

Assuming that women have already succeeded as professional authors, Leigh Smith focuses on *new* professions for women, as her colleague Parkes would later do in *Essays on Women's Work* (1865) and contributors to the *English Woman's Journal* would similarly focus in articles published in the late 1850s and early 1860s. (For instance, the two-part "What Can Educated Women Do?" of 1859 cites Jameson's *Communion of Labour* and suggests these new fields for women's work: hospitals, prisons, reformatories, workhouses, educational institutions, and factories.[113] Relatively little is said about journalism, novel writing, or other forms of paid literary work.)

For this younger generation of women authors and artists, literature is simply treated as an accessible profession. They cite it as a field in which women have already demonstrated success. Leigh Smith asserts, in the parliamentary petition she spearheaded in 1856 for the Married Women's

Property Bill, that "married women of education are entering on every side the fields of literature and art, to increase the family income by such exertions" and that "professional women [are] earning large incomes by pursuit of the arts."[114] Parkes remarks in *Essays on Woman's Work* (1865),

> Literature again is followed, as a profession, by women, to an extent far greater than our readers are at all aware of. The magazines of the day are filled by them; one of the oldest and best of our weekly periodicals owes two-thirds of its contents to their pens. Even the leaders [editorials] of our newspapers are, in some instances, regularly written by women, and publishers avail themselves largely of their industry in all manner of translations and compilations.[115]

As a thirty-five-year-old journalist, Parkes in 1865 sounds remarkably like Lewes in 1847: claiming the status of professional, detailing achievements in the field, and emphasizing the role of periodicals in the development of the woman author. She resembles Lewes in another way, by pointing out that literature can never become a profession that employs a large number of women.

> But the number of women who are adopting pursuits connected with literature and the arts must not blind us to the fact that they will always constitute the minority among even "skilled labourers." For the smallest aptitude with the pen, and what would appear to be a very average power of arranging ideas in sequence, is not a very widely diffused intellectual gift. Among men, how small is the *comparative* number of artists and authors!—the hacks may perhaps be reckoned by thousands, the average writers by hundreds, the geniuses by tens. But when we speak of unemployed women, it is a question of *tens of thousands.*[116]

Parkes's observation—really an aside in a chapter on "the profession of the teacher"—raises a conundrum that mid-Victorian women faced as they claimed literature as a profession. If they argued that authorship was an extension of women's traditional abilities and duties, how could they limit the profession to the worthy or, as Lewes would put it, exclude the idle and unfit? How could they elevate themselves above the low level of hackwork and claim high literary achievement? Parkes's reference to *genius* gives a clue to her strategy—a strategy also deployed in *The Life of Charlotte Brontë* and by its successors (chapter 4). Her colleague Anna Mary Howitt proposed another strategy—collaboration—which built on her literary training and extended it to women's artistic practice (chapter 3).

What we find at mid-century, then, are different models for professional literary work, different myths of the woman author, yet all drawing to a greater or lesser extent on the overlapping discourses of work as public service and work as self-realization, self-help, and self-dependence. At the same historical moment, we find different attitudes among professional women toward institutional affiliations and rewards. Perhaps because writers felt less need for the Society of British Authors (SBA) than did painters for the Royal Academy, there was less impulse to incorporate women of letters into professional institutions (though the SBA lists fifteen women among its initial one hundred members, including Miss Edgeworth, Mrs. Jameson, Miss Mitford, and Miss Martineau).[117] Finally, at mid-century we find women articulate, on the one hand, about the need to earn money and retain legal control of their incomes, yet reticent, on the other, about how much they need to earn. Leigh Smith may have been willing to state that married women earned money "to increase the family income by such exertions" or that "professional women [are] earning large incomes by pursuit of the arts," but she didn't state how much—at least not publicly.

The Era of Professionalism: The Society of Authors, the Debate over "Literature," and the Rise of the Woman of Letters

"The 1880s were a crucial decade for the profession of authorship"—so writes Victor Bonham-Carter in *Authors by Profession.*[118] Bonham-Carter privileges this decade because the year 1884 marks the founding of the Society of Authors, under whose aegis his two-volume study was published and whose history he tells. The decade also saw historic developments in copyright law, with three international conferences on copyright occurring in Berne, Switzerland, and nine countries ratifying the international copyright agreement in 1886. (The United States held out until 1891.) As opposed to the individualism of the 1840s and 1850s, the 1880s was a decade of institutionalization—when authors organized to declare themselves a professional group, appoint a president and honorary secretary, set up a committee of management, start a journal, disseminate information about professional issues and activities, lobby for improved copyright laws, and thereby (they hoped) protect their rights. As W. Martin Conway explained in *The Nineteenth Century*, the Society of Authors was founded "for the furtherance and protection of [authors'] just interests and rights. It exists to gather information and to give its members advice and help. It examines agreements and points out their actual meaning, and how they will work out. . . . It exists and prospers because it supplies a demand and does work that needs to be done."[119] As Walter Besant, its motivating force and editor of its journal, the *Author*, proudly reported at the annual meeting of 1892: "In the first year, 1884, there were only 68 paying members; in 1886 there were only 153—and that in the third year of our existence; in 1888 there were 240;

in 1889, 372; in 1891, 662; and in 1892, this year, up to the present day, there have been 870."[120]

From a sociological perspective, authorship came of age as a profession with the establishment of these institutions and initiatives; it moved from "status professionalism" to "occupational professionalism," to adopt Sheldon Rothblatt's terms.[121] From a historical perspective, we might say that authorship came fully to embrace the model of the man of letters as the man of business, initially limned in the *Fraser's* portrait of William Jerdan. But we would need to add that a simultaneous, sometimes paradoxical and often oppositional, response to *remove* literature from the realm of business also emerged in the 1880s—whether in the aestheticism (art for art's sake) of Walter Pater, Dante Gabriel Rossetti, and Oscar Wilde or in the consecrating efforts of men like John Morley, whose *English Men of Letters* series provided biographies of the great prose writers and, by extension, a history of the achievements of the true literary profession: Samuel Johnson (published 1878), Edward Gibbon (1878), Walter Scott (1879), Edmund Burke (1879), John Bunyan (1880), John Locke (1880), John Dryden (1881), Charles Lamb (1882), Thomas DeQuincey (1882), and others.[122] As a writer for the *Cornhill Magazine* observes, in "A Man of Letters of the Last Generation," "A powerful sense of brotherhood clings to all the veritable members of the fraternity, whose highest diploma is posthumous."[123] The fin de siècle saw a remarkable urge to award such posthumous diplomas and in so doing raise professional authors to the status of men of letters—at this point, a category of literary distinction and recognition of the role of the public intellectual in British culture.[124]

For women writers, too, the 1880s proved a crucial decade in professional recognition. Although they were not included in the early organizational meetings of the Society of Authors, initially held at the all-male Savile Club, women were asked to join from its official founding.[125] Early records show that Charlotte Yonge was recruited to be among the sixty-eight founding members to represent fiction, along with Wilkie Collins, Charles Reade, and R. D. Blackmore. By the late 1880s, and in part because of their insistence that they participate actively in governance, women authors sat on the Committee of Management: Henrietta Stannard (John Strange Winter) in 1888, Mrs. Humphry Ward in 1891, and Marie Corelli in 1892.[126] By 1896 this committee elected women to the council, which held the controlling interest, among them Charlotte Yonge, Eliza Lynn Linton, and Mrs. Humphry Ward. This official representation in the Society of Authors was matched by a complementary recognition in books and periodicals. Walter Besant addressed his advice book, *The Pen and the Book* (1899), to "young persons" to whom "the Literary Life offers attractions," and in this number he included young women. His vast "literary army"—"this thousands of pens . . . at work every day"—incorporates "clergymen in their country parishes" as well as "the wives and daughters of clergymen," "professional men, civil service men, clerks" as well as "daughters of the middle class in town or country" and "elderly single women who ardently desire to add a little to their incomes."[127] Whereas Lewes had used the military metaphor in 1847 to rebuke the "innumerable host of angry pretenders" who are "like the army of Xerxes,"[128] Besant in 1899—and in the decade prior—was happy to celebrate a vast literary army, from the bottom ranks writing for penny papers up through journalists, novelists, and poets, whatever their sex.[129]

Besant's strategy—including women in the Society of Authors, recognizing all sorts and conditions of writers in his articles and books, encouraging "solidarity" (his word) within the ranks—reflects his view that authors should cease attacking one another in private and in print and instead unite as a group against publishers and booksellers. To adapt Pierre Bourdieu's model in *The Field of Cultural Production*, Besant attempts to efface the differences among authors based on a hierarchy of genres (poetry at the top, serial fiction and popular drama at the bottom) and refuses to recognize an opposition between "symbolic credit" and "economic credit" whereby, in Bourdieu's scheme, "*discredit* increases as the audience grows and its specific competence declines."[130] Instead, in a conceptual mode resembling that of the modern book historian Robert Darnton,[131] Besant recognizes a variety of participants in book production and explains their functions in *The Pen and the Book*, creating oppositions between groups with competing interests rather than among authors themselves. As the title of a report from the 1887 conference of the Society of Authors makes evident, *The Grievances between Authors & Publishers*, the goal is to redirect authors' attention to external enemies. For Besant, authors are the "producers" or "creators" of literary property, "something which has a marketable value and is openly bought and sold in the same manner as the kindly fruits of the earth"; publishers are only "the administrators of the great literary property created by the authors."[132] In the "Prospectus of the Society of Authors," widely distributed by mail, then published in the *Author*, and later included as an appendix to *The Pen and the Book*, Besant stresses that the founders of the society "were actuated by two leading principles": "that the relations between author and publisher require to be placed once for all upon a recognized basis of justice" and "that questions of copyright—domestic and international—require to be kept steadily in the public mind."[133] Besant's oppositions look to the larger field of power rather than to lesser struggles within artistic hierarchies.

Despite the founding of the society, or perhaps because of the periodical debate surrounding it, conceptions of authorship and the status of the author were widely discussed, though they remained unsettled during the 1880s and 1890s. As editor of the *Author*, Besant put on a confident face, pointing to the great progress that nineteenth-century writers had made in income, status, and social reward. He declared that the profession of letters "does really in the long run confer more dignity and respect upon a man than any other line of work, unless it be the Church."[134] He rewrote the career of a modern Chatterton by showing him in a developmental sequence, starting with journalism so that "he was not in the least danger of starving" and working his way up through book publication to the editorship of a periodical or "great morning newspaper."[135] Besant dismissed anxiety about an over-crowding of the profession by looking confidently to expanding global markets, setting "a popular writer's possible audience, at the present day, at the enormous total of 120 millions"—in comparison with 50,000 in the year 1830.[136] And he cited the example of Tennyson, raised to a peerage in 1883, as a modern example of social distinction far different from the paltry pensions conferred by George IV.[137] (He also wisely persuaded Tennyson to become the first president of the Society of Authors so that a peer and poet would officially represent the group.) For Besant these financial, professional, and social rewards were open to the young man or woman with talent who approached the literary life in a business-like way, "in a spirit of seriousness."[138]

Besant's confidence provoked cautionary—and sometimes caustic—words. Most notably, publishers took umbrage at the Society of Authors as de facto a trade union. In June 1884 the *Bookseller*, a professional organ of publishers, reported facetiously on the formation of a "Society for the Prevention of Cruelty to Authors," whose aims included "compelling publishers to publish all manuscripts sent to them; establishing perpetual copyright; introducing the custom of daily payments to authors and furnishing them with daily accounts of sales; providing that copyrights should revert to authors when publishers seemed to be making too much profit out of their books," and so on.[139] In the same vein, the *World* published a satirical poem.

> Some Literary Gents the other day did meet
> All in a private chamber, which looks on Garrick Street;
> There they did meet together, and solemnly they swore
> That as they had been done enough they would be done no
> more[.][140]

Even a decade later publishers continued to sneer at the activities of the society as low-minded and pecuniary—as in T. Werner Laurie's "Author, Agent, and Publisher, by one of 'The Trade,'" published in the *Nineteenth Century* in November 1895. The publisher of such Edwardian and modernist writers as George Moore, Arnold Bennett, and William Butler Yeats, Laurie dismissed the "professionalism" of the society and attributed its "success" to the pleasure of amateurs at "being able for a small sum per annum to put a few initials after their names, and obtain a sort of license to call themselves authors."[141] He also attacked the agent, another figure of professionalization, as a "parasite" and an "unpleasant excrescence on literature"—an attack Besant answered in the December issue by arguing that the function of the agent was to manage the author's business and keep him free from "friction and worry" to pursue a life of the imagination.[142]

These disputes between authors and publishers, which make amusing reading for the modern scholar, have provided the focus for recent studies of fin-de-siècle professionalism.[143] They pit the authors (the "profession") against the publishers (the "trade"). But they should not obscure the more subtle, intractable questions about authorship that emerged (or reemerged) in this period: questions about the origins of literature and literary creativity, about the difference between financial and artistic achievement, about popular success versus *succès d'estime*.

Indeed, Literature (with a capital *L*) and author (with a capital *A*) became recurring topics of analysis in the periodicals. An unsigned essay in the *Quarterly Review*, "On Commencing Author," for instance, reviewed the first seven volumes of the *Author* (1890–97), edited by Besant, and challenged the business-like approach to literature that dominated its pages. Making a now common distinction between "Journalism" and "Literature"—the former as "the business of the day" or "saying a thing of the hour in the manner in which a clique of the hour wishes to have it said," the latter as "verbal expression . . . in such shape that, though the matter may grow archaic, the form will preserve its interest . . . in subsequent generations"—the reviewer (C. S. Oakley) argues that journalistic writing might be approached as a business in the mode advocated by Besant, but that literary writing has its origin in other impulses: "there are numerous motives operating on the true man of letters—of literature as distinct from journalism—urging him to exercise his vocation and to exercise it to the very best of his power, without being paid for it at all."[144] The initial motive for all true literary labor, Oakley insists, is contained in the half-line *Facit indignatio versum*—with *indignatio* variously rendered in the course of his essay as disagreement, outrage, resentment, a fire in the belly, or a need for utterance.[145] The allusion to Juvenal's satire, *Si natura negat, facit indignatio versum* ("Though nature says no, indignation shapes my poetry" [I, 79]), suggests the reviewer's insistence on an older, more traditional conception of the author and on the elements of thought and emotion that spur "genuine men of letters to work." In his unidentified, untranslated allusion, Oakley suggests that great authors of the past better understand the true basis for authorship than lesser, modern writers of Besant's stature. (If you can't read this Latin line, you eliminate yourself from the category of "genuine men of letters.") His use of "vocation," followed by a discussion of authorship as "a priestly office in a wider natural Church," reinforces the high calling of the literary author and, by contrast, dismisses the "commercial aspect" of journalism with its lower or secondary motives.[146] Mowbray Morris, a regular contributor to *Macmillan's Magazine* in the 1880s, echoes this distinction between literature and journalism in "The Profession of Letters" (*Macmillan's*, 1887), using the older word "Letters" to signify the learning that has been lost in modern periodical writing.[147]

These binaries—literature versus journalism, priestly vocation versus business or trade, high art versus commercial production, literary classic versus ephemeral writing—all now seem familiar. On the one hand, they look back to Romantic conceptions of the author, with his natural genius, artistic suffering, priestly vocation, and service to his audience; on the other, they look forward to modernist distinctions between high and popular art, the alienated artist versus the successful bourgeois professional, the Joycean creator of *Portrait of the Artist* versus the hack of Gissing's *New Grub Street*. They seem to correlate as well with the two "principles of hierarchization" in Bourdieu's analysis of the nineteenth-century French literary field: "the heteronomous principle, favorable to those who dominate the field economically and politically (e.g. 'bourgeois art'), and the autonomous principle (e.g. 'art for art's sake'), which those of its advocates who are least endowed with specific capital tend to identify with a degree of independence from the economy, seeing temporal failure as a sign of election and success as a sign of compromise."[148] Yet, for all the apparent familiarity, I want to pause over this debate of the 1880s and 1890s to understand it not in simple binaries but in the complexities and confusions with which it unfurled, and to tease out the implications for fin-de-siècle authors' self-conceptions and public self-presentations, especially those of women. For in the 1880s, the literary field in England was not so clearly delineated as these theoretical models assume.[149]

In Besant's view, journalism and literature were not binaries but elements in a professional sequence; not incompatible modes of literary production but reconcilable authorial endeavors. In *The Pen and the Book* Besant imagines the man or woman of letters as working on both journalism and literature at once. He depicts the "kind of life led daily by the modern man of letters" and shows this man—"or this woman, for many women now belong to the profession"—going "into his study every morning as regularly as a barrister goes to chambers." Like a barrister with a variety of briefs, the modern professional author takes up a variety of literary tasks:

> two or three books waiting for review: a MS. sent him for an opinion: a book of his own to go on with—possibly a life of some dead and gone worthy for a series: an article which he has promised for a magazine: a paper for the Dictionary of National Biography: perhaps an unfinished novel to which he must give three hours of absorbed attention.[150]

For Besant, some tasks may tend toward the "journalistic," others toward the "literary" (though he eschews these terms), but they do not necessarily separate into oppositional modes of work. Nor are they all *l'art moyen*, to quote Bourdieu, "characterized by the subordinate position of cultural producers in relation to the controllers of production and diffusion media."[151]

Even Oakley, the conservative *Quarterly* reviewer, does not object to journalism per se; he notes that Coleridge was "truly a great man of letters" and "also a distinguished journalist," thus suggesting that a man of letters may be *both/and* not *either/or*. Nor does Oakley suggest that earning money is incompatible with producing great literature: "unless men will starve, arrangements, of course, must be made about cheques."[152] Rather, Oakley objects to the modus operandus that Besant publicizes and encourages young aspirants to adopt—the journalist "supply[ing] a publisher with a thousand words for two shillings" or the essayist or poet writing on an assigned topic: "An emphatic protest must be made against the growing habit of regarding the writer's business as the business of finding out what the public wants and supplying it as rapidly as possible, in order to become rich." For Oakley, as for Carlyle whom he quotes, "a real book comes out of the fire in a man's belly."[153] More satirically he adds, "If we were a publisher, and a man offered to supply us with a thousand words for two shillings, we would far rather give him four shillings to supply us with none at all, and we would take out the money and tell him so."[154] What Besant and Oakley dispute is the way the author imagines his life, the mode in which he produces his work and from which good work will result, and the self-construction the author offers to himself and presents to the public. Their differences anticipate the modernist distinction between the suffering, alienated artist and the successful, middle-class author, but the two have not yet parted ways.

As for the now common opposition between financial and artistic achievement—success in the "subfield of large-scale production" versus success in the "subfield of restricted production," in Bourdieu's terms—Besant does not recognize this distinction as an opposition. While he separates literary value from commercial value for the purpose of discussing an author's rights, he does not treat them as binaries, nor does he suggest that *any* ratio can be articulated between them. In "The Maintenance of Literary Property" (1887), for example, he declares that "there are two kinds of Literary Property": one kind, "symbolized by the Laurel," the author "cannot be deprived of when he has once made it for himself"; the other, commercial property, which may be "the lower and less noble kind," is "the profit of trade in the author's production"—and of this the author can, and frequently is, deprived.[155] In *The Pen and the Book* (1899), Besant omits reference to commercial value as "the lower and less noble kind," but still insists that authors keep "quite separate and distinct . . . the literary value of a work and the commercial value of a work. *There need not be any connection at all between the two*" (my italics).[156] His approach avoids the binary of high versus popular art, often advanced by modernist writers, or the ratio of "the economic world reversed" in the production "symbolic goods," articulated a century later by Bourdieu.

Why does Besant insist on dissociating literary value from commercial value? It is a strategic rhetorical maneuver—in that he wishes his fellow authors to pay attention to the commercial aspects of their literary property. But it is also, I believe, based on a historically informed analysis of nineteenth-century authorship. Besant admits that many poems "of the very highest value" were "published in a cheap magazine" or "bought for the merest trifle": "Milton got £10 for his 'Paradise Lost'; Johnson, £10 for his 'Satire of London'; Oliver Goldsmith, £60 for his 'Vicar of Wakefield.'" (Note that these examples represent seventeenth- and eighteenth-century literary works, written in a pre-professional era.) Yet, Besant adds, after citing these examples of literary merit unrewarded by commercial success, "the feeling that literature ought not to be even remotely connected with money" is a "false and foolish prejudice": "What was not beneath the dignity of Dryden, Pope, Johnson, Goldsmith, Byron, Thackeray, Dickens, need not surely be beneath the dignity of ourselves."[157] Here Besant lines up the canonical names who foreshadow the modern professional author, the heroic figures in the history of the man of letters—Dryden, Pope, Johnson—and completes the lineage with authors whose work had, in their day and after, both commercial and literary value—Byron, Thackeray, Dickens.

Though Besant does not cite financial figures, we know that the publisher Murray paid £15,000 for the copyrights of Byron's poems; that Dickens typically earned £10,000 for a novel during the 1850s; and that Thackeray, a writer's writer better known for the *succès d'estime* than the best-seller, received a fee of £1,000 per year for editing the *Cornhill Magazine* and died with an estate valued just short of "the £20,000 he had set himself to save."[158] Besant might have added the examples of Scott, who in some years earned £15,000 for his novels, "rewards on a scale unattained hitherto in the profession"; or of the Poet Laureate Tennyson, whose income during the publication of the *Idylls of the King* surpassed £10,000 a year; or of George Eliot, the most intellectual of Victorian novelists, who balanced the commercial and aesthetic demands of authorship by taking £7,000 instead of £10,000 for *Romola* so that she could control the length of its installments in the *Cornhill*.[159] He might have pointed out that Carlyle's innovative work of genius, *Sartor Resartus*, appeared in a periodical, *Fraser's Magazine*, in 1833–34; that Matthew Arnold's *Culture and Anarchy* did also, in the *Cornhill* of 1867–68; and that Walter Pater's high-culture *Studies in the History of the Renaissance* had its genesis in the *Westminster Review* and *Fortnightly Review* in 1867–71. In the 1870s and 1880s periodicals became the vehicles for high-culture production, art for art's sake. Indeed, it was in periodicals that writers initiated and launched these concepts.

In other words, while we might read Besant's insistence that there can be no predictable relationship between literary and commercial value and his assumption that writers who produce journalism might also—indeed, frequently do—produce high art, as an atropopaic gesture, as a denial of certain brutal economic facts in an era of industrial art, we would in so doing miss the complexity of the late nineteenth-century literary field that his essays delineate. For what Besant recognizes is that the great literary figures of the nineteenth century achieved aesthetic success by working within new commercial forms—indeed, that they often helped create those forms. Scott invented the historical novel and a readership for it; Dickens created the serial novel as a powerful commercial form; Moxon adapted the illustrated volume of poetry (a form rooted in the popular literary annual) to secure Tennyson's poetic reputation in the 1850s; and Tennyson revived serial publication in *Idylls of the King* in the 1860s and 1870s for both literary and commercial success. Their symbolic capital (accumulated prestige or honor) cannot be easily separated from their economic capital (material wealth, literary property).[160] The relationship is not inverse, but intertwined. For the modern man or woman of letters, symbolic and economic capital will be intertwined as well, perhaps inextricably so.

This is not to say that Besant's view dominated late Victorian conceptions of authorship and literary production. These conceptions remained unsettled and were regularly and repeatedly debated in the periodical press. Unlike the inclusive Besant, some professional authors still complained that the untrained and unfit drifted into literature and clogged the market with shabby goods. In "The Profession of Letters" (*Macmillan's*, 1887), for instance, Mowbray Morris notes, "The noble profession of Letters is the only one that needs no capital, no testimonials, no examinations, no apprenticeships."[161] In "The Trade of Author" (*Fortnightly Review*, 1889), an anonymous essayist bemoans the fact that "any man (or woman) who can hold a pen and spell decently (I am credibly informed even the latter qualification is politely waived in the case of ladies) can become an author at his (or her) own sweet will." He cleverly adds that modern authors suffer an unfair "Competition of the Dead," in that publishers can choose to reprint older works rather than pay living men and women to produce new ones, thus not only lowering remuneration but also limiting the possibilities for modern authors to create great literature.[162] And his title implicitly laments the lowering of the profession of letters to a trade. These debates might be translated into Bourdieu's observations that "the *boundary* of the field is a [site] of struggles," that "the 'profession' of writer or artist is one of the least professionalized there is," and thus that the literary field, which is not "protected by conditions of entry that are tacitly or practically required . . . or explicitly codified and legally guaranteed," will "attract agents who differ greatly in their properties and dispositions."[163] But whether we use the language of nineteenth-century men of letters or of modern literary sociologists, the fact remains that the category of authorship was highly contested and the meaning of professionalism, contested also at the fin de siècle.

On women writers the effects were complex. Some were, no doubt, still seen as untrained and unfit, though men became more hesitant to say so in public venues and limited their disparagements to private communications.[164] (Gaye Tuchman and Nina E. Fortin cite the reader's reports of Mowbray Morris, author of "The Profession of Letters" and principal reader for Macmillan from 1891 to 1911, who dismissed the manuscript of Miss E. F. Buckley on mythology, among others, as "not woman's work": "a woman has neither the knowledge nor the literary tact necessary for it.")[165] Yet women writers nonetheless entered, and succeeded in, predominantly masculine preserves—such as newspaper journalism and periodical criticism. Perhaps on their own initiative, perhaps on the encouragement of Besant in the *Author*, perhaps because of expanding markets, late Victorian women worked as journalists, magazine columnists, and art, literary, and cultural critics in increasing numbers—as Barbara Onslow documents in *Women of the Press in Nineteenth-Century Britain*.[166] In "Journalism as a Profession for Women," published in the *Contemporary Review* of 1893, Emily Crawford describes the excitement of her career as a newspaper reporter and declares the special fitness of women for this profession.

> It is impossible to doubt that women write well. . . . [T]hey have, in a greater degree than men, the faculty for throwing life into what emanates from their pen. . . . [T]here are few of them that can be ranged among the "dryasdusts." . . . Dryasdust writers are those, of all others, whom the Editor should keep out of his newspaper.[167]

From one perspective, this may represent an instance of a field becoming feminized and thus losing status,[168] or another reason for the increasing conceptual divide between literature and journalism. But to conclude so is probably to misinterpret the late Victorian literary field, certainly to miss the complexity of Crawford's gesture. Women writers understood that they needed not only to enter new arenas and tackle high-culture genres, but also to stake their claim to distinguished achievement. In a telling example, Crawford cites as key historical evidence the work of Harriet Beecher Stowe before the American Civil War and of Madame de Séverine during "the tempest of the Commune" in 1870–71—that is, she cites two women journalists who altered the course of politics, each of whom revealed herself to be "a finished craftswoman."[169] Crawford celebrates their work in order to name distinguished forerunners and claim a legacy of distinction in what was paradoxically a new field for women. Hers is a consecrating gesture. The women of letters I discuss in chapters 5 and 6—Charlotte Riddell in *A Struggle for Fame* and Alice Meynell in the *Scots Observer*—similarly understood the need to meet the terms of the market but also to advance their professional status by what I have called "myths of authorship." Meynell succeeded in being named, by her elder contemporary George Meredith, "one of the great Englishwomen of letters."[170]

At the same time, as Tuchman and Fortin have shown for late Victorian fiction, there were countermoves to edge women out of their traditional strongholds and exclude them from high-culture genres. This maneuver may have occurred behind the scenes (as in Morris's reader's reports for Macmillan), or it may have appeared subtly in the periodical press. In the "The Profession of Letters," published without signature, Morris debates Besant's optimistic view that increasing literacy and a burgeoning readership for print materials represent an improvement for professional authors. Writing an open letter to a university man bent on a literary career, Morris begs to doubt "whether the great spread of education our age has seen has not somewhat lowered the standard of what in my time was meant by what you now call culture."[171] Morris does not directly link women to this lowered standard, but he does so indirectly by adding, "There are many more people in search of a livelihood, womenfolk especially; and, as I have already pointed out to you, the pen is an instrument that can be employed by many who would be physically or financially incapacitated from pursuing other vocations": "the Church, the Army, the Government Services, Law, Commerce."[172] The diminutive "womenfolk," the reference to those "physically incapacitated" for the traditional professions, and a subsequent comment that a classical education no longer aids a university-educated writer in the literary marketplace all suggest that Morris engages in quiet warfare against women and working-class authors who are entering and succeeding in his profession. (In the second installment of his article, Morris expresses "grave doubts on a man's place in the scale of intelligence who prefers . . . "Romola" to "Old Mortality" or "Mansfield Park" to "Vanity Fair"—another denigration of women authors.)[173] In other words, Morris also creates a myth of the author—one that gives preference to classical and manly endeavors over modern popular and feminine ones.

What we can conclude from these periodical debates is that all fin-de-siècle authors, whether male or female, needed to assume a position in relation to the debates, decide on their self-constructions as "professional" writers or more "literary" artists, and negotiate the possibilities of enacting these self-constructions in the literary marketplace.[174] Women authors, no less then men, needed to conduct themselves professionally in the modern sense and imagine measures that would bestow those "posthumous diplomas" so necessary for permanent recognition. Perhaps a few women still felt held back by social conventions from presenting themselves as professional authors. In a witty essay for *Temple Bar*, "How I didn't become an Author," Norley Chester (pseudonym of Emily Underdown) enumerates the many pitfalls that face aristocratic women who wish to sell a painting or publish fiction over their signature—from an elder sister's objections to disgracing the family name, to a younger sister's anger over revealing a secret love affair, to an aunt's distaste for "so unmaidenly" a story, to the loss of a legacy for going professional.[175] But the very fact that the fictional author *is* aristo-cratic, held back by a family of "the old-fashioned type," signals the satire on this backward-looking attitude toward women's professionalism. By 1900, when this essay appeared, women of letters were already an established part of the contemporary English literary scene and several already incorporated into the *Men of Letters* tradition.[176]

2

INVENTING THE WOMAN
OF LETTERS

Harriet Martineau in the Literary Marketplace
of the 1820s and 1830s

During her fifty-year literary career, Harriet Martineau (1802–76) wrote hundreds of periodical articles and newspaper leaders, dozens of didactic tales, parables and biographies, several books of travel writing, a ground-breaking series on political economy, and seminal studies in sociology, biblical narrative, and British political and imperial history. She published her work in radical magazines (the *Monthly Repository*, the *People's and Howitt's Journal*, the American *Liberty Bell*) and major Victorian periodicals (*Westminster Review*, *Athenaeum*, *Household Words*, *Once a Week*). She placed books with educationally oriented publishers (Houlston, Darton and Harvey, Charles Knight) and with large commercial houses (Chapman and Hall, Saunders and Otley, Smith, Elder). She was the quintessential Victorian woman of letters—working in multiple print media, managing the literary and financial aspects of her career, and successfully filling the role of *dottoressa* to the nation.[1] How did she become an author?

If we credit the account in her *Autobiography*, the process followed a common nineteenth-century pattern: anonymous submission to and acceptance by a periodical, the *Monthly Repository*; a continuing relationship with that periodical, including useful professional advice from its editor and positive response from readers; then, the development of a similar relationship with a book publisher, on whom she could count to place her work. As Martineau narrates the story of her first appearance in print, her initiation sounds simple, even natural. She notes that as a child, she revealed to her mother a desire that "I should be an authoress"; she explains how her brother James, on his departure for college, advised her "to take refuge . . . in a new pursuit" and encouraged her "in an attempt at authorship"; and she adds the approval of her elder brother Thomas who, when he read her anonymous print debut on a Sunday after church services, praised her essay and "said gravely (calling me 'dear' for the first time) 'Now, dear, leave it to other women to make shirts and darn stockings; and do you devote yourself to this.'" "That evening," Martineau concludes, "made me an authoress,"[2] using a feminine designation and creating a family-sanctioned narrative of her literary pursuits.

This episode may have made Martineau "an authoress," but as I shall suggest in this analysis of her early career, it did not make her a woman of letters. That process of professional acculturation was considerably more complex, requiring an education in the conditions of the literary marketplace and the construction of a new model for the Victorian woman author. In undergoing this more complex process, recorded in her letters and autobiography, Martineau redefines authorship away from Romantic conceptions of genius, originality, and inspiration and toward a new Victorian understanding of authorship as engagement with what Robert Darnton has called the "communications circuit," what she would have called simply "the market."[3] Martineau's reconception shows the effects of her entry into the profession of letters in the 1820s, the heyday of the literary periodical; indeed, she addresses many of the professional questions—sometimes provocatively—raised by the *Fraser's* portraits of the 1830s and the mid-century periodical debates that I examined in chapter 1. Yet in her new understanding of authorship—and, with it, her invention of the Victorian woman of letters—Martineau also incorporates the lessons that she extracted from the lives of eighteenth-century and Romantic writers, many of whom she reviewed during her literary apprenticeship with the *Monthly Repository*. From these lessons Martineau formulates the terms by which she would transform herself from an "authoress" to a "professional son," from a "daughter of Mrs. Barbauld" to a "citizen of the world,"[4] from a female writer of didactic tales and treatises to a major Victorian author of periodical essays, histories, biographies, novels, and sociological, political, and economic studies—that is, she remolds herself into a heroic (wo)man of letters.

Understanding the Literary Marketplace

In his seminal essay, "What Is the History of Books?" Robert Darnton offers the "communications circuit" as "a general model for analyzing the way books come into being and spread through society." Although this process varies from place to place and period to period, Darnton suggests that modern printed books "pass roughly through the same life cycle": "[It] runs from the author to the publisher (if the bookseller does not assume that role), the printer, the shipper, the bookseller, and the reader. The reader completes the circuit, because he influences the author both before and after the act of composition."[5] What Darnton's model articulates is the immersion of the author within the systems—economic, technological, social, cultural, political—that produce literature. What his illustration of the "communications circuit" visualizes, albeit imperfectly, are the relationships of the author with others in the marketplace: editors, publishers, reviewers, and readers most obviously, but also printers, booksellers, advertisers, and other middlemen (see figure 12). His is a non-individualistic account of writerly activity, one that treats the author as negotiating a complex web of forces.

In its full version Martineau's account of coming to professional authorship reads like Darnton *à la lettre*. As the *Autobiography* reveals, she submitted her first manuscript for publication in 1822, at the age of nineteen, when her brother left for college and she, in the hope of carrying on her own intellectual life, made "an attempt at authorship."[6] Her manuscript, "Female Writers on Practical Divinity," was a critical review of works by Hannah More, Anna Laetitia Barbauld, and other women predecessors, which she submitted under the pseudonym "V. of Norwich" to Robert Aspland, then editor of the *Monthly Repository*, and which appeared in the November and December 1822 issues. But "Female Writers" was more than a review. Like its sequel, "On Female Education," this two-part article analyzes the possibilities for women in the literary marketplace. The first installment, "Mrs. More," notes that "some of the finest works on the subject of Practical Divinity are by female authors," and attributes their achievement to "the

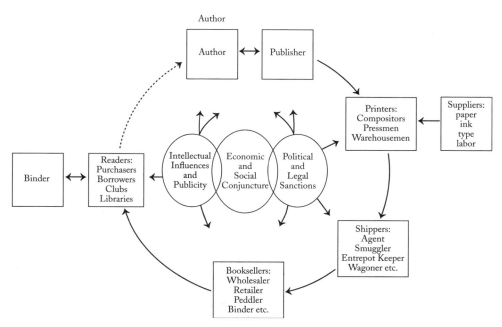

FIGURE 12. Robert Darnton, "The Communications Circuit," in "What Is the History of Books?" *Daedalus* III (Summer 1982), 68. Courtesy of Robert Darnton.

peculiar susceptibility of the female mind, and its consequent warmth of feeling." Signing herself "Discipulus," Martineau promises to consider More's work "as doing justice" to her achievement but also "as exciting the emulation of those of their sex who are capable of imitating such bright examples."[7] These twin goals merge in the second installment, "Mrs. More and Mrs. Barbauld," where she links literary achievement with "the services [More] has rendered to religion by her literary labours," services that poetesses like Barbauld have also made and that others should attempt for "the improvement of mankind."[8] The third article, "On Female Education," written presumably after Martineau had read More's *Strictures on the Modern System of Female Education*, considers the intellectual achievements of distinguished eighteenth-century women (More, Barbauld, Hamilton, Edgeworth, Carter, Talbot, Elizabeth Smith, Chapone, Grant, Aikin, and Cappe). Again, Martineau treats these women as examples of "worthy emulation." Perhaps thinking of her own exclusion from college education and her desire for an intellectual career, she urges "our earnest endeavours to the promotion of women's best interests."[9]

It is worth noting—and asking why—Martineau makes periodical publication so pivotal in her autobiographical account of professional authorship, given that the women writers she surveys produced mainly poems, novels, plays, and didactic treatises.[10] At this early stage in her career, Martineau also successfully negotiated two other modes of publication: independent, self-financed publishing and sale of copyright to an established publishing firm.[11] These two forms involved book format (often considered the mark of enduring achievement) and financial profit (often the mark of professional versus amateur work). Why periodicals?

Historically, Martineau came to authorship during the age of the periodical; as Lee Erickson notes in *The Economy of Literary Form*, "writers were best paid by periodicals between 1815 and 1835," when the market for books declined and when magazines "had not yet had their circulation undermined by the literary weeklies and newspapers."[12] Although Martineau contributed to a periodical that paid far less than leading organs like the *Quarterly Review* and *Edinburgh Review*, the *Monthly Repository* was entering a phase of cultural and political prestige, especially when W. J. Fox assumed its editorship and recruited such writers as John Stuart Mill, Harriet Taylor, Thomas Noon Talfourd, and Robert Browning.[13] These historical circumstances to some extent determined Martineau's perception of the professional author's development. Further, in 1855 when she composed her autobiography, she may have intended to reinforce the view of authorship set forth by G. H. Lewes in *Fraser's Magazine*: that, in England, periodicals rather than books had raised authorship to the status of a profession and allowed able writers to attain solid middle-class status.[14] As Lewes declared in his opening statement in "The Condition of Authors in England,

Germany, and France," "Literature has become a profession. It is a means of subsistence, almost as certain as the bar or the church."[15]

Yet periodical publishing also allowed Martineau to emphasize something absent from Lewes's account but evident in Darnton's: the roles of editor and readers in the formation of a literary career. From various anecdotes in her *Autobiography*, it is clear that external validation of her literary achievement, especially by respected men of letters, was crucial to Martineau's decision to take up her professional pen. The account of publishing her first essay includes, for example, not only Aspland's acceptance of her anonymous submission but also his request, in the "Notices of Correspondents," "to hear more from V. of Norwich" (I, 119). It includes Fox's statement, as incoming editor of the *Monthly Repository*, "that he wished for my assistance from the moment when he, as editor, discovered from the office books that I was the writer of certain papers which had fixed his attention" (I, 140). Martineau includes, too, as I have noted, her beloved elder brother's reading of the anonymous article, his praise for the "new hand" at the magazine, and his sanction of her exchange of domestic life for an authorial career (I, 119–20).

While such details recall Charlotte Brontë's acknowledgment of the help she received from an editor at Smith, Elder, who discussed her novel's "merits and demerits so courteously, so considerately, in a spirit so rational, with a discrimination so enlightened, that [his] very refusal cheered the author,"[16] Martineau's account expands the role of editor and reader from validator of literary achievement to instructor, mentor, and even collaborator in the realm of professional letters. Like Brontë, she acknowledges Fox's first letter to her as "so cordial that I was animated to offer him extensive assistance; and if he then had no money to send me, he paid me in something more valuable—in a course of frank and generous criticism which was of the utmost benefit to me" (I, 140). Unlike Brontë, however, she credits Fox with more than a sympathetic response to budding literary genius: "His editorial correspondence with me was unquestionably the occasion, and in great measure the cause, of the greatest intellectual progress I ever made before the age of thirty" (I, 140). "Occasion" and "cause" incorporate the editor as an informed reader into the process of professionalization. Martineau transforms authorship from a solitary to a social enterprise, from a matter of genius to a process of education and acculturation—just as her emphasis on "intellectual progress" raises it from hackwork to a respectable profession. That Martineau sent Fox "Essays, Reviews and poetry (or what I called such)" (I, 140)—that is, work in multiple genres—confirms that he was training her to be a full-fledged woman of letters (even as he was more practically filling the pages of his magazine).

Martineau's writing for the *Monthly Repository* played another crucial role in her professional development: it enabled her to analyze the woman writer's opportunities in the literary marketplace and imagine how they might be expanded. Darnton's analysis of the "communications circuit" excludes consideration of gender, except as it implicitly figures in the influences sketched in the center of his diagram: "economic and social conjuncture" and "political and legal sanctions." In her *Autobiography*, Martineau treats gender explicitly, though at times her discussion is muted because, even as she acknowledges her position as a woman, she tends to present herself in the role of "professional son."[17] She admits that certain social expectations (making shirts, darning stockings) inhibit the woman writer, just as the Brontës acknowledged that cultural assumptions about "authoresses" tended to prejudice editors and reviewers against them. And just as the Brontës adopted the pseudonyms "Currer, Ellis, and Acton Bell" to avoid the gender problem, so Martineau used anonymous submission and the pseudonyms "V. of Norwich" and "Discipulus" for her early work.

Yet many of the subjects on which Martineau wrote for the *Monthly Repository* suggest that she was thinking about the role of gender in professional authorship more cannily than did the Brontës and consciously seeking to insert herself into the nineteenth-century "communications circuit." Her first three articles have the woman writer's professional achievement at heart: they consider how to prepare for authorship, what genres to attempt, what subjects by authoresses appeal to readers, and what success can reasonably be expected. Several subsequent articles take up topics traditionally associated with female philanthropy: slavery, prisons, and lunatic asylums.[18] Other contributions include didactic parables, moral essays in the tradition of Hannah More, and Unitarian poetry in the tradition of Anna Laetitia Barbauld.[19] When Martineau observes that Fox "paid me in something more valuable" than money, she might have included the opportunity of learning from the reviews that she wrote of others' work, and thus of analyzing the marketplace and discovering what succeeded and what didn't.

That Martineau took her research to heart is clear from her next publishing ventures: *Devotional Exercises* (1823) and *Christmas Day* (1826). *Devotional Exercises*, written immediately after her articles appeared in the *Monthly Repository* or possibly assembled from existing personal meditations with a new concluding essay, embodies the practical divinity of her female literary predecessors. With its fourteen "prayers" and "reflections," two sets for each day of the week, and its "Treatise on the Lord's Supper,"[20] a reflective essay on the relationship of private worship to liturgical practice, this slender volume is Hannah More Unitarianized. So, too, *Christmas Day* and the other didactic tales Martineau sold to the Shropshire publisher Houlston and Sons take a lesson from More's *Cheap Repository Tracts* (an influence explored more fully below). Although these new publishing ventures reflect the concerns of the *Monthly Repository* articles, they differ in one significant way: for them Harriet Martineau received payment.

Making Money

In her account of coming to authorship, at least in the official *Autobiography*, Martineau underplays the importance of professional remuneration. Unlike Anthony Trollope, whose *Autobiography* (1883) shocked readers with its detailed accounts of production and profits, Martineau remains decorously subtle about what she earned, joking about her "first piece of pecuniary success" as a £5 note enclosed from the publisher Houlston (I, 134), and mentioning Fox's payment of £15 per year and his advice "more valuable" than money (I, 140). Later in the account, she stresses the "need for utterance" as the mark of true authorship, rather than the desire for money or fame that marks the "literary adventurer" (I, 188, 421). Yet Martineau unquestionably made money from her early publishing ventures—if not from the *Monthly Repository*, then from her self-financed book and the sale of copyright of her didactic tales. Indeed, with her father's death in 1826, she needed to supplement the mere pittance he had left her; even before his death, she was earning profits from *Devotional Exercises*. These ventures taught her useful lessons about other participants in the literary marketplace, including printers, booksellers, and advertisers; from them she learned how books were made and how to negotiate the terms of publication.

From the archives in the Birmingham University Library, we can calculate that Martineau made about £70 from the early editions of *Devotional Exercises* (1823, 1824), her first book.[21] With her brother Henry's assistance, she contracted with S. Wilkins, a Norwich "Bookseller, Printer, Stationer, and Binder," to print this volume at her own expense and to bind the sheets; she also engaged the London bookseller Rowland Hunter to sell the book directly or in response to advertisements placed in the *Monthly Repository*.[22] Martineau incurred expenses of £20 4s (1823) and £37 10s (1824) for sales of a volume that, over the nine years from 1824 to 1832, produced an income of £128 15s.[23] The fact that she retained the financial records of this first self-financed publishing venture suggests that she valued the professional experience, even if she claimed in her *Autobiography* that she "now remember[s] nothing" of it (I, 120).

We know less about Martineau's professional dealings with the firm of Houlston, that "solemn old Calvinistic publisher . . . of Wellington in Shropshire" who took what she calls the "dull and doleful prose writings" of her early years (I, 134). A letter of 3 January 1824 to her sister-in-law mentions that she is "writing a little story . . . about £5 worth" for the Tract Society: "I do not know how I shall manage, but I generally make my stories so <u>vulgar</u>, worse than Mrs. H. More's,"[24] she adds. Her financial records confirm that she sold copyright of her didactic tales typically for £5 or £10 a manuscript; that she recorded a total profit of £75 from Houlston; and that she credited her tales *The Rioters* and *The Turn-Out*, which Houlston published in 1827 and 1829, as her first works on political economy.[25] But her *Autobiography* minimizes these financial exchanges, noting only, "I remember the amusement and embarrassment of the first piece of pecuniary success. As soon as it was known in the house that the letter from Wellington contained five pounds, everybody wanted, and continued to want all day, to borrow five pounds of me" (I, 134–35). Her relations with Houlston continued "on good terms" during the 1820s, so much so that when her family suffered the last of its financial crises in 1827 and "lost our gentility," everyone assumed she was well supplied with cash "through Houlston's recent payment for one of my little books" (I, 142–43).

Martineau would eventually include professional payment in her account of authorship, taking special pleasure in what she earned and comparing her profits with those of other writers. In the *Autobiography* she notes, for instance, that she "earned altogether by my books somewhere about ten thousand pounds" (I, 268); her private tally shows a total income of 9396£, 3s, 9d.[26] Writing more privately to Richard Henry [Hengist] Horne in 1844, from her sickbed in Tynemouth, she discussed her earnings in greater detail: "I have been reckoning up my earnings (still flowing in slowly, however) & I find them between £5000 & £6000"—not quite as much as Hannah More's reputed £30,000, she noted, but nonetheless a rare achievement for any woman.[27] Yet she also told Horne that she "never looked closely after money, but kept an easy mind by always making my publishers mention the terms." This disclaimer may seem disingenuous, given the running total of profits she kept and later showed to John Chapman, but we might provisionally accept the remark and ask why Martineau minimized money in her public life writing and what she emphasized instead.

It is tempting to read Martineau's discretion about money matters as a lingering trace of the "proper lady," the woman writer who writes from a sense of selfless duty rather than from pecuniary motives. Yet the "outing" of Hannah More as an author who made large profits suggests that Martineau meant to debunk this feminine myth. (How she learned that Hannah More earned £30,000 from her writing remains an intriguing mystery, since no early nineteenth-century biography of this Evangelical woman writer mentions any profits at all.)[28] I suggest two reasons for Martineau's treatment of money matters in her *Autobiography* and letters, one conceptual, the other historical. I have already noted that Martineau conceived of authorship in terms that anticipate Darnton's "communications circuit," especially as they foreground the roles of editor, publisher, and reader in professional development. Beyond the editor as skilled reader and family members as sympathetic readers, the common reader, or reading public, figures largely in Martineau's self-conception as an author. She does not think of her readers as consumers, as purchasers of her books and thus the source of financial gain. Rather, readers are the minds and hearts on whom she as author wishes to act. The ability to convince readers, to move them not just to feel but also to take action, plays a crucial role in her conception of authorship, even more so than it does in Darnton's model.

This view is nascent in the tale of her brother's response to her *Monthly Repository* article, but it becomes emphatic in the autobiographical letter to Horne about her *Illustrations of Political Economy* (1832–34) and, more generally, her literary career. To Horne she comments,

> The Amer[ica]ns told me that every tale of mine, & every manifestation of opinion was followed by something perceptible in Govt or Parlt. I laughed at first; but, on thinking, it seemed to be true.— Whence Guizot had his informa[tion] I know not. . . . but he said, before coming over, that mine was a new case;—that in all history there was no preceding case of a woman having solid political influence otherwise than through some clever man[.][29]

Influence in the public sphere, influence on society and government—these could be most readily achieved through periodical publication in the 1820s and 1830s. Or they could be most readily witnessed, given the mode of rapid writing, printing, and response that this mode required. Whereas the *Devotional Exercises* that she self-financed might influence the spiritual life of a reader, or the didactic tales that Houlston published might affect an individual's moral action, Martineau's work in periodicals came to have repercussions in the larger world. In her early career, books were associated with the private sphere, periodicals with the public.[30] Within Darnton's model of the "communications circuit," we might say that periodicals made more visible than books the connections between the author and her readers.

We can also contextualize Martineau's account of authorship within debates of the 1840s and 1850s about the status and worth of the profession of letters. In "The Condition of Authors" (1847), Lewes devotes much attention to the relative incomes of authors in modern European nations, ultimately to document the English author's class status and improve his working conditions. Despite his fascination with earnings, Lewes concludes with an apologia for—indeed, an almost Shelleyan defense of—the modern man of letters as an important contributor to the well-being of the nation-state.

> The man who has devoted his talents and energies to the laborious task of improving and amusing mankind, has done the State as much service as the man who has marched at the head of a regiment, even if every march had been followed by a victory. . . . [H]e . . . has battled worthily for our intellectual liberty, . . . has expanded and refined our souls, . . . has helped make us wise, moderate, and humane, . . . has charmed so many a weary hour, and peopled listless days with "fond, familiar thoughts;" . . . has made us kind and gentle, far-thoughted, high-thoughted.[31]

Lewes intends his peroration to bolster an argument that authors should receive endowed professorships and government pensions, a position with which Martineau disagreed. Nonetheless, his catalogue of the author's contributions to the well-being of the nation accords with her own. Writing in the *Autobiography* about her *Illustrations of Political Economy*, she stresses the importance of readers in conceiving this seminal project, even as she acknowledges the market conditions of the early 1830s that made it so difficult to bring it to fruition.

> I thought of the multitudes who needed it,—and especially of the poor,—to assist them in managing their own welfare. I thought too of my own conscious power of doing this very thing. Here was the thing wanting to be done, and I wanting to do it[.] (I, 171)

Similarly, when she discusses her decision to write for Dickens's *Household Words* in the 1850s, she says nothing of professional fees (though her records show payment of £200) but instead mentions the "wide circulation" of the periodical that allowed for a wide influence (II, 329).[32] Like Lewes and later Darnton, Martineau understood the "economic and social conjunctures" that impinge upon the author, but she was also determined to exert an influence quite apart from the matter of remuneration. She intended her writing to have an impact in the public sphere.

Within the broad mid-century debates about the profession of letters, Martineau takes a position similar to that of the reviewer of William Jerdan's *Autobiography* (1852) in the *Westminster Review*. After chastising Jerdan for emphasizing professional fees and annual income in his argument against literature as a profession, this reviewer shifts the focus to other professional criteria, most important, the author's "mission."

> If the aim and end of literature were to accumulate money—as it is of cotton-spinning and glass-blowing—it would be rightly applied, and Mr. Jerdan's lamentations would have a curious grain of truth in them. . . . What, after all, is his complaint against literature? That it is not as productive of money as the cotton-mill or the smelting-house. . . . [B]ut there are other compensations in it of a higher kind, which should not be overlooked in the estimate of its good and its evil—the power it wields over society, its boundless influence in the extension of education and the diffusion of knowledge. The literary man may be justly proud of his mission, even should it not prove the most bountiful of paymasters.[33]

It is tempting to suggest that Martineau wrote this anonymous review, with its knowledge of factory production (her brother Robert was a Birmingham manufacturer of brass products) and its emphasis on social mission and public service. Martineau was, by this point, writing regularly for the *Westminster*.[34] But whoever the reviewer might have been, the sentiments expressed echo the principles she propounds in her *Autobiography* and the self-construction of authorship she adopted throughout her career. Martineau understood the private need to earn money, yet she emphasized the need for Victorian professionals to render public service. To quote Harold Perkin, a social historian, on the development of the professions, "It is important to note that it is not the knowledge itself or even the service as such . . . that matters, but the belief in it on the part of the client or employer and society, and thus the active steps which the profession is forced to take to inculcate that belief."[35] In a less cynical vein, Martineau anticipates this sociological insight about the importance of public service in the formation of professional identity.

Redefining Genius, Recognizing Professional Authorship

Martineau served a decade-long apprenticeship as a reviewer for and contributor to the *Monthly Repository*, during which she published almost every conceivable form of periodical writing: critical reviews, philosophical and moral essays, didactic fiction, parables, and even poetry. According to her records, she contributed "innumerable articles" to the magazine, as many as fifty-two in a single year, receiving a flat fee of £15 per annum during the editorship of W. J. Fox. The best of the *Monthly Repository* pieces were collected in a two-volume *Miscellanies* (1836), published in the United States where readers had not previously had access to them. Although the preface to the *Miscellanies* classifies this work under the theme of "The Progress of Worship" and suggests that it was "the one presiding idea [which] must have been in my mind during the composition of the whole," many of the pieces have little to do with "worship" and much to do with Martineau's future career.

Most obviously, her review of Thomas Cooper's *Lectures on the Elements of Political Economy*, published in 1832 with the title "On the Duty of Studying Political Economy," anticipates the series that she would launch that year.[36] Less obviously, but perhaps more significantly for her authorial self-conception, a two-part essay on Walter Scott, titled "The Characteristics of the Genius of Scott" and "The Achievement of the Genius of Scott," formulates the principles by which she would conduct her future career and judge the literary achievement of others.[37] The Scott essays revise Romantic accounts of authorship to suit the modern Victorian professional. Like the articles in the series "Female Writers on Practical Divinity" with which she began her literary training, the essay on Scott inaugurates her mature work of the 1830s and beyond.

In this essay Martineau continues a nineteenth-century tradition of treating authors as the "unacknowledged legislators of the World" or, in Wordsworthian terms, as "joint laborers" in the work of redeeming humankind.

> Prophets of Nature, we to them will speak
> A lasting inspiration, sanctified
> By reason, blest by faith: what we have loved
> Others will love, and we will teach them how[.][38]

Yet unlike Romantic myths, Martineau's version does not valorize inspiration, originality, or genius. Although she may have written in fits of inspiration, her *Autobiography* does not begin, as *The Prelude* does, with a meditation on the gentle breeze of nature and the correspondent breeze of the imagination. Nor does it emphasize, as Charlotte Brontë did in her "Biographical Notice of Ellis and Acton Bell," the "original mind" and "very real powers" of the literary genius.[39] Martineau is (in)famous for denying, in the *Daily News* obituary she wrote for herself, that she had any originality at all: "Her original power was nothing more than was due to earnestness and intellectual clearance within a certain range. With small imaginative and suggestive powers, and therefore nothing approaching genius, she could clearly see what she did see, and give clear expression to what she had to say."[40]

This self-composed obituary has sometimes been used to deprecate Martineau's achievement, but, in fact, her modesty reflects her redefinition of "genius" for the Victorian age. In the essays on Walter Scott, written after his death in 1832 as an appraisal of his life and work, Martineau cites Scott's *modesty* as "closely allied with the purity of Scott's *genius*" (my italics).[41] Unlike Byron, who was all too well-known for self-display, Scott wrote privately and published anonymously, and even when the authorship of *Waverley* became public, he was reluctant to drink from "the delicious cup which his brethren of the craft are usually all too ready to drain before it is half full."[42] Thus, as early as 1832, Martineau made it part of her conception of professionalism to dissociate authorship from self-importance and self-aggrandizement and to see the writer's work instead within larger social and political networks—as she would do again in the essay "Literary Lionism," written in 1837 after she had achieved fame with the *Political Economy* series.[43]

Tellingly, in the Scott essays Martineau treats literary genius not as a native gift or innate condition but as a training and an action; understanding genius requires both an inquiry into its "discipline" and "an estimate of the service that genius has rendered to society."[44] This dual inquiry determines the two parts of the Scott essay: an assessment of the "characteristics" of mind and experience that prepared Scott for authorship (like Wordsworth's self-assessment in *The Prelude*) and an inquiry into the "achievements" of Scott's literary work, by which his genius can be confirmed (unlike anything Wordsworth attempted, given that *The Prelude* ends with a promise only).

Some characteristics attributed to Scott recall common myths of literary genius: for example, that Scott learned more as a boy by "lying about in the fields" than he did by studying "his Latin grammar" or that early "vicissitude," his "ill health" and "lameness in childhood," caused the growth of "compassion" and "genius of a benignant character."[45] Other characteristics reject myths of authorship that circulated after the deaths of Shelley and Byron: for instance, that "licentious intrigues" mark the man of genius. Quite the contrary, Martineau argues; it is "not true genius which defiles its own aliment for its own pleasure."[46] (In this rejection of Byronism, her analysis is compatible with the ideology of the *Fraser's* portraits, which similarly wage war on Byronism, dandyism, and narcissism.)

The most interesting characteristic that Martineau identifies, however, both for her own self-conception and her redefinition of nineteenth-century authorship, involves Scott's class status, anticipating modern scholarly studies of professional life. According to Martineau, authors are unlikely to emerge from either the aristocratic or working classes: "the lordling knows nothing of reality" and hence has only "spurious experience" on which to build his work; the worker has only "a scanty and unfruitful power" and hence is "for ever laying a foundation on which nothing is seen to arise."[47] The "most efficacious experience of reality" occurs between the highest and lowest classes, producing the best foundation on which to build a literary career. Unlike Isaac Disraeli, who found his geniuses in all walks of life,[48] Martineau argues for the emergence of authors like Scott—and, by implication, like herself—from the middle ranks. This is what she means when she states that "Walter Scott was happy in his parentage and condition in life."[49]

Her view encompasses authorship within the larger professionalization of nineteenth-century society. According to Perkin in *The Rise of Professional Society: England since 1880*, "a professional society is one structured around career hierarchies rather than classes, one in which people find their place according to trained expertise and the service they provide rather than possession or lack of inherited wealth or acquired capital."[50] Although Perkin dates this professionalization from the 1880s, we can trace its features in Martineau's essays of the early 1830s. Perkin's "trained expertise" is a later version of Martineau's "discipline of genius," which includes not only Scott's moral and mental training but also his "industry" in literature and "practical character" in "occasions of daily business."[51] The "service provide[d]" becomes the subject of the second essay, "The Achievements of the Genius of Scott," in which Martineau details Scott's contributions to the state and society.

He has softened national prejudices; he has encouraged innocent tastes in every region of the world; he has imparted to certain influential classes the conviction that human nature works alike in all; he has effectively satirized eccentricities, unamiableness, and follies; he has irresistibly recommended benignity in the survey of life, and indicated the glory of a higher kind of benevolence; and finally, he has advocated the rights of woman with a force all the greater for his being unaware of the import and tendency of what he was saying.[52]

Scott was able to render these services because of the special ability of literature, especially drama and fiction, to instruct its readers—far more effectively, according to Martineau, than "the whole living phalanx of clergy, orthodox and dissenting, of moral philosophers, of all moral teachers, except statesmen and authors of a high order."[53] In this judgment, Martineau ranks authors above the traditional profession with which it was usually compared: the clergy.

Most important was the service Scott rendered to authors themselves: "He has taught us the power of fiction as an agent of morals and philosophy." This lesson of service—really a lesson in how best to have an effect on one's readers, a lesson in *professional* writing—was one Martineau would take to heart in *Illustrations of Political Economy* (1833–34) and throughout the rest of her career. When James Mill advised Martineau that her "method of ex-emplification,—(the grand principle of the whole scheme) could not possibly succeed" and her publisher Charles Fox asked her "to change my plan completely, and issue my Political Economy in didactic form!" she refused to alter her mode, having learned the power of fiction from the critical assessment of Scott she was composing at the same time. (Later, when "meddlers and mischief-makers" urged moving to a "larger house in a better street," she again applied Scott's "awful lesson": "never to mortgage my brains.")[54]

Martineau uses Scott's life and career, exemplary of the modern literary professional, to launch her own career as a woman of letters. The essays on Scott function, in Janice Carlisle's phrase, as an act of "specular autobiog-raphy," whereby a writer sees, comprehends, and creates the self by mir-roring the life of another.[55] In a letter to Lord Brougham, written on 10 October 1832 in response to his praise for the early numbers of her *Political Economy* series, Martineau included a bit of personal history, calling herself "a solitary young authoress, who has had no pioneer in her literary path."[56] Her self-conception as a literary pioneer emerged, I think, from her shrewd reading of the publishing market in the 1820s and 1830s: in her shift from poetry, that high Romantic genre, to prose; in her privileging of editors, readers, and publishers in her account of authorship; in her preference for the periodical over the book; and in her recognition that the anonymity of the periodical could become, paradoxically, a way for a woman writer to "make a name." Even so, the statement that she "had no pioneer in her literary path" is not quite accurate. As her critical reviews of women writers in the 1820s and of Walter Scott in 1832 reveal, Martineau studied long and hard the maps that other authors had left, even as she forged into new territory.

Forging into New Territory, Reshaping
a Women's Tradition

Martineau devised the scheme for her *Illustrations of Political Economy*, the twenty-five-part series that made her name and fame, during the summer of 1829—two and a half years before the Scott essays and her first political economy tale appeared in print. In letters written to her brother James, then serving as a Unitarian minister in Dublin, Martineau describes the reduced family finances that require her to work, discusses the possibility of conducting a school for girls "by correspondence," and sketches her plans "for literary work, with present leanings to political economy, as in her books of the 'Turn-out' and the 'Rioters.'"[57] As she contemplates this literary venture, in no sense does she imagine herself as transgressing gender norms or forging a new career model for women. The Political Economy Tales, as she then called them, build on the success of Mrs. Marcet's juvenile textbook, *Conversations on Political Economy* (1816),[58] extend the mode of her didactic tales for Houlston, and put her in the role of "governess to the nation," in Shelagh Hunter's apt phrase.[59]

Martineau conceives of her projected work as consonant with the resolutions of a private memorandum she wrote also in the summer of 1829, as she committed herself to "literary pursuits." (It is likely that she wrote this memorandum as she devised her political economy scheme.) Among the ten resolutions, most involving aspects of moral and intellectual character, is this ninth: "To consider my own interests as little as possible, and to write with a view to the good of others; therefore to entertain no distaste to the humblest literary task which affords a prospect of usefulness."[60] In other words, at the outset (and in the midst) of publishing *Illustrations of Political Economy*, Martineau imagined her work as a continuation of her earlier didactic tales and of a women's literary tradition that had preceded her. Only in one matter did Martineau potentially depart from gender norms: she contemplated— indeed, desired—a move to London. Urged by Fox of the *Monthly Repository* to accept an editorial position in the city, she expressed this desire in 1830 letters to her brother "as essential for a literary career," and to her mother as necessary for "continual access to the Museum and other libraries."[61] Her mother forbade the plan, wrongly imagining that her daughter planned to live "in lodgings" and sent "peremptory orders" to return home (*Autobiography*, I, 149), then compromising with an arrangement that allowed Harriet to spend three months a year in London living with an uncle, aunt, and cousins.

In retrospect, we can see that publishing the *Illustrations* was groundbreaking in multiple ways: conceptually, as political intervention and industrial fiction; personally, as an entrée into London literary society; and professionally, as opening up new literary ventures and requiring a new conception of the woman writer. But in medias res, as her letters reveal, Martineau did not fully comprehend the significance of what she undertook. By 1855 when she composed her *Autobiography*, however, she had acknowledged its professional import, revised the arc of her literary career, removed many traces of her links to eighteenth- and early nineteenth-century women's literature, and perhaps even forgotten the publishing contexts from which her tales emerged. She had, in short, revised herself into a "solitary young authoress" with no predecessor to show the path, a heroic woman of letters who had forged her way through a literary wilderness. She had created a new myth.

This self-revision provides the focus of the remainder of this chapter, which analyzes the professional and political significance of the *Illustrations*, seeks the motives for Martineau's erasure of their humble literary roots, and charts her radical departure from the emulation of Hannah More so clearly expressed in her debut essay, "Female Writers on Practical Divinity" (1822). In the *Autobiography* we can find traces of this erasure in Martineau's comments on the tracts and tales she wrote for the Shropshire publisher, Houlston; in her silence about the influence of More's seminal *Cheap Repository Tracts* on her didactic fiction; and in her emphasis on her innovation, as a woman writer, during the era of the First Reform Bill of 1832. That she *did* innovate is unquestionable, but that innovation had its roots in the literary past and her early career.

As Martineau narrates the story of her literary apprenticeship, she minimizes her dealings with Houlston during the 1820s, recalling them with "amusement and embarrassment" (I, 134). The embarrassment can be traced, I think, to an alliance with an Evangelical publisher whose ideology soon became alien, even antithetical to her own. Houlston published a tract series that built on the success of More's *Cheap Repository* (1795–98) and attracted such Evangelical writers as Mary Martha Sherwood, Lucy Lyttleton Cameron, and George Mogridge—all clouded by a "gloomy Calvinism" that Martineau identified with More and her sect.[62] The tracts dominating Houlston's Shropshire and London bookselling trade were religiously and socially conservative; typically, they taught the lessons of personal endurance, reliance on providence, and acceptance of one's earthly status. Their narrative mode employed personal experience and testimony—not, as Martineau would soon learn from studying political economy, for understanding the individual case within the context of larger economic and political forces, what she considered "laws," but for placing it within a biblical framework. Houlston's tracts, including those that Martineau contributed, were all published in the same format: as "little books," duodecimos of approximately 3 ½ × 6 inches, with a frontispiece or title-page illustration, a short didactic tale, and an endlist advertising other tracts in the series (see figures 13–15).[63] Their common form thus suggested a common religious perspective and social ideology—a commonality reinforced by the publisher's series, which numbered the tracts sequentially, and by the practice of readers, who often bound tracts together.[64]

Mrs. Sherwood's *A Drive in the Coach through the Streets of London* is representative of the Houlston series, "A Story Founded on Fact" as its subtitle asserts. In the frontispiece, we see "Julia and her Mamma in the

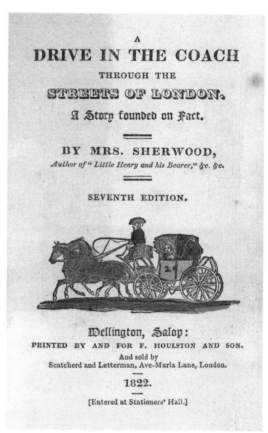

FIGURES 13 AND 14. Frontispiece and title page, Mrs. Sherwood, *A Drive in the Coach*. Courtesy of the Beinecke Rare Book and Manuscript Library, Yale University.

FIGURE 15. Frontispiece, Harriet Martineau, *The Rioters* (1827).
Courtesy of the Yale University Library.

Bookseller's Shop," an illustration of an episode in the tale. On the title page, between the story title and the publisher's signature, appears a small woodcut of a coach and horses in which a child sits—the same format used on title pages of More's *Cheap Repository* (see figure 16). In the tale itself, a little girl begs her mother to be taken along on a ride, with the understanding that she will "behave wisely in the streets" and "not give [her] mind to self-pleasing."[65] As soon as the girl reaches the shopping district of the city, however, she forgets her promise and engages in exuberant window-gazing, asking her mama for object after object of desire. So, with a lesson in mind, her mama consents to let her choose one gift from each shop window—provided that she choose something from *every* window that they pass. And the little girl chooses—a writing table, blue satin boots, a penknife, a cap with artificial flowers, and so on until she reaches an undertaker's shop and must choose a coffin. The lesson? That all things of this world come to naught, that our certain death should teach us to value the things of heaven, not the commodities of earth. The mama, who delivers this lesson, quotes 1 Timothy 5:6: "But she that liveth in pleasure is dead while she liveth."

The interpretive frame of this tract, like that of others in the Houlston series, is biblical; the little girl learns not only the lesson of her mortality but

FIGURE 16. Title page, Hannah More, "Turn the Carpet;
or, The Two Weavers," *Cheap Repository Tracts* (1796). Courtesy
of the Yale Center for British Art, Paul Mellon Collection.

also the more general lesson of subjecting her actions and expectations to
biblical rule. The rhetorical mode of the tracts, as social historian Susan
Pedersen has noted of More's *Cheap Repository*, involves either an omni-
scient narrator who comments on the protagonist's course of action, as in
A Drive in the Coach, or the personal testimony of lived experience, as in the
evangelical confession of sin and repentance.[66] Occasionally, the tracts take a
question-and-answer form—as in the Anglican catechism or didactic school-
books. Whatever the rhetorical mode, the Houlston tracts do not attempt to
analyze the individual case within social, economic, or political contexts. The
context for understanding is pre-ordained in and by the scriptures, the first
and final authority for human action.

Thus, when Martineau discusses her early work for Houlston in her *Autobiography*, we can infer why she minimizes her early tales (*Christmas Day* and its sequel, *The Friends*) and maximizes the later stories that foreshadow her writing on political economy (*The Rioters* and *The Turn-Out*): the former represent a hermeneutic practice she subsequently renounced, whereas the latter anticipate a scientific perspective she would champion. In the *Auto-biography*, Martineau does not even name the two "little eightpenny stories" she first sent to Houlston. Elsewhere she dismisses the first, *Christmas Day*, as "a trumpery story" (I, 113)—"trumpery" meaning either a "fraud," a bit of "deceit," or "something of little value, rubbish, trash" (*OED*). In fact, these early tales were deeply autobiographical, thinly disguised accounts of Mar-tineau's personal experience, including her physical infirmity and family misfortune, and thus true to her lived experience. They are not "frauds" in the sense of relating false facts or false experience, but "frauds" in the sense of relating erroneous interpretations or deducing false lessons from experience.

In *Christmas Day* (1826), the protagonist Sarah Brunton becomes a gloomy, morose creature after her father catches fever and dies, and she and her mother must economize by taking a smaller house—details not unlike those of Thomas Martineau's death in 1826 and the family's financial crisis after the crash of 1825–26. Sarah is coaxed out of her despairing state by an exemplary cousin, Margaret—a figure probably based on Ann Turner, the minister's daughter who helped Harriet take charge of her moral and emo-tional state. As Martineau explains in her *Autobiography*, "I am sure I must have been somewhat happier from that time . . . when Ann Turner and her religious training of me put me, as it were, into my own moral charge. I was ashamed of my habit of misery,—and especially of crying. I tried for a long course of years,—I should think from about eight to fourteen,—to pass a single day without crying" (I, 62). Predictably, little Sarah learns to stop crying and count her blessings, and—in the common mode of Evangelical tracts—to approach her "calamities" with a reliance on God and biblical wisdom. *Christmas Day* ends with the moral, "Whether our outward situation be prosperous or not, we may be happy in dependence on an un-changing Friend, and his care."[67]

Its sequel, called *The Friends* (1826) and covering the next phase of Sarah Brunton's life, in which she goes blind (as Harriet went deaf) but learns to become a music teacher to young girls, ends with a quotation from the Psalms, "the Lord raiseth up all them that he bowed down." The school-mistress who hires Sarah observes, "What a privilege it will be to my pupils to have continually before them such an example of resignation and pious cheerfulness under circumstances of severe privation."[68] This didactic use of calamity is not quite as extreme as the episode in Mrs. Sherwood's *History of the Fairchild Family* (1818), a popular Houlston publication in which Mr. Fairchild shows his children a rotting corpse hanging from a gibbet as a warning against family quarrels, but it projects a heavy-handed moralism and, from Martineau's later perspective, a "metaphysical fog."[69] The tale fails to treat Sarah Brunton's case within the context of the economic forces that caused her family's calamity or to offer her—or the reader—a way out of the financial predicament that keeps the mother and daughter dependent on friends' charity.

In later tales for Houlston, *The Rioters* (1827) and *The Turn-Out* (1829), Martineau swerves away from individual morality, religious piety, and philosophic resignation, and redirects her protagonists toward economic knowledge and political consciousness. These longer tales for Houlston are the ones she acknowledges as professionally significant: they showed how to analyze economic issues and participate in the public sphere. Yet, like the later *Illustrations of Political Economy*, they, too, adopt the rhetorical techniques that More had used in her *Cheap Repository* and that Sherwood replicated in the Houlston tracts: what Susan Pedersen identifies as the "simple plots, vivid language, and a moral message made clear through action rather than words."[70] In *The Rioters; or, A Tale of Bad Times* (1827), Martineau employs a first-person, eyewitness account of the hard times during a depression of wages. The tale begins as a middle-class London businessman travels to Manchester, hears of an act of loom breaking, and visits the site to learn more about the riot and the fate of the workers. The workers testify to their plight in vivid terms, and the Londoner listens, offering advice to the arrested workers and assistance to their impoverished families. The first half of the tale uses the common narrative mode of personal testimony, though privileging the Londoner's better-informed understanding of the events. This privileging—in effect, an acknowledgment of the need for economic theory—dominates the second half of *The Rioters*, which consists primarily of a didactic dialogue in which the Londoner explains to disaffected workers how "the market" works, how competition in trade affects the price of goods and the level of wages, and how the European market impacts the British mill owner and worker alike, quite beyond their control.[71]

In *The Turn-Out; or, Patience is the Best Policy* (1829), Martineau again employs a dialogue, but now a more equal one between Mr. Wallace, a mill owner, and Henry Gilbert, a spokesman for the workers. (In this adjustment of technique, she seems to have intuited a problem that Greg Myers associates with didactic tales using a dialogue format, which "profess to teach learning by experience but actually teach learning by authority.")[72] Both men express their views on the state of the depressed trade in worsted wool, and if Mr. Wallace's reasoning wins out, it is only after Henry Gilbert fully expresses his frustration and grief. Martineau implicitly agrees with the subtitle of one of More's *Cheap Repository* poems, "Half a Loaf is better than no Loaf," but she reaches her conclusion differently—not by having Tom, the rebellious worker, declare, as in More, "Thou are right, If I rise, I'm a Turk: / So he threw down his pitchfork, and went to his work," but instead by tracing the life courses of three workers—Henry, who urges a strike; his brother James, who wants to work but quits when fellow workers threaten him; and Maria, fiancée of James, who suffers much deprivation during the strike. These life stories introduce the compelling plots that More understood were essential to popular literature, yet by allowing the working-class characters to voice their complaints without authorial critique and by investigating the motives for their actions, Martineau gives their radical politics more sympathetic treatment, even as their economic and political misjudgments are exposed. Maria, who voices the woman's predicament, loses all her savings by acquiescing in the men's decisions and comes to see that if the brothers could "temper each others' character," "much sorrow might have been avoided."[73] James, who strikes against his better judgment, concludes, "Though it is a hard-ship to have low wages, any thing is better than a TURN-OUT" (135). Henry, the spokesman and advocate of the strike, remains silent, feeling guilty about the damage done to others but not relinquishing his political position. This tale of 1829 makes no allusion to the goodness and wisdom of providence; rather, it explains economic matters wholly within the theories of free trade, supply and demand, and a global market for goods.[74]

No doubt, "Old Houston," as Martineau called him, found these tales compatible with others in his series, most likely because they illustrate the errors of machine breaking, striking, and inciting mob violence. Nevertheless, by writing for Houlston and studying the tracts in his series, Martineau not only learned practical lessons about the production of popular, didactic literature but also how to take a book form intended for one purpose and turn it to another.[75] Although she claims not to have known the term "political economy" when she wrote these industrial tales of the 1820s, her *Autobiography* links *The Rioters* (1827) and *The Turn-Out* (1829) with the series that would transform her into a professional author, *Illustrations of Political Economy* (1832–34). This unlikely connection is, I think, one source of Martineau's "amusement": the fact that writing tracts for a socially and religiously conservative Evangelical publisher eventually led to her own socially progressive and politically radical fiction of the 1830s.

In this turn of the screw, Martineau repeated in the 1830s what More had done with the didactic tract in the 1790s: she transformed a publishing form identified with one political ideology for use in aid of another. In the early 1790s, More had used popular fiction to support a Tory ideology. Fearful of the growth of revolutionary political movements and of the racy, Jacobin literature that circulated among the rural poor, she and her sisters had drawn up a plan for producing and distributing "safe and salutary reading" to charity children, Sunday schools, and the rural poor.[76] As More's Victorian biographer William Roberts explains, "[T]he school of Paine had been labouring to undermine, not only religious establishments, but good government, by the alluring vehicle of novels, stories, and songs[;] she thought it right to encounter them with their own weapons."[77] After securing over £1,000 in subscriptions from wealthy philanthropists, mostly Tories, More produced *The Cheap Repository of Moral and Religious Tracts* (1795–98), a series of moral tales, didactic poems, and Bible stories modeled on the popular chapbooks (stories) and broadsheets (songs) of her day and intended to stifle the revolutionary impulses of the working classes by diverting them into religious channels.[78]

Martineau's *Illustrations of Political Economy* adopt the literary techniques that More had employed in the *Cheap Repository*, that successors had imitated in various British tract series, and that she had honed to effective use in her own tales for Houlston.[79] Although Martineau minimizes the influence, More remains, ironically, a primary literary source for the *Illustrations*— though, in repeating in the 1830s the gesture that More enacted in the 1790s, Martineau would radicalize the little book, revise its political ideology, and propel herself as a writer into the political arena.

Entering the Political Arena, Becoming a Woman of Letters

What led Martineau to transform the evangelical tract into the radical political tale? No doubt she was personally motivated to read political economy and write her tales in an effort to comprehend what had happened to her father's business and family's fortune. Thomas Martineau had been a manufacturer of bombazine and camlet in Norwich until "the speculations, collapse, and crash of 1825 and 1826" caused "the deterioration in the value of his stock," and the family "began to contemplate absolute ruin" (*Autobiography*, I, 128–29).[80] The collapse of the market in worsted cloth provides the setting for *The Turn-Out* (1829), in which a manufacturer and worker discuss the effects on wages in theoretical terms. A minor character, Miss Wallace, explains the law of supply and demand more concretely, vivifying the sudden shift in the market from worsted wool to silk in language available to the common reader: "I can answer for the ladies, at least. Every lady would rather wear silk than bombazeen, if she could get it at the same price, or cheaper" (39). The laws of political economy—of production, distribution, exchange, and consumption—make a difference in everyday life.[81]

Beyond personal enlightenment, the turn to political economy and radical politics in the late 1820s reflects Martineau's new affiliation with the *Monthly Repository* under W. J. Fox, its editor as of 1828. Under Fox's editorship the magazine moved beyond its function as a religious "house organ" with advanced social views to advocate a full set of reforms: education for women and the working classes; an untethered search for truth in religion and philosophy; a faith in science and support for technology; an endorsement of "the spirit of the age and the principle of utility"; and an agenda of political radicalism, including "the amelioration of the criminal code, the abolition of various restraints on commerce, the progress towards a better system of taxation, the repeal of the Test Act, and the emancipation of Catholics."[82] As Francis Mineka has suggested, W. J. Fox was "the bravest of all" Unitarian radicals, participating actively in reform politics in the 1820s and 1830s and publishing views so advanced that he "frighten[ed] away many of the douce, respectable folks among his subscribers," including the pro-reform Whigs.[83]

When Fox assumed the editorship of the magazine, he issued a call for "voluntary assistance to render the work a worthy organ" of the Unitarians[84]—to which Martineau responded. During the next four years she contributed over two hundred tales, poems, sketches, articles, and reviews, becoming the magazine's chief reviewer and almost its coeditor.[85] While Fox tended to write the political columns of the magazine, assigning Martineau topics on biography, theology, and moral and mental philosophy, she nonetheless used this work to deepen her knowledge of English radical politics and political economy—and to articulate a link between the two. She was influenced by the agenda of the philosophical radicals, who wrote for the *Repository* and who in the 1820s and 1830s explored, as Donald Winch has suggested, "the possibilities of combining a political economy embodying the population principle with a case for democratic representation."[86] Indeed, by 1831 Martineau had formulated a civic rationale for her Political Economy Tales, and introduced it in one of her last articles for the magazine.

In January 1832, as Fox wrote the leading article, "On the State and Prospects of the Country," in support of the Reform Bill and further measures "which relate to voting by ballot and the duration of parliaments," Martineau contributed "On the Duty of Studying Political Economy,"[87] ostensibly a review of Thomas Cooper's *Lectures on the Elements of Political Economy*. Cooper's *Political Economy*, based on lectures to students at South Carolina College, was intended for lay readers; disclaiming originality, he drew freely on the concepts of Adam Smith, David Ricardo, Thomas Malthus, and James Mill (the middle two of whom had close ties with Unitarians in Britain, which may explain how the book came to the attention of Fox and Martineau).[88] Following Cooper, Martineau argues in this review that "every member of society who studies and reflects at all [must] inform himself of its leading principles," given how relevant they are to "social duty and social happiness" in government, philanthropy, and family life.[89] Her examples—illustrating the principles of supply and demand, the ill effects of protective tariffs, and the negative consequences of ill-informed philanthropy—anticipate the series she would launch later that year and explain their relevance to political reform:

> Many popular representatives prefer shooting and billiards to studying Ricardo, as much as Charles Fox preferred tending his geraniums to

reading Adam Smith. We hold, however, that the blame does not chiefly rest with these gentlemen themselves. . . . It is true that the representatives of the people ought to be able to point out to their constituents the origin and nature of the evils they know only in their effects. This is the only way of making representation as enlightened and effectual as it might be. . . . Nor is this less necessary, supposing the ruling portion of the commonwealth as well-informed respecting its duties as it ought to be. The execution of their measures depends upon the people, and enlightened cooperation is essential to their success.[90]

That is, both political representatives and ordinary citizens, MPs and those who elect them, must understand the principles of political economy in order for political reform to occur; without mutual understanding, wrong representatives will be elected or wrong measures passed, or bills passed will not be put into effect, or they will be subverted by the countermeasures of private citizens.

This articulation typifies the "radical unitarian" approach of the *Monthly Repository*, with its emphasis on an enlightened leadership, a populace educated in scientific principles, and an extension of education to the "people," by which was usually meant (as Kathryn Gleadle notes) the lower-middle class and labor aristocracy.[91] It differed from the position of many political radicals of the former generation, most notably William Cobbett, who "loathed the political economists and their reification of human relationships" and who, in the 1810s and 1820s, subjected their writings to a steady stream of abuse in his *Political Register*.[92] (When Malthus issued a new edition of *An Essay on the Principle of Population*, Cobbett published an open letter "To Parson Malthus" in the *Weekly Political Register*: "Your book on POPULATION . . . could have sprung from no mind not capable of dictating greater acts of cruelty than any recorded in the history of the massacre of St. Bartholomew.")[93] The "radical unitarian" position differed as well from the educational project of the Whiggish Mrs. Marcet in *Conversations on Political Economy* (1816), the book that introduced Martineau to this body of theory but used political economy to justify wealth and considered its subject unsuitable for the working classes. (When Caroline asks her teacher Mrs. B. whether she would teach political economy to the working classes, the answer is "No.")[94] Martineau's project, like Fox's in the *Monthly Repository*, reflects the beliefs of the radical Unitarian circle in which she participated: that, as W. H. Ashurst explained, "The discoveries of Science have opened the way to the unity of humanity," and that, as W. B. Adams insisted, scientific and industrial advance should benefit workers, not cause more suffering.[95]

By the summer of 1831, Martineau had sketched out the plan for her Political Economy Tales "in a very small blue book," and by autumn she had "strengthened [her]self in certain resolutions," vowing "that no power on earth should draw me away." When faced with refusals by several publishers, she determined that her project must be carried out: "The people wanted the book; and they should have it" (*Autobiography*, I, 160–61). This represents an extension of her personal use of political economy in the Houlston tales to a more general, public application—an opportunity for "the multitudes" to "manage" their own welfare (*Autobiography*, I, 171), to act according to scientific laws in daily life, as she had done after studying economic theory.

Why did the need to publish her Political Economy Tales become so urgent in 1831? What does the historical context reveal about Martineau's conception of her series? If we look to the *History of England during the Thirty Years' Peace, 1816–1846,* which Martineau wrote in 1848, a year of European revolutions, we find a key: she conceived of the era of the First Reform Act as the English equivalent of the French Revolution. In the chapters on 1830–32, the years of George IV's death, Lord Grey's Whig prime ministry, and the debate over parliamentary reform, Martineau designates 1830 as "year One of the people's cause"—echoing the practice of the French Revolution in dating events from the end of the monarchy. Martineau describes the fifteen prior years of Tory rule as "dark and troubled," "discouraging and exasperating," noting the suppressions of liberty and the "vicissitudes of fortune" that the people had suffered, but also noting that they "had learned striking and virtuous lessons about their own power—lessons which had prepared them to require wisely, and conduct magnanimously, the greatest revolution in the history of their country."[96] For 1831–32, she records "the great stir among the middle classes which kept the country for nearly two years in a state which was called revolutionary, and with justice," and notes (positively) "the determination of the political unions to march on London in case of need."[97] Again, in her account of the parliamentary battle for reform, she repeats the language of revolution: "In all preceding 'revolutions,'—to adopt the term used by the anti-reformers—[the people] had acted, when they acted at all, under the direction of a small upper class who thought and understood for them, and used them as instruments. Now, the thinkers and leaders were of every class, and the multitude acted, not only under orders, but in concert."[98] In sum, in conceptualizing the years 1830–32, the period in which she planned *Illustrations of Political Economy* and published its first installments, Martineau envisioned an English revolution—not one of regicide and lawless violence (though she describes the riots in Derby, Nottingham, and Bristol that erupted against anti-reformers and depicts the divestment of William IV's power) but a war of ideas in which thinking men and women of all classes would usher in a new political era.

In this context, Martineau's *Illustrations of Political Economy* become the literary agent of a political revolution in the 1830s, just as More's tracts had suppressed revolution in the 1790s. Indeed, the opening tale of the

Illustrations, Life in the Wilds (1832), depicts a social upheaval in the British colony of South Africa that demonstrates the value of all useful citizens and the folly of social pretensions that refuse (or inhibit) productive labor. An attack by Bushmen on a British settlement results in the destruction of houses, cattle, working implements, and other goods, and the settlers must rebuild from a virtual state of nature. Those useful in the rebuilding are settlers "excited by the novelty of their situation, and full of a spirit of enterprise"; those useless (or worse) are settlers "ready to plead their rights, to refuse any employment they might fancy degrading, and to resent any hint that the less was now said of distinction of ranks the better."[99] While the explicit purpose of this tale is to illustrate the production of wealth and the division of labor, an implicit purpose is to demonstrate the crucial contribution made by the middle and working classes to the welfare of the British nation and thus their legitimate claim to full political participation. Significantly, in her depiction of "the beneficial power" of labor, Martineau acknowledges agricultural and manufacturing workers, teachers, preachers, members of Parliament, and even the king, but pointedly ignores wealthy aristocrats and landowners as contributing any form of "productive" or "unproductive" labor. Published in February 1832, just as Lord Grey "made the expected declaration that a measure of parliamentary reform was in readiness to be brought forward,"[100] the first tale participates in the movement for political reform.

If, moreover, we consider Martineau's account of the Reform Act of 1832 in *A History of the Peace* in conjunction with her 1832 review essay on Walter Scott, the last review she published before embarking on the *Illustrations*, we gather another clue to Martineau's conception of her series and her authorial work. The Scott essay articulates the contributions that authors can make to the modern nation-state—from satirizing follies to reforming prejudices to advancing the cause of women and workers. In its closing paragraphs, Martineau observes that Scott has had many imitators but that "the progression of the age requires something better than this imitation": "the serious temper of the times requires a new direction in the genius of the age."[101] This new direction is "to employ his method of procedure" to "new doctrine and other materials," to expose to consciousness the fact that in Scott "one class is in a state of privilege, and another in a state of subjection, and that these things ought not to be." The modern age requires another kind of fiction than the historical novel of knights and ladies: "We have yet to wait for the philosophical romance, for the novels which shall relate to other classes than the aristocracy."[102]

Although Martineau would not attempt a philosophical romance until *The Hour and the Man* (1841), her account of the black revolutionary hero Toussaint L'Overture, she did write fiction about those "other classes" when she embarked on the *Illustrations of Political Economy*. The tales take their heroes from factory workers and colonial settlers, middle-class bankers and progressive scientists, ordinary London merchants and illegal coastal smugglers. These characters become heroes not because of aristocratic birth but because of the productive labor that they contribute to the community—as in *Life in the Wilds*, where Mr. Stone, "the best educated man in the settlement," turns his hand to digging an irrigation trench, and Mrs. Stone, "by common consent called the Lady of the settlement," refuses the title because she "thought there was no reason for such a distinction in a place where all were obliged to exert their own power for their own subsistence."[103] In Martineau's conception, the English political revolution of 1832 was to have its parallel in an English literary revolution of the same era—by turning away from the historical novel and the hero of high birth and turning instead to ordinary heroes in everyday life.

In choosing middle- and working-class characters, her *Illustrations* enact this turn: Martineau makes parallel in fiction the political shift in power from the aristocracy to the middle classes in the 1832 parliamentary reform. So, too, in the shift from a biblical interpretive framework to the secular principles of political economy, she makes parallel the shift from the Anglican bishops in the House of Lords to the people in the House of Commons. In *A History of the Peace*, Martineau underscores the recalcitrant action of the bishops, all of whom except the Bishop of Norwich opposed the Reform Bill.

> Twenty-one—exactly enough to turn the scale—voted against the bill. . . . It was proclaimed over the whole kingdom, and it will never be forgotten, that it was the bishops who threw out the Reform Bill. Newspapers in mourning edges told this, in the course of a day or two, to every listener in the land. . . . While they imputed their yielding to a love of peace, they could not complain if the people assigned it to a lack of courage. Whether the deficiency was of sagacity, or knowledge, or independence, or principle, it did more to injure the Church throughout the empire than all hostility of Catholics and Dissenters together.[104]

In her reading of the literature and politics of the 1830s, here as elsewhere, the revolution comprised a democratization and secularization in multiple realms. She saw her work as participating in the progress of history.

This view of early nineteenth-century British literature was not wholly original, of course, though Martineau articulated it forcefully for prose fiction. In prefaces to poetry anthologies of the period, editors frequently explained the rise of Romantic poetry in terms of a revolutionary impulse. In *The Book of the Poets* (1842), for instance, an anonymous editor treats political agitation as a catalyst for artistic production and posits "a literary revolution in England," like "that political change which had convulsed France"; it was "in the first instance a work of violence and havoc, in which the necessary task of destruction was to precede that of renovation."[105] The editor enumerates the literary features of this "emancipation" as a change in subject matter: a new interest in "the short and simple annals of the poor," as evidenced in Crabbe and Wordsworth; a redeployment of the political energies of the French Revolution to English nationalism, as exhibited in the verse of Scott and Southey; and a return to domestic virtues, as exemplified by women poets and minor writers such as Milner, Heber, and Pollok.[106] Martineau's agenda for prose fiction caught a similar revolutionary impulse.

It might be argued that this literary revolution was a metaphorical one, analogous to the political perhaps, but not fundamentally so—possibly even dampening actual revolution by suggesting that representation in literature was constitutive of political representation. But Martineau would not have accepted this valuation of literary revolution as merely metaphorical, though she would admit in her 1849 *History of the Peace* that the 1832 Reform Act had not fully succeeded, that the Whigs had bungled it, and that the landed interests were "brought down" only "some little way."[107] Like Shelley in *The Defense of Poetry* (written 1821, published 1840), she pondered the role of the author in the modern nation, but whereas Shelley viewed poets as "the unacknowledged legislators of the world," Martineau conceived of her work as *visibly* engaged in shaping legislation and government policy. Thus her *Illustrations* treat topics of current political interest: free trade and protective tariffs, bank crashes and bills of exchange, colonial settlement and slavery, strikes and wages, poor laws and pauperism, overpopulation and birth control, tithes and taxation.[108]

In gauging the political and social effects, Martineau cites the enormous quantity of letters from readers and blue books from MPs that came in the mail—"to the astonishment of the postmaster, who one day sent word that I must send for my own share of the mail because it could not be carried without a barrow" (*Autobiography*, I, 179). When she moved to London to complete the series "on the spot," she received visits from politicians with causes they wished her to promote. She met regularly with her political friends and acquaintances, including Lord Durham, known as "Radical Jack," and with Whigs in the Lord Advocate's chambers and at evening parties to discuss current parliamentary debates. While she did not wish to be identified with a single political party, for fear that it would harm the sale of her series and compromise her independence of view,[109] she firmly believed that her Political Economy Tales had an impact on the Reform of 1832 and on subsequent reforms of the poor laws and laws of taxation—as in her letter to Horne: "The Amer[ica]ns told me that every tale of mine, & every manifestation of opinion was followed by something perceptible in Gov[ernmen]t or Parl[iamen]t."[110] If Martineau envisioned a link between literature and politics more direct, less complicated, and less ambivalent than those conceived by writers and critics of later eras, she nonetheless articulated a conception of fiction and a role for the professional author that would come to dominate the Victorian period. Her conception was essential to the formation of the woman of letters as a social and political critic, as (in our modern phrase) a public intellectual.

Recognizing the Woman of Letters

When the periodical press reviewed Martineau's *Illustrations of Political Economy*, several writers noted the significance of the author's gender. Among the positive reviews, *Tait's Edinburgh Magazine* observed that "the ladies seem determined to make the science of Political Economy peculiarly their own," referring to the achievements of Marcet's textbook, Edgeworth's fiction, and Martineau's *Illustrations. Tait's* found the confluence of domestic economy and political economy, of woman as household manager and as imperial governess, entirely appropriate: "The economy of empires is only the economy of families and neighborhoods on a larger scale."[111] The *Westminster Review* introduced the note of gender as a matter of national pride: "What a country is England! Where a young lady may put forth a book like this, quietly, modestly, and without the apparent consciousness of doing any extraordinary act."[112] For yet other reasons, Joseph Conder in the *Eclectic Review* praised "our fair *Dotteressa*" and "the delightful Political Economy made easy by Professor Harriet Martineau," observing that "many female tale-writers in the present day" have "similar knowledge of human nature and fertility of imagination," but that Martineau excels because she combines "a feminine power of illustration" with "a masculine faculty of abstraction"; her tales "indicate a clearness and comprehension of thought in relation to abstruse subjects of inquiry."[113] For Conder it is not so much English national culture or women's extension of their traditional domestic roles as it is this particular woman writer's abilities that contribute to her success.

These positive reviews appeared in periodicals with Radical or Whiggish leanings, as suggested by their endorsement of political economy and a woman writer's publishing fiction to exemplify its doctrines. They found the doctrines useful in an era of political reform and approved the work of those aiding reform. Presumably, they did not object to the mode of self-enfranchisement that Martineau's series enacted, with its direct influence on politicians, statesmen, and government officials. The negative reviews came, predictably, from periodicals with Tory leanings. William Maginn, editor of *Fraser's Magazine* and a vehemently anti-Utilitarian, pro-Tory writer, parodied the *Westminster Review*'s exuberant praise.

> What a frightful delusion is this, called, by its admirers, Political Economy, which can lead a young lady to put forth a book like this!—a book written by a woman against the *poor*—a book written by a young

woman against *marriage*! And what is more, where a long tirade against all charity, and an elaborate defence of the closest selfishness, is received with acclamation by those who profess themselves the friends of the people and the advocates of the distressed.[114]

A year later Maginn would produce the verbal sketch in *Fraser's* "Gallery of Illustrious Literary Characters" that derided Martineau as "the idol of the *Westminster Review*" and a follower of "Mother Wollstonecraft" and her "shameless books."[115] In a similar vein, the notoriously negative review in the *Quarterly* by George Poulett Scrope (and likely John Gibson Lockhart, the editor, who interlarded Scrope's manuscript with ribald satire) chastised Martineau for "the unfeminine and mischievous doctrines on the principles of social welfare" she endorsed and dismissed the "absurd trash which is seriously propounded by some of her characters."[116] Clearly, these Tory reviewers did not find Martineau's entry into the arena of political economy—on the domestic, national, or imperial level—exemplary. It is less clear whether they would have denounced *any* political writing by a woman or whether they meant primarily to target views identified with Radicals and Whigs.

The debates over Martineau's *Illustrations* reveal the intensely political affiliations of magazines and periodicals in the 1830s, and the virtual inability of reviewers to evaluate fiction apart from its political ideology. But what these periodical debates also reveal is an unsettling of "the relatively smooth ideological field" that Marlon Ross describes, in *The Contours of Masculine Desire*, for the "generation of feminine writers like Baillie, Hemans, and L.E.L."[117] If there was a designated "cultural space for feminine poetry," as Ross argues, there was only contested space for the wide-ranging prose of an author like Martineau. And the terms on which that cultural space might be won for the woman of letters were uncertain. Was a woman author allowed to move into the public, political arena as an extension of her recognized domestic roles (as *Tait's Edinburgh Magazine* suggests in its link between domestic and imperial economy) or because of an enlightened national English conception of womanhood (as the *Westminster Review* suggests), or could a woman writer do so only (as Joseph Conder hints) if she possessed hybrid features, masculine intelligence merged with feminine imagination?

At this phase in the history of women's authorship, it is telling to observe Martineau's negotiation of these possible strategies. In dealing with hostile reviewers like Lockhart, Scrope, and Maginn, she claimed her rights as a woman to respectful social treatment, especially in a private setting. When Lockhart requested an introduction at a social gathering, "professing great admiration and good-will, and declaring that I must know his insults to be mere joking," Martineau refused, telling the hostess who wished to introduce him, "I will never knowingly meet Mr. Lockhart; . . . if I find myself in the same house with him, I will go out at one door of the drawing-room when he comes in at the other" (*Autobiography*, I, 207). In private life, she consistently applied the principle of feminine rights and responsibilities, and assumed a womanly role. Yet, in her reflections on the experience of being hostilely reviewed, she creates a hybrid of the heroic man of letters and the forgiving Christian woman. In the *Autobiography* this professional initiation by Lockhart and the *Quarterly* becomes a "testing" and "trial."

> I remember thinking . . . that the feelings called forth by such usage are, after all, more pleasurable than painful; and again, when I went to bed, that the day had been a very happy one. The testing of one's power of endurance is pleasurable; and the testing of one's power of forgiveness is yet sweeter: and it is no small benefit to learn something more of one's faults and weaknesses than friends and sympathisers either will or can tell. The compassion that I felt on this occasion for the low-minded and foul-mouthed creatures who could use their education and position as gentlemen to "destroy" a woman whom they knew to be innocent of even comprehending their imputations, was very painful: but, on the other hand, my first trial in the shape of hostile reviewing was over, and I stood unharmed, and somewhat enlightened and strengthened. (I, 206)

The experience both tests her "power of endurance," as a male warrior might be tested, and calls forth her "compassion," as an ideal Victorian woman might show under spiritual trial. Alternatively, we might read her behavior as an *imitatio Christi*, genderless in the sense that all Christians must expect to be unfairly tested yet respond with "forgiveness."

In her public role as an author, however, Martineau assumes a masculine stance, most notably as she negotiates to publish the *Illustrations*. When she recounts the difficulty of securing a publisher for the series, she reports this exchange with her mother.

> "You know what a man of business would do?"
> "What?"
> "Go up to town by the next mail, and see what is to be done."
> (*Autobiography*, I, 164)

When her series proves a success, she writes to her mother, "I fully expect that both you and I shall occasionally feel as if I did not discharge a daughter's duty, but we shall both remind ourselves that I am now as much a citizen of the world as any professional *son* of yours could be."[118] And when she learns of the attack planned by the *Quarterly Review*, she writes to her brothers, "earnestly desiring that they would not read the next Quarterly": "I told them that the inevitable consequence of my brothers taking up my quarrels would be to close my career. I had entered upon it independently, and I would pursue it alone" (*Autobiography*, I, 205). In such instances, she refuses to be treated as a dependent sister or daughter, but stands firm as a "professional son," a woman of letters with her own career, her own views, and an ability to manage even the most difficult aspects of the literary marketplace. Her actions represent what today we would term "professional" behavior.

In adopting a masculine professional model (or, more properly, what was in its day considered masculine), Martineau meant to demonstrate that women writers could compete in the marketplace, negotiate the intricacies of the "communications circuit," and contribute national service as readily as could men of letters. In a letter to an unnamed woman admirer, dated 25 May 1833, she wrote, "None of the many rewards of my humble exertions gratify me more than the appreciation by my own sex of my endeavours to prepare a way for them to more elevating objects & more extensive usefulness than at present. . . . I wish the timid & doubting of my own sex would take the assurance of my experience in this matter."[119] When she presented herself to Lord Brougham in a letter of 10 October 1832 as "a solitary young authoress, who has had no pioneer in her literary path but steadfastness of purpose," then, she was not merely erasing traces of her literary predecessors; she was also planning to chart a path by which future women writers might raise themselves to "more elevating objects." That charting—her mythmaking on behalf of the woman of letters, her repeated shaping of the narrative of her professional career—would occur in private letters (like the mini-biography written for Richard Hengist Horne in 1844) and in her *Autobiography* (written in 1855, published posthumously in 1877). It was a retrospective self-creation or re-creation.

The *Autobiography* includes the fullest version of Martineau's self-creation—a mythmaking that consciously invokes Carlyle's account of the modern author in *On Heroes, Hero-Worship, and the Heroic in History* (1841). Martineau did not hear these lectures, delivered in London in May 1840, in that she was already an invalid under a physician's care in Tynemouth, but we know that she read manuscript versions before the lecture series began—as she wrote to the Carlyles on 26 April 1840: "You are well off in your subject this time. I imagine you c^d hardly have better suited yourself or your hearers. I have been reading your Johnson twice,—your best, I think, of that kind."[120] "Your Johnson" refers to Carlyle's fifth lecture, "The Hero as Man of Letters," in which Samuel Johnson represents the modern author as "a Heroic Soul": "He, with his copy-rights and copy-wrongs, in his squalid garret, in his rusty coat; ruling . . . from his grave, after death, whole nations and generations who would, or would not, give him bread while living."[121] Carlyle depicts Johnson struggling with publishers, booksellers, and the literary marketplace: "Wet feet, mud, frost, hunger or what you will; but not beggary. . . . Rude stubborn self-help here."[122] Commenting on Johnson's era, Carlyle insists, "His time is bad: well then, he is there to make it better."[123]

Martineau's account of her early literary career in the *Autobiography* echoes Carlyle's account of the heroic man of letters struggling in the literary marketplace. She depicts herself as a latter-day Johnson, struggling against a depressed book trade and reluctant publishers to bring forth a series she knows the public wants and needs. We know that Martineau began writing an autobiography twice before she finally produced the 1855 version that we now have: "once in 1831, and again about ten years later, during my long illness at Tynemouth"—that is, in 1841. This 1841 attempt, I believe, adopted the Carlylean category of "heroic" and influenced (or was incorporated into) the official published version of her life in the *Autobiography*.

The heroic Martineau emerges most prominently in the section recounting the publishing history of the *Illustrations of Political Economy*, the series that fulfilled her apprenticeship of the 1820s and consolidated her position as a woman of letters. Despite its ultimate success, getting the series produced was no easy matter; it required heroism equal to Johnson's. As Martineau recalls, in the early 1830s, the era of the First Reform Bill, no publisher could be convinced that the reading public wanted pamphlets about the classical economic theories of Smith, Ricardo, Mill, and Malthus. They feared that the market was bad for all books, including hers: "they brought out a long string of objections, beginning with my proposed title, and ending with the Reform Bill and the Cholera" (I, 162). Yet Martineau believed that her Political Economy Tales would sell and that the middle and working classes needed to understand political economy as it affected their everyday lives: "I thought of the multitudes who needed it,—and especially of the poor,—to assist them in managing their own welfare. I thought too of my own conscious power of doing this very thing. Here was the thing wanting to be done, and I wanting to do it" (I, 171). As she tells her tale of obstacles encountered, humiliating rejections, ceaseless hard work, and ultimate vindication, the mythmaking emerges with drama and verve. Her story of trudging "day after day," "many miles through the clay of the streets, and the fog of the gloomiest December I ever saw," and coming home "weary with disappointment . . . but ready to work . . . in case of a publisher turning up," sounds remarkably like Carlyle's heroic Johnson with his "Wet feet, mud, frost, hunger or what you will." Martineau suffers a blow more devastating than anything Carlyle reveals of Johnson's dealings with booksellers when her publisher, Charles Fox, insists that "the work should be published by subscription" (I, 167)—an outdated mode associated, by the 1830s, with amateur authors and unsuitable as a professional contract.

Yet Martineau's vision of the "supreme importance of the Man of Letters in modern society" remains Carlylean, with the periodical press surpassing "the Pulpit, the Senate, the *Senatus Academicus* and much else" in its role of setting *"light* on high places."[124] In her presentation of the modern woman of letters, however, she is less gloomy, more optimistic than Carlyle in his treatment of Johnson (or Rousseau or Burns, his other exemplary men of letters). In the *Autobiography* Martineau ends her tale of struggles in the literary marketplace with the astonishing success of her first pamphlet, *Life in the Wilds*, which sold over five thousand copies in the first week of publication and sent her to London as a full-fledged professional author. In charting the path of a solitary young authoress, she was also presenting a "Hero as Woman of Letters" to the Victorian reading public. De facto Martineau was bringing her into being.

WORKING COLLABORATIVELY
Mary Howitt and Anna Mary Howitt
as Women of Letters

Mary Howitt (1799–1888) entered the literary marketplace in the same decade as Harriet Martineau: the 1820s. Like Martineau, she wrote in many of the genres associated with women: poetry, didactic fiction, sketches of rural and domestic life, and children's tales. So, too, Howitt espoused—and published on behalf of—many of the radical causes that inspired Martineau: the education of women and workers, the abolition of slavery, the extension of the vote to the middle and artisanal classes in the era of the First Reform Bill and during the Chartist Movement, the Married Women's Property Bill in the 1850s and the enfranchisement of women in the 1860s. During their literary careers, both women wrote for major literary periodicals, including the *Athenaeum*, *Chamber's Edinburgh Journal*, and Dickens's *Household Words*, and in the 1840s Martineau even contributed a regular column, "From the Mountain," and a series of essays under the rubric "Household Education" to the *People's and Howitt's Journal*, a short-lived radical periodical edited by Mary's husband, William. In their day, both Martineau and Howitt were considered women of letters.

Yet Howitt never achieved the fame, momentary or lasting, that Martineau did. When Martineau was a rising star with her *Illustrations of Political Economy* (1832–34), Howitt was contributing to literary annuals, writing children's tales, and hoping for success with a book of poetry. Corresponding with her sister Anna Harrison in February 1833, Howitt cautiously expressed her literary ambition: "When my book will be published I know not, for the times are sadly against poetry. A part of it is now in London & has been seen by some of our literary friends who give it such extraordinary praise as almost terrifies me. I fancy myself it is the best thing I ever did."[1]

Private praise for *The Seven Temptations* (1834), the book she so valued, never materialized into public acclaim or financial success, nor did Howitt's later and better *Hymns and Fire-side Verses* (1839) secure her a high poetic reputation (though Elizabeth Barrett admired her imaginative gifts, and Howitt's ballads, uncollected until the 1840s, secured the admiration of readers as diverse as Thomas Campbell, Allan Cunningham, and David Moir).[2] During the 1830s, when Martineau followed her achievement in the *Illustrations* with seminal books on American society that publishers vied for (*Society in America, Retrospect of Western Travel*, and *How to Observe Manners and Morals*), Howitt turned to (or remained trapped in) literary annuals, children's literature, and verse for periodicals. At her death in 1888, her fellow writer Margaret Oliphant nostalgically recalled the "mild individual note" and "gentle inspiration" of Howitt's early poetry, but sadly observed, "But for [her] Autobiography we should have been disposed to say that they [Mary and her husband, William] had long ago melted away out of mortal ken. They have, we fear, save in name."[3] Today, Howitt is known, if she is remembered at all, as the English poet "second in popularity only to Mrs. Hemans in 1835"[4] or as the author of the child's verse, "The Spider and the Fly."

Why, then, should a chapter be devoted to Mary Howitt as a Victorian woman of letters? It would be easy to dismiss her as a writer who made an ill-advised professional choice in the 1830s, when the market for poetry was bad, by failing to shift to more popular genres or, like Martineau, reinvent an old genre for the modern day. But the case of Mary Howitt is more complex than that of a woman poet in an age of prose. Her vast output of over one hundred volumes of novels, tales, travel and nature writing, biography, and translation, as well as her verse and journalism, make her a prominent early Victorian literary figure. As I shall argue, she embodied the dominant early to mid-Victorian model of the professional woman author and, with her daughter Anna Mary Howitt Watts (1822–84), articulated an ideology of collaborative work to support it. As Brian Maidment has suggested, Mary and her husband, William, represent important examples of authors dedicated to progressive social and political reform[5]—a commitment expressed in the kinds of periodical and book production they chose and, I would add, in the collaborative model of literary work they advanced. It is Howitt's literary practice and ideology of work that bear scrutiny, both for the possibilities they opened for women's authorship and for the limitations they imposed.

Mary Howitt viewed writing as a family business, as a professional endeavor pursued by father, mother, and children gifted with literary ability. This model of authorship emerged early in the century among the "professional artist-classes" (the phrase is Oliphant's) and rose to prominence at mid-century, as authors carved out studies and workspaces in their homes and as painters transformed their houses to incorporate studios and salesrooms, with the ground floor becoming the workplace, the sales place, and the place of contact between the artist and audience.[6] The Howitts encountered this model of familial collaboration in their contacts with literary friends—the Chorleys of Liverpool, whom Mary recalled in her *Autobiography* as "the gifted Quakeress, Jane Chorley, her highly endowed children, William, John, Henry, and Mary Ann, forming the literary staff of the 'Winter Wreath'";[7] Alaric and Zillah Watts, for whose literary annuals and other publishing ventures the Howitts wrote in the 1820s and 1830s; Anna and Samuel Carter Hall, writers and editors whose acquaintance the Howitts made in London in the 1830s; and sisters Margaret and Mary Gillies, one a painter, the other a translator and writer, who became lifelong friends and contributors to *Howitt's Journal*. To this list of acquaintances, we might add other literary families or collaborative partnerships that were prominent at mid-century when the Howitts lived in London: Captain Frederick Marryat and his daughters Florence, Augusta, Blanche, and Emilia, all novelists; the Strickland family, including the popular historians Agnes and Elizabeth and their Canadian siblings, Samuel Strickland, Susannah Moodie, and Catherine Parr Traill; and the Rossetti family, with whom the Howitts became friends through their artistic daughter Anna Mary. Mary and William Howitt practiced literary collaboration themselves and later inducted their daughters into their work.

It is not only the model of family business that makes Mary Howitt and her daughter Anna Mary important in the history of women's authorship; it is also their articulation of an ideology of collaborative work—indeed, a myth of artistic achievement by means of collaboration. Many of Mary and Anna Mary Howitt's narratives enact forms of collaboration that bind the family—the domestic unit, the female community, the national family—together. Their book prefaces and autobiographical writings explain this collaborative model not merely as useful or strategic for the woman of letters (though it was), but more provocatively as enabling a high quality of artistic production. Yet the collaborative ideology that the Howitts espoused created tensions within, and sometimes obstacles to, the achievement of the individual woman artist or author. Mary Howitt's writing reveals points at which the collaborative project breaks down, requires a revision, or reaches an impasse and, as I shall suggest in this chapter, produces a reconsideration of what it means to be a woman of letters.

Collaborative Writing as Family Practice

Howitt began writing collaboratively in her childhood. In a chapter of her *Autobiography* (1888), "Early Days at Uttoxeter," she recalls how she and her sister Anna studied, played, and wrote poetry together. So closely were the two sisters linked that despite a two-year age difference, they learned to speak at the same time and invented a private language.

[A]fter we could both talk, being chiefly left to converse together, our ignorance of the true appellations for many ordinary sentiments and actions compelled us to coin and use words of our own. To sneeze was to us both *akisham*—the sound which one of our parents must have made in sneezing. Roman numerals, which we saw on the title-pages of most books, conveyed no other idea than the word *icklymickly-dictines*. Italic printing was *softly* writing.[8]

Howitt attributes the development of this private language to the lack of "an open communicative spirit in the family" (I, 24) and to their isolation as Quakers from other children, but it was also spurred by an intense sisterly desire to share experience empathetically and linguistically. As they matured, the sisters became coauthors, some of their verses finding their way into print in local newspapers and periodicals. An early letter from Mary to Anna, written 15 November 1822, reveals Mary copying eight of her sister's poems for the *Kaleidoscope*, a regional weekly, though not revising them as was their common practice: "[I] am possessed," Mary explains, "with great admiration for them, . . . and wisely thinking I could not improve them, have copied them verbatim."[9]

Only Mary pursued a literary career, but throughout their lives the sisters corresponded about literary affairs, Mary discussing current work and professional ambitions, Anna providing critical response and often material for poems and stories. When her *Seven Temptations* (1834) was curtly reviewed by William Jerdan, Mary wrote to Anna about the "malicious, unmanly, abusive review" in the *Literary Gazette*, but she also requested her sister's opinion of the volume, "the plan, execution, etc. etc.," "how you like it & what you like in it."[10] Anna's response must have been unequivocally positive, as Mary's subsequent letter ends with gratitude for their friendship: "I never loved a woman as I have loved thee, never had a truer, kinder friend."[11] The sisterly relationship was not only emotionally supportive; it was also creative and inventive. In September 1834, in one of several instances documented by their letters, Anna supplied Mary with material—a "beautiful & sad tale" of a "poor lost child," "worthy to be a ballad of Wordsworth's." "I wish I could do it justice," Mary says, as she turns the tale into "a ballad of the little girl who was lost on Easter Monday" and plots to get it produced in a "lovely edition" with "sweet wood-cuts."[12] (The ballad was eventually published as "Lilien May: An Easter Legend" in *Ballads and Other Poems*.)[13]

When Mary Botham married William Howitt in 1821, she in turn collaborated with him on poetry, journalism, and natural history. In 1821, under the pseudonym Wilfred Wender, William published articles in the *Kaleidoscope* about Mary's native territory, Uttoxeter, Staffordshire, which he called Deckerton. In 1822 they toured Scotland and in 1824 jointly published, under the names Wilfred and Wilfreda Wender, "A Scottish Ramble" in a Staffordshire paper, the *Mercury*. In the same period they wrote poetry, jointly publishing volumes in 1823, *The Forest Minstrel, and Other Poems*, and in 1827, *The Desolation of Eyam and Other Poems*.[14] In these works, they make no distinction between their poems or sketches, using a joint "we" in their prefaces and omitting individual signature (even though it is clear that a poem like "A Sister's Recollections: To A. H." is Mary's). From the beginning, the Howitts' model of authorship included joint publication and, more broadly, an approach to authorship as a family endeavor. Throughout their careers, they would revise and amplify each other's work and even write whole chapters or tales, if the other hadn't time to do so.[15]

Indeed, Mary might not have embarked on a literary career had she not married William, as her Quaker parents frowned on frivolous literary reading and would not have sanctioned their daughter's independent literary ventures. It was William who introduced Mary to the modern poetry of Walter Scott and William Wordsworth. It was William also who decided not to pursue his training as a builder but instead work as an apothecary while trying his hand at literature. This decision required the couple's joint literary endeavors since to supplement their income during the 1820s, while resident in Nottingham and running an apothecary's shop, they needed to place and publish as many pieces as they could: poems, essays, reviews, sketches of regional life, and especially their beloved natural history. Home and work, domestic and professional, were not separate (as we typically think of Victorian "separate spheres") in the lives of the Howitts, but compatible and intertwined.

If the collaborative model of writing was financially essential to the Howitts, it was emotionally and conceptually important to Mary, who had come to love literature through shared reading and writing. The dedication of her *Ballads and Other Poems* (1847) reads:

TO WILLIAM HOWITT

MY BEST COUNSELOR AND TEACHER;

MY LITERARY ASSOCIATE FOR A QUARTER OF A CENTURY;

MY HUSBAND AND MY FRIEND;

THIS VOLUME

IS AFFECTIONATELY INSCRIBED.[16]

William and Mary did indeed work as associates for the first twenty-five years of their marriage—and beyond, with both coediting *Howitt's Journal* (1847–48) and Mary editing and placing William's Australian travel writing of the 1850s in Victorian periodicals. Yet, arguably, by the time this dedication was written, Anna Mary, the Howitts' oldest child, had replaced both sister and husband as Mary's chief collaborator. By the late 1830s Anna Mary became the intellectual companion of—and a literary collaborator with—her mother. The family model of joint production was extended to this daughter and eventually to her younger sister, Margaret.

As early as 1833, when Anna Mary was ten years old, Mary wrote to her sister Anna about her daughter's help with drawings for a manuscript.

> I wish I could send you some specimens of Anna Mary's drawings. She is now illustrating my "Seven Temptations." She designs heads to illustrate the different characters. William has them with him in London, and has astonished several artists with them. Dear child! it is a fine talent, and, I doubt not, given for a good purpose.[17]

Five years later, when Anna Mary was in her mid-teens, she was illustrating and designing features of both parents' work (figure 17). Again to her sister, Howitt wrote,

> She is a dear, lovable girl, with a fine poetical spirit. In a little volume, which I hope shortly to send you, you will find some of her designs for the principal poem ["Marien's Pilgrimage" in *Hymns and Fire-side Verses*]. I think you will like them. They represent the spirit of Christianity under the guise of a child, in different scenes and circumstances of human life. There is also in her papa's book [*The Boy's Country-Book*] an embellishment, a tail-piece to Chapter XVI. from a drawing of hers—the runaway boys shelling peas at the cottage-door.[18]

While these letters might be dismissed as parental bragging, they in fact express Howitt's sense of the site of authorship as the home and her conception of artistic production as familial work, with children encouraged to learn and participate in their parents' endeavors. Howitt increasingly came to see this participation as professional training essential to her daughters' careers. When she sends a sample drawing to her sister in 1833, she mentions Anna Mary's "portfolio" and adds, "I hope in time she will be an excellent drawer—or more properly artist."[19] Later, after London artists have confirmed her daughter's talent, she writes, "It will be like a fortune to her."[20] By the 1840s, Mary had recognized Anna Mary's talent as grounds for a career as a professional painter and encouraged her to train at Sass's Academy as well as pursue journalistic work.

In the retrospective *Autobiography* (1888) Howitt treats this collaborative work—between husband and wife, mother and daughter, parents and children—conceptually as the basis of women's authorship. In a birthday letter written to her daughter in 1870 and quoted in the *Autobiography*, Mary recalls the origins of *The Seven Temptations*, the first volume that Anna Mary illustrated. Mary connects its inspiration to her reading of the Bible and her own poetry to her children.

> What an age it seems since you were a little child, and used to sit with me in the Nottingham drawing-room, and we read the Gospels

FIGURE 17. Anna Mary Howitt, illustration for "Marien's Pilgrimage,"
in Mary Howitt's *Hymns and Fire-side Verses* (1839).
Courtesy of the Yale University Library.

together, and I used to read you my poems, often written from thoughts
suggested by you! Some of those Sunday evening readings remain most
lively in my mind as little bits of Heaven, when illumination seemed
almost to come down from above to us. I remember how "Thomas of
Torres," in "The Seven Temptations," was the fruit of our reading

together the parable of the man who built the barns and laid up the treasure, and then his soul was called away. I wonder whether you remember those times, and how you illustrated "The Seven Temptations," with heads of all the characters?[21]

Howitt's association of Bible reading and poetic production, the first inspiring the second, reflects her religious (Quaker) convictions that authorship should extend the good words of the sacred text. Equally important is the exchange between mother and child, an exchange in which the child as listener inspires and enables the mother's literary work. Here as elsewhere, Howitt conceptualizes her authorial work as an extension of her familial role. In prefaces to books, she frequently notes that tales or poems were written originally for her children or even that a book was the result of observing and listening to her children—as in the preface to *The Children's Year* (1847):

I resolved, therefore, to try the experiment of keeping for one whole year an exact chronicle, as it were, of the voluntary occupations and pleasures, and of the sentiments and feelings, as far as I would gain an accurate knowledge of them, of my two youngest children. This little book is the result; everything which it contains is strictly true.[22]

Authorship as an extension of the maternal role was a model commonly adopted by British women writers from the early to mid-nineteenth century,[23] as I noted in the introduction. Anna Jameson articulates its basis in *The Communion of Labour* (1855), the "communion" depending on the extension of "domestic life" into the "social community." "As civilization advances," Jameson argues, "as the social interests and occupations become more and more complicated, the family duties and influences diverge from the central home,—in a manner, radiate from it."[24] Howitt's version of this model, which predates Jameson's and perhaps influenced it, incorporates features of an artistic practice that she came to understand when the family moved to London in the late 1830s and had greater social contact with other professionals. Family networks, as art historian Deborah Cherry explains, were crucial in the training of nineteenth-century artists, especially women painters: "From the later eighteenth century the practice of art was . . . shaped by kinship links, intermarriage, familial training and an increasing professionalisation. Artist dynasties assisted in the formation of an occupational group with strong familial and professional ties."[25] Howitt means to suggest, I believe, a parallel model of literary production. In thinking of her family, she envisions a group of writers, artists, translators, and editors, all of whom contribute to the domestic economy and the literary field.

This collaborative model was not without its difficulties, and even impossibilities. Although Mary was deeply committed to her husband, her letters occasionally reveal a personal ambition that is individualistic rather than collaborative. When in 1827 the *Eclectic Review* cites Dr. Moir's praise of "The Two Voyagers" as "one of the finest ballads in the English language," Mary quotes the praise to her sister, adding, "Pray don't think me grown altogether egotistical & I will have done at once."[26] The comment both acknowledges her ego—the "I" who has written the ballad singled out for praise—and represses it, by cutting off the letter immediately after the acknowledgment. Similarly, in 1839, when Mary has negotiated a literary project "which will occupy me about two years but which will bring me in a thousand pounds," she returns a £25 loan to her sister and proudly notes that she is now "a well-doing person": "I am quite astonished when I think of it, & sometimes half-afraid that I shall fail in it but of course I shall endeavour to do my best." Then, as if afraid of too much pride (the "pride that goeth before a fall"), Mary turns to her husband's achievements: "All the prosperity however does not abide with me—William has quite an equal share."[27] The "equal share" was certainly not £1,000, but a contract (or possibly payment) for a second edition of his *Rural Life of England* (1838).

Modern theories of collaborative writing treat such difficulties as inevitable. Although feminist and other scholars have used collaboration to challenge the dominant model of the solitary Romantic author and have celebrated alternative models of creativity, most continue to analyze collaborative relationships in terms of the power dynamics of the writing pair. As Holly Laird explains in *Women Coauthors*, the "intra-poetic relationships" and "anxiety of influence" theorized by Harold Bloom, as well as the less confrontational, more cooperative feminist revisions of critics like Sandra Gilbert and Susan Gubar, involve dual concepts of "collaboration": collaboration as working *with* someone else, collaboration as working *against* *someone* or as working *with the enemy*. These dual meanings repeatedly surface, producing binaries of dominance-subservience, originality-imitation, primary-secondary, professional-amateur, or composer-editor.[28]

In large part, the Howitts escaped these binaries, perhaps because they began their literary careers together, perhaps because they both saw themselves as professional authors, perhaps because they both sought to produce original work (even if much of it seems, in retrospect, secondary or derivative). Oliphant's obituary review suggests another possibility: that Mary was the more original writer of the pair, thus redressing the normative gender imbalance with greater genius. Oliphant calls William Howitt "a conscientious and persevering book-maker, producing in a laudable and workmanlike manner many volumes," but she praises Mary for having "something more—a mild individual note, a gentle inspiration, such as made the young reader especially love her name." "Mary Howitt," Oliphant states, "had a gentle potency in literature."[29] The pair seem to have acknowledged this difference by allowing Mary to continue her poetic work in the 1830s and by sending William in the direction of historical research and political analysis suited to his "book-making."

Nonetheless, by the 1840s Mary Howitt faced a crisis of ideology—a crisis that erupted when her professional writing, sometimes pursued with her husband, sometimes on her own, came into conflict with the domestic economy that she and her husband shared. We can find traces of this conflict in Howitt's letters to her sister, where she confesses that she likes and needs the "handsome pay" she receives for doing literary translations but admits the fatigue of balancing this work with her maternal responsibilities: "I am tired mentally and bodily," she tells Anna.[30] The *Autobiography* articulates the conflict explicitly when Howitt describes her son Claude's illness from a leg infection. Caught between a need to produce income and a desire to devote attention to her ailing son, Howitt here configures the professional and the domestic in opposition:

> Poor dear Claude! at this very moment I see the unfinished translation lying before me, which was broken off by his death. Alas! I could have shed burning tears over this. How often did he beg and pray of me to put aside my translation just for one day, that I might sit by him and talk or read to him! I, never thinking how near his end was, said, "Oh no, I must go on yet a page or two." How little did I think that in a short time I should have leisure enough and to spare! (*Autobiography*, II, 17–18)

Citing this passage in *Representing Femininity: Middle-Class Subjectivity in Victorian and Edwardian Women's Autobiographies*, Mary Jean Corbett concludes that Howitt, like other Victorian women authors, "subordinates her writing to her woman's role, which is itself defined as subordination to the needs of others."[31] Yet the passage does not suggest "subordination" so much as unanticipated conflict, the "agonising feelings" (*Autobiography*, II, 18) that suddenly afflict Howitt when she can no longer maintain the complementary relationship of writing and parenting that had sustained her career for nearly twenty years. The ideology of collaborative work—in which each family member participates by contributing to the domestic economy, whether by writing or studying, providing domestic labor or professional work—breaks down in 1844 when her son falls ill and dies.

As I explore the source of this breakdown in the section that follows, I want to suggest that it was not so much gender subordination that caused it as a collision of Howitt's model of work with the demands of the literary marketplace. During the 1820s and 1830s Howitt managed to operate successfully within the collaborative model she and her husband had constructed at their marriage, but by the 1840s, this model failed. Howitt's myth of authorship came head on against some unpleasant facts of the market.

Writing Poetry, Understanding
the Literary Marketplace

Mary Howitt wanted, above all, to be a poet. Her great-grandniece and biographer, Amice Lee, recounts a family story in which Mary, "aged 17, a slight, bright-eyed girl in drab Quaker dress and close-fitting cap, standing under an apple-tree, uttered a prayer that she might some day be a famous writer."[32] Whether or not this episode is apocryphal, it is a fitting story-of-origin for a young poet, recalling Wordsworth's self-dedication to poetry at sunrise in *The Prelude* and Aurora Leigh's self-crowning as a poet in spring "with its multitudes / Of nightingales all singing in the dark, / And rose-buds reddening where the calyx split."[33] Howitt's first literary productions were poetic—the verses written with her sister, the volumes published with her husband. Her best mature work, too, in the eyes of her Victorian readers, was poetic. In the estimate of David Moir, lecturing in 1851 on the literature of the first half of the nineteenth century, it was Howitt's success in the early collaborative volumes of verse that led her "to the fortress of her main strength, ballad poetry, in which she has few contemporary rivals, whether we regard her pictures of stern, solitary nature, or of all that is placid, gentle, and benignant in the supernatural."[34]

By the 1830s, however, publishing poetry had lost its financial viability. Aspiring poets had either to pay for the publication of their volumes or publish on the half-profits scheme, whereby the author and publisher shared costs and then divided profits, if there were any. Most likely, the Howitts published on one of these schemes, hoping to break even. *The Forest Minstrel, and Other Poems* (1823), their first volume, was issued by Baldwin, Cradock, and Joy, a London firm based in Paternoster Row and specializing in religious literature.[35] They sent their second manuscript, *The Desolation of Eyam and Other Poems* (1827), to this firm also but with little hope "of their making us any offer we are likely to accept"; it was published by a lesser firm, Wightman and Cramp, also based in Paternoster Row.[36] Mary's letters give no indication that the couple made any profits from their early poetry. Even her later, more ambitious *Seven Temptations* (1834), admired by their London literary friends and published by the commercially oriented Colburn and Bentley on the half-profits scheme, seems to have made no money.[37] In a letter to her sister Anna written just as the volume appeared, Mary observes, "I hope most earnestly it will be a successful volume. The cry is 'poetry don't sell!' & perhaps it does not as much as it did."[38] From the silence of subsequent letters, it seems it did not.

In quoting the commonplace wisdom "poetry don't sell," Howitt recognizes the state of the literary market in the early 1830s, which took a downturn after the bank crash of 1826, cholera epidemic of 1831, and political instability during the agitation for the First Reform Bill of 1832. Book historian Lee Erickson has documented this downturn, especially for poetry, when he notes that "the market for individual volumes of poetry collapsed in the late 1820s" and that "the shift from the Romantic to Victorian poetry market stemmed directly from the [rise of the] literary Annuals."[39] For the years 1815–19, Erickson cites the publication of more than 225 volumes of poetry, 155 of which were first editions, in contrast to only 127 volumes, 91 of which were first editions, in 1826. After the bank crash of that year, "the general market for books recovered quickly and began to expand rapidly," but "the market for individual volumes of poetry never did, gradually falling off to a low of 110 volumes in 1832, of which 77 were first editions."[40] By 1832, then, when Howitt set seriously to work on *The Seven Temptations*, most publishers would simply not risk publishing an individual volume of poetry with a limited projected readership and print run of 500 volumes. Poets could not pursue professional careers solely by writing verse. There were exceptions, of course, including William Wordsworth, who was already well established, carefully managed his copyrights, and planned new editions to maximize profits.[41] Felicia Hemans may have been another exception because she had achieved a high reputation before the market turned downward and because, according to Paula Feldman, her continuing relationship with *Blackwood's Edinburgh Magazine* provided a steady income.[42] But in the late 1820s and early 1830s, the Howitts were unknown provincial poets, writing on rural subjects and placing their verse mostly in regional newspapers and magazines. As Mary lamented to Anna in 1827, "Were I to send the most beautiful poem to any of the first magazines, the chances are a hundred to one it would never be read."[43]

Howitt negotiated the difficulties of the literary marketplace in a financially sensible, if not artistically high-minded way: she placed her poems in literary annuals. The market for annuals—collections of tales and verse, often written to accompany steel-plate engravings and advertised as giftbooks—began in the mid-1820s and rose to great commercial success in the 1830s. In her introduction to a facsimile of *The Keepsake*, one of the most popular annuals, Feldman cites sales of 10,000 to 15,000 copies for editions selling at the extravagant cost of a guinea (1£ 1s).[44] Editors of annuals solicited poems from major literary figures, sometimes paying them high sums despite low quality—for example, £500 to Walter Scott for three tales, 100 guineas (£105) to William Wordsworth for five poems, and £50 to Samuel Taylor Coleridge for five contributions.[45] Lesser or unknown writers were paid far less, but at least they earned money. In the 1820s, the Howitts met several of the innovators and editors of literary annuals: the Chorleys of Liverpool, friends of Mary's sister Anna and editors of *The Winter Wreath*; Alaric and Zillah Watts, who read the Howitts' early verse, admired it, and solicited poems for *The Literary Souvenir*, *The Literary Magnet*, and *The Poetical Album*; the S. C. Halls, who edited *The Amulet*; and the publisher Ackermann, who produced *The Forget-Me-Not*. As early as 1824, Mary mentions sending poems to these albums, and by 1826 she was contributing to *The Literary Souvenir*, a commercially successful gift-book selling close to 10,000 copies per edition.[46] She received professional remuneration for her poems, and both she and William kept their eye on profits: "There is to be another Children's Annual next Christmas by Ackermann (The Forget Me Not)," she wrote to her sister; "we are enlisted in the corps for good promised hire, & every body says Ackermann pays well. I wish everybody else did."[47]

While we might be tempted to dismiss Howitt's verse for the annuals as literary hackwork, it is not clear that this conclusion holds—or that writing for the annuals necessarily produced inferior poetry. For one thing, Howitt recognized the mediocrity of much verse in the annuals, including *The Literary Magnet* produced by their own publisher, Wightman and Cramp: "I think myself it is by no means a first-rate periodical," she admitted to her sister. Yet Howitt also understood the necessity of staying visible in the literary arena, of maintaining ties with editors and publishers who supported her work, and of doing her best, despite the venue: "I will not willingly desert the Watts. They have been the first who noticed me & gave me a kind word of encouragement & thro' good report & thro' evil I will be true to them."[48] Moreover, the kinds of poetry Howitt preferred to write—brief lyrics, descriptive rural scenes, and especially ballads—were the preferred genres of the annuals. Because annuals were organized around costly engravings, the editors solicited poetry that conformed to a "pictorial aesthetic" or that created stirring narratives to complement the illustrations. Howitt's ballads were perfectly suited to this literary culture and to her own taste. As she states in the preface to *Ballads and Other Poems* (1847), all her life she has been "a passionate admirer of ballad-poetry": the first book she read, "when I had my free choice in a large library," was "Percy's Relics of Ancient English Poetry"; and when, in the first years of her marriage, she gave "vent to my own peculiar fancies," she "took to writing ballads."[49] Many of Howitt's ballads might have been leading pieces in a literary annual—including "The Two Voyagers" praised by David Moir. Some, like "Tibbie Inglis" for *The Forget-Me-Not* and "The Faery Oath" for *The Literary Souvenir*, actually were.

In terms of Howitt's professional development, then, it seems more likely that writing poetry for literary annuals and regional periodicals aided her literary career. She could place poems in these venues for payment, gauge the response of her readers, and save up the best for published collections—as she did for *Hymns and Fire-side Verses* (1839) and *Ballads and Other Poems* (1847), where "Tibbie Inglis," "Lilien May," "Far-Off Visions," "The Faery Oath," and other poems initially published in annuals appear.[50] With this practice, Howitt avoided the embarrassment that faced young poets who launched slender volumes of verse before they had sufficient material of quality—including Alfred Tennyson, whose 1830 *Poems* included many slight lyrics never reprinted and whose 1832 *Poems* included several, like

"O, Darling Room," that invited the ridicule of John Wilson Croker of the *Quarterly Review*. Howitt wisely let her mediocre poems lie buried in the ephemeral annuals where they originated.

In praising these tactics, common among shrewd men of letters in the 1830s, I am countering Carl Woodring's suggestion in *Victorian Samplers: William and Mary Howitt* that in the 1820s and 1830s Mary was "turning out poems like thumbtacks for the gilt and satin annuals"[51]—an analogy that suggests piecework or hackwork. On the contrary, I would argue, Mary's letters suggest that she wrote poetry when a local tale or scene in nature inspired her and that she saved up her manuscripts for later placement. Artistry moved her to write, economics to place and publish. Only when she edited *Fisher's Drawing Room Scrap-book* from 1839 to 1841, a task she assumed after Laetitia Landon's death, did Howitt feel pressure to write many new poems to fill up the volume. (And then William assisted with the work.) During the heyday of the annuals, however, which corresponds to the first decade of her career, Howitt shows herself capable of producing popular verse forms and doing professional, even exemplary literary work.

To complicate the case further, I believe that Howitt did her least successful work when she wrote poetry without regard to the marketplace. For *The Seven Temptations*, Howitt retrospectively tells us, "I resolved to put forth my whole strength into one effort, which should afford me free scope for working out character, and for dramatic effect, at which I had always aimed, even in the simplest ballad."[52] This "whole strength" effort, implicitly in contrast to the sporadic verse writing she had previously done, failed in the eyes of its readers—and not just because William Jerdan placed a malicious notice in the *Literary Gazette*. The seven long poems, each illustrating a form of temptation from avarice to despair and linked together by the evil machinations of Achzib, the tempter, make dull reading. As Howitt aspires to psychological intensity, she loses the compelling narratives, sharp details, and vigorous pace of her ballads; instead, she introduces long soliloquies and meditative passages, as in "The Poor Scholar," where a sickly scholar contemplates death in pious clichés, echoes of Pope, and (perhaps) anticipations of Tennyson.

> Oh, I should long to die!
> To be among the stars, the glorious stars;
> To have no bounds to knowledge; to drink deep
> Of living fountains—to behold the wise,
> The good, the glorified! To be with God,
> And Christ, who passed through death that I might live!
> Oh I should long for death, but for one tie,
> One lingering tie that binds me to the earth!
> My mother![53]

Jerdan was on target when he criticized the plan and execution of the work. He comments:

> We cannot congratulate the accomplished, and, on most occasions, delightful author of this volume, either on the design or execution of this Heptalogy. The former is radically defective and vicious; and the latter, consequently, every way unworthy of her talents. . . . It is too dull and trite to do good, too poor as a composition, though there are a few poetical passages to add a laurel to Mary Howitt's justly high reputation.[54]

Carl Woodring also targets a flaw when he notes that "Mary's conception of an evil spirit trying his strength against humanity owed much to Goethe's *Faust* and to Byron's *Manfred* and *Cain*; . . . the scheme of trial by seven different temptations was based on the attempted emotional spectrum of

FIGURE 18. "The Annals of 1830." Courtesy of the Lewis Walpole Library, Yale University.

Joanna Baillie's *Plays on the Passions*."[55] That is, the concentrated effort by which Howitt hoped "to achieve a name among the poets of my country" was derivative—too obviously like what the great poets before her had achieved, not sufficiently like what she did best. Her best poetry came in bursts of inspiration and composition, usually appearing as fugitive pieces in annuals and periodicals, then reappearing in her collections of lyrics and ballads.

But the market for the annuals was unstable even in the 1830s and eventually faltered in the 1840s, when the fashion for these gift-books abated. We catch a glimpse of this ever-threatening instability in a print showing *The Winter's Wreath*, edited by her friends the Chorleys, sinking beneath thin ice, and new ventures being sold as "hot ones" (see figure 18).[56] As the market fluctuated and the fashion for literary annuals declined, Howitt turned to other kinds of work—some pursued jointly with her husband (guidebooks and collections like *The Homes and Haunts of the Most Eminent British Poets* of 1847 and *The Literature and Romance of Northern Europe* of 1852), some undertaken independently (her novel *Wood Leighton* of 1836, her children's tales of the 1840s, and her translations of Hans Christian Andersen and the Swedish novelist Frederika Bremer, commissioned by Bentley in the mid-1840s). In expanding her range and changing her focus, Howitt was acting professionally as a mid-Victorian woman of letters. She was interpreting literary trends, varying the genres, producing work suited to her interests within the constraints of the literary market, and, as we shall see, working for the "progress of the age."

Negotiating the Demands of Collaboration

When Howitt describes, then, the tension she felt in 1844 as her son Claude fell fatally ill, the crisis was not simply that she, as a woman writer, felt obliged to subordinate her literary art to her domestic duties. (After all, her husband, William, felt a similar tension between family and work; his poem "A Father's Lament" records his grief.)[57] Neither did Howitt feel that in doing translation she had accepted a lesser form of literary work, though we might now judge so.[58] About this work she wrote to her sister in 1844: "Between thee & me I am to receive 18 guineas a week for the translations I give them—it is very handsome pay & I only wish I had full employment at that rate all the days of my life."[59] Rather, I suggest that Howitt's model of literary production as family business and her ideology of collaborative work hit a crisis point. With Claude dangerously ill, professional and familial desires no longer aligned. And Howitt's model, involving the full family, broke down.

The writing that follows this rupture—*The Children's Year* (1848), *Our Cousins in Ohio* (1849), and the columns of "The Child's Corner" (1847–48) in *Howitt's Journal*—represents Howitt's attempt to reenvision collaborative work, create a new kind of writing project to encompass every family member, and reestablish the collaborative ideology of the past on a firmer basis. The books of this period are, at root, family memoirs: *The Children's Year*, a record of the two youngest children's lives, written by Mary and illustrated by her daughter Anna Mary; *Our Cousins in Ohio*, the transformation of letters from Mary's sister Emma about the lives of her American nieces and nephews, with illustrations by Anna Mary (English edition) or her sister (American edition); and the columns of "The Child's Corner," a thinly fictionalized record of life in the Howitt household. In reenvisioning the family's work as collaborative life writing, Howitt incorporates her younger children (who would otherwise be excluded from the professional work of the household) and focuses on domestic incidents (rather than on the professional achievement of its individual members). This re-focus makes the family rather than the singular subject the unit of study, even as it treats one particular unit (the Howitt family) as exemplary of the larger English national family.

Howitt presents *The Children's Year*, for example, as juvenile literature that endeavors to "enter fully into the feelings and reasonings of the child." She begins with a chapter titled "The Children's Home," follows with another that depicts the family reading together, and describes the setting up of a "house" by Meggy and Herbert, in which the children reproduce common domestic activities, from decorating and gardening to cleaning and repairing to entertaining guests at dinner or tea. It is as if Howitt, the writer of the book and "mama" of the narrative, needs to assure herself that Herbert and Meggy are "very happy little children": "they had kind parents, a pleasant home, a kind brother and sister older than themselves, good health and loving hearts."[60]

Howitt engages the children in activities resembling "work." Although she describes her children "playing at living in a house," their play in the "little tool-house" reproduces the work of the "big" house and prepares them for the real work of the world they will soon enter (see figure 19).[61] In this narrative, the collaborative work of the Howitts becomes living exemplary lives that can be recorded for, written about, and imitated by other English households. Not only their household but the nation is conceived as engaged in a collaborative project. The young British readership of *The Children's Year* is encouraged, through sympathetic imagination and action, to reproduce the model of the Howitt household in family units throughout Britain.

Such didactic writing was, of course, common in children's books of the 1840s, just as Howitt's conception of the national household was common in writing by radical authors of this period.[62] Yet along with its mid-century resonances, Howitt's didacticism includes a peculiarly personal element, even as it furthers her political goals. In *The Children's Year*, Howitt incorporates the work of every family member, including the servants, so that the book becomes a collaborative project to which all can contribute: the father

FIGURE 19. Anna Mary Howitt, illustration for Mary Howitt's
The Children's Year (1847). Courtesy of the Yale University Library.

by reading stories or retelling histories of the Viking and Norman invasions, which are then incorporated into the text; the elder daughter by sketching the younger children's activities, some of which find their way into the published account; the elder son, by arranging educational excursions, which are retold for inclusion in the book and thus for the reader's edification; and the servants, by inviting the children to tea in the kitchen or to holidays at their families' homes, so that other levels of British domestic society can be integrated. Howitt's goal of making *The Children's Year* a fully collaborative narrative leaves no one out. She thus reassures herself of domestic harmony, even while encouraging a model of family life and work in others.

For, if the book enabled Howitt to overcome a personal crisis in collaboration, it also allowed her to advance the political goals that she and her husband shared and articulated in their writing of this period, especially in their magazine *Howitt's Journal*. These goals included the education of the working and middle classes, the political advancement of workers, the professional advancement of women, and (in their words) "the universal progress by mental, moral, and physical education of the human race."[63] *The Children's Year* advances these goals by concentrating on the domestic household rather than on public institutions, as articles in their journal tend to do. It attempts to inspire its audience to achieve these goals, beginning with its initial assurance that its young readers will "very likely . . . find that they have thought and done the very same things themselves" and continuing to its final wish, "Would that all children might be as happy as their age and nurture are capable of!"[64]

When Howitt wrote her columns for "The Child's Corner" in *Howitt's Journal*, she continued the ideological project of *The Children's Year*, appearing in the persona of "the poet," with Meggy and Herbert as the poet's children and Anna Mary sketching their activities. When Howitt composed *Our Cousins in Ohio* (1849), she expanded the range of domestic models to include colonial families like her sister's in a larger collaboration. This American book, based on a transatlantic epistolary exchange between the two families, engages in the project of nation-building through the creation of "imagined communities," to use Benedict Anderson's phrase.[65] Yet unlike Anderson, who emphasizes the public monuments, institutions, and movements that construct the "imagined political community," Howitt focuses in *Our Cousins* on domestic space, on the private home as the site of national origin; she imagines the national community as arising from, and consolidating the values of, local domestic communities. These books and columns were Howitt's contributions, as a woman of letters, to the larger social and political issues of her day. They were her means of advancing Quaker and Radical perspectives, commenting on civic debates such as slavery and abolitionism, and articulating a model of collaboration for herself and her readership.

Mother-Daughter Productions: Training the Professional Artist

Howitt transmitted her model of collaborative work to her daughters, involving them in professional apprenticeships at an early age and training them to become financially independent women. When Anna Mary showed a talent for drawing, Howitt engaged her in illustrating stories and magazine articles, thus initiating her daughter's career as an artist. Later, she engaged both daughters in writing and translating, providing them with a literary apprenticeship unavailable in her youth and still unavailable to most women.[66] Whether they were to marry or remain single, the Howitt daughters were to become professionals, Anna Mary as an artist and author, Margaret as a translator and biographer. To her sister, she wrote in 1844, "Girls must be made independent. I am bent on A. M. making £300 next year by translating; experience shows me that 9/10ths of the troubles and discomforts of families in this country come from lack of money. When I think of some, how wretched and hopeless does the lot of woman seem!"[67] As this and other letters reveal, it was in the 1840s, as Mary considered her daughters' careers, that the word *professional* entered her vocabulary and the phrase *literary property* began to shape her conception of her own work. When Anna Mary became engaged to Edward La Trobe Bateman, a decorative designer and illuminator, poor "but sure to make a great name and money," Howitt comments, "A. M. is resolved to be as good an artist as possible as a means of wealth to her husband. This will be her dower."[68] Proudly, she reports, "Anna Mary works hard as ever at her own profession. She is mostly away the whole of four days in the week—but she is getting on very well—though as yet she is only drawing anatomical studies which though valuable are not beautiful, at least to common eyes."[69] And when Anna Mary fixes up the "old nursery" into a "painting room," Howitt tells her sister, "It looks quite professional."[70]

Both parents encouraged their children's literary and artistic pursuits, took them to Germany for three years to study its language, art, and literature, and (at least in Anna Mary's case) incorporated juvenile productions into their books. As the Howitt letters document, Anna Mary began to design book illustrations while a teenager. Even so, her drawings for her mother's *Hymns and Fire-side Verses* (1839) and her father's *The Boy's Country-Book* (1839) can at best be called amateur productions: they are mostly unsigned or signed as "Anna Mary"; they are not acknowledged on the title page; and they were presumably reworked by a professional engraver. By the late 1840s, however, after she had attended Sass's Academy, Anna Mary's illustrations become more professional—not only in that they represent better artistry but also in that they are publicly acknowledged as the work of "A. Howitt" or "Miss Howitt."

Periodical publication provided the turning point in this developmental progress, as it so often did for women authors and artists.[71] On 29 May 1847, Anna Mary published an illustration to her mother's column, "The Child's Corner," in *Howitt's Journal* (see figure 20).[72] Like other radical magazines intended for the betterment of the working classes, *Howitt's Journal* was understaffed and underfunded. With the financial strain of publishing a monthly journal and the threat of bankruptcy looming, the Howitts needed all the help they could get, and their daughter's artistic contributions were welcome. As Deborah Cherry notes, "Anna Mary Howitt was expected to work and contribute to the family business of cultural production."[73]

FIGURE 20. Anna Mary Howitt, illustration for "The Child's Corner,"
Howitt's Journal 1 (1847), 303. Courtesy of the Yale University Library.

Yet, whatever the practical reasons for her involvement, Anna Mary's inaugural illustration for *Howitt's Journal* was conceived of—and produced
as—a professional contribution. It was delineated by John Absolon, a well-
established illustrator and watercolor painter, and engraved by William
Measom, a wood engraver who worked regularly for the *Illustrated London
News*.[74] While this publication process makes it more difficult to evaluate
the merits of the original drawing, it nonetheless represents an acknowledgment that Anna Mary's art was to be treated like that of other professional artists who appeared in the journal: William Bell Scott, Margaret
Gillies, William Wilkie, and Wilhelm von Kaulbach, with whom she would
later study. The illustration bears her name as inventor: "Miss Howitt."

This illustration is more professional than earlier work, too, in the sense
that Anna Mary interprets her mother's story and produces a perspective
complementary to, but different from, the narrator's. Mary's column, "The
Young Turtle-Dove of Carmel," tells the story of a turtle-dove's home in a
monastery on Mount Carmel, Syria, and then of its migration to Surrey,

FIGURE 21. Anna Mary Howitt, "Dr. Jack's Death Bed," illustration for Mary Howitt's *Our Cousins in Ohio* (1849). Courtesy of the Yale University Library.

England, where it is caught by two well-intentioned children. "It shall live with us; it shall love us; it shall have a mate and be so happy," say the children, but the captive bird becomes "sick at heart" and dies within its cage.[75] The adult narrator intends a factual lesson in natural history and a moral tale about leaving wildlife alone. Anna Mary's drawing captures the bewilderment of the children as they contemplate the dead bird; in a scene not narrated in the tale, they hold the corpse and, in their regret, comfort each other. As illustrator, Anna Mary has achieved an independent perspective on the episode, sympathetically providing a child's vision to complement her mother's voice.

This success in *Howitt's Journal* enabled more extensive work in book illustration—another venue for professional women artists.[76] Anna Mary provided designs for her mother's next book, *The Children's Year* (1847). In the preface Mary Howitt explains that she "wished that in books for children the writer would endeavor to . . . look at things as it were from the child's point of view rather than from his own."[77] Anna Mary embraces this artistic goal by foregrounding the children's actions and capturing their perspectives in her illustrations to the tales. The success of *The Children's Year* led to a contract for another book based on the real-life experiences of children: *Our Cousins in Ohio* (1849). As in *The Children's Year*, Anna Mary's artistic work was featured in *Our Cousins*: in the former, the title page reads, "with four illustrations by John Absolon from original designs by Anna Mary Howitt"; in the latter, it becomes "with four illustrations on steel, from original designs by Anna Mary Howitt."[78] The designs for *Our Cousins* are well-executed pieces, entering into the spirit of the tales yet rendering what to the artist were visually dramatic moments. In the illustration "Dr. Jack's Death Bed" (figure 21), for example, Anna Mary creates a scene unnarrated in the story but important to understanding the children's act of charity and to embodying cultural values about death and dying.[79] She makes the illustration an artist's interpretation of the essential moment rather than an accurate reproduction of her aunt's letters or her mother's tale. Here the apprentice has become fully professional—except, perhaps, in payment for her work. We do not know whether Anna Mary was remunerated for her illustrations in *Howitt's Journal*, *The Children's Year*, or *Our Cousins in Ohio* or whether her work was an unpaid contribution to the domestic economy.

Mother-Daughter Productions:
Training the Professional Journalist

Perhaps because Mary Howitt understood the importance of financial independence, Anna Mary's professional training included not only drawing and painting lessons but also lessons in the literary marketplace. Among these were lessons in transforming personal experiences into articles or tales and placing them in appropriate magazines, often through personal contact with editors. Soon after *Our Cousins* appeared, Anna Mary decided to devote herself to painting and in 1850 traveled to Germany with fellow artist Jane Benham, their plan being to study at the Munich Art Academy. Whatever the artistic value of her German sojourn, it added the important function of becoming an apprenticeship in journalism. Like her mother, Howitt became a skilled correspondent and from Munich regularly sent letters home detailing her experiences and surroundings. Either at her mother's suggestion or by her own initiative, or perhaps after writing an article for Henry Chorley, who asked her to visit and describe Oberammergau for *The Ladies' Companion*, she soon began to write up her Munich experiences, which her mother then edited for Dickens's new periodical, *Household Words*, and for the well-established *Athenaeum*.[80]

The "Bits of Life in Munich," as *Household Words* titled them, represent another form of mother-daughter collaboration. In 1850 Dickens had written to the Howitts, asking them to contribute to his new venture; they both did so, William with "The Miner's Daughter" and a Christmas story for 1850, Mary with "a fresh ballad."[81] Almost simultaneously, and capitalizing on this open invitation, Howitt began editing her daughter's letters for *Household Words*; the series appeared in eight numbers between 2 November 1850 and 14 June 1851[82]—some in the same numbers as her parents' work, a fact readers could not know given the magazine's practice of anonymous publication. We can sense Mary's professional hand in the editing for periodical publication. The topics are chosen to appeal to Dickens's working- and lower-middle-class readers: accounts of German customs at Christmas, Easter, and other native holidays; descriptions of Munich streets, homes, and scenery; articles about ordinary domestic life and a fancy dress ball. Details about German art are omitted and personal responses, modified or generalized. Especially interesting are the omissions of Anna Mary's tale about a "fearful man" rumored to be stalking young women and of her emotional, almost visionary response to a Catholic mass at Easter.[83] Perhaps the one was too sensational for an English publication, the other improper for a Quaker daughter or inconsistent with Dickens's consistently anti-Catholic stance.

In addition to the series in *Household Words*, Howitt placed some of her daughter's letters in the "Foreign Correspondence" section of the *Athenaeum*. Except for the first, which describes local celebrations on All Souls' Day, the *Athenaeum* letters focus on German art, notably the work of Ludwig von Schwanthaler and the revival of a mode of fresco painting called Stereochromic.[84] This high-art writing must have had less appeal (even for *Athenaeum* readers) than the more popular accounts in *Household Words*, for the columns soon ceased. Anna Mary must have ceased writing them, too, for the book version of her German experiences, titled *An Art-Student in Munich*, actually includes very little about art and considerably more about ordinary German life and customs—a balance resulting from the easier access to *Household Words* during composition and the principles of bookmaking her mother taught her.

Whether taken directly from her daughter's letters or reshaped for *Household Words* as reports home by "a young lady who is studying art,"[85] the "Bits of Life in Munich" represent another version of family collaboration. Not only do they use the genre of familiar correspondence, they also were edited by Mary as she sat in Anna Mary's painting room. This site seems to have re-created the close mother-daughter bond that Mary craved and that enabled her own literary work. In a letter dated November 1850, written just as her daughter's first article was appearing and as she was producing her own contributions for *Household Words*, Mary wrote to Anna Mary,

> I work always in your painting-room, in which I have made no alterations. I venerate the old things and the old memories. But I am getting over my intense longing for you. I can take up beautiful thoughts of you and lay them down at will, and not be ridden, as it were, by them, driven by them, haunted by them till they become a dreadful nightmare. Oh! that was dreadful. If I were a painter, I should paint a Ceres mourning for the lost Proserpine. . . . I can see the wonderful head of the maternal Ceres, with her heart, not her eyes, full of tears, revealing inexpressible love, and yet desolation. Don't imagine that I am such an one now. I am very happy; nor would I wish my Proserpine to be here.[86]

The allusion to Ceres and Proserpine reveals that Anna Mary's decision to study for an artistic career had traumatically disrupted their close bond and left the mother desolate, even periodically unable to write. The passage hints of an unproductive Ceres, and the phrase, "If I were a painter," of an unbridgeable distance now existing between mother as writer, daughter as painter, each practitioners of a different art. (Who or what functions as Hades is unclear: the art of painting? a masculine grip on English art schools that excluded women painters? a model of professionalism that compelled Anna Mary to travel to Germany?) Yet as Howitt revises the myth, the return to her daughter's painting room re-creates the bond between mother and daughter, enabling them again to collaborate. Working in the room allows the mother to think of herself as a painter (thus imaginatively participating in her daughter's art form); it allows her to transform her daughter into a writer (by editing her daughter's letters and turning them into literature). Ideally, Howitt suggests, by working in the old room and venerating the "old memories," she can resist "alterations" in their familial and artistic relationship.

After Anna Mary returned from Germany, the familiar collaborative practice was physically reestablished—at least from the mother's point of view. In her *Autobiography* Mary reports on the period in the early 1850s when her husband and sons traveled to Australia, and she and her daughters worked together at home: "For upwards of two years my daughters and I dwelt alone at The Hermitage, busily occupied in writing, painting, and studying." To her husband she wrote, "Sometimes Annie and I sit together in the same room, each at our table, for an hour or two, never speaking. Then we say, 'How quiet and pleasant it is, and what a holy and soothing influence there is in this blessed work!'"[87] "Blessed" work because once again originating at a sacred site: the home.

It was a productive period, individually and collaboratively, for both mother and daughter. Mary Howitt continued her translations of the Swedish novelist Frederika Bremer, her contributions to *Household Words* and other periodicals, her editing of the *Dusseldorf Artist's Album*, and her work in juvenile literature. Out of Anna Mary's literary apprenticeship came the expanded *An Art-Student in Munich* (1853); a memoir of the artist Thomas Seddon for the *Athenaeum* (1856); and *A School of Life* (1855), a collection of tales originally sent to her brother Alfred during his travels in Australia.[88] And the 1850s were productive years for Anna Mary's painting as well: in 1854 she exhibited *Margaret Returning from the Fountain* at the National Institution; in 1854 she began *The Castaway*; and in 1856 she sent to the Crystal Palace exhibition *Boadicea Brooding over Her Wrongs*, for which her friend and fellow artist Barbara Leigh Smith modeled the warrior queen. The epitome of this period is Anna Mary's novella *The Sisters in Art*, published in the *Illustrated Exhibitor and Magazine of Art* in 1852. In this utopian fiction Anna Mary represents the principles and practice of artistic collaboration and articulates a theory of collaboration as a feminist mode of production that would undergird the next generation of professional women.

Collaborative Work as Feminist Ideology

The Sisters in Art (1852) consolidates the familial model of work with which Anna Mary Howitt grew up and gives an idealized account of her friendship and professional work with Bessie Rayner Parkes and Barbara Leigh Smith, founding members of the feminist Langham Place Group, better designated at this period as "the women artists of Scalands," Smith's Sussex retreat. At Scalands, sometimes also in the company of Adelaide Procter and Lizzie Siddal, these young women poets and artists wrote and painted, lived and worked together. Their practice and theory of work extends what the Howitts had lived as a family. It includes political and social efforts, as well as artistic labor, first in their circulating of a petition to Parliament for the passage of the Married Women's Property Bill, later in their founding of the *English Woman's Journal* and its efforts on behalf of women's education, professional training, and legal rights.

The narrative of *The Sisters in Art* recounts the artistic development and communal work of three women: Alice Oliver, a naturalistic painter; Esther Beaumont, a classically and scientifically trained painter; and Lizzie Wilson, a designer. Alice is an idealized version of Anna Mary, a young woman raised in the rural north on natural landscape and Romantic poetry. Esther is a version of Barbara Leigh Smith, later Bodichon, the well-educated and financially independent daughter of the Radical politician Benjamin Smith, who formally trained as a painter and exhibited publicly in the 1850s and 1860s. Lizzie Wilson is probably a version of Lizzie Siddal, the working-class fiancée of Dante Gabriel Rossetti and a fellow artist whom the Scalands group befriended during the 1850s.[89]

Just as Anna Mary had worked alongside her mother at home in the 1840s, so in the 1850s she translated this familial model into a painterly practice with other women. Mary Howitt had written of working with her daughter: "Sometimes Annie and I sit together in the same room, . . . [and] say, 'How quiet and pleasant it is, and what a holy and soothing influence there is in this blessed work.' "[90] When Anna Mary describes the mutual life and work of Alice, Esther, and Lizzie in *The Sisters in Art*, she echoes this sacralizing language: "Time with them had effected no other change than to draw them together into a holier and truer communion of sympathy, taste, and pursuit, and to evolve from the unity of separate talents a result, of which singly they were not capable."[91] Anna Mary's conception of collaboration draws, too, on language that Barbara Leigh Smith had used to express her dream of an "Inner and Outer Sisterhood":

> The Inner to consist of the Art-sisters bound together by their one object; . . . the Outer Sisterhood to consist of women, all workers, and all striving after a pure moral life, but belonging to any profession, any pursuit.[92]

The exchange and interchange of language, like their professional exchange in the visual arts, undergirds the collaborative model of these young founders of British feminism.

What makes *The Sisters in Art* important in the history of women's authorship is that the Scalands group not only practiced collaborative writing and painting but also theorized collaborative work as superior to individualistic endeavor. Howitt's narrative begins as if it were meant to be the developmental tale of an individual artist, Alice Oliver. But as Alice accumulates friends and fellow workers, the narrative abandons its singular focus. By the fifth installment, the three women whose stories have been separately told come to live and work together in their own house-studio. In the sixth, they articulate their belief in the superiority of collaboration, and prove it by joining forces for—and winning—a design competition sponsored by a Belgian firm. The manufacturer who awards the prize and seeks them out for further contracts praises their art: "it brings together," he says, "three truths rarely found so united in design—the natural, the scientific, and the artistic."[93] This ideology of collaborative work—viz., women working together do better than men or women working alone—further leads them to found a women's college of art, where they teach together and create a broadly intellectual curriculum, including reading in literature, history, and philosophy as well as specific training in painting, pottery, and design.

In a sense, these young professionals were justified in promoting women's collaboration as superior to men's individualistic endeavor: unlike the men who attempted to found the Society of British Authors in the 1840s but failed, Howitt, Parkes, Leigh Smith and their colleagues successfully used their groups, formal and informal, to lobby for legislation on the Married Women's Property Bill and for women's admission to art classes of the Royal Academy. Yet, for all its endorsement of collaboration, *The Sisters in Art* acknowledges the difficulties of the project. For most of the novella, the collaborative life and narrative hold, with the self-elected sisters working together as artists, educators, and feminist reformers. Yet the narrative breaks down in the utopian fiction as it did in real life. *The Sisters in Art* is prescient, almost prophetic, of the lives of Howitt, Smith, and Parkes after the mid-1850s and of the dispersal of their working community. The narrator notes that for three years the women studied together in Rome, where "they had many friends, some who, as acquaintance ripened, gave signs of intentions more than friendly, but as when they met at Padua, they agreed, indeed vowed, to lay aside all mere personal considerations till the great purpose of their study and life was accomplished, namely— the establishment of an advanced School of Female Art in their own country."[94]

What interrupts the collaborative narrative is the marriage plot, the conventional ending (or beginning) of the individual heroine's life. Alice marries Dr. Beaumont, an anatomist; Esther marries a sculptor whom she has met in Rome; and Lizzie marries the son of an eminent potter, the marriages thus disrupting their shared house-studio and dispersing their life stories. In real life, if we may make such a distinction, the same sort of dispersal occurred: Smith collapsed after an unhappy liaison with John Chapman, went to Algiers where she met Dr. Eugene Bodichon, and married him in 1859. Howitt, in distress over her friend's abandonment and despair over a bad review by John Ruskin, retreated into silence and soon married a family friend and fellow journalist, Alfred Alaric Watts. Parkes continued editing the *English Woman's Journal* during the 1850s and went on to write *Essays on Women's Work* in 1865, marrying Louis Belloc in 1867 after her conversion to Roman Catholicism.

What my invocation of the marriage plot obscures is that it was not simply marriage that ended the collaborative effort of these women artists but, significantly, a disagreement about women's work. The ideology that had allowed them to work together became an ideology that all could not fully embrace; as a result, their collaboration broke down. As Joanne Shattock has noted, Parkes and Smith advocated professional work for women, but their views on this issue gradually diverged: "[Parkes's] views were qualified. . . . She did not believe in complete equality of the sexes, seeing women's 'delicate' organization of both brains and bodies as preventing equal competition and therefore separating herself from the more advanced views of contemporaries like Smith Bodichon."[95] Smith continued to advocate for women's full participation in professional careers, whether as single or married women, and after her marriage she pursued an independent career as a landscape painter.

Anna Mary Howitt's views on women's professional work also diverged from those of Parkes, though not in Smith's direction. Under the influence of mesmerism and spiritualism, she and her family began to practice "automatic" writing and drawing. The beautiful effects of spirit drawings, her own and her father's, came to challenge her assumptions about the value of professionalism. Her father, William, without training as an artist, having "never received a single lesson in drawing," nonetheless produced spirit drawings that, his daughter testified, "from their remarkable accuracy and infinite variety of rich and elegant combination of line and jewel-like ornamentation, are highly noteworthy."[96] These amateur productions gave access to spiritual meaning—access highly valued by the women of Scalands and their mentor John Ruskin—that the "ordinary arena" of art might aspire to, but not necessarily attain. Thus the spiritualism of the late 1850s came in conflict with the apprenticeship in journalism and painting that had seemed so important to Anna Mary's professional development in the late 1840s. Writing and drawing "automatically" led Howitt to abandon her artistic career, her collaboration with the women artists of Scalands, and the professional ideology of work that they had shared. Instead, she turned to collaboration with otherworldly spirits and with her new husband, Alfred Alaric Watts, who shared her religious views.[97]

Presenting the Woman of Letters: Mary Howitt's *Autobiography* (1888) as Collaborative Mythmaking

When Mary Howitt came to compose her *Autobiography* in the 1880s, three decades after these events, she re-created the collaborative model that had motivated her authorial career. Early in the 1880s, in the company of her daughter Margaret, she sifted through family memorabilia and professional correspondence to assemble facts, anecdotes, and quotations for her narrative. From her sister Anna, she solicited a history of their father's family, including records from the Quaker monthly meeting books of their native Nottinghamshire. During a visit by Anna Mary, she requested sketches of Marienruhe, the Howitts' retirement home in Switzerland, to complement the earlier drawings her daughter had made of family homes in Nottingham and London. Howitt published her account in the periodical *Good Words* as "Some Reminiscences of My Life" (1885) and "Reminiscences of My Later Life" (1886); later, it was amplified and revised by her daughter Margaret, whose name appears on the title page of *Mary Howitt: An Autobiography* (1889) as its editor.[98] Despite its singular title, Howitt's *Autobiography* may be the most remarkable example of collaborative life writing produced in

Victorian England.[99] Unlike the *Autobiography* of John Stuart Mill, to which Harriet Taylor contributed behind the scenes, or *The Autobiography of Elizabeth Davis*, for which the Welsh historian Jane Williams served as amanuensis, Howitt's text was conceived and executed as a collaborative project.[100]

In composing this family memoir, Howitt faced a version of the narrative dilemma that had confronted Anna Mary in *The Sisters in Art*. Collaborative life writing requires not only a shared life story but a shared ideology—in this case a set of beliefs about the value of collaborative work, shared family endeavor, and a professional career pursued jointly with others. Howitt articulates her beliefs in the passage of her *Autobiography* quoted earlier: working together within a family is "a holy and soothing influence"; it is "blessed work," sacred because it emerges from the domestic heart and hearth. Yet, as she well knew, the family had divided on the issue of work in the late 1850s when William committed himself to the work of spiritualism and journalism on its behalf, and when Anna Mary abandoned her professional career as an artist and also committed herself to spiritualism. That William and his daughter Anna Mary conceived of their commitment as a new form of communal effort is evident from the title of the biography Anna Mary wrote of her father: *William Howitt and His Work for Spiritualism* (1883). In effect, from the late 1850s onward, Anna Mary shifted her ideological commitment from professionalism to spiritualism, from achievement in the public sphere to development in an inner, non-material realm.

Mary Howitt minimizes this familial division in her *Autobiography*, presenting the work as a memoir of the "professional artist class" with which she and her husband identified and for whom collaboration was a common practice. This class, named by Margaret Oliphant in a review of memoirs by Fanny Kemble and Anna Jameson,[101] included Victorian intellectuals who valued not only the art they produced through collaboration but also the professional training they transmitted from one generation to the next. When Howitt composed her autobiography, she wished to re-create the life of this "professional artist class," repeating episodes and details that signal family harmony and striving to include all family members in the history.

Howitt begins with a portrait of Marienruhe, the Swiss home built on a site that she, her husband, and daughter Margaret discovered in 1874, came to love for its natural beauty, and built with their literary profits.[102] She incorporates a mini-biography of her husband, William, as if both to record his independent history before their marriage and to consolidate their long domestic and professional partnership. And she includes numerous drawings by Anna Mary of earlier family homes: the Howitt homestead in Heanor, West End Cottage in Esher, "our first home in Heidelberg," the Elms in Lower Clapton, the Hermitage in Highgate, and various views of

THE ELMS, LOWER CLAPTON.

FIGURE 22. Anna Mary Howitt Watts, "The Elms, Lower Clapton,"
illustration for Mary Howitt's *Autobiography* (1889).
Courtesy of the Yale University Library.

Marienruhe (see figures 22–24). These drawings document the family's life
together and testify to their achieved middle-class status—both matters of
crucial importance to the formation of the Victorian man and woman of
letters. The gracious home of the Howitts' retirement testifies to the success
of their professional careers.

The most difficult narrative task emerges when Howitt must account for
her daughter's decision to abandon her career as a painter and take a different
path, spiritually and professionally. When Howitt writes of Anna Mary's
decision, she sees not an ideological rift within the family but an attack from
outside. According to the *Autobiography*,

> Our daughter had, both by her pen and pencil, taken her place among
> the successful artists and writers of the day, when, in the spring of 1856,
> a severe private censure of one of her oil-paintings by a king among
> critics so crushed her sensitive nature as to make her yield to her bias

WILLIAM AND MARY HOWITT AT THE HERMITAGE.

FIGURE 23. Anna Mary Howitt Watts, "The Hermitage," Highgate, illustration for Mary Howitt's *Autobiography* (1889). Courtesy of the Yale University Library.

FIGURE 24. Anna Mary Howitt Watts, "Marienruhe," illustration for Mary Howitt's *Autobiography* (1889). Courtesy of the Yale University Library.

for the supernatural, and withdraw from the ordinary arena of the fine arts. After her marriage in 1859 to her contemporary and friend from childhood, Alfred Alaric, the only son of our valued associates, Mr. and Mrs. Watts, they both jointly pursued psychological studies. (II, 117)

This interpretation blames John Ruskin, the "king among critics," for ending Anna Mary's artistic career; less vehemently, it explains Anna Mary's new direction in terms of the marriage plot. Following Howitt's lead, art historians tend to blame Ruskin—or, more generally, patriarchy—for the loss of a potentially great woman artist. Deborah Cherry, for instance, suggests that in *Boadicea Brooding over Her Wrongs* Howitt and Ruskin were confronting each other head on about the legitimacy of women artists entering the masculine domain of history painting and, thus quite consciously, rewriting British history.[103] Who would dispute this conclusion? It is reported that Ruskin, the man whose words provided the epigraph for *An Art-Student in Munich*,[104] wrote to Anna Mary after viewing her painting, "What do you know about Boadicea? Leave such subjects alone and paint me a pheasant's wing."[105] Yet Pamela Gerrish Nunn is also right to suggest that it wasn't Ruskin alone who caused the demise of Howitt's career, but that another (perhaps unwitting) culprit was Alfred Alaric Watts, Anna Mary's husband.[106] Whether stern critic or loving husband, patriarchy functions as the agent in most accounts of Anna Mary's professional crisis and withdrawal.

What both versions obscure is the division that spiritualism caused within the family, a division that set father and elder daughter on one side as spiritualists, mother and younger daughter on the other as (eventually) Roman Catholics. In the *Autobiography* Howitt simply narrates the end of Anna Mary's career in one paragraph and in the next takes up the matter of spiritualism, as though the two were unrelated.

> In the spring of 1856 we had become acquainted with several most ardent and honest spirit-mediums. It seemed right to my husband and myself, under the circumstances, to see and try to understand the true nature of those phenomena. . . . The system was clearly open to abuse. I felt thankful for the assurance thus gained of an invisible world, but resolved to neglect none of my common duties for spiritualism. (II, 117–18)

The passage disguises the fact that Anna Mary chose to redefine those "common duties" and, in so doing, abandon her artistic career. An independent letter by Margaret, the younger daughter who assisted with the composition of the *Autobiography*, assesses Anna Mary's decision differently; Margaret blamed spiritualism for ending Anna Mary's professional career, asserting that "my pure & most sensitive sister was 'gassed' by the poisonous miasma of spiritualism."[107] If Margaret's version is accurate, then Anna Mary's life story cannot be easily incorporated into a professional family memoir; it becomes a potential tangent, an alternative narrative that gives evidence against a family history of harmonious collaboration. Unlike Howitt's earlier ideological crises, which required the reintegration of domestic and professional labor, this crisis involves two ideologies that define distinctly different kinds of collaborative work.

Perhaps this is why it was so important for Howitt to include her elder daughter's work in the final auto/biographical collaboration. By inviting Anna Mary to Switzerland, where the writing occurred, and by asking her to bring her old sketches and make new ones of the family home, Marienruhe, Howitt could recuperate her daughter for the joint familial project. As she explains, "She [Anna Mary] came to Meran at the time of roses, bringing with her a collection of drawings and sketches, which she had earlier made of her parents' 'Homes and Haunts.' She began at once to make sketches of our present surroundings, with a sense of their being needed."[108] It is significant, of course, that Anna Mary contributes sketches of the family homes, the sites of past and present collaboration (figures 22–24). It is significant, too, that Mary Howitt refers to them as "her parents' 'Homes and Haunts.'" The phrase alludes to the title of the first important book on which Anna Mary collaborated with William and Mary: *The Homes and Haunts of the Most Eminent British Poets* (1847).[109] By drawing her parents' home, Anna Mary collaborates once more in a family project. By including her daughter's drawings as the "homes and haunts" of the British authors that the *Autobiography* commemorates, Mary Howitt confirms the family's professional work and its status in the literary world of Victorian Britain.[110] The ideology of collaborative work may have been challenged during the family's lifetime, but it is reaffirmed in the final version of this woman of letters' life history.

❊ 4 ❊

PARALLEL CURRENTS
The Life of Charlotte Brontë as
Mid-Victorian Myth
of Women's Authorship

Charlotte Brontë was not a professional woman of letters—at least not in Victorian terms. During her lifetime she copublished *Poems of Acton, Currer, and Ellis Bell* (1846) with her sisters, Anne and Emily, and as Currer Bell produced three highly acclaimed novels: *Jane Eyre* (1847), *Shirley* (1849), and *Villette* (1853). Once, in August 1849, she penned an indignant response to the *Quarterly Review*, addressed to the reviewer (Elizabeth Rigby, later Lady Eastlake) whose notice of *Jane Eyre* had called the novel "unchristian" and the novelist a "strange man" or, if a woman, someone who had "long forfeited the society of her own sex."[1] But this biting "Word to the 'Quarterly'" was intended as a preface to *Shirley*, not as a letter to a periodical, and in any case was never printed.[2] Brontë never wrote articles, columns, or reviews for periodicals nor, as far as her letters reveal, was she ever asked to do so. Although her publisher, George Smith, often sought her response to books his firm had published and to manuscript segments of Thackeray's novels, most famously *Henry Esmond*, Brontë never expressed her literary opinions in print, nor did she receive payment for her unofficial, private work as a publisher's reader. She lacks (and perhaps avoided) work in those genres that crucially mark the nineteenth-century man and woman of letters.

Nevertheless, Brontë as a literary figure—and *The Life of Charlotte Brontë* as a biography—had remarkable influence on mid-Victorian conceptions of women's authorship and on aspiring young women who sought a model for literary success and, in subsequent decades, became women of letters in their own right. In *A Literature of Their Own: British Women Novelists from Brontë to Lessing*, Elaine Showalter chooses Brontë as the seminal figure in the emergence of a distinctly female literary tradition, and in her discussion of the legend of Charlotte Brontë and its impact, Showalter quotes Margaret Oliphant's astute estimate in an 1855 review: "Perhaps no other writer of her time has impressed her mark so clearly on contemporary literature, or drawn so many followers onto her own peculiar path."[3] Oliphant was referring to Brontë's mark, via *Jane Eyre*, on the trajectory of the nineteenth-century novel. But we might also speak of Brontë's life as it "impressed its mark" on women of letters via the biography that Elizabeth Gaskell, her friend and fellow novelist, wrote after her death: *The Life of Charlotte Brontë* (1857). This masterful biography constructed the woman writer in terms of a "parallel currents" model: "her life as Currer Bell, the author; her life as Charlotte Brontë, the woman." It separated the identity of the author from that of the woman, even while emphasizing the importance of "duty" in the woman writer's work and revealing the intermingling of domestic tragedy with literary triumph in the life of its subject. Gaskell's model—its rationale for women's writing and its continuing influence on myths of women's authorship—dominated the mid-Victorian period, and it provides the focus of this chapter and the next.

Before the *Life*: Romantic and Early Victorian Biographies of Literary Women

Brontë died on 31 March 1855, and when Gaskell learned of her death, she resolved to write a memoir of her friend and fellow novelist. On 31 May 1855 she wrote to their mutual publisher, George Smith of Smith, Elder, "if I live long enough, and no one is living whom such a publication would hurt, I will publish what I know of her, and make the world (if I am but strong enough in expression,) honour the woman as much as they have admired the writer."[4] The opportunity came sooner than she expected. The next month, on 16 June 1855, the Reverend Patrick Brontë, Charlotte's father, addressed a letter to Gaskell, with a request "to write a brief account of her life and to make some remarks on her works"; he added, "You seem to me the best qualified for doing what I wish should be done."[5]

When Gaskell agreed to write a biography of Brontë, the models for writing a woman author's life history were few, and none distinguished. Alexander Dyce had published *Specimens of British Poetesses* (1825) and Anne Katherine Elwood, *Memoirs of the Literary Ladies of England* (1843)—the first an anthology of representative poems with biographical headnotes, the second a collection of short biographies describing the author's life circumstances and chief literary works.[6] Both were informational, the second inspirational to scribbling young women. As Elwood acknowledged in her preface, her *Memoirs* were for the amateur, "intended only for such of her own sex, who, not feeling themselves equal to profound and abstract subjects, can derive amusement and information from what is professedly too light for the learned, and too simple for the studious."[7] Yet Elwood also knew that women with writerly ambition would scour them for hints about success in a literary career, as she herself seems to have done with the printed biographical notices she used for this collection.[8]

The authorized biographies of nineteenth-century women writers were not much superior to Elwood's, though they set the agenda for subsequent life writing about professional women artists and authors. After Laetitia Landon's death in 1838, Emma Roberts, a friend and minor author, prefixed an account of the poetess's career to *The Zenana and Minor Poems* (1839), testifying to Landon's exemplary domesticity and countering claims that she had committed suicide after an ill-advised marriage to George MacLean, governor of Cape Coast, Africa.[9] Laman Blanchard, another literary friend, then issued his *Life and Literary Remains of L.E.L.* (1841), amplifying the account with further instances of Landon's talent, achievement, and tragic death.[10] In the same decade, Henry F. Chorley published *Memorials of Mrs. Hemans* (1836), a personal reminiscence with a selection of literary letters, and the sister of Felicia Hemans followed with a hagiographic account of the poetess's life in her *Memoir* (1840), assuring the public of the domestic woman behind the literary author and revealing the dutiful daughter, affectionate sister, and solicitous mother who, more than any individual, "would have shrunk more sensitively from the idea of being made the subject of a biographical memoir."[11] These biographies presented woman writers of originality, even genius, who were also, invariably, domestic paragons.

Nineteenth-century fictional accounts of the woman artist were better as literary productions but discouraging as models, whether hagiographic or scandalous. Following Madame de Staël's *Corinne* (1807, trans. 1833), women novelists and poets presented the artistic woman as distinctly different from the domestic daughter, wife, and mother. *Corinne*, with its Scottish hero attracted to the dark half-Italian, half-English poetess but committed to marrying his fair, pure English betrothed, taught the lesson of their incompatibility and the fate of the artistic woman as decline and death. In effect, it created a binary: the artistic woman versus the domestic woman. Landon promulgated the Corinne myth in many poems, most notably "A History of the Lyre" (1829), where Eulalie, a poetess, wastes away after her English lover returns to his Emily and, in the final scene, erects "a sculpted form" that is both her grave marker and a monument to fame.[12] Gaskell's Mancunian counterpart, Geraldine Jewsbury, modified the Corinne tradition in *The Half Sisters* (1847) to proclaim the lesson of the complementarity of the two female types, the artistic and domestic as two "sisters," but Jewsbury's novel does not suggest a wholly satisfactory life course for her artistic heroine. When Bianca, the actress-protagonist of *The Half Sisters*, decides to marry "Viscount Melton, of Melton Hall, in Staffordshire, and of Fort Vernon, in Scotland," she gives up her career. The novel's final chapter tells of the "bitter lamentations for the irreparable loss the stage had sustained from the abdication of its high-priestess," and Bianca appears instead in a cozy domestic scene, "working a cushion in crochet for Lady Vernon."[13] While Bianca assures us that "genius" can be shown in more than "one special mode of manifestation," it is hard to believe that Jewsbury meant this domestic finale unironically. In any case, it does not present a model for the sustained achievement of the woman writer; it separates the artistic life from the domestic and reads them oppositionally (or sequentially).

Romantic and early Victorian biographies of women authors influenced Gaskell as she contemplated her *Life of Charlotte Brontë*. In their focus on an author's domestic life and circumstances and in their concern with characteristics of the woman of "genius," such memoirs raised questions that Victorian biographers and their readers felt the need to address: questions about the relationship of the private woman and the public author, the domestic and the literary, and the compatibility or incompatibility of the two. As Gaskell addresses these enduring questions in *The Life of Charlotte Brontë*, she disrupts the oppositional mode of the earlier nineteenth century to reformulate the artistic and the domestic as "parallel currents." Perhaps speaking for herself as much as for Brontë, Gaskell suggests that there are "separate duties belonging to each character—not opposing each other; not impossible, but difficult to be reconciled."[14]

Exemplary Domesticity and the Woman Writer

One reason Gaskell felt pressed to present Brontë as exemplary in her femininity and domesticity is that these qualities had been challenged in reviews of *Jane Eyre*. Brontë's debut novel was praised as "a work of great promise," even genius, but the novelist was also chastised for "masculine hardness, coarseness, and freedom of expression."[15] Elizabeth Rigby in the *Quarterly Review* condemned the novel's protagonist, Jane Eyre, as "the personification of an unregenerate and undisciplined spirit. . . . She has inherited in fullest measure the worst sin of our fallen nature—the sin of pride."[16] These judgments died down with the publication of *Shirley* and *Villette*, but they surfaced again in the obituaries and omnibus reviews published after Brontë's death.

It was Ellen Nussey, Charlotte's friend of thirty years, who urged the Reverend Arthur Nicholls, Charlotte's widower, to authorize a biography in order to refute errors in fact and judgment that were circulating in the obituaries—errors that she believed could be disproved by the publication of her extensive correspondence with her friend. Particularly irksome was an article in *Sharpe's London Magazine* for June 1855, "A Few Words about 'Jane Eyre,'" that "hurt and pained" Nussey in its "tissue of malign falsehoods."[17] Written anonymously,[18] the article revived many of the rumors about "Currer Bell" that had circulated at the publication of *Jane Eyre* and included suggestions of impropriety and coarseness, based on the character of

Mr. Rochester who used "real wicked oaths, like a bold, bad, live man" and on the 1848 *Quarterly* speculation that the novel was written by a "strange man" or by a woman who had "long forfeited the society of her own sex": "Of course, it was a man's writing, no woman *would* have written such a book."[19] The *Sharpe's* article also introduced inaccurate details about the Brontës' lives, including the marriage of Patrick Brontë at Penzance, his severance of ties with his wife's relatives, his abandonment of his children and their education to his servants, and his daughters' abject poverty. This revival of old wounds led Nussey to urge the need for "a just and honourable defence," which could be best mounted, she urged, by the novelist Mrs. Gaskell.

Nussey pledged her support, in terms of both her personal testimony and her cache of letters—an offer of great importance to Gaskell, who constructed much of the biography from these materials. Nussey prepared her letters for Gaskell's use—arranging her collection, selecting over three hundred, erasing many of the proper names to preserve anonymity, and perhaps destroying some that she felt might do damage. In her note acknowledging receipt, Gaskell assured Nussey, "They gave me a very beautiful idea of her [Charlotte's] character."[20] As the reader of the *Life* readily grasps, these letters were ideal for projecting one strand of Brontë's life that Gaskell intended to highlight: her character as a dutiful daughter, loving sister, and faithful friend.[21] As Gaskell would phrase it in the second volume, in an oft-quoted passage of the *Life*,

> When a man becomes an author, it is probably merely a change of employment to him. He takes a portion of that time which has hitherto been devoted to some other study or pursuit; . . . But no other can take up the quiet regular duties of the daughter, the wife, or the mother, as well as she whom God has appointed to fill that particular place: a woman's principal work in life is hardly left to her own choice; nor can she drop the domestic charges devolving on her as an individual, for the exercise of the most splendid talents that were ever bestowed. (II, ii, 223)

In the first volume of the biography, Gaskell extracts from Brontë's letters to show her subject fulfilling a "woman's principal work," even as she hints of the "splendid talents" that are simultaneously developing, to be fully revealed in the second volume where Brontë emerges as a literary phenomenon.

Throughout the *Life* Gaskell stresses Brontë's exemplary domesticity. Her first extract from the Brontë-Nussey correspondence depicts Charlotte and her sisters living an ordinary life of middle-class femininity at the Haworth parsonage: reading, writing, drawing, walking, sewing, and doing "a little fancy work" (21 July 1832). In the next extract, Gaskell quotes a letter written in French, "for the sake of improvement in the language," and for the "happy little family picture" it "presents us" (18 October 1832).[22] Other early letters reveal Charlotte analyzing novels, plays, biographies, and history books (4 July 1834); moralizing on the temptations of London, "the great city . . . as apocryphal as Babylon" (19 June 1834); confessing her spiritual faults and admiring Ellen's ability to set her face "Zionward" (10 May 1836); and submitting to "duty—necessity . . . stern mistresses, who will not be disobeyed," as she leaves for a position as governess at Roe Head School (6 July 1835). As Rosemarie Bodenheimer has noted, "Charlotte's first letters to Ellen Nussey might have been conduct-book models of an 'improving' correspondence."[23]

Although the Brontë-Nussey letters became more intimate (and witty) as their friendship progressed, and their subjects more varied as they moved into wider social circles as adults, Gaskell maintains the focus on duty, familial responsibility, and moral integrity as she selects and quotes from these letters. It is not that Gaskell alters or "improves" Brontë's language or sentiments—as John Gibson Lockhart did in his *Memoirs of the Life of Sir Walter Scott* (1837–38) or John Forster in the *Life of Charles Dickens* (1872–74); throughout *The Life of Charlotte Brontë*, Gaskell quotes responsibly,[24] allowing herself a biographer's freedom to combine selections from several letters, make smooth transitions between extracts, and continue the narrative thread without unnecessary digressions. Rather, it is Gaskell's understanding of the biographer's need to shape the plot and interpret her subject's life that motivates her selections. Gaskell selects (positively) to emphasize Charlotte's deep commitment to her dying siblings and ailing father, and she omits (more complexly) to observe the Victorian convention that nothing offensive about the living should appear in print and to avoid narrative paths she wishes to avoid, especially those that involve Brontë in a romantic attachment with her Belgian teacher, Constantin Heger.

The emphasis on familial duty begins in volume I, chapter 8, as Gaskell shows Charlotte leaving home "with necessity 'as her mistress'" for a schoolteacher's life "as monotonously and unbroken as ever" (early June 1837), then returning home to care for their servant Tabby who has broken a leg (29 December 1837), and serving as housemaid at Haworth by "cleaning, sweeping up hearths, dusting rooms, making beds, etc." (15 April 1839). Gaskell reinforces this exemplary feminine character by quoting Charlotte's exchange with the poet laureate Robert Southey, who advised that "Literature cannot be the business of a woman's life, and it ought not to be. The more she is engaged in her proper duties, the less leisure will she have for it"—to which Charlotte replied, "I have endeavoured not only attentively to observe all the duties a woman ought to fulfill, but to feel deeply interested in them."[25]

The theme of womanly duty becomes most intense in the opening chapters of the second volume, as Brontë nurses her aged father through cataract surgery, even as she receives publishers' letters rejecting *The Professor* and begins the novel that will become *Jane Eyre*, and then as her siblings

Branwell, Emily, and Anne succumb to consumption. Gaskell reinforces the commitment to duty as a *Christian* virtue in volume II, chapter 3, as she quotes from Anne's last verses, Charlotte's letters to Ellen Nussey, and Nussey's account of Anne's death, which begins, "Her life was calm, quiet, spiritual: *such* was her end. Through the trials and fatigues of the journey, she evinced the pious courage and fortitude of a martyr." Nussey has been derided as a pious spinster who misunderstood Brontë, or at least understood only one side of her friend's character, and who wished primarily to refute "the oft-made charge of irreligion"[26]—an estimate that is no doubt true. Yet Nussey's position as conventional reader and recipient of a female friend's letters produced essential evidence for the rebuttal that Gaskell wished to make against reviewers who had wrongly depicted the author of *Jane Eyre* as unfeminine and unchristian. As Gaskell wrote to George Smith on 19 August 1856, when she was halfway through the *Life*, she planned a "tirade against Lady Eastlake," the worst of the reviewers and the one who, in the *Quarterly*, had most injured Brontë's private character; "whatever Miss Brontë wrote Lady E. had no right to make such offensive conjectures."[27]

In advancing this interpretation of the woman writer as one who fulfills the "quiet regular duties of the daughter, the wife, or the mother," Gaskell had also to diminish the view that Brontë, like the heroines of her novels, was overly and obsessively concerned with romantic love. Harriet Martineau had privately chastised Brontë for this defect and repeated it (though less fulsomely) in her obituary in the *Daily News* in April 1855: "Though passion occupies too prominent a place in her pictures of Life, though women have to complain that she represents Love as the whole and sole concern of their lives, . . . it is a true social blessing that we have had a female writer who has discountenanced sentimentalism and feeble egotism with such practical force as is apparent in the works of 'Currer Bell.' "[28] Gaskell minimizes the romantic aspect of the correspondence by excising phrases or sentences from Brontë's letters that reveal an interest in courtship and love—for example, "We write of little else but love and marriage" in a letter of 15 May 1840—and by omitting anecdotes of social life that involve flirtation or erotic playfulness—for example, in a letter of 3 March 1841 when Charlotte asks Ellen whether she has received a Valentine "from our bonny-faced friend the curate of Haworth," a man she had a year earlier dubbed "Miss Celia Amelia," a nickname Gaskell carefully omits by extracting the letter to read, "Mr. W. delivered a noble, eloquent high-Church, Apostolical succession discourse" (7 April 1840).

Of course, Gaskell was also mindful of the sensitivities of the Reverend Arthur Nicholls, Charlotte's widower, who had mistrusted his wife's friendship with a Unitarian and resisted the biography. In treating the three proposals of marriage prior to his, Gaskell discretely underplays their romantic significance and waits for her moment to present Nicholls as a Jacob serving seven years for his beloved Rachel. The first proposal, from Ellen's clergyman brother Henry Nussey, receives mention with little elaboration: "her first proposal of marriage was quietly declined and put on one side. Matrimony did not enter into the scheme of her life, but good, sound, earnest labour did." The second, from the Reverend David Pryce, curate at Colne in Lancashire, appears in a letter of 4 August 1839, introduced as evidence of Charlotte's "power of attraction . . . when she let herself go in the happiness and freedom of home." The third, from James Taylor of Smith, Elder,[29] provides a refutation of the assumption that "some are apt to imagine, from the extraordinary power with which she represented the passion of love in her novels, that she herself was easily susceptible of it," to which Gaskell adds Brontë's testimony that "each moment he came near me, and that I could see his eyes fastened on me, my veins ran ice" (9 April 1851). Not fire or passion as in Martineau's assessment, but ice and coldness in Gaskell's *Life*.

Further, the *Life* avoids mentioning a fourth possible candidate for Brontë's hand, George Smith, publishing head of Smith, Elder, to whom Brontë was certainly attracted. Modern biographers have speculated that Smith's mother intervened when the attachment between author and publisher became too close.[30] Gaskell may not have detected this incipient romance, however, since Smith did not permit full access to his personal correspondence with Brontë.[31] But Gaskell certainly recognized that Smith and his mother were prototypes for Dr. John and Mrs. Bretton of *Villette*, for in a letter to Nussey, she refers to Smith's "very pretty, Paulina-like little wife."[32] So whether deliberate or unwitting, the downplaying of Smith's romantic interest complements Gaskell's insistent presentation of Brontë as dedicated to family duties, committed to useful work, and uninterested in courtship or marriage for their own sake. For this interpretation she had not only Nussey's letters but also the testimony of Mary Taylor, their mutual friend, sent in a letter from New Zealand: "She thought much of her duty, and had loftier and clearer notions of it than most people, and held fast to them with more success. . . . All her life was but labour and pain; and she never threw down the burden for the sake of present pleasure."[33]

The manuscript of the *Life* shows that Gaskell debated where to place Taylor's testimony, ultimately deciding to quote it in the penultimate paragraph of the biography.[34] In this key location, the assertion "She thought much of her duty" reinforces the theme that Gaskell is at pains to underscore throughout: that the exemplary woman writer is exemplary not only in literary terms, but also in domestic. The effect, as Lucasta Miller has observed, is to create a "saintly heroine, . . . a quiet and trembling creature, reared in total seclusion, a martyr to duty and a model of Victorian femininity."[35] Another effect, as Linda Hughes and Michael Lund have added, is to assure the Victorian reading public that the biographer herself is an exemplary woman writer; Gaskell's representation of Brontë is "self-defense as well as defense, self-advertising as well as rescue of a beloved friend and sister novelist."[36] An ongoing effect was to convince scribbling young women that domestic life and literary life were separate, yet compatible arenas in which they might succeed.

Elizabeth Gaskell as Mid-Victorian Woman of Letters

In constructing Charlotte Brontë as a figure exemplary in her domesticity and committed to lofty and clear notions of duty, Gaskell was working through issues about women's authorship that she had pondered in terms of her own life and career. Writing to Eliza Fox in February 1850, after the success of *Mary Barton* and as she began to contribute regularly to Dickens's *Household Words*, Gaskell insisted that both "home duties" and "the development of the individual" were values to be pursued: "assuredly a blending of the two is desirable." Yet Gaskell also acknowledged that the "blending" would be different for women than for men: "One thing is pretty clear, *Women*, must give up living an artist's life, if home duties are to be paramount. It is different with men, whose home duties are so small a part of their life."[37] As Gaskell considered the legitimate claims of home and family on the woman author, she reached a conclusion in this 1850 letter that parallels the affirmation of women's work in Anna Jameson's 1856 lecture, *The Communion of Labour*: that for neither men nor women should "Self" be "the end of exertions"; that "we have all some appointed work to do, . . . what *we* have to do in advancing the Kingdom of God."[38] (Jameson would argue, as I noted in chapter 1, that the world needs the labor of both men and women, but that men and women contribute differently to the world's work, with women's contributions extending their responsibilities in the domestic realm to the world at large.)[39]

Gaskell's authorial career had been founded on this sense of "appointed work," committed to a "professional ideal" that stressed "ideality" more than "materiality" (to adopt Susan E. Colón's useful terms).[40] Gaskell's initial model of authorship was closer to Mary Howitt's than to Charlotte Brontë's; indeed, her biographer Jenny Uglow argues that Howitt was "her model of a professional but socially motivated woman writer."[41] Certainly, Gaskell was influenced by the Howitts, with whom she corresponded, exchanged visits, and used as literary agents for placing *Mary Barton*. Gaskell's first publication, "Sketches among the Poor, No. 1," was a poem coauthored with her husband, William, and published anonymously in *Blackwood's Edinburgh Magazine* in January 1837. The sketch depicts a solitary working-class woman who has lost her family, including a beloved sister now sleeping "beneath a grassy tomb," but who finds her purpose in life by serving others as a "fond nurse" who "lulls the tired infant to its quiet rest" or as a companion to the aged and dying who rely "on her counsel day by day."[42] In this fictional woman's acts of selfless labor lie a parallel to the writerly acts of William and

Elizabeth Gaskell, the clergyman and his wife who labor for the betterment of the Manchester poor. The couple intended the *Blackwood's* poem to be the first in a series; as Gaskell later explained to Mary Howitt, "We once thought of *trying* to write sketches among the poor, *rather* in the manner of Crabbe . . . but in a more seeing-beauty spirit. . . . But I suppose we spoke of our plan near a dog-rose, for it never went any further."[43] Despite the aborted plan, the impulse behind "Sketches among the Poor" continued to motivate the Gaskells' work—in various modes. In 1838 William gave a series of lectures to Manchester weavers on the "Poets and Poetry of Humble Life." Elizabeth wrote a now-lost series of articles, presumably prose versions of "Sketches among the Poor," which she sent to John Blackwood but which were, she later acknowledged, "both poor & exaggerated in tone; and they were never inserted."[44]

It seems that Gaskell envisioned the sort of husband-wife collaboration that she recognized in the Howitts. In May 1838, just after the Howitts had published *The Rural Life of England* and as William Howitt embarked on *Visits to Remarkable Places*,[45] she wrote to the couple, thanking them for "their charming descriptions of natural scenery and the thoughts and feelings arising from the happy circumstances of rural life" and describing her own youth in a "little, clean, kindly country town."[46] The Howitts encouraged her writing, for Gaskell sent "Clopton Hall," a description of her schoolgirl visit to an old Warwickshire country house, which William included in the third chapter of his *Visits*, "Visit to Stratford-on-Avon and the Haunts of Shakespeare."[47] Later, he incorporated Gaskell's "Cheshire Customs" into an expanded and revised edition of *The Rural Life of England* in the "Lingering Customs" section.[48] In her *Autobiography* Mary Howitt recorded that her husband was so impressed with Gaskell's "powerful and graphic" depictions that he urged her "to use her pen for the public benefit."[49]

This use of authorship "for the public benefit" reveals itself in Gaskell's authorial debut. Although she continued to write during the subsequent decade, perhaps helping her husband with his anonymously published *Temperance Rhymes* (1839), more likely composing stories and sketches on her own, especially after the death of her infant son Willie, Gaskell did not appear in print again until 1847.[50] In that year, she published "Life in Manchester: Libbie Marsh's Three Eras" in *Howitt's Journal of Literature and Progress*, jointly edited by William and Mary. These three linked stories, like "Sketches among the Poor" a decade prior, depict the acts of selfless labor of a Manchester spinster—working as seamstress to support herself, saving hard-earned money to buy a Valentine gift for a crippled boy, aiding his embittered mother to lead a more tranquil life, and showing such "peace shining on her countenance" that the plain heroine becomes almost beautiful to those who know her.[51] The moral, or "concluding sentence of the story," hesitantly offered as something readers tend to skip, expresses the author's and her heroine's rationale: "She has a purpose in life; and that purpose is a holy one."[52] This sense of a "holy purpose" authorizes Gaskell's authorship. As she would put it to Eliza Fox, "I do believe that we have all some appointed work to do, . . . and that first we must find out what we are sent into the world to do, and define it and make it clear to ourselves."[53] As Alexis Easley notes, hereafter Gaskell would see herself as a social investigator and reformer, "wander[ing] through urban landscapes, documenting the harsh reality of working-class poverty," and "describing her philanthropic activities in Manchester" to literary friends.[54]

Although her husband, William, discontinued his work at authorship,[55] except for the occasional religious or civic address,[56] Gaskell continued to offer fiction to *Howitt's Journal*, a radical periodical "devoted to the people and their cause," "to promot[ing] their education and their self-education."[57] When *Howitt's Journal* foundered in 1848, she turned to industrial fiction in *Mary Barton: A Tale of Manchester Life* (1848), *Ruth* (1853), and *North and South* (1854–55), and to reformist tales for Dickens's *Household Words*, a less radical but still progressive magazine. The exemplary domesticity of Gaskell's working-class heroines in her debut fiction mirrors the exemplary model of women's authorship she attempted to enact in her early career and depict in her biography of Charlotte Brontë. Gaskell acknowledged that she couldn't live up to her ideal: "my books are so far better than I am that I often feel ashamed of having written them and as if I were a hypocrite."[58] Yet despite the impossibility of achieving the saintly selflessness of Mary in "Sketches of the Poor" or Libbie Marsh in "Life in Manchester," Gaskell did project herself as "a high-profile social reformer and woman of letters," to quote Easley.[59] As Angus Easson further observes, in the first half of her career Gaskell was "as concerned with the didactic as the aesthetic function of the novel"; in her early work "moral and aesthetic feeling" are closely linked, and she views "success" as "moral rather than financial."[60]

This linkage of the moral and aesthetic influences Gaskell's representation of Brontë as literary worker, especially in the emphasis on "duty." Yet Brontë was not so easily assimilated into a Victorian model of authorship that posited literary labor as an *extension* of a woman's domestic work. As Gaskell recognized, Brontë's precedents for authorship were Romantic, her impulses for writing linked to inspiration, imagination, and genius. And this difference between their authorial orientations, whatever their domestic similarities, led to the "parallel currents" model that Gaskell advanced in *The Life of Charlotte Brontë*.

Literary Genius and the Woman Writer

Gaskell does not introduce the model of "parallel currents" until the second volume of the *Life*, the point at which she turns to Brontë's success as a novelist and her career as a literary figure. In the biography's most famous passage, Gaskell writes of her subject as a woman with a divided existence: "her life as Currer Bell, the author; her life as Charlotte Brontë, the woman."[61] In volume I, Gaskell concentrates on the "quiet regular duties of the daughter, the wife, or the mother"; in volume II, she turns to the responsibilities of the gifted writer who, "possessing such talents," must not hide her gift in a napkin" but labor "for the use and service of others." Practically speaking, she makes this turn to Brontë's literary life by diminishing the letters to Ellen Nussey (which had continued as regularly as ever) and by selecting instead from letters to George Smith, Brontë's publisher; two members of his firm, W. S. Williams and James Taylor; and various literary acquaintances with whom Brontë corresponded after the publication of *Jane Eyre*. Conceptually, Gaskell makes the turn by meditating on the important but problematic concept of "genius."

As she shapes and interprets Brontë's literary career, Gaskell enters into a mid-century debate about the role of the woman writer and the grounds of her authority. Unlike Mary Howitt and other mid-Victorian women, Gaskell does not present Brontë's authorship as an extension of a woman's maternal or domestic duties; in her subject's experience, home and work, domestic and professional, are not intertwined but separate: "two parallel currents."[62] Neither does Gaskell present womanly experience (erotic, marital, or maternal) as enabling or enriching the woman writer's work—as in Elizabeth Barrett Browning's *Aurora Leigh* where the artist-heroine concludes,

> Passioned to exalt
> The artist's instinct in me at the cost
> Of putting down the woman's, I forgot
> No perfect artist is developed here
> From any imperfect woman.[63]

Instead, Gaskell presents Brontë's talent as something distinct from her womanly character—not unfeminine or unwomanly, but ungendered, unsought, and God-given. In alluding to the New Testament parable of the talents, she conveys both her sense that artistic genius is a gift and a belief that it must serve a purpose beyond the self. To quote Gaskell's letter to Eliza Fox, "I believe that we have all some appointed work to do, wh[ic]h no one else can do so well; Wh[ich] is *our* work; what *we* have to do in advancing the Kingdom of God."[64]

Despite what Gaskell presents as an implicit agreement with Brontë about the purpose of women's art, her interpretation of Brontë's literary life varies noticeably from her own in one significant respect. Gaskell famously advised a young wife and mother with literary ambition to wait until her children were older to begin a career.

When I had *little* children I do not think I could have written stories, because I should have become too much absorbed in my *fictitious* people to attend to my *real* ones. . . . yet . . . everyone who writes stories *must* become absorbed in them, (fictitious though they be,) if they are to interest their readers in them. Besides viewing the subject from a solely artistic point of view a good writer of fiction must have *lived* an active & sympathetic life if she wishes her books to have strength & vitality in them. When you are forty, and if you have a gift for being an authoress you will write ten times as good a novel as you could do now, just because you will have gone through so much more of the interests of a wife and a mother.[65]

Gaskell does not make this link between womanly experience and depth in art for Brontë—perhaps because she wished to suppress a connection between her subject's life and art to avoid exposing the autobiographical basis of *Villette*, or because she suspected that, in Brontë's case, marriage to Nicholls had put an end to authorship, or because she had evidence of Charlotte's early genius in juvenilia that exhibited "creative power"[66] with little need for the womanly maturation she elsewhere advocated.

For, if Gaskell wrote the *Life* to defend Brontë's domestic character, she also intended to display her subject's genius and claim this trait for women authors. In the early nineteenth century, following Isaac Disraeli's *The Literary Character; or, The History of Men of Genius* (1795),[67] biographers compiled anecdotes to demonstrate evidence of genius in their literary subjects. Lockhart, for example, notes characteristics of Scott that fulfill common myths of literary genius: that Scott had an "extraordinary genius" as a boy for reading poetry, that he learned more by "roll[ing] about in the grass all day long" than by studying his Latin grammar, or that early "vicissitude," his ill health and lameness in childhood, caused the growth of compassion and genius of a benignant character.[68] Henry Chorley similarly notes traits of genius in young Felicia Hemans: her ability as a child to quickly memorize and recite long poems, her juvenile verse "prophetic of the style in which the poetess was one a future day so signally to excel," and two prize poems, "Wallace" and "Dartmoor," that were awarded top honors by the Royal Society of Literature in 1821 when Hemans was not yet thirty.[69] Indeed, Chorley makes female genius a key theme of his biography, prefacing his narrative of her life with the assertion that "genius is of no sex" and that, despite prejudice, women writers "are winning day by day, in addition to the justice of head commanded by their high and varied powers, the justice of heart which is so eminently their due."[70] *Genius*, a Romantic emphasis, had been lost in early Victorian accounts of women's authorship, and Gaskell reclaims it strategically in *The Life of Charlotte Brontë*.

The word *genius* appears sixteen times in the *Life*. Half of the uses occur in Brontë's letters, in references to the other artists and authors, from

William Thackeray (whom she much admired), to James Hogg and Sydney Dobell, to her sister Emily, to the actress Rachel. In these cases, *genius* emerges as a key term in Brontë's lexicography, revealing her immersion in Romantic literature and culture. Gaskell's use of the word *genius* clusters in two distinct places: in her description of Brontë's juvenilia in volume I and at the publication of *Jane Eyre*, *Wuthering Heights*, and *Agnes Grey* in volume II. In volume I, following the conventions of Romantic biography, Gaskell demonstrates the Brontë siblings' youthful genius and gives "curious proof how early the rage for literary composition had seized upon her [Charlotte]" (I, v, 54). She reproduces the fourteen-year-old Charlotte's "Catalogue of my Books, with the period of their completion up to August 3rd, 1830" (I, v, 54–55), quotes from her adolescent diaries and tales, and provides a facsimile of the juvenilia with "the extreme minuteness of the writing" (I, v, 54). In volume II, Gaskell takes up the question of genius as she narrates the story of the extraordinary publication of *Jane Eyre* and the revelation of its success to Charlotte's father, noting that no family friend or acquaintance guessed its authorship: "No one knew they had genius enough to be the author" (II, ii, 217). In these key places, the *Life* confirms the genius of its subject and implicitly furthers Chorley's claim that "genius is of no sex."

Even so, Gaskell treats the concept of "genius" warily, as if she worries about its possible connotations of waywardness or imaginative extremity. In a letter to George Smith, written just after she (with the help of Sir James Kay-Shuttleworth) had wrested the juvenilia from Haworth parsonage, Gaskell describes Brontë's Angrian tales as "the wildest & most incoherent things, . . . all purporting to be written, or addressed to some member of the Wellesley family"; she adds, "They give one the idea of creative power carried to the verge of insanity."[71] In another instance, when she writes of Brontë's experience at the Cowan Bridge School and her depiction of its founder, William Carus Wilson, as the Reverend Brocklehurst in *Jane Eyre*, she comments, "I cannot help feeling sorry that, in his old age and declining health, the errors, which he certainly committed, should have been brought up against him in a form which received such wonderful force from the touch of Miss Brontë's great genius" (I, iv, 45). These instances reveal Gaskell's fear that "genius" might take an author in a wrong direction and that Brontë's habit of "making out" might (and did) lead to unfortunate effects. More often, however, Gaskell tames the concept of genius by associating it with other virtues—as in the "brave genius" with which Brontë faced her sisters' ill health, her father's blindness, and the rejection of her manuscript of *The Professor* (II, i, 202). Similarly, in a letter to Charlotte Froude, Gaskell described Brontë's "strong feeling of responsibility for the Gift, which she has [been] given."[72]

Gaskell's association of "genius" with "duty" and "responsibility" is a classic mid-Victorian gesture, one that has drawn sharp criticism from modern scholars. Deirdre d'Albertis has argued, for instance, that Gaskell substitutes her own conception of "duty" with its "unambiguously public values" for Brontë's different conception of "genius" as "a responsibility only to realize the individual's full artistic potential."[73] This is a fair critique of a slippage in Gaskell's treatment, a collapse or conflation of an author's social responsibility with her aesthetic and imaginative commitment. Yet the concepts of "genius" and "duty," "talent" and "responsibility," were intertwined in both writers' work. Brontë, for instance, praised Thackeray as "the first social regenerator of the day" and linked his social critique to "an intellect profounder and more unique than his contemporaries have yet recognized."[74] Similarly, for Gaskell, "duty" was linked to the author's social role and to the relationship she envisioned between the domestic and literary in the life of the woman author; as she argued to Eliza Fox, women need to attend to "the development of the individual," not just the fulfillment of "duty." Thus, as Gaskell understood Brontë's life course, it had produced "two parallel currents": "her life as Currer Bell, the author; her life as Charlotte Brontë, the woman." This model was Gaskell's resolution to—and advancement on—the earlier, less fruitful nineteenth-century models that saw literary genius and domesticity as oppositional.

Yet Gaskell's motives extend beyond these mid-century debates over women's authorship and seek to honor a distinction that Brontë repeatedly articulates in her letters: the right of an author to be considered, and her work evaluated, apart from the question of gender. Brontë's initial letters to Smith, Elder make this distinction with their instructions to "address Mr. Currer Bell, under cover to Miss Brontë, Haworth, Bradford, Yorkshire."[75] This continues in the amusing episode of Charlotte and Anne's first encounter with George Smith, when they refuse to meet London literary figures because it would reveal their physical (sexual) identities. The distinction becomes emphatic in Brontë's exchanges with G. H. Lewes, who favorably reviewed *Jane Eyre* for *Fraser's Magazine* (December 1847) and the *Westminster Review* (January 1848), and sent a private letter of "cheering commendation and valuable advice."[76] Despite their congenial correspondence on wide-ranging topics of literary influence and achievement, the two fell out over Lewes's notice of *Shirley* in the *Edinburgh Review* (January 1850). Prior to its appearance, Lewes had written to Brontë of his intention to review her new novel; she answered with a firm statement that she desired gender-neutral treatment, that she wished "you did not think me a woman" and that "all reviewers believed 'Currer Bell' to be a man."[77] Nonetheless, Lewes explicitly raised the gender question in his review, expressing his opinion that "the grand function of woman" "is, and ever must be, *Maternity*" and remarking that, though women have achieved some distinction in literature, they might have ranked even higher "had they not been too solicitous about male excellence,—had they not written from the man's point of view, instead of from the woman's."[78]

Lewes's review, it now seems, as it must then have seemed to Gaskell who read the correspondence, introduced the question of the author's sex more to pursue his own masculine agenda and alleviate personal anxieties than to shed light on women's authorship.[79] Certainly, he did not respect Brontë's authorial persona, by which she constructed herself publicly as "Currer Bell." In contrast, throughout the biography Gaskell observes the distinction between "Currer Bell" and "Charlotte Brontë" in presenting the letters to publishers and literary acquaintances as those of the author, "Currer Bell." Pointedly, she includes the signature "Currer Bell" in quoting Brontë's letters to Lewes.[80] Implicitly, she counters Lewes's claim that the "grand function of woman" is "Maternity" by showing the genius of her subject. The grand function of the woman of genius in the *Life* is the production of great literary works.

Gaskell, Brontë, and the Professional Woman Author

In the mid-1850s, when Gaskell wrote her biography, young women artists and authors had begun pressing for a professional view of women's work in the public sphere. As I noted in chapter 1, Barbara Leigh Smith, Bessie Rayner Parkes, Anna Mary Howitt, and others in the Langham Place Group urged the improvement of education for women, professional training for women artists, and access to forms of employment reserved for men. In *Essays on Woman's Work* (1865), an expansion of her ideas in *Remarks on the Education of Girls* (1854), Parkes advanced six fundamental propositions: "Let women be thoroughly developed, thoroughly rational, pious and charitable, properly protected by law, have a fair chance of a livelihood, and have ample access to all stores of learning."[81] Education and livelihood were key items in this mid-Victorian feminist agenda. Though Parkes and her circle concurred with Gaskell in treating women's work as a contribution to the social good, they nonetheless took a more professionalized approach to issues of employment—emphasizing practical matters from training and education to payment and public recognition.

Literary professionalism is underplayed in *The Life of Charlotte Brontë*. The term *professional* appears in only four instances, all in reference to male employment. Gaskell refers to the dwellings of lawyers and doctors, the "professional middle-class" that live in "our old cathedral towns" (I, i, 11); she describes the local curates in "their professional character" (I, ix, 122); she mentions the Brontë sisters' training in French by "professional masters" (I, x, 133); and she quotes "professional critics" in their estimates of *Jane Eyre* (II, ii, 213). Gaskell associates professionalism, in other words, with the traditional male professions of the church, medicine, law, and literature. Nowhere does she claim professional status for "Currer Bell," despite Brontë's keen interest in the professional practices of authors, editors, and publishers, expressed in numerous letters to her publisher George Smith and his reader W. S. Williams.

In composing the *Life* and selecting from the correspondence, Gaskell suppresses or minimizes aspects of Brontë's letters to George Smith, Thomas C. Newby, and even herself that dwell on professional aspects of authorship. She omits discussions of royalties, payments, and publishers' dealings with their authors—omissions as small as the amount of a bank draft sent by her publisher (£100) or as significant as the information she and Brontë exchanged about the differences between working for Chapman and Hall (then Gaskell's publisher) and Smith, Elder (Brontë's publisher).[82] Instead, Gaskell highlights Brontë's intellectual responses to literary work—from Thackeray's novels and lectures on eighteenth-century literature, to Ruskin's *Stones of Venice*, Emerson's *Representative Men*, and Wordsworth's post-humously published *The Prelude*, to lesser works like Sydney Dobell's *Balder* and Lewes's *Ranthorpe*. In the case of letters to George Smith, the publisher of Brontë's novels and of the *Life*, Gaskell's choices may have been made by mutual agreement; the manuscript of the *Life* reveals points at which Smith excised details about himself and his dealings with Currer Bell.[83] In the case of Newby, who had published *Wuthering Heights* and *Agnes Grey* and scandalously failed to pay the authors their earnings, it may have been fear of a lawsuit, given Gaskell's expressed desire to "gibbet" this shady publisher and Smith's cautious warnings against libel.[84] In quoting letters to herself, Gaskell may have felt it unseemly to include details of the more niggardly royalties that Chapman and Hall paid her, the more generous treatment of Brontë by Smith, Elder, and the possibility of shifting publishers in the early 1850s. Or Gaskell may simply have believed that Brontë's responses to literary works were more interesting than concerns about literary production or payment—and thus the letters to W. S. Williams, who often appears in the *Life* as "a literary friend," become especially important, as he regularly sent boxes of books to Haworth for Brontë's perusal and for their mutual discussion of contemporary literature.[85]

Whatever the case, Gaskell seems reluctant to associate the woman writer with the professional author—and here she differs from her subject and imposes her own ambivalent views on the *Life*.[86] From recent work by Carol A. Bock on the Brontës' entry into authorship, we know that Charlotte Brontë was, in fact, more "professionalized" than the *Life* acknowledges—that she carefully studied the *Fraser's* articles of the 1830s on authorship, compared books of verse for matters of paper, typeface, and layout, bought *The Author's Printing and Publishing Assistant* (1839) to inform herself in publishing the sisters' *Poems*, and exchanged letters with Smith and Williams on matters of copyright and royalty, especially as she negotiated a second edition of *Wuthering Heights*.[87] Brontë was not a Victorian woman of letters in a fully professional sense, but neither was she merely a gifted amateur. Margaret Smith's edition of the *Letters* reveals Brontë's considerable interest in Victorian publishing practices, especially in a sequence of letters she sent to Smith and Williams that discuss a reissue of her sisters' novels and that cover questions of copyright, royalties, advertising expenses, and author's rights.[88] Yet this sequence is represented in the *Life* by only one letter to Williams of 29 September 1850, stating her intention to write a preface to the reissue; it is followed by a letter to Nussey of 3 October 1850, expressing her sense that she undertakes "*a sacred duty*" that is "exquisitely painful and depressing" (II, ii, 293). Duty trumps professionalism in Gaskell's presentation of Brontë.

It is unclear whether Gaskell avoids the mid-nineteenth-century discourse of professionalism because she felt it inappropriate for women or because the label "professional" indicated a lesser status (in Bourdieu's terms, applicable to the "sub-field of large-scale production" rather than a designation of high or canonical status)[89] or because she felt that Brontë's character might be injured by the association. After all, reviewers had criticized *Jane Eyre*, along with *Wuthering Heights*, as "coarse" and "unfeminine," and they might find further ammunition in a construction of Brontë's authorial self as "professional" and implicitly "masculine." Then, too, Gaskell may have recognized in Brontë's letters an association of authorship with Romantic claims of genius, inspiration, and self-expression, rather than with mid-Victorian interests in professional status, intellectual property, and fair payment to authors. Even in the literary phase of Brontë's life, Gaskell underscores the theme of duty and minimizes the professional aspects of Brontë's career—a decision based on a lingering association of business and finances with "coarseness" and on a desire to preserve for Brontë the Romantic claim to "genius," a category that soars above material concerns.

Gaskell's *Life* (1857) thus projects a different view of the mid-Victorian woman author from that presented in Harriet Martineau's *Autobiography* (written in 1855, published in 1877). Whereas Martineau traces her professional progress as "a solitary young authoress, who has had no pioneer in her literary path," and revels in charting the steady accumulation of her earnings, noting that she "earned altogether by my books somewhere about ten thousand pounds,"[90] Gaskell minimizes the professional aspects of Brontë's career, excludes financial details from Brontë's letters to her publisher, and shows her subject as much more interested in ideas than in profits. In the *Life* we never learn that George Smith purchased copyright of *Jane Eyre* in September 1847 for £100 but sent Brontë a second payment of £100 in February 1848 in acknowledgment of its success; or that Smith, Elder ultimately paid £500 each for *Jane Eyre*, *Shirley*, and *Villette*; or that Brontë and W. S. Williams exchanged letters about whether she should buy the books Smith, Elder sent to Haworth out of her profits or accept them as gifts.[91] The *Life* creates a mid-Victorian model of the woman artist as one more concerned with artistic expression than with professionalism, a woman who both fulfills her "quiet regular duties" and expresses her "splendid talents," thus answering critics who did not think this combination possible. Gaskell argues that it *was* true of Charlotte Brontë and implies that it is also true for herself. As she concludes in the final passage of the *Life*, the biography appeals to readers who know "how to admire generously extraordinary genius, and how to reverence with warm, full hearts all noble virtue" (II, xiv, 370).

The Brontë Myth

The model of the Victorian woman writer that Gaskell constructed in the *Life* soon became a myth—or, more accurately, a cluster of myths. Elaine Showalter has described one as "the myth of the novelist as tragic heroine"; Lucasta Miller has elaborated others as the "positive myth of female self-creation" and a conflicting myth of the "saintly heroine," "a martyr to duty and a model of Victorian femininity."[92] To these we might add the myth of self-help, a female version of the "rise and progress" tale made famous by Samuel Smiles in his collective biography of successful Victorian men, *Self Help, with Illustrations of Character and Conduct* (1859).[93] This self-help aspect of the Brontë myth was important in the history of women's authorship for its apparent accessibility, its imitable pattern for young women writers. *The Life of Charlotte Brontë* locates the origin of literary genius in an ordinary parsonage in an isolated Yorkshire village; it shows its subject as an avid reader and scribbling adolescent who, with her sisters, writes romantic tales and secretly publishes a book of poems, even as she labors as a schoolteacher; and it traces a meteoric rise to fame with a pseudonymous novel, *Jane Eyre*, and its successors, *Shirley* and *Villette*. Although great struggle is required of the heroine and many obstacles are placed in her way—from virtual poverty to lack of literary friends and London contacts to indifferent publishers who reject the manuscript of her first novel, *The Professor*—Charlotte Brontë succeeds by dint of her determination and literary genius.

The next chapter traces the problematics of Gaskell's model for subsequent women of letters. But before ending this one, we might note the specific problem posed by the biography's ending. *The Life of Charlotte Brontë* does not end with a triumphant literary career but with a wedding and a funeral. This conclusion of the *Life* was inevitable, given Brontë's marriage to the Reverend Arthur Bell Nicholls in June 1854 and her death nine months later in March 1855. Yet Gaskell uses the inevitable facts to return to the theme of "parallel currents," the shape of a woman writer's life, and the intersection of human tragedy and triumph.

The final two chapters of the *Life* turn from Brontë's letters to her London publisher and his circle, to more intimate letters addressed to old Yorkshire friends, and to Gaskell herself, a new Mancunian friend. These letters begin with one from Brontë to Gaskell, written soon after a visit to

Gaskell's Manchester home, Plymouth Grove, in which Brontë wonders if her fellow novelist "find[s] it easy, when you sit down to write, to isolate yourself from all those ties, and their sweet associations, so as to be your *own woman*, uninfluenced or swayed by the consciousness of how your work may affect other minds" (II, xiii, 353). Gaskell leaves unanswered this expression of authorial unease, written after Nicholls had proposed marriage but before Brontë had formally accepted; she does not tell us whether she, as a writer, felt herself to be "her *own woman*"—or whether Brontë did after she accepted Nicholls's proposal. Instead, Gaskell follows with her own letter to an unknown correspondent, composed soon after a visit to Haworth and recording details of life at the parsonage and conversations between the two women authors about books, fame, and human fate. These and the letters that follow to Margaret Wooler, Ellen Nussey, and Laetitia Wheelwright complicate Gaskell's assertion that the woman and the author, and the "separate duties belonging to each character," are "not opposing each other; not impossible, but difficult to be reconciled." Even as we see Brontë acceding to Nicholls's proposal and entering into the joys and duties of married life, we sense through the letters the end of a literary career. "My dear Arthur is a very practical, as well as a very punctual and methodical man," Brontë writes to her former teacher, Margaret Wooler: "Of course, he often finds a little work for his wife to do, and I hope she is not sorry to help him" (II, xiii, 365). In the separation of the "I" and "she," Brontë registers a self-division.

Gaskell leaves it to her readers to decide whether the literary self would have persisted. After the narration of Brontë's marriage and wedding tour, she closes "the sacred doors of home . . . upon her married life," with "her loving friends, standing outside," catching "occasional glimpses of brightness, and pleasant peaceful murmurs of sound, telling of gladness within" (II, xiii, 364). There is no further narration of a literary career, even though Nicholls claimed he did not stifle his wife's writing and, in 1860, offered "The Last Sketch," a manuscript Charlotte had read to him in 1854, to George Smith for the *Cornhill Magazine*. Gaskell ends the *Life* with the "tragedy and triumph" motif that she had used to close volume I; but now she reverses the domestic tragedy and (potential) literary triumph of volume I to a domestic triumph and (potential) literary tragedy in volume II. In so doing, she reveals how problematic her model of women's authorship actually was.

5

CHALLENGING BRONTËAN MYTHS OF AUTHORSHIP

Charlotte Riddell and
A Struggle for Fame (1883)

In the opening chapter of Charlotte Riddell's 1883 *kunstlerroman*, *A Struggle for Fame*, a young Irishwoman leaves Ulster and heads to London, secretly hoping to become an author and ease her aging father's financial and physical distress. The date the novel gives for this pilgrimage is notably precise: 17 October 1854. So, too, is the date it gives for its heroine's first meeting with a London publisher: February 1855. Given that the narrative is based on Riddell's experiences as a struggling author, we might assume that the dates record her own departure from Carrickfergus, County Antrim, and her early encounters with the publisher Thomas C. Newby, who treated her politely but declined to accept a juvenile novel. Yet they do not. According to her biographers, Riddell moved to London in 1855 or 1856 with an invalid mother (not father) and published her first novel soon thereafter.[1] Why, we might ask, should Riddell have included these two specific dates in a fiction of female authorship? If they are not strictly autobiographical, what other reference might they intend?

In this chapter I shall argue that Riddell sets *A Struggle* in the mid-1850s not only because it coincides with her own entry into the profession of letters but, more important, because 1855 recalls the most famous authorial life and death in nineteenth-century women's life writing and the most influential account of women's authorship in the Victorian period: Elizabeth Gaskell's *Life of Charlotte Brontë* (1857). In *A Struggle for Fame* Riddell invokes— indeed, reproduces and interrogates—this seminal narrative as it influenced a generation of mid-century women writers, popularized a "parallel currents" model of authorship, and then came into conflict with the professional realities of the later nineteenth-century literary field. Riddell did not achieve the meteoric rise to fame that Brontë did with *Jane Eyre* in 1847. Yet her own career was not without its professional successes and literary glory. During the decade between 1857 and 1867, when Riddell entered the literary marketplace, she published ten creditable novels, some meriting multiple printings and second editions; she placed her fiction in well-known periodicals, including *Once a Week* and *Tinsley's Magazine*; achieved critical acclaim with *George Geith of Fen Court* (1864), an innovative fiction of City life that was later dramatized, also to critical acclaim; and gained the editorship of *St. James's Magazine* in 1867, a mark of her perceived literary status and professional ability.

Most analyses of *A Struggle for Fame* and its author's career have focused on the conditions that impeded Riddell in the literary marketplace. In a study of the reception of her work of the 1860s and 1870s, for example, Patricia Srebrnik has argued that Riddell's novels appealed to readers from the social classes they depicted (the "middling" and lower-middle classes that included junior and senior clerks, solicitors, civil servants, accountants, engineers, and tradesmen and their wives) but that the periodical reviewers who passed judgment on Riddell's fiction represented a new "urban gentry" who saw themselves as "upper professional gentlemen" and did not wish to identify with her middling heroes or acknowledge familiarity with the milieus in which such characters operate. Srebrnik suggests that Riddell was, in fact, ahead of her time and would have found a more receptive audience in the 1890s when reviewers began to call for fiction with insight into "the habits of thought and habits of action" of the "commercial and professional" classes,[2] but being too far ahead, Riddell failed. More recently, Margaret Kelleher has applied Bourdieu's opposition between the "sub-field of large-scale production" and the "sub-field of restricted production"—fields differentiated by popular and economic success versus symbolic criteria of lasting value—to explain the rise and fall of Riddell's popular fiction and its writer's reputation. As one of Bourdieu's most famous essays argues, "the field of cultural production 'reverses' the economic world in giving a higher status to symbolic success than to material reward"—hence Riddell's fall from popular success to low (or no) critical esteem by the end of the century.[3]

Yet, for all that *A Struggle for Fame* engages with the market conditions that confronted writers of Victorian fiction and influenced the status of her own professional work, the novel also engages with the symbolic myth-making about authorship that occurred during the later Victorian period. In *A Struggle* Riddell reinscribes myths of women's authorship made famous in Gaskell's *Life* and other nineteenth-century memoirs of women writers: myths of genius and vocation, of domesticity and duty, of solitude, loneliness, and tragedy. At first glance, Riddell's choice might seem historically out of sync, even nostalgic, especially after the publication of Harriet Martineau's highly professional, market-savvy *Autobiography* of 1877, and during the professionally self-conscious decade that saw the founding of the Society of Authors in 1884. Nonetheless, I shall suggest that Riddell provocatively drew on earlier nineteenth-century models of women's authorship to lay claim to the symbolic capital those myths had accrued, as well as to test the validity of the myths and, in the final volume of her novel, to reintroduce valuable insights from her predecessors' lives that had been lost in the movement for professionalization.

Rewriting Brontë's Life, Accruing Literary Value

In the first volume of Riddell's *kunstlerroman* the narrator distinguishes between "nowadays," the 1880s, when "the smallest child has some idea of 'how books are made'" and the 1850s, when "the ordinary details of the literary profession" (I, 226) were unknown, unrecorded, and thus unavailable to aspiring writers like Glenarva Westley, the heroine.[4] Riddell is no doubt thinking about the explosion of professional literature distributed by the Society of Authors in the 1880s, with its pamphlets on copyright and literary property, on publishers and agents, and on practical matters of book-making—in contrast to the paucity of information available when she began her literary career in the mid-1850s. When young Glen asks the old-fashioned publisher, Mr. Vassett, "If you only tell me what I ought to do I will try to set about it at once" (I, 122), he claims that he cannot give such advice.

> If I could publish a key to the problem you want to solve[,] it would sell so well, I should never need to bring out another book. The land you want to enter has no itinerary—no finger posts—no guides. It is a lone, mapless country, and if you take my advice you will keep out of it. (I, 123)

Authorship is terra incognita—or so Vassett claims. By the 1860s, however, as Riddell well knew, publishers *had* brought out such guides as Vassett claims couldn't be written. Members of the Langham Place Group, for example, published articles, pamphlets, and books on women's work, including authorship, as in Emily Faithfull's *Choice of a Business for Girls: Artistic and Intellectual Employments* (1864) and Bessie Rayner Parkes's *Essays on Woman's Work* (1865). In the periodical press of the 1860s and 1870s, journalism was analyzed as a profession (or trade), including by Riddell herself in an 1874 article in the *Illustrated Review*: "Literature as a Profession."[5] By the 1880s and 1890s, magazines and books were offering practical advice to women on entering the profession of letters, as in Emily Crawford's "Journalism as a Profession for Women" in the *Contemporary Review* (1893) or Arnold Bennett's *Journalism for Women: A Practical Guide* (1898).[6]

Drawing on the history of nineteenth-century authorship through which she had lived, Riddell establishes a contrast between an amateur "then" and a professional "now," between a gentler (and more gentlemanly) era when "in the literary world females still retained some reticence, and males the traditions at least of self-respect" (I, 103) and the current professional era when authors are more business-like and market-conscious, if also more "pushing" and "hopelessly impecunious" (I, 103). The names Riddell conjures up to represent the former era include Brontë's and V's (Mrs. Archer Clive): "Oh days that seem gone so long! When 'Jane Eyre' and 'Paul Ferroll' were titles as familiar in men's mouths as 'Lady Audley's Secret' and 'The Woman in White'" (II, 68–69).[7]

Despite the neat antithesis between "then" and "now," aspiring women writers of the 1850s did, in fact, have some "fingerposts" and "guides" with which to begin their literary careers. In the autobiographies and memoirs of other writers—from Isaac Disraeli's *The Literary Character; or, The History of Men of Genius* (1818, rpt. 1840), to the periodical articles of the 1830s in *Fraser's Magazine* on Laetitia Landon (L.E.L.), Harriet Martineau, Caroline Norton, and Mrs. S. C. Hall, to new anthologies of and about women writers such as Anne Katherine Elwood's *Memoirs of the Literary Ladies of England* (1843) or Jane Williams's *The Literary Women of England* (1861)[8]— they had access to the lives of women authors, and from them could glean models on which to base their careers. Some of these lives—perhaps all such lives—created myths of female authorship, even as they conveyed some facts about publishing. Indeed, it is part of my argument that the myths were as important as the facts, both to Riddell as an aspiring author and to Glenarva Westley, her protagonist in *A Struggle for Fame*.

We do not know which books, articles, or memoirs Riddell read before emigrating to London: hers is a scantly documented life. But from the evidence in the novel itself we can deduce that Riddell drew on the most important of these memoirs, *The Life of Charlotte Brontë*, and the obituaries that shaped it. For a young woman writer in 1855, the lives of the Brontë sisters would have presented a pattern of extraordinary literary and cultural success, if also personal tragedy. The three sisters had risen from poverty and obscurity in their remote Yorkshire village to national fame, if not actual wealth. Biographical details of their lives had circulated in London periodicals even before Charlotte Brontë died in 1855, particularly tales of their lonely, restricted domestic life and their sudden burst upon the London literary scene. As Linda Hughes and Michael Lund have demonstrated, the biographical mythmaking began in earnest with obituaries published immediately after Charlotte's death in 1855 and continued with the publication of Gaskell's *Life* in 1857. These mid-century accounts created the enduring myths of the Brontës and female authorship that we still encounter today. They emphasized the isolation of the family amid rough, rude Yorkshiremen; the genius of the young children, playing games and writing little books among themselves; the naiveté of the sisters in the London publishing world, "as truly innocents abroad, stumbling into the precincts of Paternoster Row";[9] and, especially in Gaskell's *Life*, the domestic commitment and feminine propriety exhibited by Charlotte Brontë before, during, and after her struggle for authorship.

As Joanne Shattock reminds us, in her study "Victorian Women as Writers and Readers of (Auto)biography," "autobiographies and biographies [of women writers] purported to offer real-life heroines and role models" to other women, a substitute for access to the university training, literary society, and private London clubs available to men.[10] Living in a remote district of Ireland, Glenarva Westley needs such models. Early in *A Struggle* she dedicates herself to authorship in a scene of vocation that echoes Romantic auto/biographies. As she contemplates nature from her bedroom window, where "beneath her lay the ocean, calm as a sleeping child," she wonders what she might do to reverse the family's loss of fortune. "Standing in a flood of moonlight," she vows, "I will write," and "opening her desk there and then, she began" (I, 223–25). This scene draws on Wordsworth's silent dedication to poetry in *The Prelude* (Bk. IV), Aurora's self-crowning in Barrett Browning's *Aurora Leigh* (Bk. II), and possibly Charlotte Tonna's midnight inspiration, also on an isolated Irish estate, in her *Personal Recollections* (ch. VI).[11] It also mythologizes the author's actual experience. As Riddell told a female journalist about "writing her first story": "It was on a bright moonlight night . . . —I can see it now flooding the gardens—that I began it, and I wrote week after week, never ceasing until it was finished."[12]

In *A Struggle* this Romantic scene is followed by a specifically Brontëan moment. According to Gaskell's biography, the Brontë sisters kept their writing a secret from their father, "fearing to increase their own anxieties and disappointments by witnessing his." Eventually, Charlotte revealed her success by marching into her father's study with a copy of her work.

> "Papa, I have been writing a book!"
> "Have you, my dear?" (He went on reading.)
> "But, papa, I want you to look at it."
> "I can't be troubled to read manuscript."
> "But it is printed."
> "I hope you've not been involving yourself in any such silly expense!"
> "I think I shall gain some money by it; may I read you some of the reviews?"[13]

Glen Westley similarly surprises her father with the secret of her writerly endeavors.

> "I think I can make a future for myself," she cried, with a trembling exultation in her voice, and then she told him all. . . .
> "Write!" he repeated. "Is it possible?" (I, 282–83)

Although Glen lacks a printed book at this stage in her career, she nonetheless has favorable testimony from publishers about her ability, which she, like Charlotte, offers to her father.

"Should you like me to read you some of the things I have written?'
she asked eagerly. . . .
"Not tonight, my love," answered Mr. Westley, meanly deferring
the evil day. (I, 285)

Mr. Westley, like the Reverend Patrick Brontë, plays the predictable role of
the father who fears his daughter's failure or, worse, loss of womanliness in
her success.

Riddell also echoes tales of Charlotte Brontë's naïve attempts to place
her first novel with a London publisher. According to the *Life*, the manuscript of *The Professor* made its rounds "slowly and heavily from publisher
to publisher," and by the time it reached 65 Cornhill, the office of Smith,
Elder, "there were on it those of other publishers to whom the tale had been
sent, not obliterated, but simply scored through, so that Messrs. Smith at
once perceived the names of some of the houses in the trade to which the
unlucky parcel had gone, without success."[14] Glen Westley is less naïve,
perhaps having learned from Brontë's experience to send her manuscript
in a clean, new, brown paper parcel, but her book manuscripts similarly
make their unsuccessful rounds—first from Ireland to London, Dublin,
and Edinburgh, from which "they almost all returned to her with terrible
promptitude, not one bear[ing] an olive-branch of promise back with it" (I,
235), and then from her new home in "stony hearted London" (I, 293),
where Glen personally trudges from one publishing house to another "in
quite a regular and systematic . . . round of the trade" (I, 307).[15] In both
cases, it is a sympathetic publisher's reader—W. S. Williams at Smith,
Elder, Mr. Pierson at Vassett's—who recognizes the young writer's ability
and turns the tide. At stake is not the actual publication of the manuscript
submitted (for Smith, Elder did not publish *The Professor*, nor does Mr.
Vassett publish Glen's Irish tale, "The Hanes of Carrigohane") but the
recognition of genius. As Mr. Pierson observes of Glen and her father,
"They are quite new; we have not had anything like them in Craven Street
before" (I, 106).

Finally, Glen's first publishable novel is "a story of sin and sorrow and
injustice" (possibly a Brontëan theme) with characters "planted on a wild
portion of the Yorkshire coast" (certainly a Brontëan setting) (II, 137–38).
Echoing the reviews as well as Gaskell's *Life of Charlotte Brontë*, Riddell
records the disbelief of "sophisticated" London critics who cannot fathom
how a young woman from the provinces, surrounded by rude, unlettered
hinds, might produce a book of genius. In the *Saturday Review* obituary of 4
April 1857, the writer recalled, "When the public heard that the author of
Jane Eyre was a plain little woman, the daughter of a clergyman living in the
remotest wilds of Yorkshire, it was natural to wonder whence came this
astonishing knowledge of the workings of fiery passions. Did she write from
memory—or was she taught by the inspiration of a creative mind?"[16] Gaskell

echoes this wonder in the *Life*, using the primitive culture of Yorkshire, "its lawless yet not unkindly population,"[17] to emphasize the Brontës' unprecedented case and to explain away the elements of "coarseness" that some critics had found in the Brontës' novels. In *A Struggle for Fame* such disbelief is expressed by a priggish young clergyman, Mr. Dufford, who wishes to marry Glen, debar her "from association with those dreadful [Ballyshane] boys," and place her "where she would have the advantage of mixing in polite society" (I, 243). An amateur author himself, Dufford cannot recognize Glen's genius and wishes only to "mould, and train, and fashion her . . . into the conventional pattern" (I, 252)—much as some London reviewers had criticized Charlotte's wildness and passion and judged it by their own conventional literary and moral standards.

The fact that Dufford is "the son of a rich but honest tradesman of Cork" (I, 239)—that is, of a class inferior to Glen, who is impoverished but nonetheless of the gentry—gives point to Riddell's satire and adds a twist to Patricia Srebrnik's argument that the periodical reviewers of Riddell's fiction represented a group who styled themselves to be "urban gentry" or "upper professional gentlemen." In Riddell's satire, critics who fail to recognize women's genius—like Glen's, Brontë's or her own—but instead try to push women writers into a conventional mold are, like the priggish Dufford, betraying their lower-middle-class conventionality; though rich or professionally successful, they are nonetheless tradesmen at heart.

In these echoes of Brontë's life, Riddell emphasizes the genius of her young protagonist and draws on cultural capital that bears Brontë's imprint. Glen Westley, like her real-life predecessor, is portrayed as a rarity in the publishing world, and her literary ability, not just her popular success, is underscored. On this Romantic model—of genius, inspiration, and literary talent—the novel insists. We might place this insistence in the context of Riddell's own literary production which, as Margaret Kelleher argues, typically falls into Bourdieu's "sub-field of large-scale production," the realm of popular but ephemeral literature. At the very least, Riddell suggests, her career originated in genius, aspired to greatness, and produced some works of true merit. Even Barney Kelly, the successful but irremediably lower-class Irish journalist who writes a "stinging article, entitled 'Fame and Notoriety'" out of pique at Glen's literary success (III, 267), must finally acknowledge the lasting value of her work.

We might also place Riddell's insistence in the context of late Victorian publishing practices. As Gale Tuchman and Nina Fortin have argued, the shift from the triple-decker format of the mid-nineteenth century to the "high-culture" novel of the 1880s and 1890s tended to "edge women out" of the literary marketplace. Whereas the triple-decker had been amenable to women's reading practices and, indeed, was associated with the fiction of women writers, "the high-culture novel was imbued with the supposed virtues of culturally elite men."[18] Thus, when Macmillan, a university press, bought out Richard Bentley and Son, a major supplier of the triple-decker novel, women novelists like Riddell (who published *A Struggle for Fame* with Bentley in 1883) often found themselves without a publishing venue.[19] In effect, the shift in the late Victorian market for fiction created a split between high and popular art, with the fiction of many women writers consequently lowered in prestige. Riddell's *kunstlerroman* reflects these broader changes in the literary market and decries evaluations of writers' work based solely on gender or current publishing trends.

Literary Markets, Male Reviewers, and Women's Achievements

In modern histories of the Victorian novel, *A Struggle for Fame* is typically treated as a fiction about the mid-Victorian publishing market, and Riddell praised for writing "one of the finest Victorian novels about writing Victorian novels."[20] While this assessment is valid, we might also note that Riddell associates a market-conscious, commercially driven attitude to writing not with her heroine, Glenarva Westley, but with her male counterpart, Barney Kelly, the Irishman who journeys from poverty in Ulster to a successful career in London as a journalist and magazine editor. Kelly makes his way first by composing comic sketches for a new magazine, *The Galaxy*; then by publishing a historical study of old English dramatists with the respectable Mr. Vassett (the publisher Charles Skeet); later by moving to the trendy firm of Felton and Laplash (a thinly disguised version of Tinsley Brothers); and eventually by landing himself an editorship that did "not necessitate the eternal turning out of 'copy'" (III, 23). Kelly represents the successful Bohemian author who approaches the literary marketplace in terms of its trends and produces whatever story, article, or book the newest magazine or most fashionable publishing house might need. His approach is stridently professional.

Margaret Kelleher has offered the journalist and novelist Edmund Yates as the real-life model for Kelly, perhaps because Yates came from a theatrical family, spent much of his early literary career writing for popular periodicals like *Bentley's Miscellany*, and then rose to become editor of *Temple Bar*, a rival to Thackeray's *Cornhill* and Riddell's *St. James's Magazine*.[21] Another possibility is George Augustus Sala, Yates's friend and fellow Bohemian, whose career began as an illustrator before Dickens signed him on as a contributor to *Household Words* and whose novel *The Seven Sons of Mammon* was the first triple-decker issued by the innovative Tinsley Brothers in 1861.[22] But might we not include Thackeray and Dickens themselves in the originals for Barney Kelly and, indeed, read Riddell's narrative of Kelly's career as an exposé of the more mysterious—or mystifying—aspects of these greater Bohemians' literary lives?

Thackeray, like Kelly, began as a freelance journalist and kept company with Bohemian artists and authors of the sort Riddell depicts in the Dawtons, Kelly's South Lambeth friends. As John Carey notes, in his early days Thackeray "wrote with immense, if spasmodic, energy, turning out book reviews and art criticism and comic sketches and burlesques for *Fraser's* and *Punch* and the *Times* and the *Morning Chronicle* and any other paper that would take his stuff." Once he made his name, Thackeray dropped his Bohemian acquaintances, offending his *Punch* colleagues Mark Lemon and John Leech "by deserting them at the theater and going to sit in a stage box with Count d'Orsay and the Earls of Chesterfield and Granville" and in general, as Carlyle put it, preferring "dinner-eating in fashionable houses" to serious literary work.[23] Barney Kelly's career in volume III follows a similar path. Once he gains a place on *The Galaxy* and expands his range to include respectable publishing firms like Vassett's, he stays away from the Dawtons and their Bohemian home, the Wigwam. Although initially willing to accept their help "touching up his stories" (III, 3), he decides "it is a sort of life that would not suit me, . . . referring to life in Bohemia" (III, 7). Kelly, moreover, prefers the "easy berth" of an editorship to the serious labor of authorship, perhaps a swipe at Thackeray's *Cornhill* days. And, like Thackeray after the success of *Vanity Fair*, Kelly turns his back on satiric work, despising his early sketch "How's Maria?" (III, 2) in the same way that Thackeray came to hate *The Book of Snobs*.[24]

If Barney takes his moral character from Thackeray, he learns lessons in professional character from Dickens. Unlike Thackeray, Dickens maintained his friendships with Bohemians like Yates and Sala, drawing them into his periodical ventures and even defending Yates in a dispute that followed a "very impertinent and unfriendly sketch of Thackeray."[25] It is not Dickens's bohemian life but aspects of his alter ego David Copperfield that influence Kelly's depiction. Kelly may lack "genius," says the narrator, "but he made up for the want of a gift which does not always enable its possessor to compass worldly success, by indomitable perseverance and a determination to try all the gates of fortune till he found one that yielded to his hand" (III, 3). Riddell has altered the metaphor, but in Kelly's perseverance we hear echoes of David Copperfield's determination to "clear my own way through the forest of difficulty" and his pleasure, when his secret authorship comes to fruition, in reporting, "Altogether, I am well off; when I tell my income on the fingers of my left hand, I pass the third finger and take the fourth to the middle joint"—the same £300 plus income that Kelly desires and achieves.[26] Kelly, moreover, achieves his success by adopting Copperfield's quiet, self-effacing manner: " 'It does not matter,' " he decides, " 'what a man does or leaves undone, so long as he can *keep it quiet.*' . . . So, Mr. Kelly, looking around, saw there was a great field in London open for any man who liked to push his way steadily and unpretentiously" (III, 6). Like Glen who has learned from Brontë, Barney Kelly has learned from Dickens a successful way into the profession of letters—a way that assures his respectability and ultimately his professional success.

The extreme version of "keeping it quiet" is Mat Donagh, the Irishman who tells his family that he is "in literature," implying that he is a fine writer and key contributor to *The Galaxy* (I, 174), while in fact he works as an "advertisement canvasser" (II, 5). Although the revelation of his real work embarrasses Donagh, who once aspired to "make a great splash in literature" (II, 7), the importance of Donagh's commercial contribution to the periodical is underscored by Will Dawton, who explains that *The Galaxy* might exist "without its 'crack' novelist or sledge-hammer leader-writer, or sportive essayist, or tender poet, or cynical reviewer," but "it could not live without Mat" (II, 6). Donagh's silence about his true work parallels the larger silence of male authors about the commercial underpinnings of their success and their negotiations in the literary marketplace. From *David Copperfield* a reader would scarcely guess at the commercial genius of Dickens, its author, or of the market realities that Dickens skillfully manipulated to gain literary fame. As Mary Poovey has pointed out, "the individualization of authorship," as in *David Copperfield* and other mid-Victorian *kunstlerroman*, attempted to "'solve' the contradiction between two images of the writer—the 'genius' and the cog in the capitalist machine—at the same time that it assured the writer a constructive and relatively lucrative social role."[27] The autobiography of Mat Donagh is an extreme version—almost a parody—of the mystifying fictions that Victorian male authors told of their work, and Riddell exposes the paradoxes of their role in the mid-Victorian marketplace, even as she retains her belief in genius.

My point in drawing these parallels is less to uncover the real-life counterparts to Riddell's fictional characters than to explore her motives in aligning Glenarva Westley with Romantic, Brontëan authorship and Barney Kelly with a market-driven, Bohemian model. I have already suggested that Riddell accrues cultural capital for the woman author by setting her work within a paradigm of genius, inspiration, and high vocation. Kelly lacks such symbolic capital, opting instead for immediate economic reward; whatever his material success, the novel makes it clear that his *fame* will never last, however successful his professional *struggle*. In Poovey's terms, *A Struggle* retains the two images of the writer, but reverses the usual gender alignments by affiliating Glen with genius and Kelly with the cog in the capitalist wheel. The novel thus mounts a challenge to male authors and critics like Coventry Patmore, who maintained that women were naturally inferior as artists and authors, debarred by their naturally limited abilities from the "properly masculine power of writing books."[28]

The novel further suggests that authors like Kelly, whose books lack genius, will deeply, almost involuntarily hate authors like Glenarva because they recognize the difference between wheat and chaff, their ephemera and her "original books" (III, 226). When Kelly's own novel falls flat, "a dead failure" (III, 229), he savagely reviews Glen's *Heron's Nest* because he envies its achievement. A "well-known essayist" later admits to Glen that "we all hated you then"—the "we" of the "Burleigh Street fraternity" (III, 204) being the Bohemian authors published by Felton and Laplash (Tinsley Brothers). In the literary world of *A Struggle* there is an irreconcilable opposition between authors of genius and authors of the marketplace, between workers in Bourdieu's "sub-field of restricted production" and those in the "sub-field of large-scale production."

Riddell reverses the usual gendering of these categories, but she is honest enough to acknowledge that she cannot reverse a gendered double standard. Kelly maintains "a certain chivalrous sympathy" for Glen so long as she publishes loyally with Vassett, lives quietly at home, and stays out of the literary limelight (III, 234). Once she moves to the glitzy firm of Felton and Laplash, and "see[s] a little of life, and mix[es] in society" (III, 226), he shows no mercy, treating her as he would any professional rival, perhaps even treating her worse for abandoning the domestic sphere. As he says to his wife, using a debased version of Gaskell's "parallel currents" model, "She ought to stop at home and write her books and mind her house, and see her husband's slippers are warmed" (III, 240). Riddell underscores the effects of this double standard, noting that Kelly can get ahead because he starts "in the race unweighted" (III, 9), whereas women authors carry the burden of their households with them. She also underscores the irony of male reviewers like Kelly, most of them unsuccessful as novelists, imperiously judging women's fiction as "popular" and thus denying them the status of high art.

Facing Facts of the Market

In separating Glenarva Westley, the gifted Brontëan novelist, from Barney Kelly, the market-conscious man of letters, Riddell was virtually separating two aspects of her own career. Riddell began as a novelist—selling her first book in 1855 to Thomas C. Newby, the publisher notorious for his shady dealings with Emily and Anne Brontë; placing her next novel with the reputable Smith, Elder, publisher of Charlotte Brontë's fiction; and then moving in sequence from the conservative Charles Skeet (1858–63), to the flashy Tinsley Brothers (1864–77), to the well-established publisher of triple-decker novels, Richard Bentley and Sons (1880–91). Yet Riddell had another sort of career. After the success of *George Geith of Fen Court* (1864), which Tinsley bought for an astonishing £800, she moved beyond novel writing into the realm of magazine writing and editing, regularly placing stories in Christmas annuals, collecting them for book volumes, serializing novels in popular magazines, writing essays on domestic and professional topics, and assuming half-proprietorship and editorship of *St. James's Magazine* in 1867.

She became, in other words, a Victorian woman of letters—doing most of the literary work she associates with Kelly, except perhaps for regular reviewing.[29]

It is interesting to speculate why Riddell does not present Glenarva as a full-fledged woman of letters, why she varies her heroine's life course so noticeably from her own and from the dominant pattern of the period. By the 1880s, when *A Struggle* appeared, the woman of letters was a common figure on the literary scene—from Eliza Lynn Linton (1822–98), novelist, essayist, and crack journalist for major periodicals; to Frances Power Cobbe (1822–1902), feminist journalist, essayist, and lecturer on major social problems; to Margaret Oliphant (1828–97), novelist, biographer, and principal reviewer for *Blackwood's Edinburgh Magazine*; to Anne Thackeray Ritchie (1837–1919), novelist, essayist, and biographer. A simple answer lies in Riddell's Brontëan model and its association of women's achievement with the novel. This association would have been reinforced by the life and career of George Eliot, who had died in 1880, three years before Riddell published *A Struggle*. Marian Evans had risen from the literary drudgery of translation and editorial work for John Chapman on the *Westminster Review* to high acclaim as the novelist of *Adam Bede*, *Middlemarch*, and *Romola*—a formidable figure in the history of (women's) authorship and a pattern for the commonplace view that the novel represents the Victorian woman writer's highest form of achievement.[30] Riddell, too, identifies women's artistic achievement with the novel and makes Glenarva its exemplar.

A more complex answer lies in Riddell's assessment of the effects of the professionalization of letters, identified with the "now" of the novel's opening scenes and the founding of the Society of Authors in the 1880s. Although Riddell would later profit from the beneficence of the society, receiving £60 annually from 1901 until her death in 1906 from a pension fund it administered, in the 1880s she lamented the change that the Society of Authors had made in authors' attitudes to their work. To her friend Victoria Matthews, she wrote in 1886,

> What is needed now in literature is a GREAT writer. . . . I can only hope that in some public place—looking with bright young eyes on the stream of London life, or taking a lesson from the mountains and the silent moors and the lovely lakes—there are lads who will arise as prophets in 1900, teaching the world that money is not all and success is not all, that to an author his Art ought to be as near and dear to him as his God.[31]

The sources of inspiration for these imaginary "lads" are the sources that had inspired Dickens at mid-nineteenth century and the Romantic poets at the beginning of the century. They are the same sources that inspired Riddell's best work: the "stream of London life" she depicts in her City novels of the

1860s and the natural beauty of her native Ireland in *Berna Boyle* (1884) or of rural Middlesex in *Daisies and Buttercups* (1882). "When I look back and consider the authors there were even in my time, and think of those who immediately preceded them," she adds, "I feel the century is getting so old as to be doting."

The negative effect of the modern race for wealth and popular acclaim, Riddell suggests, is imitativeness, derivativeness, and lack of originality. These she illustrates in the same letter to Victoria Matthews by analyzing Frances Hodgson Burnett's best-seller, *Little Lord Fauntleroy* (1886), which brought the author instant fame and over £20,000 in profits. In Riddell's estimate *Little Lord Fauntleroy* is a case of "poaching on another's manor." Burnett had borrowed, wittingly or unwittingly, from Juliana Ewing's *Jackanapes* (1883) and Rhoda Broughton's *Nancy* (1873). Burnett's book, like that of many contemporaries, "make[s] up for paucity of original thought by talking a great deal about thoughts that are not original." In contrast, the "old authors" each show "the 'grip' of his subject . . . even in the shortest sentence. It is as when a master lays his hands upon the piano."[32]

While these assessments involve nostalgia, in that they look retrospectively to the mid-Victorian novel as the height of artistic achievement, they are not wholly nostalgic. With them Riddell also engages in contemporary literary debates. She articulates the same warnings that other men and women of letters voiced with the founding of the Society of Authors and with Walter Besant's emphasis on professionalism, literary property, and its commercial value. As I suggested in chapter 1, in the 1880s Literature (with a capital *L*) became a recurring topic of analysis. When an essay in the *Quarterly Review*, "On Commencing Author," reviewed the first seven volumes of the *Author* (1890–97), edited by Besant, it challenged the business-like approach to authorship that dominated the journal's pages. Making a distinction between "Journalism" and "Literature"—the former as "the business of the day," the latter as "verbal expression . . . in such shape that, though the matter may grow archaic, the form will preserve its interest . . . in subsequent generations"—the reviewer argues that journalistic writing might be approached as a business in the mode advocated by Besant, but that literary writing has its origin in other impulses: "there are numerous motives operating on the true man of letters—of literature as distinct from journalism—urging him to exercise his vocation and to exercise it to the very best of his power, without being paid for it at all."[33] Arthur Waugh, commenting on the Society of Authors in the *National Review*, would make a similar point and argue that writing "pot-boilers" leads to "a loose, irresponsible habit of work," whereas, "in the realm of art, everything should be done as well as we can do it."[34] Although Riddell would not have agreed with all points made by the *Quarterly Review* or *National Review*, especially not with the former's anti-feminist sentiments, she maintained the same distinction between literary work that lasts and ephemeral writing that does not—a distinction that echoes widely in periodical literature of the 1880s and 1890s.

In so doing, Riddell questions the decision she made in the 1860s to shift from the reputable, if conservative publisher Charles Skeet to the up-and-coming firm of Tinsley Brothers. According to S. M. Ellis, Skeet was "old-fashioned," "more a seller of old books than a publisher of new ones"; when he "did not respond to Mrs. Riddell's suggestion that she ought to receive better terms than he had hitherto paid her," she decided in a business-like way to leave the firm.[35] After the success of *Too Much Alone* (1860), she determined to play the market and walked into the offices of Tinsley Brothers, where she introduced herself to Edward Tinsley. In his *Recollections* William Tinsley recalls the scene: "'*What?*' shouted the publisher. '*Here!* Bill!' he [Edward] bawled to his brother in the back sanctum; 'here's *Too Much Alone!* By God! I have been wanting to find her.'"[36] In negotiating with the Tinsleys Riddell left the gentler, kinder world of mid-Victorian publishing, where relations between author and publisher were cordial, if sometimes also paternal, and entered the emerging new world of market-driven choices, industrialized production, and commercial profit over literary product. This is the literary field of the 1870s and 1880s that Riddell analyzes in the second and third volumes of *A Struggle for Fame*, a field that had both rewarded and punished her for participation. In these volumes she questions whether she had made the right professional decisions, as in this analysis of Glen's recognition of selling herself short:

> What better was she for all the prizes she had won—all the money she had earned—all the people she had seen—all the flattery, all the praise which once seemed so sweet? How much better—nay, rather, how much worse! If no one knew the fact, Glen was fully aware that she had not done herself justice, that she owned higher capabilities than, so far as it now seemed, the world was ever likely to be wot of. (III, 299–300)

If the language of this passage is archaic, the questions that emerge from it are not: whether modern women authors are unwise to abandon the old model wholly, even with its double standard, or whether they might wisely maintain certain aspects of the model of authorship that Gaskell had advanced in her mid-Victorian biography of Charlotte Brontë.

Reevaluating Brontë's Life, Revising
Myths of Authorship

In *The Life of Charlotte Brontë* Gaskell identified two "parallel currents" in her subject's life: the professional current, "her life as Currer Bell, the author," and the domestic current, "her life as Charlotte Brontë, the woman."

In discussing these distinct identities, Gaskell insists that the woman author must "take up the quiet, regular duties of the daughter, the wife, and the mother" but must also use her special talents: "she must not hide her gift in a napkin." She acknowledges that the two currents are "difficult to be reconciled" but "not impossible" (I, ii, 223). As if following Brontë's example, in the first two volumes of *A Struggle for Fame* Riddell shows Glen taking responsibility for her ailing father, then marrying a husband of whom her father approves and caring for him in illness, even as she faithfully continues to write novels and seek publishers. Indeed, Riddell not only repeats the theme of the "two currents" but even shifts the gender of her surviving parent—from her own mother to Glen's fictional father—in order to reproduce Brontë's life more precisely and explore its narrative of literary success to its end.

This exploration occurs in volume III, as if Riddell means to write beyond the two-volume ending of Gaskell's *Life* and consider its implications for the women writers of her own generation who succeeded Brontë. One question that the Brontëan reinscription raises is whether the professional and domestic currents can, in fact, be reconciled as Gaskell claims. At a pivotal moment early in volume III, as Glen begins a new novel for Mr. Vassett, she finds herself distracted by domestic life and unnerved by skeptical comments from her in-laws; the narrator comments, "though she did not, like Charlotte, 'go on cutting more bread and butter,' she proceeded to pour out more tea . . . and took refuge in silence—an asylum she latterly somewhat affected" (III, 48). If Riddell reproduces in this scene an episode from her domestic life, which was plagued by financial worries and her husband's difficult relatives, she does so while thinking of "Charlotte." Here as elsewhere, volume III of *A Struggle* suggests that the two currents do not run smoothly parallel for some (perhaps most) women authors. For "want of ready money," Glen "spend[s] her strength in effecting petty economies instead of concentrating her energies on the exercise of her profession" (III, v, 156). Although she has achieved a measure of literary success, she must now write "by fits and starts" because she also serves as her husband's secretary and clerk: "she allowed every social, domestic, and business matter to take precedence of her own legitimate employment" (III, v, 155–56).

A conflict between the professional and the domestic plagued Riddell's career, as it did those of her contemporaries Mary Elizabeth Braddon (who for twenty years of married life "was forced to work off John Maxwell's debt by slavishly writing both novels and serials, and actually had to use her savings to keep the household afloat") and Margaret Oliphant (who in her *Autobiography* wrote of the family crises that forced her "to give up what hopes I might have had of doing now my very best").[37] The Riddell Papers at the University of Texas include a wrenching testimony to this conflict. In a memorandum of agreement, dated 24 July 1871, "between Mr. Joseph Hadley Riddell, acting for himself as for his wife Mrs. Charlotte Riddell residing at

St. John's Lodge, Hanger Lane, Stamford Hill, and Messieurs Henry S. King & Co. of Cornhill, London," the Riddells accepted a loan of £285 in exchange for "the copyright, stereotype plates and moulds" of a dozen novels, including her famous *George Geith of Fen Court*.[38] The materials would revert to the owner, according to the agreement, if the loan were repaid by 1 March 1872 (as presumably it was not, given that Joseph Riddell filed for bankruptcy in September 1871). In effect, Riddell's entire professional achievement was mortgaged to save her husband's failing business.

For Brontë, who, though poor, had sufficient family means to underwrite publication of the *Poems of Currer, Ellis, and Acton Bell* and who, dying within a year of marrying the Reverend Nicholls, never really tested the compatibility of the professional and domestic within marriage, this sort of crisis was inconceivable. Brontë never faced a publisher who said, as Laplash does, "you're not what you once were" (III, 325) or creditors who insist "Your wife's income must pay your debts" (III, 317). Nor did Brontë live long enough to fall out of fashion or hear her publisher advise, "You'll have to run your stories through the country newspapers; that's what they all do now—Collins, and Braddon, and the rest. And why not you?" (III, 326). Riddell's literary life simply could not fulfill Gaskell's model.

If the professional and domestic currents fail to run smoothly in Glen's life, the marketplace of the 1870s and 1880s adds another snag. Whereas Brontë could stay modestly at home in Haworth, making an occasional trip to London to meet her publisher and a few literary figures, Glen, like her author, must become a public presence in her role as modern professional author. When she joins the "stable" of Felton and Laplash, she must also accept Felton's hospitality, immerse herself in the "social life of Bohemia" (III, 206), and play by the new rules of celebrity publishing. "The New Firm," as volume III, chapter iv calls it, instigates a "mode of doing business" that "consisted in looking out for names and trying to bag them" (III, 108). In this brave new world of publishing Glen is forced to give up the privacy and anonymity so valued by herself and women authors of mid-century: "Thanks to Messrs. Felton and Co., she was now common property"—and thus subject to "everyone who pleased to stare at [her] and criticize" (III, 201). Despite her heroine's distaste for the limelight, Riddell understood keenly that modern authorship required publicity and that the private, domestic sphere was a myth of the past. Like others of her generation, she had photographs taken for *cartes de visites*, allowed herself to be interviewed for magazines such as the *Pall Mall Gazette* and *Lady's Pictorial*, and attended soirées where she was one of the literary lion(esse)s.[39]

Yet Riddell questions the wisdom of this path to fame. In the presence of her bullying publishers, Barney Kelly advises Glen, "I hope Mrs. Lacere will not abandon her old ideas till she is very sure the new are better. If she take my advice she will stay quietly at home, and leave general society to those who do not need time for thought, or leisure in which to produce original books" (III, 226). Although Kelly often serves as a mouthpiece for conservative views of womanhood and female authorship, here he openly states what Glen cannot: that the new celebrity mode of authorship is destroying her originality and cultural worth. The narrator comments, "she and Mr. Kelly did not differ greatly in opinion concerning the demerits of the clique with which, against her better judgment, she had become acquainted" (III, 227). Kelly further articulates an older nineteenth-century view of literary achievement in his essay, "Fame and Notoriety," where he distinguishes between the two concepts and contends that "the moment an author came prominently before the public he compassed Notoriety," whereas "the author's work alone was capable of securing Fame" (III, 268). According to Leo Braudy in *The Frenzy of Renown: Fame and Its History*, this view of fame was dominant in the early nineteenth century when "an increasingly fame-choked world [began] to reach out for solace and value to anonymity and neglect as emblems of true worth";[40] it represents an attempt to separate fame from celebrity, true success from mere visibility, the *succès d'estime* from commercial reward. This view became a feature of myths of the Brontës, especially in the neglect of Anne and Emily's novels by their first critics. Riddell suggests that women authors of the later nineteenth century might wisely retain the distinction between fame and notoriety, as the achievement of celebrity status could not win them genuine, lasting fame. Indeed, when Glenarva succumbs to the values of Felton and Laplash, she suffers a breakdown, not only losing her income and public status but ruining any chance of true literary distinction.

In the end, Riddell's engagement with *The Life of Charlotte Brontë*, particularly the model of "parallel currents," raises the question of whether the life of the woman author must inevitably produce tragic death. Gaskell may not have intended this interpretation of her model, but her reconstruction of Brontë's life in Glen's fictional career brings it to the fore. In the *Life*, Gaskell had detailed Charlotte's care for her father, interspersing accounts of her writing *The Professor* and *Jane Eyre* with scenes of nursing and mourning. That these two were mingled is one of Gaskell's points: "All this time, notwithstanding the domestic anxieties which were harassing them—notwithstanding the ill-success of their poems—the three sisters were trying that other literary adventure to which Charlotte made allusion [writing novels]."[41] So, too, as Gaskell reads Brontë's literary career, public success is punctuated by personal tragedy: the deaths of Branwell and Emily just as the sisters' first novels appear, the death of Anne as Charlotte composes *Shirley*. Again, Gaskell stresses the intermingling of personal and professional: "She went on with her work steadily. But it was dreary to write without any one to listen to the progress of her tale, . . . as in the days that were no more" (II, iv, 380).

Riddell employs a similar pattern in *A Struggle*. Throughout the first two volumes Glen serves as a faithful companion and nurse to her father, just as

Charlotte conscientiously nursed Patrick Brontë through surgery for blindness and her siblings through the consumption that led to their deaths. But in the final volume this intermingling becomes formulaic; literary success and familial sickness or death meet in an equation—first with the death of Glen's father at the very moment a publisher buys her novel *Tyrrel's Son*, again with the death of her husband just as Barney Kelly writes a glowing review and a new magazine editor solicits her work. As the penultimate chapter phrases it: "Once again FAME had crossed the threshold hand-in-hand with DEATH!" (III, 346).

Modern readers of *A Struggle* are often embarrassed by this equation of a woman author's fame and the death of her husband or family member. Has Riddell overidentified with Brontë and lost artistic control? In seeking pity for her predicament, has she fallen into sentimentality? Or, in a clever, if more cynical, reading, does the ending betray Riddell's guilty desire to free herself from domestic responsibility by killing the father and the husband who have held her back from literary fame? While there may be elements of sentimentality or guilt or both in the ending, I would suggest that Riddell makes the penultimate chapter formulaic because she intends a critique of Gaskell's *Life* and the myth of authorship it constructs. Glenarva's life course, based on Riddell's own, has shown the parallel currents—of the woman and the author, the domestic and the professional—to be impossible, not just difficult, to reconcile. If the modern woman author is to have a chance at literary achievement, she must write beyond the ending of Brontë's life—as Riddell gestures in her conclusion. When Glenarva turns down an offer of marriage from her childhood friend Ned Beattie, now a wealthy successful colonialist, she also turns her back on Gaskell's myth. "It is very certain I am not going to marry you or anyone else," she writes to Ned, even as she seems to say to us, "I am sorry you have forced me to say this" (III, 351).

After *A Struggle*

The deathbed scene in the penultimate chapter of *A Struggle* transmutes the death in 1880 of Joseph Hadley Riddell, the author's husband, into a tragic closure of a woman writer's *kunstlerroman*. It echoes the closure of Gaskell's *Life of Charlotte Brontë*, garnering pity for the bereaved novelist yet holding out the possibility of a new phase of literary work. The final chapter opens "thirty months" after the deathbed scene—that is, at roughly the time Riddell composes the novel. When in the final vignette Glenarva Westley stands on a riverbank, "with the sluggish river to her left hand and the darksome pine-woods to the right, with the sun westering behind the spot where she stood calmly waiting" (III, 357–68), we assume that she draws from nature not only restorative power but also artistic inspiration, that her calm waiting is not only resignation in the face of tragedy but also expectation of future artistic achievement.

Riddell in effect "fulfilled" this final scene of expectation in the next phase of her career—by using the natural scenery of Middlesex to inspire some of her *Weird Stories* (1884) and by returning to the natural beauty of Ireland in *Berna Boyle* (1884). While her work of the 1880s may not have won the high critical acclaim or financial success that had rewarded her earlier novels of urban life, it was published by the respectable firm of Richard Bentley and Son, serialized in major magazines, and recognized as the work of a literary craftswoman. She was written up in the *Pall Mall Gazette* in 1890, "Lady Novelists—A Chat with Mrs. J. H. Riddell," and in the *Lady's Pictorial* by Helen C. Black, who included the interview in *Notable Women Authors of the Day* (1893).

Riddell's closure to *A Struggle* includes a marriage proposal that, by all biographical accounts, never occurred in her own life. In this episode, she again echoes Gaskell's *Life*, with its proposal from the patient, devoted curate Arthur Nicholls, who waited long to marry Charlotte Brontë. Ned Beattie, Glenarva's suitor, is a childhood friend who, we are made to believe, has loved her during his long years in colonial service and who returns in hope of finally winning her hand. But Ned departs with a refusal and a final view of "his brave, lonely Glen, who never for ever might be his wife" (III, 357). This is not faithfulness to the memory of a dead husband so much as Riddell's rejection of marriage and domestic life as incompatible with a literary career. Financially, Riddell never recovered from the debts accrued by her husband; professionally, she never fully recovered either. S. M. Ellis records that "her financial troubles only increased with the death of Mr. Riddell, for quixotically and without any legal obligation, she took upon herself to pay off liabilities due to her late husband's relatives."[42] This decision made Riddell's life as a widow "a sad and lonely one" and her work as an author "none too prosperous, for though her books were selling well, she did not find writing lucrative, . . . and there was a quixotic and heavy drain on her financial resources."[43]

The ending of *A Struggle for Fame* is more than autobiographically revelatory, however; it passes a general judgment on mid-Victorian myths of authorship. As its author knew, she was not the only woman author who had found domestic life incompatible with sustained literary achievement. Her fellow novelist at Tinsley Brothers, Mary Elizabeth Braddon, had also been constrained by her husband's debts. Another widowed novelist, Margaret Oliphant, had for over forty years supported her family and that of her brother Frank by reviewing steadily for *Blackwood's Magazine* and writing, almost ceaselessly, over a hundred books of fiction, biography, history, and travel. As Oliphant lamented in her *Autobiography* (1899), in comparing her life and work with George Eliot's: "it is a little hard sometimes not to feel with Browning's Andrea, that the men who have no wives, who have given themselves up to their art, have had an almost unfair advantage over us who have been given more than one Lucrezia to take care of." Oliphant also acknowledged, in comparing her life and work to Charlotte Brontë's, "my work to myself looks perfectly pale and colourless besides hers."[44] Like Riddell, Oliphant knew that marriage meant carrying a little world on one's back in the race of life.

These women writers were not alone in recognizing the difficulties of the married woman author or the impossibility of modeling a personal life and professional career on Gaskell's "parallel currents." The model had collapsed by the end of the nineteenth century. In a twentieth-century reminiscence, *Some Victorian Women*, the caricaturist Harry Furniss recalls many of the late Victorian authors he had sketched, including Oliphant and Riddell. In concluding his sequence, "Some Women Who Wrote" and "More Women Who Wrote," Furniss observes,

> Writing for one's living is a strenuous life. It takes more out of a woman than managing a hotel or running a scholastic establishment: there is not only the brain fag for the actual authorship, but there is the more important business side of the work. Some famous women, like George Eliot, are lucky in having a business partner, but most women who write have to divide their work between domestic duties and business worries and their profession, and one or the other is in consequence bound to suffer.[45]

Here the verb *divide* separates "domestic duties" from "business worries" as incompatible "currents": one or the other will suffer. More tellingly, the stream of "talent," so crucial to Gaskell's myth of the woman author, has dropped out of Furniss's account, overwhelmed by the ever-present "domestic duties" of the mother, wife, sister, and daughter and the newer "business worries" of the late Victorian professional woman of letters.

TRANSFORMING THE POET
Alice Meynell as Fin-de-Siècle
Englishwoman of Letters

In 1875, a young poet named Alice Thompson (soon to be Alice Meynell) published *Preludes*, a slender volume of lyrics illustrated by her sister Elizabeth, a professional painter. In its material form the volume signals its poetic intentions, its affiliations with nineteenth-century lyric traditions, and its author's aspirations. The cover prominently displays five gold-embossed symbols: a lyre, pen, acanthus, urn, and pair of turtle-doves, the first two representing modes of literary production, the second two, symbols of the arts and artistic achievement (see figure 25).[1] The fifth, deriving from the "voice of the turtle" in the Song of Songs, is special, if not unique, to *Preludes* and suggests that the young poet, newly converted to Catholicism, desired a Christian lyric figure as well.[2] In its symbolism, the volume seems overdetermined, announcing itself not only as about poetry, but also as about poetic achievement.

The title of the volume also announces Meynell's literary aspirations—what she late in life, half laughingly, recalled as her "childhood confidence in a future genius."[3] Most likely, given the serious musical training of the Thompson women, the title recalls Chopin's musical *Preludes* (1838), those brief lyrical pieces composed when Chopin was twenty-seven, covering all twenty-four musical keys and demonstrating, as one critic has put it, an "astonishing variety and vividness of mood . . . achieve[d] in little more than a blink of an eye."[4] Meynell's *Preludes*, written in her mid-twenties and published when she, too, was twenty-seven, similarly aims at variety and vividness of mood, meter, and stanzaic form, all achieved within the brief compass of lyric verse. Of course, the title makes a literary allusion as well: to William Wordsworth's autobiographical *The Prelude* (1850), a personal epic tracing the "growth of a poet's mind." Meynell's *Preludes* suggests a similar focus on the origins of poetic power and identity—a focus confirmed by the nature lyric that opens the volume, the multiple allusions to Romantic poets

FIGURE 25. Cover of *Preludes* (1875) by A. C. Thompson.
Courtesy of the Yale University Library.

throughout, and the epigraphs that establish its author's poetic lineage. Yet whether *Preludes* intends a musical or literary allusion, the title suggests, more fundamentally, a first book of poetry, a book launching a literary career and anticipatory of a later, larger poetic achievement.

If *Preludes* announced Meynell's aspirations—her youthful ambition to write poetry, to launch a career as a poet, to achieve a high place in literary culture—its prophecy failed, or seemed to. In a personal copy retained in the Meynell library, a note is penciled on the title page: "Preludes to Silence."[5] We know, in retrospect, that the volume was not a prelude to a long, unbroken career as a poet, for Meynell soon ceased writing verse and turned instead to prose, becoming an important late Victorian journalist, critic, and essayist. In the 1880s and 1890s she pioneered in modern art criticism, in the reflective essay, and in the mode of the "common reader" of literary works. As her elder contemporary George Meredith pronounced, Meynell's work as an essayist demonstrates "that she will some day rank as one of the great

Englishwomen of Letters"; as Joanne Shattock, a modern literary historian, comments in a typical assessment of Meynell's career, she was "an accomplished essayist, her work at its best equal[ing] that of Virginia Woolf in its range, poise, and style."[6] Yet, accurate as these judgments may be, they do not account for Meynell's ambitions in 1875 when "A. C. Thompson" entered the literary field, nor do they explain her decision to turn from poetry, her chosen form, to the essay, a form she took up for financial reasons but in which she made her most significant contribution to English literature. What motivated Meynell's transformation from a lyric poet into a professional reviewer, journalist, and essayist, ultimately to become (in Meredith's phrase) a "great Englishwomen of Letters"?

In her maturity Meynell dismissed her *Preludes* as insignificant, saying, "My first book of verse was accepted by a publisher only because my elder sister, who had just made a great reputation as a battle-painter, was kind enough to illustrate it."[7] Her daughter Viola reported that her mother would never acknowledge the merit of these early poems: "Hardly without a feeling of treachery can a member of her family pronounce their achievement already fine, so thorough was her own repudiation of them later, . . . [f]or in maturity she liked in her own work only that which had more compact thought in it."[8] We might be tempted to explain Meynell's dismissal of her early work in terms of the archetypal encounter of a young woman artist with a strenuous male critic—in this case, with Coventry Patmore, who praised her prose but said of her poetry "that though it was true, beautiful, and negatively almost faultless, it did not attain the classical and only sound standard."[9] In this analysis, Meynell abandoned poetry because she wrote better prose (or because a male critic told her she did).

Yet Meynell's disavowal of *Preludes* derives, I believe, not from a sense that she was a better essayist than poet, but from a sense that her youthful poems were not what they claimed—or she hoped—them to be: that is, not preludes to a future of verse. Her volume suggests an uncertainty about the direction her own—and, more broadly, late Victorian—poetry might take, about its relations to a nineteenth-century Sapphic tradition and to the nature poetry of Romantic predecessors whose work she admired. In this chapter, I shall suggest that Meynell left poetry for both financial and intellectual reasons, that she became a woman of letters in part as a "lucky necessity,"[10] but that also, during her years writing reviews, articles, and essays for periodicals, she resolved the conceptual questions that plagued her at her 1875 poetic debut: What lyric traditions might a late Victorian writer continue and develop in the modern age? What women's literary traditions might profitably continue and even thrive? What role might poets play in the modern profession of letters? I shall argue, in other words, that to become a modern poet Meynell had to become more comprehensively a woman of letters—in her definition, expressed in an assessment of the American writer James Russell Lowell, "judicious, judicial, disinterested, patient, happy, temperate, delighted."[11] Meynell's work in the reflective essay represents, in and of itself, a solution to the questions raised by her inaugural volume of poetry, just as her career represents a solution to the practical quandary of making money while also winning the high cultural prestige associated with poets and poetry. The larger arc of this chapter traces Meynell's origins as a poet and her return to origins—but with a difference. It suggests a model of professional achievement and cultural prestige impossible for Mary Howitt in the 1830s and 1840s, but possible for Alice Meynell in the very different literary field of the 1880s and 1890s.

Working Collaboratively, Mastering
Professional Journalism

In one version, the story of Alice Thompson's transformation from poet to journalist, essayist, and woman of letters can be simply told. The young author laid aside poetry in 1877 when she married Wilfrid Meynell, a fellow writer with no independent income. Alice's father, Thomas James Thompson, initially opposed the marriage on the grounds that Wilfrid's "financial prospects [were] too uncertain,"[12] but the couple's resolve, evidenced by their practical efforts to secure journalistic work and (for Wilfrid) an editorial position on the *Lamp*, a Catholic magazine, eventually won over Thompson père. At her marriage Alice's father promised to allow her £150 a year—"so little," she noted in a love letter to Wilfrid, "that I shall have the happiness of depending on you almost entirely."[13]

In fact, Alice Meynell also depended on herself and her writerly skills. In 1877 £150 was insufficient income for a literary couple with middle-class expectations and hopes (soon realized) of a family, so the Meynells took on whatever professional work came to hand—from freelance and commissioned articles for magazines as diverse as the *Magazine of Art*, *Art Journal*, *Tablet*, *Spectator*, *World*, and *Saturday Review*; to their own short-lived venture called *The Pen: A Journal of Literature*, officially founded and edited by Wilfrid but de facto produced by both; to editorial work on the Catholic *Weekly Register*, which required reporting on ecclesiastical affairs, translating papal encyclicals, and soliciting material from Catholic writers; to reviewing art exhibitions and writing artists' biographies, which provided a stable, substantial portion of the couple's income. Indeed, the art reviewing was so crucial to their household finances that Alice and Wilfrid scheduled their marriage around press days of the spring exhibitions, bringing forward the wedding date by a week so as not to lose this important source of income.[14] In this phase of Meynell's career, as in the early careers of all the women of letters studied in this book, financial necessity pushed the pen.

Like the Howitts before them, the Meynells worked as a team. Both reviewed art exhibitions; both wrote, edited, and produced the short-lived

Pen and the long-lived *Weekly Register*, both contributed regularly to the *Magazine of Art* and the *Art Journal*, and both assembled deluxe volumes for the book market, notably *Some Modern Artists and their Work* (1883), *The Modern School of Art* (1886), and *London Impressions* (1898).[15] Letters from Alice to Wilfrid, still preserved in the library of their country house in Greatham, West Sussex, include many references to bringing out the *Weekly Register*, dubbed the "*Reggie*," and often to Alice's doing so single-handedly: "Never again shall I fear taking the *Reggie* for you; I am going at it at a canter with both hands down." At other times, Alice enlisted the aid of Francis Thompson, the poet the Meynells had rescued from drugs and despair: "I am perfectly capable of turning out an amusing *Register* with no help except that of F.T."[16] Later, when the aging (and admiring) Coventry Patmore offered to visit and write copy or read proofs, Alice turned him down, explaining how she scanned foreign papers for Catholic news and adding, "These little things require no talent, but they do require a knowledge of current things, and a perfect familiarity with the habits of a paper."[17]

In undertaking this journalistic work, Meynell provided herself with an apprenticeship essential to becoming a professional woman of letters—a version of the training Harriet Martineau received under W. J. Fox on the *Monthly Repository* and that Mary Howitt provided her daughter by editing Anna Mary's letters on German culture for *Household Words* and the *Athenaeum*. Yet in this apprentice phase, the Meynells had more than financial survival or personal fame in view; they cared about advancing the profession generally, aiding other young writers to find their way, and nurturing belles lettres and poetry in writers of genius.[18] Under the pseudonym John Oldcastle and probably on Wilfrid's initiative, they assembled a small how-to book, *Journals and Journalism: With a Guide for Literary Beginners*,[19] first published in 1880 and continuing into multiple editions during the next decade. The book offered advice on beginning a career with "journalism" rather than "literature," submitting manuscripts to editors and publishers, handling rejections and correcting proofs, and understanding the laws of copyright (or lack thereof). The volume included a "Dictionary of the Periodical Press," with short entries on the principal London periodicals, office addresses, editors' names, and the editorial mission—a list no doubt useful to the Meynells themselves, just as the advice they gave reflected lessons they had recently learned. In the 1880s Wilfrid participated in the founding of the Society of Authors, attending the first organizational meetings and providing professional advice (though not, as far as I can determine, contributing to its magazine, the *Author*).[20] Alice became president of the Society of Women Journalists in 1897.[21]

During these early years, Meynell was doing more than serving a literary apprenticeship (though her hours of editing, translating, and proofreading were certainly a journeyman's work). She was also acquiring skills for innovations in art and literary criticism, building a deep knowledge of literature and life essential to composing personal essays and public commentary, and making contacts with editors and publishers for placing her mature work. And these things—"in ripeness, not rawness, consists the excellence," to quote her essay on Lowell's literary development—involve a more complex story of Meynell's conversion into a woman of letters, a story with intersecting but distinct paths as art critic, literary essayist, and poet, and with a public self-construction as a professional writer that belies the "angel in the house" label with which she is often tagged.

As Meaghan Clarke has documented, Meynell did seminal work in Victorian art criticism, beginning with contributions to the *Magazine of Art*, founded in 1878 just after she married, and the *Art Journal*, newly re-launched under the editorship of Marcus Huish when Samuel Carter Hall retired in 1880.[22] Both Meynells contributed regularly to these periodicals, as well as to the Catholic *Tablet*, sometimes with unsigned reviews of contemporary exhibitions, sometimes with signed articles using their own names or substituting the pseudonyms Alice or John Oldcastle (the latter used by both). Alice's early signed contributions tend to be biographical: short profiles for "Our Living Artists," featured in each issue of the *Magazine of Art*; obituary notices for its "Bundle of Rue" column; and longer accounts of artists' careers, such as the two-part history of Benjamin Hayden, "Story of an Artist's Struggle" for the *Magazine of Art*, or the three-part "George Mason: A Biographical Sketch" for the *Art Journal*.[23] Meynell developed the technique of characterizing artists' key stylistic features in the opening paragraph and positioning them within a painterly tradition or current school before moving on to discuss the primary achievements of the career. In a column on the French painter Henri Regnault (1843–71), for example, she begins with a trend in European art of which Regnault is the "chief exemplar": "Modern art has shown, in one of its contemporary Continental developments, a certain expansion of beauty in colour and execution which may be called the blossoming of painting."[24] In her discussion of the Scots painter William Quiller Orchardson (1832–1910), she observes, "When a British artist develops his own personality steadily, singly, and naturally, he does so in spite of heavy odds"—a comment intended as much to critique the national system of art education as to explain Orchardson's "primal artistic gift of seeing nature pictorially."[25] These techniques—useful later in writing literary criticism and the "Modern Men" column of the *Scots Observer*—make her art columns distinctive even at this early stage, notably superior to others.

Despite groundbreaking work as a woman art critic, Meynell considered this criticism to be ephemeral—written to a high standard but written (in the words of the pseudonymous John Oldcastle) as a "test," as "an earnest of . . . future success."[26] Very few of her early journalistic essays survive in the Meynell library (where manuscript versions of *Preludes* are carefully preserved); none is collected in later volumes of her essays; and only a few pieces were gathered for income-producing collections, such as *Some Modern Artists and their Work*, edited by Wilfrid and lavishly produced by Cassell, the publishing firm that issued the *Magazine of Art*.[27] There, along with other slightly revised columns from the magazine, her biographical sketches of G. H. Boughton and Jean Louis Ernest Meissinier (perhaps also of Frederick Leighton and her sister, Lady Butler, if she coauthored the John Oldcastle chapters) appear. Her first critical biographer, Anne Kimball Tuell, who had access to this early art criticism and interviewed Meynell late in life, praises its "evenness and temperance," and "regrets . . . Mrs. Meynell's expressed wish that her work in this field should not be seriously considered."[28]

In expressing this wish (virtually a command to a would-be biographer), Meynell followed a principle she formulated early in her career and held to throughout: she would produce journalism of high quality but would not engage in "book-making," to recall Margaret Oliphant's phrase, unless she deemed her work to have lasting value. Paraphrasing Meynell, Tuell articulates this principle: "She discarded whatever sketch or criticism might be written by any able journalist of exceptional refinement, keeping only what was her 'solitary' own, the style rich, in the unmistakable close tissue."[29] In adopting this strategy, Meynell was, I would argue, astutely managing her literary career and public self-presentation with two aims in view: always to be perceived as a professional writer, yet ultimately to become a "classic" author, an Englishwoman of letters.

Meynell pursued her journalistic career seriously: "I worked hard on journalism that I loved, on my own subjects, during the years that I bore eight children," she told Tuell.[30] She took care, as Ana Parejo Vadillo has shown, to create a public image of professional and economic success through her deployment of urban domestic space: the Meynells' homes, all located in Kensington amid professional artists and writers of the highest status, projected social and economic stability, as well as aesthetic taste and modern architecture.[31] And Meynell *looked* the part of a professional art critic—in her working mode at home and in her carefully chosen dress for public art exhibitions. As Katherine Tynan recalls, Meynell at home appeared as a working journalist.

> During those working years I can see her as she used to sit in that library at Palace Court doing her articles. . . . She worked in the library, a pleasant room, as all the Meynells' rooms were pleasant and full of interest and charm, but it was the common-room of the house and its visitors. She always wrote uncomfortably to my mind, with people talking about her, seated on an uncomfortable chair, just as she had come in, an outdoor garment laid aside, but still wearing her hat.[32]

So, too, in public spaces Meynell presented herself as a professional. As Marie Belloc-Lowndes recalls, Meynell wore, for a Royal Academy private view in the 1890s, "a flounced skirt of smoke-grey crepe and a simple black hat. She moved among the women there, many of whom wore eccentric and startling costumes, as if she were a being belonging to another, more rarified, sphere."[33] Drawing on the adjective *rarified*, some critics have read this appearance as ethereal, as part of an angel-in-the-house persona,[34] but Meynell's dress was chosen, I think, for a different purpose: to distinguish her from the "pre-Raphaelite" and "aesthetic" women who were as much the objects of attention as the pictures, and to set herself apart as the professional art critic moving among them. The "smoke-grey" color and rarified air may also recall the well-known mien of Anna Jameson, the early Victorian art historian who pioneered in Meynell's chosen field and whose professional contributions Meynell had analyzed in an article for the *Magazine of Art* in 1879, just as she began her own career.[35] Jameson was distinctive in London and continental societies as a professional authoress, with dark garb, elegant hands, and a face *"spirituelle* in its expression."[36]

In contrast to her dismissal of her art criticism, we can see Meynell's bid for literary status and lasting fame in her belletristic essays: in the delay in collecting them for book publication, in the high-quality production of the volumes, in their elegantly but not decadently designed covers, and in the frontispiece that she eventually used to represent herself to the reading public—the 1894 portrait by John Singer Sargeant, painter of major late Victorian literary figures from Coventry Patmore and George Meredith (both of whom she admired and who admired her in turn) to Edmund Gosse, Vernon Lee, and Robert Louis Stevenson. Sargeant's portrait (see figure 26) shows Meynell in fashionable but not eccentric puff sleeves and elongated skirt, hands clasped, large eyes soulful—rarified, but not angelic. Osbert Burdett describes the effect and, with it, the impression Meynell made.

> We see a tall, slender figure, the stem, as it were, of a delicate refined face, a face a little weary, as if it were masked with the ashes of a fire which had wasted the spirit within. . . . Life is a burden to this poetess, not a joy. It imposes too great a strain upon her nerves."[37]

Even if we dispute Burdett's conclusion and attribute the "strain upon her nerves" to the challenges of raising seven children while writing full-time, we can recognize that Meynell's shift from journalism to literature was self-consciously performed, that in the 1890s she came to present herself as a figure within the literary elite.

When Meynell began her work in the literary essay, then, she wrote for permanence as well as pertinence, for prestige as well as professional remuneration. This shift was influenced—in practical terms made possible—by William Ernest Henley, the editor of the *Scots Observer* who solicited her work and encouraged her to collect her best pieces in *The Rhythm of Life and*

FIGURE 26. Alice Meynell, 1894. Frontispiece portrait based
on a drawing by John Singer Sargeant.

Other Essays (1893), her first essay collection. Henley had known the Meynells during his years at the helm of the *Magazine of Art* (1882–86), possibly earlier during the brief life of the *Pen*.[38] When he assumed editorship of the *Scots Observer* (soon renamed the *National Observer*), he dissolved the conventional antithesis between "journalism" and "literature" and encouraged literary journalism or creative nonfiction, as we might call it today. According to his

friend and biographer, L. Cope Cornford, "Henley's conception of journalism was that it should be treated as an art, in intention and in effect; in
matter and in style. . . . Henley determined that criticism, as such, should
be expressed in terms of art."[39] Meynell reflects this innovative approach—in
effect, a fin-de-siècle refusal to accept the binarism of periodical journalism
versus high art—in the columns she wrote for Henley, all stylishly polished,
despite their spontaneous, almost breathless effect.

Not only a generic innovator, Henley was also recognized as "the most
influential literary editor of the day."[40] Under him, the *Scots Observer* led
with political commentary, ended with book reviews, and filled its middle
pages with the best literary work Henley could solicit: art and culture columns by Andrew Lang, J. M. Barrie, and David Hannay; poetry by W. B.
Yeats, Katharine Tynan, Graham R. Tomson, Alice Meynell, and Rudyard
Kipling (his *Barrack-Room Ballads* first appeared there); stories by Robert
Louis Stevenson, H. B. Marriott Watson, and Margaret Oliphant; a "Modern
Men" column by many hands; and essays (indexed as "featured articles") by
Barrie and Lang on professional literary matters, Tomson on dress, and Mey-
nell on triumphantly idiosyncratic topics ranging from landscape, houses,
and railways, to composure, rejection, and pathos, to elemental aspects of
nature: "The Sun," "The Flower." Meynell also contributed to the unsigned
book reviews and the "Modern Men" column, with critical reassessments of
Oliver Wendell Holmes, James Russell Lowell, and Coventry Patmore.[41]
These contributions—many no longer than three paragraphs—paid well (a
guinea a column).[42] Indeed, so determined was Henley to make the *Scots
Observer* an illustrious magazine, rival to (but aesthetically superior to) the
Saturday Review, that its backers lost over £20,000 during its five years of
publication. Henley set high literary standards; his printer Walter Blaikie
produced beautifully typeset issues; and his contributors enjoyed the freedom of publishing high-quality work without editorial amputation or undue
intervention.

The contributors also enjoyed the pleasure of being known as Henley's
"young men"—high Tory, counterdecadent, dismissive of socialism and Glad-
stonian liberalism, passionate about high art and contemptuous of "'popular
culture' . . . as the sorriest contradiction in terms," always "waging a brilliant
battle against Dulness, Decadence, Deciduity."[43] Meynell may have professed socialism and chafed at Henley's hyper-masculine attitudes,[44] but she
shared his commitment to high culture: as her essays "Decivilised" and
"New-Worldiness" attest, she too rebuked the barbaric savagery of the
"transatlantic, colonial" who thought great literature could be produced by
rejecting old world traditions, and she embraced the *Scots Observer*'s standard
of an informed, discriminating art.[45] Privately, Meynell expressed her pride
in writing for this prominent weekly paper—as a letter to her mother reveals
in its comment that she considers its staff "the foremost men in England"
and that her inclusion "put[s] my work very high in the ranks of literature."[46]

Publicly, in a retrospective dedication of *The Rhythm of Life*, she acknowledged Henley's seminal influence.[47]

Meynell's essays in the *Scots Observer*, published between February 1889, when "The Unit of the World" and "The Lesson of Landscape" appeared anonymously, to October 1892, when "Penultimate Caricature" appeared over her signature,[48] typically ran a double-columned page or less, four or five pages in her little volume, *The Rhythm of Life*.[49] Each begins with an assertion or observation—"Simplicity is not virginal in the modern world," to quote "Rejection," a contemporary favorite, or "If life is not always poetical, it is at least metrical," to quote the title essay. Meynell then illustrates, for example, "the rhythm of life" with metrical aspects of human existence—happiness or sorrow recurring in "the tides of the mind," remorse not remaining but returning, disease "closing in at shorter and shorter periods towards death, sweeping abroad at longer and longer intervals towards recovery."[50] Often, she quotes poets, essayists, and spiritual advisors—Thomas à Kempis who "knew of the recurrences" and Shelley who, like the author of the *Imitation of Christ*, "knew that what is approaching to the very touch is hastening towards departure." Her arrangement is associative rather than logical, with examples and quotations leading to further examples, quotation, reflection, and personal revelation, often expressed as generalization. "Exercises in close thinking and exact expression, almost unique in the literature of the day," the *Athenaeum* reviewer would describe them.[51]

Talia Schaffer has argued that personal revelation gave Meynell's readers "a voyeuristic thrill," despite the "oblique and self-defensive" mode of the essays, and that this provocatively half-revelatory mode accounts for their attraction.[52] Perhaps so, yet voyeurism (on the reader's part) and self-revelation (on the writer's) are intrinsic to the personal essay as a genre; indeed, Montaigne poses the question in his seminal "Of Repentance": "But is it reasonable that, being so private in my way of life, I should seek to make myself publicly known?"[53] In Meynell's case the voyeurism may have emerged from reflective writing that was, in large part, thinking aloud about her beliefs on art, poetry, human life, and culture. "The Rhythm of Life," for instance, expresses one of Meynell's most oft-quoted dicta on poetry.

> Like [the saints] are the poets whom, three times or ten times in the course of a long life, the Muse has approached, touched, and forsaken. . . . Few poets have fully recognised the metrical absence of their Muse. For full recognition is expressed in one only way—silence.[54]

Readers, then and now, have treated this comment as a sideways explanation for Meynell's long years of poetic silence, even though it actually pronounces judgment on the published poetry of *others*, who lack the "uncovenanted beatitude of sweetness" that only the Muse can bestow. Like all the essays in this early series, "The Rhythm of Life" offers personal revelation, but I would suggest that the appeal lies in the wisdom, judgment, and consolation for the changing moods and circumstances of human existence that they extend. These are not Victorian "leaders" or modern "op-eds" but, in Meynell's terminology, "commentaries."

Making Money, Winning Prestige

Meynell's contributions to the *Scots Observer* attracted the notice of admiring readers and produced, I believe, the pivotal moment in her career, allowing a transition from professional journalist to a prominent woman of letters in fin-de-siècle literary culture. In this weekly periodical, "all was powerfully, all was curiously, all was singularly written," noted her contemporary Francis Watt, but Meynell's pieces stood out. "How we shouted and wrote each other notes over Mrs. Meynell's 'Rejection,'" wrote Wilfrid Whitten in the *Academy*, recalling the heady days of the early 1890s.[55] Then prominently, in a *Fortnightly Review* article, "Mrs. Meynell, Poet and Essayist," Coventry Patmore praised her prose for its high, "classical" achievement, for embodying "new thought of general and permanent significance in perfect language, and bearing, in every sentence, the hall-mark of genius" (even though he judged her poetry as not attaining "the classical and only sound standard"). Patmore even recanted his earlier statement that "no female writer in our time had attained to true 'distinction.'"[56] Such judgments, made privately in conversation among literary friends and publicly in print to the cultural elite, consolidated Meynell's reputation. Professionally, however, the most important admirer of these belletristic essays was John Lane, publisher and partner with Elkin Matthews at the Bodley Head. Through Henley, Lane offered in 1892 to collect Meynell's essays in a small volume and, at the same time, issue a volume of her poetry—as paired books, each echoing the other in size, design, and type (see figure 27). This was the prestigious launch that made Meynell's career.[57]

Remembered today as the publisher of the *Yellow Book*, Lane was more importantly the discoverer, promoter, and publisher of poets, the fin-de-siècle equivalent of Edward Moxon, publisher of Shelley, Keats, Tennyson, and Browning. Along with his antiquarian bookselling partner Elkin Matthews, Lane published W. B. Yeats, John Masefield, Richard Le Gallienne, Oscar Wilde, Francis Thompson, Ernest Dowson, John Davidson, Lionel Johnson, and Ezra Pound, among others.[58] Lane also promoted the high-culture essay, publishing the work of George Egerton, Florence Farr, Elizabeth Pennell, Grant Allen, Edmund Gosse, and Kenneth Grahame. With handmade paper, limited editions, and book designs by Charles Ricketts and Aubrey Beardsley, Lane and Matthews's Bodley Head books were elite volumes, unquestionably aimed at what Bourdieu calls the "sub-field

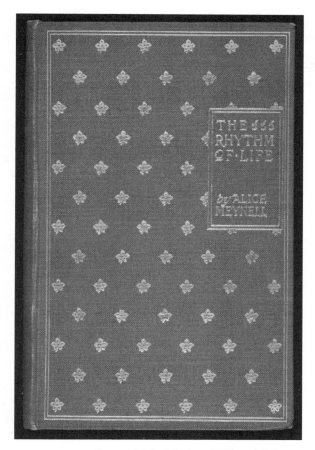

FIGURE 27. Cover of *The Rhythm of Life and Other Essays* (1893) by Alice Meynell.

of restricted production."[59] Editions were typically limited to five hundred copies.

According to his friends and some of his authors, Lane was not much of a businessman (the Bodley Head press never seemed to operate in the black and Meynell's letters remind him repeatedly of overdue accounts),[60] but he was a superb promoter of the books he produced.[61] When Meynell's essays were collected and about to appear as a book, Le Gallienne, one of Lane's authors and officially his literary advisor, produced a review of the forthcoming volumes, *The Rhythm of Life and Other Essays* (1893) and *Poems* (1893). Responding to Patmore's judgments in the *Fortnightly*, Le Gallienne echoed the praise of Meynell's prose but challenged the elder poet's underrating of her verse, defending it as "the deep cry of a heart rather in its natural language than in the queenly speech of the muse" and confessing that he preferred her poetry to her prose, which he admired for its cultivated style but thought revealed "too little joyous life, too much of the literary ascetic." Whether this was a strategic move to help Lane launch both volumes or whether it reflected an actual preference, Le Gallienne in any case pronounced Meynell a true woman of letters, quoting her own words back to her in praise:

> [T]he whole man, the very whole of him, is his style. The literature of a man of letters worthy the name is rooted in all his qualities, with little fibres running invisibly into the smallest qualities he has. He who is not a man of letters, simply is not one; it is not too audacious a paradox to affirm that doing will not avail him who fails in being.[62]

In Le Gallienne's view, Meynell had, in her very "fibres," the right stuff. She was a "man of letters worthy the name."

These reviews—by an elder statesman of poetry and a young Turk—assured Meynell's success, not only as a distinguished high-culture essayist but also as a well-paid professional author. *The Rhythm of Life* quickly went into second and third editions (if only of five hundred copies, given Lane's practice of limited issue). Henley asked for more articles, despite knowing that the *National Observer* was failing, perhaps hoping that Meynell's appearance might boost sales.[63] Other, more popular periodicals requested interviews and contributions, resulting in columns about Meynell in *Sylvia's Journal* and the *Queen* and columns by her in the *Saturday Review* and, more important, the *Pall Mall Gazette* (*PMG*).[64] After publishing a few fugitive pieces, the *PMG* enlisted her for its "Wares of Autolycus" column, a feature launched in 1895, named for that Shakespearean "snapper-up of unconsidered trifles" and intended to attract women readers with its commentary on fashion, food, china, and, more broadly, women's place in English society. Patmore, having now met the Meynells and visited their London house, wrote to his wife: "Mrs Meynell is getting all sorts of commissions to write at very high prices, and works many hours *every* day."[65]

Patmore doesn't specify figures for the "very high prices," but we know that the *PMG* articles paid well, based on Meynell's letters and account books for the late 1890s. At the start of the series, she wrote to Wilfrid, "I should much like to know what the *Pall Mall* means to pay me for the weekly articles. I shall not growl at £1 10 s; but £2 would make me very happy."[66] The records, though incomplete, suggest happiness rather than growls, with payments eventually reaching £3 per article.[67] In an account book for 1898, for instance, Meynell records debits (mainly payments to servants) and credits (royalties, commissions, and sales to periodicals). She lists her "Wares of Autolycus" essays, already published in the *PMG* and about to appear in a Bodley Head volume as *The Spirit of Place and Other Essays* (1898), as selling to the American *Collier's Weekly* for £3 per column, with a total of 52 columns for that year: "Finished up to date," she records. "If the cheques still come in spite of refusal, post 3 more <u>before</u> Jan. 6 which will make 52 in the year."[68] She also lists payments for other reviews, articles, and an unidentified story about a little boy at eight and nine guineas per installment (8£ 8s, 9£ 9s, the guinea representing a polite form of payment to artists). That year (1898) the royalties on her three Bodley Head books brought in £73.11.0—about half what she earned by reselling the *PMG* columns to *Collier's* but important to household finances nonetheless.[69] Even if Patmore exaggerated the "very high prices," he accurately reported Meynell's "getting all sorts of commissions," "work[ing] many hours *every* day," and thus earning a great deal more money than she ever had before.[70]

It is conventionally argued that for nineteenth-century authors, the *succès d'estime* was distinct from financial success—that, as Bourdieu asserts in *The Field of Cultural Production*, a fundamental opposition exists between "symbolic credit" and "economic credit," whereby "*discredit* increases as the audience grows and its specific competence declines."[71] Meynell's literary career disrupts, and partially disproves, this antithesis between "economic" and "symbolic" credit. For her the two were linked: financial success came as a result of symbolic credit, high payments followed from growing literary acclaim. This dual success came, moreover, as Meynell disrupted the traditional hierarchy of genres (poetry at the top, journalism and serial publication at the bottom). Paradoxically in her case, the essay replaced the poem as the prestigious genre; serial publication, in regular columns written for the *Pall Mall Gazette* and sold to *Collier's Weekly* for a second fee, confirmed her literary "distinction," to adopt Patmore's term. De facto, journalism led to Meynell's *succès d'estime*. The literary field of the 1890s in which she worked did not operate by the conventional rules—in part because of its new fascination with the essay, in part because of an appetite for small, aesthetically pleasing books, in part because of the opening of the American periodical market. Nor was Meynell forced to gender the distinction between market-driven writing and writing of genius, as Charlotte Riddell had done to assert her artistry in *A Struggle for Fame*. Instead, Meynell was able to work within a highly masculine context, the *Scots Observer* with Henley's "young men," and produce work that Patmore declared "classical": "the marriage of masculine force of insight with feminine grace and tact of expression."[72]

It was in these reflective essays, moreover, that Meynell worked out her views on modern poetry and her place within literary tradition—a process that enabled her return to verse writing. Several essays in *The Rhythm of Life*, the collection she made from the *Observer* columns, treat poetic matters: "Rejection," the value of simplicity in style and "the great and beautiful quality of fewness"; "Mr. Coventry Patmore's Odes," the heroic line as the fundamental "unit of metre" in English verse and the dangers of forgetting this "metrical check"; "Innocence and Experience," the regrettable practice of modern love poets who have "no reluctance in adopting the past of a multitude of people" and produce verse "full of ready-made memories"; and "The Rhythm of Life," the periodicity of poetic inspiration and the "artificial violence" of throwing one's literary life "out of metre."[73] In these essays Meynell articulates the values that tacitly explain her repudiation of *Preludes*, inform her daughter's comment that "in maturity she liked in her own work only that which had more compact thought in it,"[74] and anticipate the later achievement of her verse. Meynell came to understand (and value for its own sake) the "innocence" of her early poetry, even as she prepared for the mature work of her "experience."

Moreover, in writing these essays Meynell (re)discovered the concept of a literary career and the meaning of literary development, by which a woman of letters makes a lasting contribution to literature. From the beginning Meynell had written about literary careers, especially those of women. Her earliest journalism includes a review of Harriet Martineau's *Autobiography*; a biographical sketch of Anna Jameson, based on the recently published *Memoirs* by her niece Gerardine Macpherson; and an article for the *Spectator* on Mary Wollstonecraft.[75] Like the essays on "Female Writers of Practical Divinity" that Martineau wrote in her adolescence, Meynell's early reviews reveal a young writer seeking possible models, analyzing women's literary achievements, and exploring the confluence of personal life and professional work. But these reviews reflect the bias of youth, overly emphasizing the early writing and not yet comprehending the overarching *career*, the development by and through which a writer reaches maturity—as Meynell would learn later through her essay writing.

In her early sketch of Anna Jameson, for instance, Meynell knows that "it was late in life that the authoress entered upon the works by which her name will live" (*Sacred and Legendary Art*, *Legends of the Madonna*, and *Legends of the Monastic Orders*), but she cannot trace a professional lifeline that explains how Jameson moved from *Diary of an Ennuyée* and *Characteristics of Women* to this important work as an art scholar and critic. Meynell attributes the success of Jameson's later works to "personal research [that] was indispensable" and a "sincere and living . . . interest in that research," as "evidenced by the tears with which she is recorded to have spoken of the beautiful legends she studies."[76] That is, Meynell understands the value of hard work but still operates with a youthful view of inspiration—in women displayed by visible emotion—as the basis of authorial achievement.

In contrast, in her essays on men of letters in *The Rhythm of Life*, Meynell emphasizes "ripeness" and explores the informing contribution of a national literary tradition to a writer's achievement. Her hero in these essays is James Russell Lowell, the only man of letters America has "given to the world": "judicious, judicial, disinterested, patient, happy, temperate, delighted."[77] Meynell praises Lowell for representing "the little-recognised fact that in ripeness, not in rawness, consists the excellence of Americans." (Already, in these comments, we can sense Meynell's reassessment of her own literary development.) A scholar fluent in multiple European languages and their literatures (as she was), Lowell understands that American achievement results not from a barbaric yawp but from absorption of European culture; by his example, Meynell understands the role that history, both literary and political, plays in the making of a national literature and an individual author's oeuvre. Sketching the development of American writing from "colonial days, with the 'painful' divines," to the "experimental period of ambition," to the "civil-war years, with a literature that matched the self-conscious and inexpert heroism of the army," Meynell suggests that Lowell as man of letters was possible only because he was "the child of national leisure, of moderation and education."[78] Tellingly, she singles out his small critical books, *Among My Books* and *My Study Windows*, and his nature writing, "My Garden Acquaintance" and "A Good Word for Winter," as his highest achievements—in effect choosing the prose works that most resemble her essays of the early 1890s.

If Meynell worked out her views on poetry, prose, and the profession of letters in these critical essays, it was in other essays—particularly those meditating on the natural world—that she found solutions to the conceptual questions that marked her youthful poetry. As I will suggest in the next sections, Meynell inherited two nineteenth-century lyric traditions—of Romantic nature poetry and of Sapphic verse—in which she was deeply immersed and to which she was drawn. Yet in 1875 when she published *Preludes*, she could not locate her place within these traditions, nor foresee their continuation in modern English literature. One function of her essays was to clear the way for her future as a poet—a clearing that involved both analyzing past tradition and imagining future possibility.

Renewing the Romantic Nature Tradition

Meynell's uncertainty about nature poetry emerges in the opening lyric of her debut volume *Preludes*, "In Early Spring." The poem begins with an apostrophe and a lyric "I"—"O Spring, I know thee!"—and then catalogues the delights of spring that the nature poet knows: "the yet / Leaf-folded violet," "The cuckoo's fitful bell," the "wild hedge-roses" of June, the "songs yet half devised" of the "wild birds silent yet," and so on.[79] After twenty-six lines, however, the poem breaks from its lyric "I" and shifts to a third-person masculine.

> The poet mused upon the dusky height,
> Between the stars towards night,
> His purpose in his heart. I watched, a space[.]

The break is both grammatical and spatial, with the final twelve lines set off from the first twenty-six. The "I" emerges as an onlooker, not the lyric poet herself but someone who watches for "The meaning of *his* face," "the secret . . . / Hid in *his* grey eyes" (my italics). The disjunction between the "I" and "he" signals an uncertainty about inhabiting the lyric voice. It suggests that the young writer cannot imagine herself as a poet in the Wordsworthian tradition, that there is a secret in the nature poet that she cannot fathom, and that, while she "knows" spring, she cannot "write" it.

Meynell's uncertainty may reflect a gendered alienation from this tradition of English lyric; as Margaret Homans has argued in *Women Writers and Poetic Identity*, Romantic nature poetry utilizes (perhaps strategically creates) a gendered binary, a separation of the male poet from the natural world, the lyric "I" from the feminine object, Mother Nature. Alternatively, "In Early Spring" may signal the burden of the past that *any* young poet feels when beginning a literary career. As its speaker admits after cataloguing the season's delights,

> But not a flower or song I ponder is
> My own, but memory's.
> I shall be silent in those days desired
> Before a world inspired.

These lines, appearing just before the shift from the lyric "I" to the descriptive "he," suggest that the celebration of spring is derivative and its representations come not from nature but from a literary past. The speaker registers the difference between the "sweet surprise" of spring in "the young children's eyes" and the knowledge of spring in the older poet's experience: "I have it all by heart." The opening poem thus meditates on the richness of the poetic past and the difficulty of imagining original nature writing in the present or future. It recognizes that the things of earth are, poetically speaking, well-known: "O all brown birds, compose your old song-phrases, / Earth, thy familiar daisies!"

In this recognition Meynell joins other Victorian poets who felt the burden of the past—from Tennyson's doubt in *In Memoriam* ("What hope is here for modern rhyme?") to Swinburne's Sapphic abjection in "Anactoria" ("Men shall not see bright fire nor hear the sea, / Nor mix their hearts with music . . . But . . . Memories shall mix and metaphors of me.")[80] It is a version of the problem Meynell explores, as I noted above, in "Innocence and Experience," where she analyzes contemporary love poets whose verse "is full of ready-made memories," who have "no reluctance in adopting the past of a multitude of people to whom they have not been introduced."[81] But whereas in that mature essay Meynell critiques poets like Alfred de Musset for "so much experience, so much *déception*," here, as a young nature poet, she can do no more than acknowledge a difficulty for her own verse.

The uncertainty in this opening lyric goes to the heart of Meynell's vocation, for, as she was later to write in "Some Thoughts of a Reader of Tennyson," the English, a "vigorous little nation of lovers of poetry," are readers of nature poetry, "fostering Letters and loving Nature."[82] To succeed as an English poet required reaching that "little nation." And Meynell's uncertainty encompasses more than nature poetry per se. We can infer from other poems she wrote during the late 1860s and early 1870s but excluded from *Preludes* that she pondered long and hard about the burden of the past for the modern poet. In "Singers to Come," omitted from the volume but published in the *Irish Monthly* in 1876, she begins with a seemingly unanxious relation to tradition and an optimistic vision of future poets.

> No new delights to our desire
>> The singers of the past can yield.
>> I lift mine eyes to hill and field,
> And see in them your yet dumb lyre,
>> Poets unborn and unrevealed.

This poet confidently dismisses the past and portrays her own role in shaping the future, as Meynell represents herself as a forward-looking counterpart to "the maid who found, / And knelt to lift, the lyre supreme / Of Orpheus from the Thracian stream." Yet "Singers to Come" was excluded from *Preludes*, perhaps as too self-asserting or too self-confident of its calling. So, too, "A Song of Derivations," also written in the 1870s, was omitted. In this "Song" Meynell writes more ominously of poetry as possession—"Voices, I have not heard, possessed / My own fresh songs"—while recognizing that the past has the capacity to enrich modern poetry and make immortality possible through poetic tradition.

> . . . my thoughts are blessed
> With relics of the far unknown.
> And mixed with memories not my own
> The sweet streams throng into my breast.

As the concluding lines suggest, consciousness of the past carries a burden, what we have come to call "the anxiety of influence."[83] The mingling of "the past poets of the earth" with "my own fresh songs" inhibits or weighs down the young poet: "Heavily on this little heart / Presses this immortality." The achievement, the "immortality," of prior poets diminishes the speaker. Is her heart "little" because it is young or because it is female (and implicitly lesser and more fragile)? Is the difficulty gender, or generic tradition, or both?

Meynell would find an alternative to writing Romantic nature poetry in the essays she composed for the *Scots Observer*, collected in *The Rhythm of Life*, and she would develop this new mode of nature writing in the *Pall Mall Gazette* during the 1890s. In her essay on Lowell, we find a hint of the direction she will take when she praises those essays "when he is minded to play White of Selborne with a smile"—that is, when Lowell adapts the observational mode, "so charmingly local," of the seminal English nature writer Gilbert White.[84] White's *Natural History of Selborne* (1789), named for the parish in which the naturalist-clergyman lived and served, was famous for its close observation of plants and animals, of seasonal cycles and winged migration, of man's place within an economy of nature. Meynell's essays, beginning with "The Sun" in *The Rhythm of Life* and continuing with "Cloud," "Grass," "Rushes and Reeds," and "Winds of the World" in *The Colour of Life* (drawn from her columns in the *Pall Mall Gazette*), follow White's lead but develop their own mode of "looking closely." In "The Sun," for instance, Meynell stands on a Suffolk plain, "with its enormous sky," to see sunrise—bemused that a nature lover would ascend a mountain to see "a sun past the dew of his birth; he has walked some way towards the common fires of noon." Contrarily, she, "on the flat country," finds the "uprising is early and fresh, the arc is wide, the career is long."[85] Her observations—in a larger sense about "views" in nature, in early Victorian painting, and implicitly in nature poetry—are precise, sharp, grounded in a personal and local place, unwilling to be deceived by artistic traditions, and insistent that "all achieved works of Nature and art" reveal an "organism that is unity and life." Using verbal art to capture this unity, she concludes with the "alternative splendour" that comes from the only two "views" available to a human on the plain: "to look with the sun or against the sun."[86]

Meynell's phrase "common fires of noon" echoes, of course, Wordsworth's "common light of day" in the "Ode: Intimations of Immortality"—but with a note of critique. Whereas his phrase laments the loss of the child's rapture in nature, hers attests to the adult's continuing pleasure. Her chosen position on a Suffolk plain, the flattest of English terrains, contrasts with his ascent of Mt. Snowdon to achieve the great visionary moment of *The Prelude*. Her experience is one of "glow" and "luminosity," his of "instantly a light upon the turf [that] / Fell like a flash" (*Prelude*, XIV, 38–39); she celebrates the sun, he the moon. In "Winds of the World," another *PMG* essay, Meynell hints at the poetic attitude informing the difference: "Every wind is, or ought to be, a poet." In her view, the wind *is* the poet, not a source of the poet's inspiration or of a natural philosophy. Nature is named, described, felt, valued—not for the visionary moment, nor for the "correspondent breeze of inspiration" (*Prelude*, I, 35), but for its essential pleasure and power. As Patmore would discern, Meynell had learned "to write beautifully, profitably, and originally about truths which come home to everybody, and which everybody can test by common sense; to avoid with sedulous reverence the things which are beyond the focus of the human eye, and to direct attention effectively to those which are well within it." This achievement was more difficult than the "far easier field" of the "transcendentalism" of Emerson or (though Patmore did not say it) the natural supernaturalism of Wordsworth.[87]

In writing these innovative nature essays, Meynell speaks to an uneasiness she had registered in *Preludes*: the assumption that Nature yields up a higher meaning, a natural philosophy, to the Romantic poet. Meynell's "To a Daisy" investigates this assumption. The sonnet reproduces Wordsworth's "To the Daisy" and "To the Same Flower" but, to adopt Antony Harrison's terms, "reinscribes" a "culturally resonant text" in order to revise its meaning.[88] In "To the Daisy" Wordsworth derives from the flower "Some steady love; some brief delight; / Some memory that had taken flight; / Some chime of fancy wrong or right; / Or stray invention"—that is, what his fancy pleases, what he invests in the flower. In "To the Same Flower" he again uses the daisy to exercise his poetic fancy.

> Oft on the dappled turf at ease
> I sit and play with similes, . . .
> And many a fond and idle name
> I give to thee for praise or blame.

Then follows a catalogue of fanciful possibilities: "A nun demure of lowly port; / Or sprightly maiden, of Love's court, . . . A queen in crown of rubies drest; / A starveling in a scanty vest; / Are all, as seems to suit thee best, / Thy appellations." Meynell's "To a Daisy" refuses to exercise the poetic imagination in this mode; it remains content to acknowledge that the daisy, "slight as thou art," hides "secrets." In its final lines, the "I" "abides" to watch the daisy "grow and fold and be unfurled."

> Literally between me and the world.
>   Then I shall drink from in beneath a spring,
> And from a poet's side shall read his book.[89]

Here, as in other lyrics, Meynell displaces the work of nature poetry onto the Romantic male poet and "his book." The refusal to repeat Wordsworth's act of fancy carries with it an implicit criticism—as Le Gallienne noted when he praised Meynell's "Daisy" over Wordsworth's, which he thought had a "somewhat aimless aim" and took "several 'shots' [that] resulted in several charming but comparatively superficial reflections."[90] The concluding question of Meynell's sonnet—"O daisy mine, what will it be to look / From God's side even of such a simple thing?"—hints that Wordsworth's fancy reveals only superficial, earthly "appellations" and fails to penetrate to any true natural philosophy or transcendent meaning.

Reservations about Romantic nature poetry appear elsewhere in *Preludes*. In "To a Poet" (retitled "To Any Poet" in subsequent editions), Meynell characterizes the poet "who singest through the earth" as one whom "unfallen Nature" dumbly defies.

> Sing thy sorrow, sing thy gladness,
> In thy songs must wind and tree
> Bear the fictions of thy sadness,
>   Thy humanity.
> For their truth is not in thee.

The revelations of the nature poet are fictions or, in Ruskin's phrase, pathetic fallacies; the truth of Nature, her secrets and "silent labour," become available only after death.

> Nought will fear thee, humbled creature.
> There will lie thy mortal burden
> Pressed unto the heart of Nature,
>   Songless in a garden,
> With a long embrace of pardon.

This analysis of Romantic nature poetry—that it fails to penetrate the veil—suggests an alternative to two other positions represented in 1875: Swinburne's agnostic insistence that nature is empty, without spiritual meaning, resulting in what Susan Lorsch has called his "language of negation," and Anna Mary Howitt Watts's spiritualist belief, expressed in *Aurora*, published in 1875, the same year *Preludes* appeared, that the eternal Truth comes to those who listen to "Nature's Psalmist."

> *"They alone serve Truth,"* sings the holy Bird,
>   *"Who, awaiting ever his blissful call,*
> *At midnight arise their loins to gird,*
>   *Reckless if sorrow or pain befall;*
>   *Lo! it cometh, it cometh, the call of God,*
>   *To every Flower that springeth from Earth,*
>   *To every creeping worm of the sod,*
>   *To every Creature of mortal birth.*["]*[91]

Meynell allows neither nature's emptiness, "no transparent rapture" in Swinburne's phrase, nor human access to the "wild strains of music echoing back from hill and dale," in Howitt Watts's. But neither does "To a Poet" allow much possibility for the future of nature poetry. It ends in "Silence, the completest / Of thy poems, last and sweetest."

Silence was Meynell's response to lack of inspiration, to the departure of the Muse: "full recognition" of "the metrical absence of the Muse," as she writes in "The Rhythm of Life," "is expressed in only one way—silence."[92] Yet if the Muse seemed to be metrically absent for two decades after *Preludes*, she was not absent from Meynell's prose work. Each volume of essays, from *The Rhythm of Life* (1893) and *The Colour of Life* (1896) through *London Impressions* (1898), *The Spirit of Place* (1898), and *Ceres' Runaway* (1909), collects the best from the *Scots Observer* and *Pall Mall Gazette* columns—and always that best includes nature essays. The essays comment on elements of nature ("Cloud," "Rushes and Reeds," "Grass," "Wells," "Rain," "Shadows") and, increasingly, on human experience in nature ("July," "The Sea Wall," "The Tow Path," "The Tethered Constellations," "Dry Autumn"). In these essays Meynell forged a new way to write for an English readership that loved Romantic nature poetry and reinvented a mode of nature writing that, following Gilbert White, explored human relationships within the natural world by "looking closely." Writing about Meynell's style in *The Rhythm of Life* and *The Colour of Life*, Meredith would miss the link to White and the *Natural History of Selborne* but would recognize another important source of Meynell's innovative art: the journalism, "necessarily impressionistic," that "has added fluency and quickened the observation of the most penetrative eyes we have among us": "the writer casting an irradiation on . . . daily things does an act of beneficence," he added.[93]

In a late collection, *Hearts of Controversy* (1917), Meynell would return to the problem of modern nature poetry. She would articulate a challenge to all English poets: how, "fostering Letters and loving Nature," they might write about the natural world without falsifying or becoming "silly." In an assessment of Tennyson's achievement, she would praise the Victorian laureate for giving readers "a new apprehension of nature" and showing "the perpetually transfigured landscape in transfiguring words," while criticizing his predecessor Wordsworth for repeated falsifications.[94] Lines from "Hartleap Well" provide Meynell's test case:

> This beast not unobserved by Nature fell,
> His death was mourned by sympathy divine.

Wordsworth falsifies, in Meynell's estimate, by asking the reader to believe in an expression of divine sympathy "fatally rebuked by the truths of Nature": the poet "shows us the ruins of an aspen wood, a blighted hollow, a dreary place, forlorn because an innocent stag, hunted, had there broken his heart in a leap from the rocks above," yet we know, because we daily see, "the world blossoming over the agonies of beast and bird" and thus the world "is made less tolerable to us by such a fiction." The falsifying of nature in "Hartleap Well"—a more serious transgression than the flights of fancy in "To a Daisy"—reveals Wordsworth in an exercise of bad faith.

We are tempted to ask whether Wordsworth himself believed in a sympathy he asks us—on such grounds!—to believe in? Did he think his faith to be worthy of no more than a fictitious sign and a false proof?

The challenge Meynell poses is twofold: how to avoid the falsification of a natural supernaturalism and how to continue an expansion, following Tennyson, "of our national apprehensions of poetry in nature."[95]

In her later lyrics, as in her prose essays, Meynell would strive for accurate apprehension of nature and achieve it in a handful of poems written about the experience of nature in urban London—"November Blue," "A Dead Harvest (In Kensington Gardens)," "The Rainy Summer," and "A Thrush before Dawn." Her most intriguing response to the challenge of writing nature poetry appears in *Last Poems* (1923), in a pair titled " 'The Return to Nature': Histories of Modern Poetry."[96] The first of the pair, "Prometheus," links a masculine poetry of "Prometheus the forgiven" with the sun.

> It was the south: mid-everything,
>> Mid-land, mid-summer, noon;
> And deep within the limpid spring
>> The mirrored sun of June.

As Shelley Crisp has argued, this poem "establishes narcissism, a solipsistic use of nature to mirror only images of the self, as a principle of male poetics."[97] In contrast, the second of the pair, "Thetis," links a feminine nature poetry with "the wild eye of fancy," with "argent foam" and "silver feet"—adjectives that suggest the moon and potentially a secondary "light" or status.

> In her bright title poets dare
>> What the wild eye of fancy sees—
> Similitude—the clear, the fair
>> Light mystery of images.

> Round the blue sea I love best
>> The argent foam played, slender, fleet . . .

Yet the age-old hierarchy is not, finally, what Meynell's gendering of masculine and feminine nature poetry suggests. Rather, Prometheus's is a "mirrored" poetry, reflected and refracted through the (male) poet who has undergone the trial of being bound and returned to "splendour in freshness" only after plunging into the abyss. Thetis's poetry, in contrast, gives access to an original, "natural" poetry, achieved without violence and without a fall; as Meynell suggests in the final lines:

I saw—past Wordsworth and the rest—
 Her [the blue sea's] natural, Greek, and silver feet.

Thus the usual hierarchies—sun/moon, masculine/feminine, primary/
secondary, original/reflected—are undone as the lyric poet, here a feminine
"I," claims access to a "blue sea," the Mediterranean that gave Thetis birth
and that Meynell knew as a child. As a mature poet, Meynell has "seen past"
the Romantics to a modern mode of writing nature.

From Victorian Sapphic Poet to Modern
(Feminist) Essayist

If, in her reflective essays, Meynell resolved an ambivalence about Romantic
poetry and created a modern form of the nature essay, she also worked out
her affiliation with a nineteenth-century women's lyric tradition—what
Angela Leighton has called, in *Victorian Women Poets: Writing against the
Heart*, the tradition of "creative but suffering femininity" and Yopie Prins
has identified as a Sapphic afterlife in Victorian poetry.[98] This development
partially reflects Meynell's personal experience: her transition in the years
1875–95 from a young girl to married woman to mother of seven children.
But it also involves, as I shall suggest, her strategic use of the "Wares of
Autolycus" column in the *Pall Mall Gazette* as a site for reimagining a
women's literary tradition and rethinking women's roles as wives, mothers,
and authors.

 When Meynell resolved in her late teens to *work* at her poetry, she wrote
in her diary, "I must try to cultivate that rhyming faculty again which I used
to have, if it is not quite gone from me. But whatever I write will be melan-
choly and self-conscious as are all women's poems"[99]—as if she feared that,
as a woman, she must inevitably fall into a Sapphic strain and prove herself
unable to write in a different mode. Perhaps to resist this fall (or disguise it),
Meynell omitted two of her most intense lyric laments from *Preludes*: the
sonnet "Renouncement" and the three-stanza "After a Parting." Dante Gabriel Rossetti, who read the first in manuscript and committed it to memory,
judged it to be "one of the three finest sonnets ever written by women"[100]—a
judgment with which most modern critics have concurred. Reminiscent of his
sister Christina's poetry in its renunciation of earthly love, "Renouncement"
also recalls, in its half-willed return to the beloved in sleep and dreams, his
own sonnets in *The House of Life*.

I must not think of thee; and, tired yet strong,
 I shun the thought that lurks in all delight—
 The thought of thee—and in the blue Heaven's height,
And in the sweetest passage of a song.

"After a Parting," also omitted, similarly turns from earthly love "heaven-ward"—

> Farewell has long been said; I have foregone thee.
>   I never name thee.
> But how shall I learn virtues and yet shun thee?
>   For thou are so near Heaven
> That Heavenward meditations pause upon thee.[101]

—even as it clings in memory and imagination to the earthly beloved. These suppressed lyrics, as well as other early poems in manuscript, notably "To the Reader Who Should Love Me," suggest that Alice Thompson wrote, whether inevitably or not, in the nineteenth-century Sapphic tradition, and that this was her strong suit.[102] Such lyrics reveal, moreover, an uncanny biographical, even biological, motivation for writing Sapphic laments in that the poems emerge from an impossible, unrequited love for Father Augustus Dignam, the young priest who admitted her into the Catholic Church and with whom she fell passionately in love.

Yet even with the omission of key lyrics, many poems in *Preludes* join the Sapphic strain. "Parted," placed second the volume, begins as a muted lyric lament.

> Farewell to one now silenced quite,
> Sent out of hearing, out of sight[.]

Another lyric written after the separation from Father Dignam, "Parted" attempts a swerve away from a feminine lament to a Wordsworthian Lucy poem. Despairing of consolation, the speaker reminds herself of the natural pleasures left to her—"The morning crowns the mountain-rim; / Joy is not gone from summer skies"—and then, in a gesture repeating Wordsworth's in "Three Years She Grew," recalls her lost beloved's presence in nature, though removed from her sight.

> He is not banished, for the showers
> Yet wake this green warm earth of ours.
>   How can the summer but be sweet?
>   I shall not have him at my feet,
> And yet my feet are on the flowers.

This characteristic swerve—away from a Sapphic lament and toward a masculine tradition—recurs throughout *Preludes*. Indeed, the most critically acclaimed of her lyrics participate in a Sapphic tradition but disguise their links with nineteenth-century women's verse.

This disguise takes various forms—from the epigraphs to male poets, attendant on almost every poem in *Preludes*; to the self-conscious internal allusions, also to male poets; to the arrangement of poems within the volume. For example, "To the Beloved Dead," subtitled "A Lament," imagines the woman's body as a lyre, awaiting a "pulse" at "windy dawn," or "a strain of thee from outer air," to move her "lonely soul" to music—clearly a Sapphic theme. "Sonnet" (retitled "A Shattered Lute" in the collected *Poems*) continues the theme of the silent lute, of the abandoned poetess who stands "as mute / As one with full strong music in his heart / Whose fingers stray upon a shattered lute"—thus participating in an English Sapphic tradition forged by Mary Robinson, Laetitia Landon, Felicia Hemans, Christina Rossetti, and other poetesses.[103] Yet these two lute poems are separated in the volume, a choice that lessens their combined Sapphic impact. The second sonnet, moreover, carries an epigraph from Petrarca—"*Senza te son nulla*" ("who without you am nothing") from Petrarch's canzone 359—to suggest not an English feminine but an Italian masculine source. Like the epigraph to "Parted"—"*Come vedi, ancor non m'abbandona*" ("As you see, [Love] has still not abandoned me") from Dante's *Inferno*—the allusion to a male poet reveals Meynell's unwillingness to place her work solely within a women's tradition and her desire to see it instead as representing a major Western form of verse.[104]

Perhaps the epigraphs, often to classical but also to French and Italian poets, were meant to display the young poet's wide reading and register her ambition to join a European cadre of authors. Perhaps, too, the epigraphs were intended to make a critical point about the genre and history of the love lament—that it is not, fundamentally, a feminine form. The lyric "Regrets" self-consciously alludes to contemporary verse by male writers—to Leigh Hunt's *The Story of Rimini* (1816) and Matthew Arnold's "Marguerite" poems (1853)—and in so doing shows male poets, too, writing love laments. In "Regrets" Meynell uses the ebbing tide as a vehicle for expressing the slow, painful, but inevitable process of loss.

> As when the seaward ebbing tide doth pour
>   Out by the low sand spaces,
> The parting waves slip back to clasp the shore
>   With lingering embraces.
> So in the tide of life that carries me
>   From where thy true heart dwells,
> Waves of my thoughts and memories turn to thee
>   With lessening farewells[.]

By a conscious poetic interchange with the "ebb and swell" of feelings in Arnold's "Isolation: To Marguerite" and the "enclasping flow" of "To Marguerite—Continued," as much as to the Sapphic laments of Landon or

Hemans, Meynell suggests that passionate longing and loss appear in manly poetry as well as in feminine.[105]

Nonetheless, despite her attempt to control her poetic affiliations, readers of *Preludes* tended to associate Meynell's verse with women's lyric—as Le Gallienne implicitly did when he praised it as "the deep cry of a heart rather in its *natural* language" (my italics) or when Rossetti referred to her "little book" as "all deep-hearted speech."[106] In *Victorian Women Poets* Leighton has shown how, in later verse, Meynell moves away from this tradition and avoids the sentimentalizing poetry of motherhood that might have followed, had she simply transferred her poetic energies from romantic love into the next "natural" phase of her life: maternity. Instead of writing sentimentally about children, as do her contemporaries Christina Rossetti, Dollie Radford, and Edith Nesbit, Meynell "writes with a new restraint and skeptical distance about a subject which has conventionally lain outside the sphere of serious literature"; she "issues a quiet challenge to the still-standing icon of the sublime Madonna and perfect mother of much popular women's poetry."[107] This "skeptical distance" emerged, I believe, not so much from Meynell's poetic development as from her objective stance as a journalist, from the "quickened observation" and "penetrative eyes" that Meredith praised in her prose essays.[108] "Skeptical distance" and "quickened observation" show themselves with remarkable strength in Meynell's mid-1890s journalism about childhood, originally published in the *Pall Mall Gazette* and collected in a volume, *The Children* (1896).

In *The Children* Meynell signals a nonsentimental, objective perspective in her two-part lead essay, "Fellow Travellers with a Bird," and underscores her stance in the title of the closing piece, "Real Childhood." In "Fellow Travellers," Meynell insistently begins: "To attend to a living child is to be baffled in your humour, disappointed of your pathos, and set freshly free from all the pre-occupations." That is, to the adult who pays attention, looking, listening, and stretching toward (*attendre*) the child, conventional ideology proves false, sentimentality fails, and, more positively, as "freshly" implies, unnecessary worries dissolve. Part II of "Fellow Travellers" reiterates this perception, applying it specifically to Victorian literature: "In one thing . . . do children agree, and that is the rejection of most of the conventions of the authors who have reported them." Thus setting the stage for her more authentic reports, Meynell's essays—on the language of children, on childhood experiences, on literary and artistic representations of children—allow scope for originality and wit, as she quotes the son who reminds his father at tart time, "I hope you will remember that I am the favourite of the crust"; the daughter whose language displays involuntary "feats of metathesis" ("stand-wash," "sweeping-crosser," and "sewing chamine"); or the child who mishears an Irish maid complain about weak English tea and asks, as she brings her mother a cup, "I'm afraid it's bosh again, mother" and then adds, in a half-whisper, "Is bosh right, or wash, mother?"[109] Indeed, contemporary critics praised *The Children* for its humor—"humour un-stretched and inviolate, clear, simple, shining, and never at fault," in the words of a *PMG* reviewer.[110] But Meynell's essays also allow a testing of conventional wisdom on childhood: whether children in illness are patient (they are), whether encouraging juvenile authorship à la the Brontës fosters the imagination (it doesn't); and whether talking baby talk promotes communication with the young (it doesn't; it's merely "the excited gibberish of the grown-up").[111]

By challenging Victorian myths of childhood, these essays allow Meynell an opening for challenging Victorian myths of motherhood. The maternal speaker of "Fellow Travellers" does not feel obliged to answer the daughter who asks whether it's "bosh" or "wash," leaving her to decide for herself, "with doubts," that it's "bosh." Nor does the mother correct the child who inverts word parts by informing her that it's "wash-stand" or "crossing-sweep." In her maternal persona, Meynell feels little need to answer, instruct, or correct. Indeed, one is tempted to speculate that she had read Mary Howitt's column, "The Young Turtle-Dove of Carmel," for *Howitt's Journal* in that her "Fellow Travellers with a Bird" self-consciously eschews the lesson-driven narrative of her mid-Victorian predecessor.[112] Whereas Howitt uses the turtle-dove to deliver a factual lesson about avian migration and a moral tale about leaving wildlife alone, Meynell avoids lessons of any sort—except to correct the misapprehensions of adults. Children are "fellow travellers" with the adult. As for the "bird," a common emblem of exemplary behavior in popular natural history, it is wholly absent from the essay.

This release from conventional wisdom into penetrative observation prepares for the maternal poems of Meynell's maturity, inaugurated with the printed privately *Other Poems* (1896) and later officially published as *Later Poems* (1901) by John Lane. "Cradle-Song at Twilight" sets the tone.

> The child not yet is lulled to rest.
> Too young a nurse, the slender Night
> So laxly holds him to her breast
> That throbs with flight.
>
> He plays with her and will not sleep.
> For other playfellows she sighs;
> An unmaternal fondness keep
> Her alien eyes.[113]

In this conventionally titled but startlingly revisionary poem, the night functions as nurse of the child. Yet this substitute nurse, an analogue to the mother, gazes "unmaternally" at the child, resisting the expected role and "sigh[ing]" for other "playfellows"—perhaps lovers, as the phrase "unmaternal fondness" hints. Another verse in *Other Poems*, "The Modern Mother," overtly revises the Victorian conception of maternity, as it recalls a child's kiss, "with filial passion overcharged," and ponders the expectations of mothers about motherhood.

> Unhoped, unsought!
> A little tenderness, this mother thought
>   The utmost of her meed
> She looked for gratitude; content indeed
> With thus much that her nine years' love had bought.
>
> Nay, even with less.
> This mother, giver of life, death, peace, distress,
>   Desired ah! not so much
> Thanks as forgiveness[.]

In contemplating this scene of filial love, Meynell registers the complex response of the mother: her limited expectations of reward ("meed"), her gratitude for the child's spontaneous act of love, her knowledge that she has bargained for it ("bought" it with her own "nine years' love"), and thence her recognition that "forgiveness" more than "thanks" may be the appropriate response. As Leighton observes, "A sense of other perspectives, other pressures of the 'heart,' complicate the love which should be primary and all-engrossing."[114] In this verse as throughout *Other Poems*, there is none of Barrett Browning's fulsome celebration of "the love of wedded souls" or "loves filial," no sense that the woman poet writes in a "full-veined, heaving, double-breasted Age," none of what Meynell called, in a critical assessment of her poetic predecessor, a "positive morality."[115]

In *Other Poems* Meynell even challenges deep-seated cultural expectations about the importance of motherhood. Quoting a Roman decree—"When Augustus Caesar legislated against the unmarried citizens of Rome, he declared them to be, in some sort, slayers of the people"—she counters in "Parentage": "Ah no, not these!" This poem, the most overtly political of her 1890s verse, suggests that women acquiesce in war, violence, and death by bearing children and yielding them up to patriarchal ambition.

> But those who slay
> Are fathers. Theirs are armies. Death is theirs,
> The death of innocences and despairs;
> The dying of the golden and the grey.
> The sentence, when it speaks, has no Nay.
> And she who slays is she who bears, who bears.[116]

Fathers may form the armies, strike the deathblow, give the "sentence" that "has no Nay," but women are complicit when they become mothers. They "slay" as they bear children, and thus must doubly bear—as the repeated "who bears, who bears" of the final line insists—the pain of childbirth and the pain of grief.

Emerging from her sharply observant journalism and counter-conventional essays on childhood, Meynell's maternal poems have justifiably won the acclaim of modern scholars and critics. These poems form the basis of Meynell's revival as a preeminent fin-de-siècle poet and forerunner of modern feminism. In a seminal assessment Leighton concludes, "The 'alien' perspectives of [Meynell's] temperamental dispassionateness, on a subject that is too often awash with conventional passion, result in poems which, beneath the surface of their verbal simplicity, expressed a quite unique sense of the foreboding and misgiving in giving life itself."[117] Yet for all that I concur with this view, I want to explore, in the final section of this chapter, the effect that Meynell's essays on childhood and poems of motherhood had on her later reputation as an Englishwoman of letters—an effect not unambiguously positive. This will involve speculation about Meynell's participation in a remaking her public myth of authorship after 1895, that is, after publishing *The Children* and *Other Poems*.

Remaking Alice Meynell (Again)

In the years 1875 to 1895 Meynell began as a Sapphic poetess, became a top-tier journalist and critic on the *Scots Observer* and *Pall Mall Gazette*, and earned the status of an Englishwoman of letters of "distinction" (in the estimate of Patmore and Meredith), "the new sibyl of style" (in the phrase of Oscar Wilde).[118] During these years she produced revisionary essays and poems on childhood, motherhood, and the social roles of women (in the estimate of modern critics). Yet, paradoxically, this work remade her into a late Victorian "angel in the house" and contributed to a modernist tendency to treat her work as thematically Victorian, thus effectually depriving Meynell of the "classical," canonical status that she had apparently won.

We can begin to trace this remaking in the reviews of *The Children* and in a redeployment of Meredith's influential judgment in the *National Review* to market that volume. A review in the *Pall Mall Gazette*, as I noted above, praised *The Children*'s humor as "clear, simple, shining, and never at fault," but then diminished its realm: "Her book is a fairyland where there is, indeed, a place of rest." In a *Fortnightly* review, James Sully, professor of the philosophy of mind at University College, London, and author of a scholarly treatise, *Studies of Childhood* (1895), diminished Meynell's work even further: "To a pretty theme she has applied her prettiest of manners. . . . She comes certificated by authoritative hand, as trained by maternal sympathy in the unlocking of children's secrets"—words meant to praise, but better suited to feminine amateurism than authorial maturity and obtuse to the *lack* of maternal certification on which the essays insist. Nonetheless, and perhaps with Meynell's approval, John Lane excerpted these "Opinions of the Press" in his advertisements for *The Children* and reprinted them in other editions of her work.[119]

Even more perplexing are the excerpts that Lane took from Meredith's 1896 review of *The Rhythm of Life* and *The Colour of Life* and reused as advertisements for *The Children*. In his final paragraph Meredith had applied the Arnoldian keyword "distinction" to Meynell's prose: "The power she has, and the charm it is clothed in, shall, then, be classed as 'distinction'— the quality Matthew Arnold anxiously scanned the flats of earth to discover." Meredith imagines Arnold, in his afterlife, "lighting on such Essays as *The Point of Honour* [about Impressionism], *A Point of Biography* [about lapses and imbalances in modern biography], *Symmetry and Incident* [about Japanese art], and others" and "saying, with refreshment, 'She can write.'" Meredith also imagines Thomas Carlyle "listening, without the weariful gesture, to his wife's reading of the same, hearing them to the end, and giving his comment: 'That woman thinks!' " In these imaginary acts, Meredith makes two great Victorian men of letters approve Meynell's prose—a judgment that allows her to join their company and Meredith to prophesy that "she will some day rank as one of the great Englishwomen of Letters."[120]

Strikingly, in the "Opinions of the Press" for *The Children* cited in Bodley Head editions, Meredith's judgment is substantively altered. By selecting sentences that seem apt for a conventional collection about childhood, Lane makes Meredith endorse Meynell's maternal character.

> Her manner presents to me the image of one accustomed to walk in holy places and keep the eye of a fresh mind in our tangled world. . . . Her knowledge and her maternal love of children are shown in her ready entry into the childish state and transcript of its germinal ideas . . . only deep love could furnish the intimate knowledge to expound them so.[121]

In fact, the initial comment about Meynell's *manner* sums up Meredith's praise of her *style*—a prose style "correcting wealth and attaining to simplicity by trained art." "She must be a diligent reader of the Saintly Life," Meredith adds in gender-neutral terms, as the "attraction" of her writing "is in her reserve."[122] In the excerpted "Opinion," this statement introduces not Meynell's prose style but her womanly *ethos*, and what follows—in a misrepresentation of Meredith's words—emphasizes the writer's "maternal love." In the original, Meredith had actually stressed the "impressive reserve" with which Meynell writes of children and praised her nonsentimental approach.

There is not the word of affectionateness; her knowledge and her maternal love of them are shown in her ready entry into the childish state and transcript of its germinal ideas, the feelings of the young—a common subject for the sentimentalizing hand, from which nothing is gathered.[123]

His judgment had meant to remove Meynell from the common realm of Victorian women's writing and bestow "distinction" on her for resisting sentimentality, even as he credited her with "deep love." But the excerpt alters this intention.

The correspondence between Meynell and Lane does not reveal who chose the excerpts, but given her close involvement with the production of Bodley Head volumes and her willingness to challenge decisions she disliked,[124] we can only conclude that Meynell acquiesced in the selections from reviews. This act alone could not, however, have altered her public persona from an avant-garde essayist keeping company with Henley's men of letters and Lane's aesthetes to a late Victorian angel in the house. Equally influential were poems published in her praise by Coventry Patmore and Francis Thompson that overlooked the writer as they gazed at the woman. In "Alicia's Silence," one of many Alicia poems written in tribute, Patmore reconstructed Meynell's life history by transforming the young poetess into a woman embodying her art.

> A girl, you sang, to listening fame,
> The grace that life might be,
> And ceased when you yourself became
> The fulfilled prophecy.
>
> Now all your mild and silent days
> Are each a lyric fact,
> Your pretty, kind, quick-hearted ways
> Sweet epigrams in act.[125]

As if this transformation from artist to object of masculine art weren't dubious enough, Patmore continued in the more sensual "Alicia" poems to praise Meynell's dainty feet and figure her as "sole essential good of earth / And sweetest accident of Heaven" in a body "Sharp honey assuaged with milk, / Straight as a stalk of lavender, / Soft as a rope of silk."[126] More complexly but equally detrimental to her authorial status, Thompson paid homage in *Love in Dian's Lap* to Meynell's maternal, physical, and heavenly beauty, as in "Her Portrait":

> How could I gauge what beauty is her dole,
> Who cannot see her countenance for her soul,

As birds see not the casement for the sky?
And, as 'tis check they prove its presence by,
I know not of her body till I find
My flight debarred the heaven of her mind.[127]

While Thompson's verse does not name the object of his contemplation and emphasizes the transcendence of his response, moving from the earthly body to the heavenly mind, it nonetheless casts Meynell in an angelic mode. This is the Meynell myth that began to emerge in the mid- to late 1890s—with several of the poems in Thompson's cycle appearing in *Merry England*, the periodical Wilfrid Meynell edited. Thus, as Talia Schaffer has argued, Meynell herself helped disperse an angelic image, even while identifying with edgy journalists and fin-de-siècle aesthetes and writing proto-feminist essays in the *Pall Mall Gazette*.[128]

Meynell's poetry of the late 1890s contributes to this remaking of the public myth. When she assembled the slender volume titled *Other Poems*, privately printed in 1896 and published at the Bodley Head as *Later Poems* in 1901, Meynell introduced this new work with "The Shepherdess," a poem that became a signature piece.

She walks—the lady of my delight—
A shepherdess of sheep.
Her flocks are thoughts. She keeps them white;
She guards them from the steep.
She feeds them on the fragrant height,
And folds them in for sleep.[129]

This new image of the poet as shepherdess, gathering thoughts into a poetic sheepfold, has perplexed—and provoked—modern critics in its insistence on purity ("white," "chastest," "circumspect and right") and femininity ("lady of my delight," "maternal," and "shepherdess," a feminine noun). Why should Meynell have chosen "The Shepherdess" as an announcement of her mature poetry and poetics? Angela Leighton simply dismisses the poem for its "mincing sickliness" and blames Meynell's male mentors—Patmore and Meredith—for encouraging the stuff of "innumerable school anthologies."[130] In contrast, taking a recuperative approach and using the concept of "reinscription" whereby a poet rewrites texts "with a clearly defined significance for their culture . . . to subvert the accepted interpretation," Sharon Smulders has suggested that in "The Shepherdess," Meynell employs a "creative response to the problem of gender and genre" by "parodically engag[ing] the conventions of lyric verse" of male poets (in this case, Wordsworth and Byron) and "accommodat[ing] a distinctly feminine perspective."[131] In yet another explanation, Tracy Seeley contextualizes the poem within the rediscovery of the seventeenth-century metaphysicals in the 1890s and emphasizes Meynell's turn to a poetics of "ecstatic transport through contact with the physical world."[132] Yet, whether by evaluative judgment, subversive rereading, or historical contextualization, the fact remains that modern critics need to *explain* Meynell the poet as shepherdess and offer a rationale for this highlighted poem—with its deliberately feminine persona—in Meynell's self-construction in the mid- to late 1890s.[133]

This reconstruction will likely remain a biographical conundrum, a "silence" about Meynell's authorial self cultivated to increase its mystery. Yet, as criticism involves breaking silences and speaking answers, I want to speculate about Meynell's motives in relaunching her poetic career as a shepherdess of poetic thoughts. It may be that, having secured her place as the foremost Englishwoman of letters of the 1890s, Meynell felt free to advertise the feminine element of her style and persona. After all, in a *Pall Mall Gazette* essay of 11 October 1895, she analyzed the assets and defects of Harriet Martineau's authorial persona in "A Woman of Masculine Understanding," concluding that only limited "credit returns to the masculine understanding."[134] It may be too, having discovered the richness of seventeenth-century metaphysical devotional poetry, Crashaw's especially, that Meynell decided to launch a volume of her religious verse—as the "other" of *Other Poems* suggests in its emphasis on *difference* from the 1893 *Poems*. Yet it also seems likely that, in 1895, Meynell felt a pressing need to emphasize the purity of her poetic thoughts, the Catholicity of her verse, and the angelic effect of her person. And this need, I suggest, emerges from a specific crisis that (re)shaped the literary field in 1895.

In April 1895 John Lane, Meynell's publisher, was implicated in the scandal of Oscar Wilde's homosexuality when a newspaper headline announced Wilde's arrest with "Yellow Book Under His Arm." Though the yellow book turned out to be a French novel, not the *Yellow Book* magazine that Lane produced, the association caused an uproar at the Bodley Head offices and among its authors. Among those who wrote to express disapproval and threaten dissociation unless Lane withdrew Wilde's books from distribution were the Meynells.[135] Lane did, in fact, withdraw Wilde's books and severed his ties as publisher; Lane also sacked Aubrey Beardsley, Wilde's friend and the art editor of the *Yellow Book*, so as further to dissociate the Bodley Head from the scandal.[136] Nonetheless, though she had never published in the *Yellow Book*, Meynell seems to have worried about her links with Lane and the Bodley Head, for the next volumes of her work—the privately printed *Other Poems* (1896), *The Children* (Bodley Head, 1896), and the *Later Poems* (Bodley Head, 1901)—reveal the aftereffects of that uproar in the more decorous persona of the author as mother and in the whiter, chaster, carefully guarded "thoughts" of "The Shepherdess."[137]

Not only does that signature poem recast Meynell's image as poet and, in "The Fold," expand on its conceit of the shepherdess-poetess keeping her "flocks of fancies," the lyrics in *Other Poems* also self-consciously mark Meynell as a Catholic devotional poet: "'I Am the Way,'" "Via, et Veritas, et Vita," "The Lady Poverty"—to name three that follow "The Shepherdess" in the volume.[138] Moreover, a fourth poem, "Why Wilt Thou Chide?" echoes Psalm 85 and publicizes Meynell's rebuke of Coventry Patmore for over-stepping the boundary of friendship and proposing a more intimate love. Such poems, placed at the beginning of the volume, tend to counteract the revisionary nature of poems like "Cradle-Song at Twilight" and "The Modern Mother"—or, rather, allow the subversive aspects of these poems to be overlooked.

"The Shepherdess" would remain, until after Meynell's death, the sig-nature poem of her maturity.[139] It would retain its place of prominence in *Later Poems* (1901) and lead again in a reissue of that volume, *The Shepherdess and Other Verses* (1914), published by Burns and Oates, the Catholic press then managed by Wilfrid Meynell. This 1914 edition would include the note: "Originally published in 'Later Poems' (1902) and now incorporated in the author's complete volume of 'Collected Poems' (1913), this group of Verses, is still the subject of a separate demand which this edition is designed to satisfy"—as if to reinforce the religious quality of the volume and its special place in Meynell's oeuvre. But "The Shepherdess" would also, as numerous modern scholars have attested, alter Meynell's long-term status as English-woman of letters, almost sending her to the "dark and indescribed" spaces of literary history that she had worked so hard to illumine during her critical career.[140]

7

THE WOMAN OF LETTERS
AND THE NEW WOMAN
Reinventing Mary Cholmondeley

When Coventry Patmore conferred the honorific "distinction" on Alice Meynell as an essayist, Oscar Wilde pronounced her the "new sibyl of style," and George Meredith prophesied her lasting achievement as an Englishwoman of letters, it was already the 1890s—a point in the history of women's professional authorship when such acknowledgments ought to have been common rather than rare. For two literary generations prior, Victorian women had forged reputations as professional journalists and essayists; art, literary, and cultural critics; novelists and poets; and authors who worked adeptly in several of these genres, as their male counterparts did. By the 1850s a pioneering group of women—Harriet Martineau (1802–76), Mary Howitt (1799–1888), and Anna Jameson (1794–1860), among others—had established their names as women of letters in the Victorian literary field, negotiating the demands of the market and constructing public identities that legitimated and enhanced their authorial status. By the 1870s, the next generation of women—including Eliza Lynn Linton (1822–98) and Frances Power Cobbe (1822–1904) as journalists and cultural critics, George Eliot (1819–80) and Margaret Oliphant (1828–97) as novelists and literary reviewers, and Barbara Leigh Smith Bodichon (1827–91), Bessie Rayner Parkes (1829–1925), and Adelaide Procter (1825–64) as feminist journalists, essayists, and poets—had expanded the opportunities for women writers, demonstrating that women could not only achieve distinction in traditionally feminine genres (poetry, fiction) but also succeed in others (journalism, criticism, the essay). By the 1890s, the names of distinguished women of letters should have become even more numerous. Yet, although the number of professional women who entered the literary field increased, those who achieved recognition as women of letters diminished.

Literary historians as methodologically diverse as Elaine Showalter, Lyn Pykett, Talia Schaffer, and Gaye Tuchman and Nina Fortin have analyzed this professional erasure and discussed the diverse challenges that the 1890s presented to all women writers. In *Edging Women Out* Tuchman and Fortin point to the collapse of the triple-decker novel, a publishing mainstay of two generations of women novelists, and to the rise of a new "high-culture" novel that critics, wrongly but insistently, identified as a masculine form; in this transition women writers were edged out of the publishing market for fiction.[1] In *The Forgotten Female Aesthetes* Schaffer points to the omission of key women figures from seminal histories of the aesthetic movement, all written by male participants, all focusing on "their own and their friends' achievements," and thus all effectively excluding women from official literary history.[2] In *The "Improper" Feminine* Pykett adds that modern literary histories of the fin-de-siècle novel have scarcely been attentive to women authors: "the traditional history of the later Victorian novel is entirely dominated by male writers: the central figure of Thomas Hardy is surrounded by the attendant spirits of the three lesser Georges—Meredith, Gissing, and Moore."[3] And in *A Literature of Their Own* Showalter identifies an additional obstacle to lasting distinction as women of letters: the emphasis of New Women writers on issues of immediacy, especially political issues that became outdated or that eclipsed aesthetic concerns. This produced work that, in Showalter's terms, "leads to rhetoric but not poetry"—or, as Patmore might have phrased it, that leads to fugitive but not "classical" literature.[4]

As these literary historians attest, the 1890s witnessed a growing separation of popular from high art, mass from elite culture, the "subfield of large-scale production" from the "subfield of restricted production"—and with it a separation of popular fame and financial reward from the *succès d'estime* that made the 1890s almost modernist. Yet, as the career of Alice Meynell has shown, it was possible in the 1890s to achieve both financial success and critical esteem, to be a professional journalist yet win distinction as a woman of letters. Doing so required, however, a careful negotiation of what I have called myths of authorship and trends in the market. In this coda on a New Woman writer of the 1890s, I analyze a case of near success, but ultimate inability to achieve a lasting reputation as a woman of letters: the career of Mary Cholmondeley. A novelist who won critical esteem and transatlantic fame with her *kunstlerroman Red Pottage* (1899), Cholmondeley was unable to translate this success into a secure place in the literary field after the turn of the century—or into a lasting place in English literary history. Her case is illuminating for understanding the predicament of many New Woman writers who, as the century waned, lost their audience, both popular and critical.[5]

In analyzing Cholmondeley's career, I begin with an observation that Penny Boumelha, Lyn Pykett, and other scholars of fin-de-siècle fiction have made about a disjunction that recurs in New Woman writers' representations of the female artist—between "the woman of genius and the woman of Grub Street," in Boumelha's formulation.[6] As Pykett observes,

New Woman fiction typically presents a woman of genius who begins with high ambition but eventually fails, often to become a Grub Street hack; it depicts "the struggles of a girl alone in the world and earning her own living" and "the conflicts, frustrations, and compromised or thwarted careers . . . of the professional woman writer and the aspiring woman artist."[7] Boumelha notes that this disjunction reflects the compromises that New Women were often forced to make, "stranded between the self-sacrificing plots of womanhood and a concept of the artist that identifies commercial success with inauthentic and market-oriented mass culture";[8] their writing reveals the tensions between the demands of the marketplace and their desire to construct authorial myths expressing higher artistic ambitions, if also incomplete achievements. Cholmondeley's early career contains a similar disjunction between aspiration and achievement, between popular success as a sensational novelist and a desire for critical esteem. Yet, unlike other New Woman writers of the 1890s, Cholmondeley was able to join popular success with artistic achievement in *Red Pottage*, her first New Woman novel. In creating Hester Gresley, a "woman of genius" with no trace of the Grub Street hack, Cholmondeley devises a strategy to protest against her devaluation in the market after the collapse of the triple-decker novel and reinvents herself as an "advanced" writer in an emerging modern(ist) field of elite art—to great critical acclaim.

From Sensation Novelist to New Woman Writer

Cholmondeley began not as a professional New Woman writer but as what Vineta Colby has called a "devoted amateur."[9] In late adolescence, bored with life in a country rectory, she composed her first piece of fiction, "Her Evil Genius"—a story that she felt "half satisfied with," "half ashamed of," but still hoped to publish.[10] Despite adolescent ambition, Cholmondeley had to wait until her mid-twenties to place a story: in 1882 publishing a humorous sketch in *The Graphic* called "All is Fair in Love and War"; in 1885 a sensational tale called "Geoffrey's Wife," the narrative of a young husband who loses his wife in a Paris mob, tries to rescue her, and finds to his horror that he has saved a lower-class woman of the streets.[11] Her first novel, *The Danvers Jewels* (1887), a "mystery-sensation novel . . . on the Wilkie Collins pattern,"[12] turns on a plot of stolen Indian gems. Its sequel, *Sir Charles Danvers* (1889), reworks themes and plots of George Eliot's *Mill on the Floss* and *Middlemarch*, focusing on its heroine's matrimonial dilemma to marry for love or for money, duty, and social reform (in the latter case to a suitor who will allow his new wife to "improve" the cottages on his estate). *Diana Tempest* (1893), Cholmondeley's third, quite successful novel, protests against the marriage market, but its protest is almost overwhelmed by its sensational plot of illegitimacy, sibling rivalry, and attempted assassination of the heir.

These early works of sensation fiction were published by the firm of Richard Bentley and Son, first serially in its magazine *Temple Bar*, then in triple-decker format for circulating libraries. As the *Waterloo Directory* notes, Bentley's enterprises, including *Temple Bar*, were produced "for the comfortable, literate, but ill-educated middle-class which read magazines for pure entertainment and easy instruction."[13] Given this middle-brow audience, Cholmondeley and her early novels were not destined for distinction.

Despite the inauspicious start, by the end of the 1890s Cholmondeley had written a novel considered "advanced."[14] *Red Pottage* (1899), with its double plot of a domestic heroine learning of her lover's adultery and an artistic heroine facing her brother's treachery, offers a serious protest against the sexual double standard, commits itself to sisterhood as a source of strength and social reform, and depicts a woman novelist as a figure of genius—all features of New Woman fiction.[15] Percy Lubbock recalled the novel as "a scandal": "'Have you Read Pottage?'" he remembers asking his literary friends. "Wasn't she clever, wasn't she cruel?—but wasn't she wise and just?"[16] How—and why—did Cholmondeley come to write such a book, given her earlier works of light fiction?

Personal matters figure into the transition from imitator of Collins, Eliot, and Rhoda Broughton, a family friend and literary mentor, to New Woman novelist. In a private journal entry, written after the success of *Red Pottage*, Cholmondeley insists,

> It is not my talent which has placed me where I am, but the repression of my youth, my unhappy love-affair, the having to confront a hard dull life, devoid of anything I cared for intellectually, and being hampered at every turn I feebly made by constant constant [*sic*] illness. What I have thought, what I have felt, what I have suffered in those past years has been the "kindling" that year after year fed the flame which kept me alive.[17]

Like other New Women, she saw herself as writing of—and out of—her gendered, bodily experience; she used her fiction to "re-enact autobiographical dilemmas"—as Ann Heilmann suggests New Woman novelists often did.[18] Among these was a failed engagement, from which Cholmondeley turned to authorship as a resource and distraction. Equally important were the death of her invalid mother and the retirement of her clergyman father, which released her from a sense of family responsibility and respectability, and allowed her to move from Hodnet rectory in Shropshire to London, a relocation that put her in touch with an advanced literary set that included Howard Sturgis, Henry James, her old friend Rhoda Broughton, and the Findlater sisters.

Yet it would be a mistake to treat Cholmondeley's transformation in purely psychological terms. Of great importance was her reading of New

Woman novelists in the 1890s and her change of publishers in the same decade—a change precipitated by the crisis in publishing fiction. Writing *Red Pottage* was most likely triggered by reading Grant Allen's *The Woman Who Did* (1895), in which Herminia Barton says to Alan Merrick, as she refuses legalized marriage, "Think how easy it would be for me . . . to do as other women do . . . to be false to my sex, a traitor to my convictions; to sell my kind for a mess of pottage . . . I know what marriage is . . . by what unholy sacrifices it is sustained and made possible . . . and I can't embrace it."[19] Unlike Allen, and writing largely against him, Cholmondeley depicts not the effects of a *woman's* decision to avoid marriage but rather the effects of the sexual double standard on both men and women and the ways in which various characters sell their birthright for a mess of pottage, whether the male protagonist, Hugh Scarlett, by indulging in an affair with a married woman or female characters by marrying for money, rank, and security. In this exploration Cholmondeley extends a theme that she had introduced in *Diana Tempest*, where a young woman marries the wrong brother and wonders if "she had sold her birthright for red pottage"; a chapter epigraph subsequently confirms her fear, adapting the story of Jacob and Esau in Genesis 25: "After the red pottage comes the exceedingly bitter cry."[20]

A further impetus to Cholmondeley's new direction was Mary Harkness's *In Darkest London* (1891), a New Woman novel that influenced the depiction of Hester Gresley, the writer-protagonist of *Red Pottage*, and her friend, Rachel West. Hester's book *An Idyll of East London* pays tribute to Harkness's novel and critiques its socialist ideology, depressing (from Cholmondeley's perspective) in its unrelieved Marxism and rejection of any effective individualism. Hester and Rachel show that individual and collaborative action by and between women can alter lives and contribute to social reform—a New Woman theme that *Red Pottage* endorses.

Yet it was the demise of Richard Bentley and Son that provoked the greatest disruption in Cholmondeley's career and, I believe, instigated a change in the mode of her fiction. Broughton had introduced Cholmondeley to George Bentley in the mid-1880s, and the Bentley archive reveals a cordial correspondence between author and publisher. Bentley enthusiastically praised Cholmondeley's first novel *The Danvers Jewels* as "your bright and humorous story" and urged her "to continue to give me the benefit of such papers."[21] Bentley readily accepted her next two novels for publication in periodical and book format, paying £50 for copyright for *Sir Charles Danvers* (with a contract specifying an additional £20 for each 100 sold over the initial 550 copies of the Library edition) and increasing her royalties as her sales and reputation rose.[22] Cholmondeley received £500 for *Diana Tempest*: £250 for serial publication in *Temple Bar*, £150 for book publication, and a £100 bonus (after the novel went into a fifth edition).[23] These rates fall below those paid to Broughton, who often sold copyright of her novels for £800, but they represent Bentley's estimate of solid worth.

When George Bentley died in 1895 and his son Richard sold out to Macmillan, Cholmondeley lost a ready, comfortable outlet for her fiction. The publisher's archive does not make clear whether Macmillan tried to "edge out" this particular woman writer, as Tuchman and Fortin suggest that the firm systematically did to others,[24] or simply didn't keep up with the correspondence required by the transition. In either case, Cholmondeley felt neglected and unwanted—and so took *A Devotée* (1897), her next novel, and the plan for *Red Pottage* to Edward Arnold. In an exchange with Macmillan after *Red Pottage*'s success (it went into a fifth edition within a year), Macmillan wrote to ask why she had left the firm. She responded that she had supposed "you would have written to me had you wished for the new book on which Mr. Bentley knew I was engaged," admitting that she was "disappointed that I only heard from you when several months had elapsed, and when I was in treaty with another publisher."[25] In a subsequent letter, written after Macmillan sent an apology, she added,

> I was a very small writer and you are a very great publisher. It never entered my head to write to you. But I will frankly own I was deeply disappointed at not hearing from you.
>
> Perhaps you will say I ought to have taken for granted that you were interested in my books, but my modesty (since quite extinct) was <u>then</u> in robust health.
>
> Until I received your letter of June 24th [1900] I had remained under the impression that the firm did not value my books.[26]

Cholmondeley's impression—that Macmillan had quietly dropped her and resumed correspondence only after she had published a best-seller—seems accurate, given the five-year hiatus in the letters. Despite the belated wooing, she turned down an advance contract on her next book, telling Macmillan that their offer did "not compare favourably" with others in hand. She published her later works of fiction with John Murray.

Losing Bentley and then Macmillan dealt a blow to Cholmondeley's self-esteem—what she sometimes referred to as her "Plantagenet blood."[27] Yet the move away from Bentley benefited her professional career, opened new markets for her work, and altered the kind of fiction she produced. Her depiction of a female writer-protagonist occurs only after the loss of Bentley, and her choice of a writer of genius as heroine of *Red Pottage*, striving to create transcendent work, asserts her desire to be treated seriously as an artist. Lubbock, who as literary executor had access to Cholmondeley's journals and drew on them for his memoir *Mary Cholmondeley: A Sketch from Memory*, chose not to quote from the entries of the mid-1890s that might document this transition; instead, he passes over the crucial years, commenting, "I am not able to follow her through the years that changed this young woman."[28] But what Lubbock includes from 1900, just after the success of *Red Pottage*, reveals that Cholmondeley had determined to prove her worth: "In old days when no one thought anything of me I always had in the depths of my mind a stubborn feeling that I was worth something after all. I thought more of myself when others thought little of me."[29] With her new novel she demonstrated that she was "worth something"; yet still she wondered, "Why did they not see me then as they think they see me now? I am the same woman."[30]

The New Woman and the Writer of Genius

Hester Gresley, the writer-protagonist of *Red Pottage*, becomes the means by which Cholmondeley represents her worth and the vehicle by which she expresses her philosophy of literary creation. Hester possesses the fundamental traits of a writer of genius—and by so endowing her, Cholmondeley lays claim to her own talent. As a child Hester is a gifted storyteller, entertaining her "stolid, silent, solid" friend Rachel with tales of captive princesses, conversations between sparrows, and descriptions of city trees retreating nightly to "the green country to see their friends."[31] As a young woman, Hester is nervous, fragile, and sensitive, unlike her friend and domestic counterpart Rachel: "Rachel was physically strong. Hester was weak. The one was calm, patient, practical, equable, the other imaginative, unbalanced, excitable" (36). So, too, Hester is more verbally adept than her clergyman brother, who styles himself an author but whose prose takes "various tortuous and unnatural windings" (62) and commits every possible cliché. Like Charlotte Brontë in a state of "making out," Hester has visionary moments; when she speaks to Rachel about the book she is writing, "Everything else was forgotten. Hester's eyes burned. Her colour came and went. She was transfigured" (80). Hester, the narrator says, was one "of those who worship art" (81).

In presenting Hester as a sensitive genius, Cholmondeley risked creating an "abnormal" female character, as judged by eugenic theories of the 1890s. As Boumelha has documented, the studies of Francis Galton, Cesare Lombroso, and Havelock Ellis made "genius" near kin to "idiocy," associated it with degeneracy, and in women linked it to hysteria and madness.[32] What prevents Hester, as New Woman writer, from becoming a solipsistic visionary, decadent, or hysterical female is that her art emerges from a bond of sisterhood, a commitment to and love of her friend Rachel. Sisterly love represents a *normative* female emotion; the Victorians considered the sororal relationship, both ideal and real, to be a "bond that would transcend other earthly relationships"; "no one else, . . . not parents, children, or even a husband, could provide the same sort of support, comfort and love that a sister could."[33] This cultural belief in sororal unity, in women's supportive relationships with one another, affirms rather than pathologizes Hester as a writer.

When Rachel suffers a loss of income and social status, Hester stands by her friend, giving half her pocket money and supplying Rachel's material needs, frustrated that she can do no more. From this giving—not of money only but of sympathy and support—emerges Hester's scene of vocation.

> And as Hester leaned against Rachel the yearning of her soul towards her suddenly lit up something which had long lain colossal but in-apprehended in the depths of her mind. Her paroxysm of despair at her own powerlessness was followed by a lightning flash of self-revelation. She saw, as in a dream, terrible, beautiful, inaccessible, but distinct, where her power lay, of which restless bewildering hints had so often mocked her. (37)

Cholmondeley does not describe the composition of Hester's first novel, *An Idyll of East London*. After this visionary scene, there is a blank space, then the statement: "A year later Hester's first book, 'An Idyll of East London,' was reaping its harvest of astonished indignation and admiration" (38)—as if the significant process lies in the discovery of sympathy, the expression of desire, the revelation of vocation, not in writing itself. Like the sisterhood of Anna Jameson's *Communion of Labour* or Anna Mary Howitt's *The Sisters in Art*, the bonding of Hester and Rachel produces art that is aesthetically satisfying and socially redeeming.

In this commitment to sisterhood Hester resembles other New Women characters; in the words of Ella Hepworth Dixon, a contemporary novelist, "All we modern women mean to help each other now."[34] What makes Hester different from other New Woman *artists* is the omission of her struggle in the marketplace, the vicissitudes of fame, finances, and fickle editors that other fictional women writers typically encounter in Grub Street. Unlike Mary Erle in Dixon's *The Story of a Modern Woman* (1894), Hester does not tramp from one dingy London publisher's office to another, selling her fiction for two guineas, negotiating to write a society column for *The Fan*, or listening to male editors explain how "to write stories which other young ladies like to read."[35] Unlike Cosima Chudleigh in Emily Morse Symonds's *A Writer of Books* (1898), Hester faces no publisher who tells her to "cut out all the dissertations and all the dialogue that doesn't advance the action of the story," nor does earning money require the "slashing and mutilating [of] the offspring of her brain."[36] While we might explain such omissions by pointing to Cholmondeley's remote life in a Shropshire rectory or privileged financial status as the daughter of gentry, or by treating her as an amateur as Lubbock and Colby have done,[37] these explanations do not square with Cholmondeley's known transactions with editors and publishers, or with her intentions in *Red Pottage*. Her business correspondence shows that she understood the process of submission, acceptance, negotiation, production, and advertisement and that she bargained for fair payment, even if she never resorted to the pleading that hard-pressed women writers like Margaret Oliphant sometimes did.[38] Significantly, in *Red Pottage* the material details of literary production are relegated to a minor role and associated with hack writers—as when Hester's brother receives proofs for an article in the *Southminster Advertiser* and the siblings correct them together.

Literary production for Hester, in contrast, is represented as a divinely inspired creative process—perhaps what Ann Heilmann calls a "clever tactical move" in self-representation,[39] but also a reflection of Cholmondeley's beliefs about art. As Lubbock notes, "She made her own books in her own deliberate way; but her eye was always on her vision, her apprehension of truth, and the growing object under her hands, the book itself, was shaped in a faith of which she could give no certain account."[40]

The novel allegorizes Art as a modern Christ calling the woman writer to "walk upon the troubled waves of art" (154). It figures Hester's struggle to complete her book as the disciples' desire and fear: "So our little faith keeps us in the boat, or fails us in the waves of that wind-swept sea" (154). When Hester finally finishes, the narrator presents her struggle as a reenactment of Christ's agony in the garden of Gethsemane: "The night was over, and that other long night of travail and patience and faith, and strong rowing in darkness against the stream, was over, too, at last—at last" (153). This scene of struggle is set on a Sunday morning—in explicit juxtaposition of the woman writer's act of worship in literary creation versus the conventional clergyman's worship in a parish church.

The destructive force in the novel becomes, then, not the literary marketplace, not editors, publishers, or critics who overlook or undervalue Hester's work, but her brother James, the clergyman whose limited, commonplace views lead him to destroy the manuscript of Hester's new novel, *Husks*. James engages in an inquisitional-style book-burning, condemning the religious philosophy of the novel and telling his wife that he has "been reading the worst book I have come across yet, and it was written by my own sister under my own roof" (261). Cholmondeley thus presents a New Woman writer as stifled by resistance to her creative imagination and intellectual achievement, not by the conditions of Grub Street. And she links Hester's work to the preeminent women authors of the nineteenth century as she echoes the words of their critics in James's comments on his sister's novel: "'It is dreadfully coarse in places,' continued Mr. Gresley, who had the same opinion of George Eliot's works" (263). "Coarse" was the term of opprobrium assigned to Charlotte Brontë's *Jane Eyre* and Emily Brontë's *Wuthering Heights*—a denigration Gaskell worked hard to erase in *The Life of Charlotte Brontë*. George Eliot was Cholmondeley's model in art, the novelist who had "broadened the domain of our fiction" and "uplifted it to a moral and an intellectual eminence where it had never been before."[41] As an artist, Hester extends this distinguished literary tradition.

In her decision to present Hester as an author of genius and intellectual stature, Cholmondeley varies a strategy that Charlotte Riddell had used in *A Struggle for Fame* to resist devaluation in the literary field. Both novelists turn to the Brontës (Cholmondeley also to George Eliot) for the symbolic capital required to raise their artist-figures above the level of hack or producer of popular fiction. But whereas Riddell depicts the grinding conditions of the literary market of the 1870s in which Glenarva Westley struggles to survive, Cholmondeley dissociates her woman writer from the marketplace and emphasizes instead the deep intellectual resistance to innovative art against which Hester labors. It is as if Cholmondeley has decided that her strategy must be to represent the intellectual struggle, not the material conditions, of her work. Indeed, in *Red Pottage* the literary marketplace is represented by "the *raté*" who attend Sybell Loftus's second-rate salon: "the 'new woman' with stupendous lopsided opinions on difficult Old Testament subjects"; "the 'lady authoress' with a mission to show up the vices of a society which she knew only by hearsay"; and the male author of "Unashamed" who insists that "true art requires . . . a faithful rendering of a great experience" and then looks around, "as if challenging the world to say that 'Unashamed' was not a lurid personal reminiscence" (20, 24). Hester quietly stays in her room and writes great books—in a contrast that dissociates her from the New Women of Oxbridge education and crusading polemics, as well as from naturalist and decadent writers of the fin de siècle.

In this dissociation Cholmondeley has been criticized for validating herself at the expense of other women writers or, a lesser fault, "betraying a particular cultural anxiety."[42] Yet this may be less cultural symptom than authorial strategy—the kind of strategy that Pierre Bourdieu analyzes in Flaubert's *A Sentimental Education* for distinguishing the writer-hero Frederic Moreau, "devoted to pure art," from the popular bourgeois authors and businessmen who surround him.[43] Cholmondeley distinguishes Hester from the inferior, professionalized authors who populate Sybell's salon, thus separating the real thing from the shams who dominate the English literary field. And this distinction is reinforced by the critical estimate of *Husks* that the Bishop of Southminster offers to James Gresley ("he considered it the finest book that had been written in his day" [295]) and by the contract that Hester's publisher offers for its sale (£1,000 [297]). In this fictional realm, Hester's literary genius and devotion to art lead to critical esteem and, eventually, economic reward. That she is not silenced by her brother's act of treachery is made clear in Cholmondeley's next novel, *Moth and Rust* (1902), where the heroine Anne reads *Inasmuch*, a new, highly regarded novel by Hester Gresley.[44]

Cholmondeley's strategy in *Red Pottage* produced an immediate success. In critical terms, the *Spectator* praised the novel as "ingenious, original, and abounding in strong dramatic situations" and singled out the "extremely interesting and well-contrasted subsidiary plot" of Hester for special notice, calling the artist-heroine "a most fascinating specimen of the intellectually emancipated modern woman."[45] (No trace of the hysterical New Woman, despite Hester's physical collapse after her brother burns her manuscript.) The review in the *Academy* for 9 December 1899, written by Arnold Bennett, was even stronger. "Miss Cholmondeley," it began, "is one of the fortunate few for whom the gates of success have opened wide almost at first knock."[46] If "at first knock" was inaccurate, given the fifteen years of labor that preceded her first critical success, the rest of the review gave Cholmondeley what she wished: "plenty of invention, plenty of wit, some humour, some imagination, and a fresh touch of originality."[47] American notices went further by identifying Cholmondeley with her artist-heroine and attributing Hester's traits of genius and solid literary learning to her author: *Harper's Bazaar* noted that Cholmondeley "was brought up on a solid foundation of English literature in the very library where her great-uncle the bishop [Bishop Reginald Heber] used to write his sermons"—as if fingering his volumes might have caused literary talent to pass from his "poet's fingers" to hers.[48] Such critical judgments led to large sales—over 20,000 copies almost immediately in 1899[49]—and to solicitations for future work.

On the popular end of the spectrum, Cholmondeley found her fiction solicited by women's magazines, as did other New Woman writers who wrote best-sellers.[50] Immediately after publishing *Red Pottage*, she contracted with the *Lady's Realm* for a story of 5,000 words, and in 1906 serialized *Prisoners (fast bound in misery and iron)* in that periodical (which also featured the work of Sarah Grand).[51] On the highbrow end, she placed "The Pitfall" with Henry Newbolt in the *Monthly Review* (1901), warning him that it "is what I believe is called 'advanced.' It has already raised a blister on a sensitive mind to which I have privately administered it."[52] In her negotiations with Newbolt over payment, she explained that she had sent the story to him but asked less than usual for it (only £50 for 8,500 words instead of her usual £40 for 5,000) because "that particular story had to be placed where it would reach a cultivated reader. In ordinary magazines I am most certain it would have failed to make the impression I desired. And uneducated persons would have been offended by it."[53]

Cholmondeley's success led also to solicitations for essays on modern topics—the kind of cultural commentary that might have secured her reputation as a woman of letters.[54] In 1901 the *Monthly Review* published a satirical essay on advertisement, "An Art in its Infancy," in which Cholmondeley compared the modest ads in eighteenth-century newspapers with the modern craze for covering the landscape with posters and seeking public endorsements of new products. Under the title "Advertising and Advertisers," Cholmondeley (via her agent, Curtis Brown) sold this essay to the American periodical, *Littell's Living Age*, and reprinted it in the *Eclectic Magazine*. After the turn of the century she wrote "Votes for Men" for the

Cornhill (1909) and sold it also to the American *Harper's Bazaar* (1910).[55] This satirical piece, set in the twenty-first century, imagines a Queen Eugenia hearing the pleas of male suffragists and rejecting them with the same arguments that Edwardians used against women's suffrage (or laughing them out of court by quoting the commonplace wisdom—for instance, "You know, and I know, and every school girl knows, that what rules the birth-rate rules the world").[56] After *Red Pottage*, in other words, Cholmondeley gained a reputation as an elite novelist, enabling her to experiment with more "advanced" work even as she turned to new women's magazines for the placement of her popular short fiction.

Yet modern assessments conclude (justifiably) that Cholmondeley never managed to consolidate her gains. Carol Rhoades, in *Nineteenth-Century British Women Writers: A Bio-Bibliographical Sourcebook*, notes, "Cholmondeley's reputation was short-lived."[57] Kate Flint observes, "none of her remaining volumes—*Moth and Rust* (1902); *The Lowest Rung* (1908), a collection of novellas; and *Notwithstanding* (1913)—were as popular or well received as her earlier writing."[58] In a typical judgment Elaine Showalter states that Cholmondeley's career "declined after the success of *Red Pottage*. Her subsequent novels were ignored; by the time her 'ancient father' died in 1910, . . . the inspiration of her youth was long past."[59] While this is not quite true in that her novella *Moth and Rust* received serious critical attention, it is nonetheless the case that Cholmondeley never fulfilled the promise of the 1899 *Academy* review by Bennett:

> Miss Cholmondeley suffers from no lack of inspiration, and though she views the world with certain easily defined social prejudices, her sense of the ridiculous will save her from that narrowness into which too many novelists—especially women-novelists—have fallen step by step while catering for a large audience. . . . Gifted with plenty of invention, plenty of wit, some humour, some imagination, and a fresh touch of originality which lends allurement to everything she writes, Miss Cholmondeley has an excellent chance of taking rank with the novelists whose work is worthy of serious consideration and serious praise. It is greatly in her favour that she imitates no one.[60]

Bennett's assessment falls short of the high praise that Meredith bestowed on Meynell when he prophesied that she would "some day rank as one of the great Englishwomen of Letters,"[61] but it nonetheless hits the keynotes of distinction: "inspiration," "invention," "wit," "humour," "imagination," "originality." These were the traits that secured Meynell's reputation. Why did Cholmondeley fail to attain (or sustain) the literary rank that Bennett predicted? This is a question we might pose as well for other New Woman writers (though not in a biographical mode, as Showalter's "inspiration of her youth" implicitly does).

Some factors may be particular to Cholmondeley's case. Bennett's warning—about becoming too serious about "certain . . . social prejudices," about losing or lacking a sense of the ridiculous—sounds too much like late twentieth-century complaints that feminists can't take a joke to credit fully. Yet Bennett put his finger on a problem that Cholmondeley herself acknowledged: a tendency to "preach," an inclination to imitate the "wisdom" of George Eliot (whose work she admired), and to moralize too much for contemporary taste.[62] In a letter written before the publication of "The Pitfall," she voiced her uneasiness that she sometimes might "preach and point morals" and asked Henry Newbolt, her editor, to "be a friend and point it out" when she did.[63] In a letter of 1906, she expressed a related anxiety about the reception of her novel *Prisoners*: "I have been very nervous and depressed about it, and I was warned by the friends who read the MS. that it could never be popular as it was so grave."[64] This tendency toward *gravitas* had been balanced in *Red Pottage* by a witty satire on the clergy and middle-class domestic life. Later novels lacked this balance—and, for whatever reason, whether inability or lack of inspiration, Cholmondeley did not turn her discursive gifts toward essay writing and cultural commentary.

Yet rather than put the burden of failure solely on Cholmondeley and her art, we might consider the market conditions that she faced at the turn of the century and that posed obstacles for all women authors. These conditions in part account for her fading from view and complicate the common explanations for the New Woman writers' loss of rank and reputation, including their focus on social and political issues that became outdated or that eclipsed aesthetic concerns (what Showalter calls "a quarrel that 'leads to rhetoric but not poetry' "); their failure to produce great, lasting literary art; the deep cultural resistance to both decadent and New Woman writers and their social ideologies; or the unfortunate luck of having their literary experiments taken over by male modernists.[65] While Cholmondeley might have identified cultural resistance as the greatest obstacle to her popularity, I suggest that specific aspects of periodical and book publishing at the end of the nineteenth century directly impinged on the development of her career and that these were aspects over which she had little control.

The New Woman and the Literary Marketplace of the Fin de Siècle

One problem that all fin-de-siècle writers faced was the "momentarity" of the high-culture magazine of the 1890s, what Osbert Burdett notes in *The Beardsley Period* as "the novelty and brevity of the life of the cultural magazine."[66] We might compare, for example, the brevity of the *Scots Observer* (1888–94) or the *Yellow Book* (1894–97) with the longevity of *Blackwood's Edinburgh Magazine* (1817–1980) in which Margaret Oliphant and George

Eliot established their reputations as novelists, or of the *Westminster Review* (1824–1914), in which Harriet Martineau and George Eliot published some of their most distinguished cultural commentary. Long-running Victorian periodicals provided women authors with a regular outlet for their fiction, essays, and reviews and thus an opportunity to establish careers and build reputations. With Bentley's *Temple Bar* (1860–1906), Cholmondeley formed an association with a long-running periodical, one in which she could develop her fiction writing, if also learn to conform to a house style. But after she lost Bentley as her publisher, she was never able to establish another such continuing relationship. She made a good attempt with the *Monthly Review* (1900–1907) under Henry Newbolt, where she placed a few pieces, but he retired from the editorship in 1904, just three years after they met, and the periodical folded soon thereafter. Although she engaged an American agent, Curtis Brown, who placed many of her stories in respected, remunerative periodicals like *Harper's Bazaar* and *Scribner's Monthly*, Cholmondeley never regained a regular place in an English periodical. Unlike her contemporary Alice Meynell, who always had *Merry England* as an outlet and, in the 1890s and 1900s, got a regular berth on the *Pall Mall Gazette*, Cholmondeley lacked the professional security requisite to establishing herself as a woman of letters.

A second problematic aspect of the periodical market in the 1890s was its deployment of the "cult of personality." We need only think of Oscar Wilde and *Woman's World*, or Aubrey Beardsley and the *Yellow Book*, or Sarah Grand writing for, but also featuring as a modern female cyclist in, the *Lady's Realm*[67] to recognize the importance of marketing oneself as an "aesthete" or a "decadent" or "New Woman." Cholmondeley never found public self-display easy. After the publication of *Red Pottage*, a few periodicals, mostly American, tried to capitalize on associations between her life and fiction by printing pseudo-interviews. *Munsey's Magazine* carried a column of "Literary Chat," subtitled "Autobiography and Fiction—Mary Cholmondeley's Stories and Her Life," that drew parallels between the author and her heroine; portrayed Mary as the ward of a fashionable society woman; and tried to make Cholmondeley into a literary personality.[68] Some American reissues of her novels—a 1900 Appleton edition of *Diana Tempest*, for instance—included a similar biographical sketch and a glamorous, youthful portrait of the author, draped in a fur stole (figure 28). But this attempt at public personality never went far, whether because, in her aristocratic mode, Cholmondeley resisted it or because, in her shyness, she simply could not carry through. (Though Alice Meynell might privately have raised her eyebrows over interviews in *Sylvia's Journal* and the *Queen*,[69] she let them be printed—and then sent apologies to any friend, publisher, or fellow author whom she thought might be offended.)[70]

Cholmondeley acknowledged her difficulty in creating a convincing authorial persona in a preface to her 1908 collection, *The Lowest Rung*. She

FIGURE 28. Mary Cholmondeley, frontispiece to American edition of *Diana Tempest* (1900). Courtesy of the Yale University Library.

begins by observing, "I have been writing books for five-and-twenty years, novels of which I believe myself to be the author, in spite of the fact that I have been assured over and over again that they are not my work."[71] She continues, in a humorous vein, to enumerate the various claims made by others to authorship of her work. There is the "charming elderly man" who "discussed one of my earliest books with such appreciation that I at last remarked that I had written it," and who then "gravely and gently" told her, "I know that to be untrue." There is another man who "actually announce[d] himself to be the author of 'Red Pottage' in the presence of a large number of people"—and was routed by "the late Mr. William Sharp," who knew better. Then there are friends and relatives who acknowledge her to be an author but who deny her any originality, making such comments as "We all recognized Mrs. Alwynn at once as Mrs. —, *and we all say it is not in the least like her.*"[72] Clerical critics behave no better—one claiming, for instance, that the character of the Reverend Mr. Gresley in *Red Pottage* "was merely a piece of spite on my part, as I had probably been jilted by a clergyman."[73] Although Cholmondeley relates these anecdotes with wit, she admits "they were real enough to give me not a little pain at the time."[74]

That they continued to cause pain is evidenced by the fact that she saved them up for a preface, in which she asserted her authorial identity and literary originality. That she saw the problem as not wholly her own but as challenging women writers generally is clear from her conversation about similar experiences with Lucy Clifford, author of novels about solitary, struggling women, including *Aunt Anne* (1892), a book much admired by Arnold Bennett.[75] Presumably Cholmondeley felt that male authors suffered less from such erasure. She continued to use the prefaces to her collections as sites for asserting her authorial identity and views on art.[76] Her last volume, *The Romance of His Life and Other Romances* (1921), includes an introductory sketch, "In Praise of a Suffolk Cottage," about the place where "most of these stories were written."[77] In memorializing the author's home, Cholmondeley memorializes herself and her career, creating a final image of the writer as an Englishwoman happy in a cottage she has refurbished with the profits of her labors and with the aesthetic taste that has transformed a "forlorn, disheveled, and untenanted" house into a home "millionaires would tumble over each other to secure."[78]

Cholmondeley's case might lead us to speculate about the role of periodicals and book publishing—the very market conditions that she avoided depicting in *Red Pottage*—in the making or breaking of New Woman writers. Individually and collectively, they seem to disappear after the first decade of the twentieth century. We can, in some cases, point to specific causes: the shift from literature to activism in the suffrage campaign that dominated Sarah Grand's mature years; the marriages and divorces that forced Graham R. Tomson to change her name and lose her authorial identity; the decision of Ella Hepworth Dixon to turn from novel writing to journalism when, following in her father's footsteps, she became editor of the *Englishwoman.* Yet the erasure of the New Woman author cannot be simply a matter of biography or aesthetics, that is, of the personal tragedies, idiosyncrasies, or career diversions of individual writers or the lack of lasting literary value of their work as a group. Nor can it simply be the case that, as

Showalter argues, "all the feminist novelists had but one story to tell and exhausted themselves in its narration."[79]

Changes in fin-de-siècle book and periodical publishing suggest a more complicated story. If losing Bentley pushed Cholmondeley out of a publishing rut, it also gave her no obvious road to travel. Without a regular place in a periodical where she might develop her fiction and her reputation, she lost the possibility of becoming a permanent name. Without a regular conduit from periodical to book, it became more difficult to consolidate her fiction in a recognizably permanent form or to advance her career at the moment of highest acclaim. The expansion of American markets produced more income—as Cholmondeley's personal letters to Broughton attest.[80] But the demise of long-running periodicals and the short lives of new ones, along with the changes in the book market of the 1890s, produced a dampening effect on the careers of Cholmondeley and other New Woman authors and a decrease in opportunities to achieve distinction as women of letters. Although this study of the Victorian woman of letters disclaims any large historical arc of rise and fall, it does finally reveal that the rise or fall of any individual woman author was dependent on the literary field in which she produced her work.

❧ NOTES ❧

Introduction

1. For these examples, see Catherine Gallagher, *Nobody's Story: The Vanishing Acts of Women Writers in the Marketplace, 1670–1820* (Princeton: Princeton University Press, 1994); Betty A. Schellenberg, *The Professionalization of Women Writers in Eighteenth-Century Britain* (Cambridge: Cambridge University Press, 2005); Jan Fergus and Janice Farrar Thaddeus, "Women, Publishers, and Money, 1790–1820," *Studies in Eighteenth-Century Culture*, ed. John Yolton and Leslie Ellen Brown, 17 (1987), 191–207; Jan Fergus, "The Professional Woman Writer," in *The Cambridge Companion to Jane Austen*, ed. Edward Copeland and Juliet McMaster (Cambridge: Cambridge University Press, 1997), 12–31; and Carol A. Bock, "Authorship, the Brontës, and *Fraser's Magazine*: 'Coming Forward' as an Author in Early Victorian England, *Victorian Literature and Culture* 29 (2001), 241–66, as important examples of recent studies of women's professionalism. While I take a different approach by situating women's authorship within larger nineteenth-century debates about the profession of letters, I also draw on the methods established by these scholars for studying the material conditions of authorship, tracking women authors' identification with professional groups, and recognizing their strategies of public self-presentation.

2. Walter Besant, *Fifty Years Ago* (New York: Harper and Brothers, 1888), 262. Besant notes, "New professions have come into existence, and the old professions are more esteemed. It was formerly a poor and beggarly thing to belong to any other than the three learned professions. . . . Artists, writers, journalists, were considered Bohemian."

3. Lee Erickson, *The Economy of Literary Form: English Literature and the Industrialization of Publishing, 1800–1850* (Baltimore: Johns Hopkins University Press, 1996), 72.

4. *OED*, s.v. "profession," III.6.a. F. D. Maurice makes this distinction (cited in this entry) in his 1839 *Lectures on the Education of the Middle Classes*: "*Profession* in our country . . . is expressly that kind of business which deals primarily with men

as men, and is thus distinguished from a Trade, which provides for the external wants or occasions of men."

5. Later in the century, in a similar effort at upgrading status, publishers would refer to themselves as a profession and demote bookselling to a trade.

6. Catherine Seville, *Literary Copyright Reform in Early Victorian England: The Framing of the 1842 Copyright Act* (Cambridge: Cambridge University Press, 1999), 25. Clare Pettitt's study of the overlapping discourses of inventors and writers in the 1830s and 1840s, both working to secure ownership of their mental labor in patent and copyright laws, reveals the uncertainty of the trade-profession distinction; see her *Patent Inventions: Intellectual Property and the Victorian Novel* (Oxford: Oxford University Press, 2004), esp. ch. 2, "Property in Labour: Inventors and Writers in the 1830s and 1840s," 36–83.

7. William Wordsworth, preface to *Lyrical Ballads* (1802), in *The Prose Works of William Wordsworth*, ed. W.J.B. Owen and Jane Worthington Smyser, 3 vols. (Oxford: Clarendon Press, 1974), I, 138.

8. Thomas Carlyle, "The Hero as Man of Letters," in *On Heroes, Hero-Worship, and the Heroic in History* (Lincoln: University of Nebraska Press, 1966), 157.

9. *OED*, s.v. "professional," III.6.a.

10. [G. H. Lewes], "The Condition of Authors in England, Germany, and France," *Fraser's Magazine* 35 (1847), 285; William Jerdan, *The Autobiography of William Jerdan, with his Literary, Political, and Social Reminiscences and Correspondence during the Last Fifty Years*, 4 vols. (London: Arthur Hall, Virtue, and Company, 1852–53). This debate occurs simultaneously with (indeed, is part of) the "Dignity of Literature" debate that pitted Thackeray against Dickens in the periodical press; see Clare Pettitt, "'The Spirit of Craft and Money-Making': The Indignities of Literature in the 1850s," in *Patent Inventions*, 149–203, which draws on the earlier work of Craig Howes, "*Pendennis* and the Controversy on 'The Dignity of Literature,'" *Nineteenth-Century Literature* 41 (1986), 269–98; Michael Lund, "Novels, Writers and Readers in 1850," *Victorian Periodicals Review* 17 (1984), 15–28; and Mark Cronin, "Henry Gowan, William Makepeace Thackeray, and 'The Dignity of Literature,' " *Dickens Quarterly* 16 (1999), 104–45.

11. See, e.g., Harold Perkin, *The Rise of Professional Society, England since 1880* (London: Routledge, 1989), esp. chs. 1 and 4; A. J. Engel, *From Clergyman to Don: The Rise of the Academic Profession in Nineteenth-Century Oxford* (Oxford: Clarendon Press, 1983); and Gaye Tuchman and Nina A. Fortin, *Edging Women Out: Victorian Novelists, Publishers, and Social Change* (New Haven: Yale University Press, 1989), 1–16.

12. *OED*, s.v. "letters," II.6.b. The use of the phrase clusters in the eighteenth century; the quotation from Scott (cited in this entry) is from *Works*, IV; *Biographies* II (1870), 191.

13. "Preface to the First Edition," "The Lay of the Last Minstrel," in *The Complete Poetical Works of Sir Walter Scott*, ed. Charles Eliot Norton (New York: Thomas Y. Crowell, 1894), 4. Scott wrote, "I determined that literature should be my staff, but not my crutch, and that the profits of my literary labor, however convenient otherwise, should not, if I could help it, become necessary to my ordinary expenses."

14. John Viscount Morley, *Recollections* (London: Macmillan, 1917), I, 125. Morley is discussing the working practices of various men of letters, with John Stuart Mill illustrating the former and the historian George Grote the latter.

15. These women were, in their day, referred to as "literary ladies" or "learned ladies," rather than "women of letters"—a nineteenth-century designation.

16. Norma Clarke, *The Rise and Fall of the Woman of Letters* (London: Pimlico, 2004), 3–4.

17. Schellenberg, *Professionalization of Women Writers in Eighteenth-Century Britain*, 76–77, 97.

18. Eighteenth-century women wrote these genres, as Susan Staves's *Literary History of Women's Writing in Britain, 1660–1789* (Cambridge: Cambridge University Press, 2006) attests, but regular professional payment for such writing did not become widespread for men or women until the nineteenth century. Indeed, Schellenberg links the process of women's professionalization in part with "the generic range of [women's] publishing" (*Professionalization of Women Writers in Eighteenth-Century Britain*, 12).

19. Commenting on her subtitle, *The Vanishing Acts of Women Writers in the Marketplace, 1670–1820*, Gallagher notes, "It is a place where the writers appear mainly through their frequently quite spectacular displacements and disappearances in literary and economic exchanges" (xviii). While I would not argue that women suddenly ceased vanishing in 1820, especially given the policy of anonymity in periodical publishing until the 1860s, I suggest that, with the emergence of a recognizable profession, women authors became visible participants in the Victorian literary marketplace.

20. Julia Kavanagh, *English Women of Letters: Biographical Sketches*, 2 vols. (London: Hurst and Blackett, 1863). The phrase appears in a pre-publication review, "English Women of Letters," in the *Saturday Review* 14 (1862), 718–19. Kavanagh does not include a preface to explain her use of the phrase or the principles underlying her literary genealogy, nor does Gertrude Townshend Mayer for her later collection, *Women of Letters*, 2 vols. (London: Richard Bentley, 1894). Mayer's volume expands the genealogy to include such seventeenth-century women as Margaret, Duchess of Newcastle, and Mary, Countess Cowper, and nineteenth-century women writers such as Mary Russell Mitford and Mary Shelley.

21. James Payn, "Fraudulent Guests," *Longman's Magazine* 1 (January 1883), 335.

22. Mrs. [Margaret] Oliphant, *Richard Sheridan* (London: Macmillan, 1883). In *Victorian Biography: Intellectuals and the Ordering of Discourse* (Hemel Hempstead: Harvester Wheatsheaf, 1993), 132–37, David Amigoni argues that the *Men of Letters* series attempted to separate "feminine" literature and literary style from "masculine" history and style and that the biographers "were ever vigilant against what they saw as deviant forms of 'literary' rhetoric which threatened to subvert 'the historic idea' " (137); while this binary informs the choice of authors, in my reading the series was not entirely consistent in enforcing this principle.

23. See George Meredith, "Mrs. Meynell's Two Books of Essays," *National Review* 27 (August 1896), 762–70. Additional volumes in the *Men of Letters* series on George Eliot by Leslie Stephens (1902), Fanny Burney (Madame d'Arblay) by Austin Dobson (1903), and Maria Edgeworth by Emily Lawless (1904) appeared after Morley's death. A volume on Christina Rossetti by Dorothy Margaret Stuart was added later (1930).

24. In her important study, *The Professionalization of Women Writers in Eighteenth-Century Britain*, Schellenberg argues that the process of professionali-

zation occurred during the second half of the eighteenth century, as evidenced by the increase in "the proportion of publishing by women and in the generic range of that publishing" (12). My account does not dispute this long process of professionalization for either men or women writers, and shares Schellenberg's emphasis on "generic range." I focus, however, on the public debate over literature as a profession, the material conditions that allowed writers to rely solely on literary work for their support, and the larger nineteenth-century context in which various middle-class professions developed.

25. Mary Poovey, "The Man-of-Letters Hero: *David Copperfield* and the Professional Writer," in *Uneven Developments: The Ideological Work of Gender in Mid-Victorian England* (Chicago: University of Chicago Press, 1988), 89.

26. A. S. Collins's useful *The Profession of Letters: A Study of the Relation of Author to Patron, Publisher, and Public, 1780–1832* (New York: E. P. Dutton, 1929) stops where this study begins. J. W. Saunders's *The Profession of English Letters* (London: Routledge and Kegan Paul, 1964) gives a broad overview from the fourteenth century and the rise of vernacular literature to the present day. Other accounts include Victor Bonham-Carter, *Authors by Profession*, 2 vols. (London: Society of Authors, 1978, 1984); Nigel Cross, *The Common Writer: Life in Nineteenth-Century Grub Street* (Cambridge: Cambridge University Press, 1985); and John Gross, *The Rise and Fall of the Man of Letters: A Study of the Idiosyncratic and the Humane in Modern Literature* (London: Macmillan 1969). More recently, Clare Pettitt gives an excellent account of the emergence of literary professionalism in the introductory chapter, "Heroes and Hero-Worship: Inventors and Writers from 1818 to 1900," of *Patent Inventions*, 1–35; Jennifer Ruth discusses fictional representations of various professions in *Novel Professions: Interested Disinterest and the Market of the Professional in the Victorian Novel* (Columbus: Ohio State University Press, 2006); and Susan E. Colón treats "materialist" versus "idealist" concerns in *The Professional Ideal in the Victorian Novel: The Works of Disraeli, Trollope, Gaskell, and Eliot* (New York: Palgrave Macmillan, 2007).

27. Walter Besant, *The Pen and the Book* (London: Thomas Burleigh, 1899).

28. Coventry Patmore, "Mrs. Meynell, Poet and Essayist," *Fortnightly Review* 52 (December 1892), 762, 763; see also Patmore's "Distinction," *Fortnightly Review*, n.s., 47 (June 1890), 826–34, for his initial judgment.

29. *George Eliot's Life as related in her Letters and Journals*, ed. J. W. Cross (New York: Harper and Brothers, 1885), I, 203.

30. Pierre Bourdieu, *The Field of Cultural Production: Essays on Art and Literature*, ed. Randal Johnson (New York: Columbia University Press, 1993), 42.

31. Dorothy Mermin, *Godiva's Ride: Women of Letters in England, 1830–1880* (Bloomington: Indiana University Press, 1993).

32. Mary Poovey, *The Proper Lady and Woman Writer* (Chicago: University of Chicago Press, 1984), 41. Sandra Gilbert and Susan Gubar's influential *Madwoman in the Attic* (New Haven: Yale University Press, 1979) initiated this approach. Influenced by Harold Bloom's Freudian *The Anxiety of Influence: A Theory of Poetry* (New York: Oxford University Press, 1973) and transmitted to feminist criticism of the 1980s and 1990s, the dual consciousness approach has largely given way to models that credit the woman writer's conscious construction of her public identity and literary career.

33. Harriet Martineau, *Autobiography*, ed. Linda H. Peterson (Petersborough: Broadview Press, 2007), 126.

34. Robert Darnton discusses the "communications circuit" in "What Is the History of Books?" *Daedalus* 111 (Summer 1982): 65–83.

CHAPTER 1
The Nineteenth-Century Profession of Letters and the Woman Author

1. Erickson, *The Economy of Literary Form*, 72.

2. Ibid., 91. In his *Autobiography*, I, 157, William Jerdan notes that he made "a weekly salary amounting to above 500*l* a-year" for editing the *Sun* and earned additional income by supplying provincial papers with copy.

3. Isaac Disraeli uses this designation as a chapter title in *The Calamities of Authors* (1812; London: Frederick Warne, 1840).

4. Gross's *Rise and Fall of the Man of Letters* excludes women from his account, except for a brief mention of George Eliot; in *Authors by Profession*, I, 100–114, Victor Bonham-Carter discusses Harriet Martineau and George Eliot; and in *The Common Writer*, Nigel Cross includes a chapter titled "The Female Drudge: Women Novelists and Their Publishers"—but, by definition, the "drudge" is not a "professional." The absence of scholarship on the Victorian professional woman author has been partially redressed by Barbara Onslow in *Women of the Press in Nineteenth-Century Britain* (Houndsmill, Basingstoke: Macmillan, 2000); Hilary Fraser, Stephanie Green, and Judith Johnston in *Gender and the Victorian Periodical* (Cambridge: Cambridge University Press, 2003); and Alexis Easley in *First-Person Anonymous: Women Writers and Victorian Print Media, 1830–1870* (Aldershot: Ashgate, 2004), as well as individual articles and chapters cited throughout this book. Robert Halsband's lecture, *The Ladies of Letters in the Eighteenth Century* (Los Angeles: William Andrews Clark Memorial Library, 1969), treats women of letters in an older, amateur sense of the term. Norma Clarke's *Rise and Fall of the Woman of Letters* focuses on eighteenth-century women writers of the Bluestocking circle and argues that the "fall" was inevitable given the ascendance of Victorian "separate spheres" and the "proper woman"—a historical view I complicate and contest.

5. Patrick Leary, "*Fraser's Magazine* and the Literary Life, 1830–1847," *Victorian Periodicals Review* 27 (Summer 1994), 106.

6. Miriam M. H. Thrall, *Rebellious Fraser's: Nol Yorke's Magazine in the Days of Maginn, Thackeray, and Carlyle* (1934; New York: AMS Press, 1966), 5.

7. "The Fraserians; or, The Commencement of the Year Thirty-Five, A Fragment," *Fraser's Magazine* 11 (January 1835), 1–27. The illustration appears between pages 2 and 3.

8. The phrase is Patrick Leary's, who notes in "*Fraser's Magazine* and the Literary Life," 112, that Coleridge had published nothing at all in the magazine—nor had Robert Southey, the Count d'Orsay, and William Jerdan, also included in the portrait.

9. Judith L. Fisher, "'In the Present Famine of Anything Substantial': *Fraser's* 'Portraits' and the Construction of Literary Celebrity; or, 'Personality, Personality is the Appetite of the Age,'" *Victorian Periodicals Review* 39 (Summer 2006), 98, 123.

10. "Regina's Maids of Honour," *Fraser's Magazine* 13 (January 1836), 80. The illustration is inset opposite the text.

11. On the popular pastry, see http://www.theoriginalmaidsofhonour.co.uk/.

12. See Leary, *"Fraser's Magazine* and the Literary Life," 105–26, and Patricia Marks, "Harriet Martineau: *Fraser's* 'Maid of [Dis]Honour,' " *Victorian Periodicals Review* 19 (Spring 1986), 28–34, as well as Fisher, *"Fraser's* 'Portraits,' " 116–23, who emphasizes the strategy of defining male authorship against a feminine model and thus de-legitimating the sexually ambiguous Regency model. In *"Colour'd Shadows": Contexts in Publishing, Printing, and Reading Nineteenth-Century British Women Writers* (Houndsmill, Basingstoke: Palgrave Macmillan, 2005), Terence Allan Hoagwood and Kathryn Ledbetter read these illustrations in terms of a related contrast between "domestic gentility rather than literary genius" (47).

13. "Regina's Maids of Honour," 80. William Maginn, the editor, composed the rhyming text.

14. The text of "The Fraserians" and the letters "FR—MAGA—" in the illustration suggest that James Fraser holds *Fraser's Magazine*, but the size is that of a book.

15. "The Fraserians," 12.

16. Leary, *"Fraser's Magazine* and the Literary Life," 113–14.

17. "The Fraserians," 17. As Leary observes, the Irish antiquary Thomas Crofton Croker was "a much-loved member of *Fraser's* inner circle" but made his living for "most of his adult life as a clerk in the Admiralty office" (*"Fraser's Magazine* and the Literary Life," 114).

18. For missing writers who frequently contributed, see Leary, *"Fraser's Magazine* and the Literary Life," 114–16.

19. For Bunbury, see Leary, *"Fraser's Magazine* and the Literary Life," 119; for Downing, see Thrall, *Rebellious Fraser's*, 282. Bunbury's contributions fall mostly after the portraits were published, but so, too, did Thackeray's. At the 1835 "sitting," Thackeray was only a potential contributor, not yet an active one.

20. See William Bates, ed., "Notes" to "No. 68.—Regina's Maids of Honour," *A Gallery of Illustrious Literary Characters* (London: Chatto and Windus, [1873]), 183. This book reproduces the drawings of Daniel Maclise and biographical sketches of William Maginn from the original articles in *Fraser's Magazine* published between 1830 and 1838.

21. The *Fraserian* portraits are modern in that they depict the authors, male and female, in their characteristic dress and do not, as in Richard Samuel's portrait *Nine Living Muses of Great Britain* (1779), show women in classical dress with harps, lyres, or manuscript rolls. In imitation of *Fraser's*, and to counter its interpretations, the *New Monthly Magazine* introduced portraits in the 1830s and 1840s, but many of these, like the Samuel's portrait, show authors in classical garb or portrait busts.

22. "Advertisement" to "The Bas Bleu; or, Conversation," in *The Works of Hannah More*, 2 vols. (Philadelphia: J. J. Woodward, 1830), I, 14.

23. More, *Works*, I, 17 (ll. 254–25, 264–73).

24. Schellenberg, *Professionalization of Women Writers in Eighteenth-Century Britain*.

25. Patricia Marks, in *"Fraser's* 'Maid of [Dis]Honour," suggests that Maginn alludes to Leigh Hunt's poem, "Blue Stocking Revels," but given that Hunt

published his poem in the *New Monthly Magazine* in 1837, the influence more likely goes the other way, with Hunt picking up on Maginn's allusions and the *Fraser's* portrait.

26. Dror Wahrman, *The Making of the Modern Self: Identity and English Culture in the Eighteenth Century* (New Haven: Yale University Press, 2004).

27. Quotations from the individual portraits of authors are taken from *A Gallery of Illustrious Literary Characters*, 9–11. "No. 1.—William Jerdan" and "No. 2.— Thomas Campbell" appeared in *Fraser's* 1 (June 1830), 605–6, and 1 (July 1830), 714.

28. *Gallery of Illustrious Literary Characters*, 52, 74, 98. These portraits appeared in *Fraser's* 4 (January 1832), 672; 6 (August 1832), 112; and 7 (May 1833), 602.

29. According to Bonham-Carter, *Authors by Profession*, I, 72–73, the 1833 act was "commonly known as Bulwer-Lytton's Act." For Bulwer-Lytton's participation in the domestic copyright campaign, see Seville, *Literary Copyright Reform*, 191–92, 204–5, and her extended account, "Edward Bulwer Lytton Dreams of Copyright: 'It might make me a rich man,' " in *Victorian Literature and Finance*, ed. Francis O'Gorman (Oxford: Oxford University Press, 2007), 55–72.

30. *Gallery of Illustrious Literary Characters*, 161, 178–79. These portraits appeared in *Fraser's* 11 (May 1835), 652, and 13 (April 1836), 427.

31. Andrew Dowling uses this designation in *Manliness and the Male Novelist in Victorian Literature* (Aldershot: Ashgate, 2001); Fisher adopts it to describe male authors whom *Fraser's* satirizes for effeminacy.

32. Alexis Easley discusses the growth of this phenomenon later in the nineteenth century in "The Woman of Letters at Home: Harriet Martineau in the Lake District," *Victorian Literature and Culture* 34 (2006), 291–310. Easley focuses on literary tourism, the growth of which began in the 1840s, notably spurred by William Howitt's *Homes and Haunts of the Most Eminent British Poets*, 2 vols. (London: Richard Bentley, 1847).

33. Marlon B. Ross, *The Contours of Masculine Desire: Romanticism and the Rise of Women's Poetry* (New York: Oxford University Press, 1989), 203.

34. *Gallery of Illustrious Literary Characters*, 31. This portrait, the first of a woman author, appeared in *Fraser's* 3 (March 1831), 222.

35. *Gallery of Illustrious Literary Characters*, 35, 93, 111–12, 156–57, 189. These portraits appeared in *Fraser's* 3 (May 1832), 410; 7 (March 1833), 267; 8 (October 1833), 433; 11 (April 1835), 404; 13 (June 1836), 718.

36. Easley, *First-Person Anonymous*, 26, 30. At the end of "The Birth of a Tradition: Making Cultural Space for Feminine Poetry," the chapter in which he traces the movement from the *bas bleu* circle to the "relatively smooth ideological field" (202) of the 1830s, Marlon Ross acknowledges that the shift from conversation to print introduces a "disruptive movement" and that women must now "risk profit or ruin on the literary market" (230).

37. *Gallery of Illustrious Literary Characters*, 114–15. Martineau's portrait originally appeared in *Fraser's* 8 (November 1833), 576, at the height of her fame.

38. Thrall, *Rebellious Fraser's*, 129. Thrall's chapter, "Denunciation of Political Economists," details the stance of William Maginn, Michael Sadler, and Thomas Carlyle against the Economic Radicals and its alterative Tory approach to a more humane treatment of poverty, population, and the effects of the industrial revolution.

39. *Gallery of Illustrious Literary Characters*, 115.

40. R. K. Webb, *Harriet Martineau* (New York: Columbia University Press, 1960), 114, gives August 1833 as the date of the move.

41. "Mrs. Hannah More," *La Belle Assemblée, or Court and Fashionable Magazine* (October 1815), 144. The article also refers to More and her sisters' "profession" of schoolmistress.

42. See Margaret Beetham, *A Magazine of Their Own?: Domesticity and Desire in the Women's Magazine, 1800–1914* (London: Routledge, 1996), for a discussion of the early women's magazines, *The Lady's Monthly Museum*, the *Lady's Magazine*, and *La Belle Assemblée*, and their the negotiations of the meaning of "the lady" during decades of social change. As Beetham points out, these magazines were "in flux between an older aristocratic definition and a new set of values associated with the bourgeois family" (18).

43. [Harriet Martineau], "Female Writers on Practical Divinity," *Monthly Repository* 17 (1822), 593–96, 746–50.

44. In *The Dissidence of Dissent: The Monthly Repository, 1806–1838* (Chapel Hill: University of North Carolina Press, 1944), Francis E. Mineka list the names and contributions of authors; see "Identification of Authorship," 394–428. The *Monthly Repository* published such male authors as Leigh Hunt, Walter Savage Landor, Henry Crabb Robinson, and Robert Browning.

45. The *Wellesley Index for Victorian Periodicals* (online) shows that, in addition to Grote, Shelley, and Martineau, women authors frequently contributed unsigned reviews in the 1830s and 1840s and that doing so often led to a full-scale article, as in the cases of Anna Maria Hall, Caroline Lindley, and Margaret Mylne.

46. *Gallery of Illustrious Literary Characters*, 35.

47. Ibid.

48. Ibid., 111–12.

49. The phrase appears in Philip Elliott, *The Sociology of the Professions* (New York: Herder and Herder, 1972), who distinguishes "status professionalism" from "occupational professionalism," and in Sheldon Rothblatt, *Tradition and Change in English Liberal Education: An Essay in History and Culture* (London: Faber and Faber, 1976), whose words (184) I quote. Stefan Collini discusses the shift from the older to modern concepts of professionalism in "Leading Minds," the first chapter of *Public Moralists: Political Thought and Intellectual Life in Britain, 1850–1930* (Oxford: Clarendon Press, 1991), 27–33.

50. *Gallery of Illustrious Literary Characters*, 21; originally "No. 6.—Sir Walter Scott," *Fraser's Magazine* 2 (November 1830), 412.

51. Lewes, "Condition of Authors," 285, 288.

52. Pettitt, "Property in Labour: Inventors and Writers in the 1830s and 1840s," in *Patent Inventions*, 36–83.

53. Frank Turner, "The Victorian Conflict between Science and Religion: A Professional Dimension," in *Contesting Cultural Authority: Essays in Victorian Intellectual Life* (Cambridge: Cambridge University Press, 1993), 171–200.

54. Engel, *From Clergyman to Don*, 10. Engel provides the figures included in this paragraph, as well as an account of a royal commission appointed by Lord John Russell to inquire into university education; in 1852 it issued its own proposal for reform.

55. Seville, *Literary Copyright Reform*, 216.

56. Quoted in Harriet Martineau, *A History of the Thirty Years' Peace* (London: George Bell, 1878), IV, 194. This history was originally published by Charles Knight in 1849–50; see IV, 192–97, for her discussion of the history and reform of copyright.

57. Speech of 7 February 1842, in *The Speeches of Charles Dickens*, ed. John Squire (London: Michael Joseph, 1870), 72.

58. Thomas Carlyle to Charles Dickens, 26 March 1842, in *The Carlyle Letters Online* http://carlyleletters.dukejournals.org (accessed 31 July 2008). Walter Besant provides a history of this 1837–42 attempt to secure American copyright in "The First Society of British Authors," *Essays and Historiettes* (London: Chatto and Windus, 1903), 271–307, where he quotes Carlyle's letter more fully: "In an ancient book it was thousands of years ago written down in the most decisive and explicit manner '*Thou shalt not steal.*' That thou belongest to a different 'nation,' and canst steal without being certainly hanged for it, gives thee no permission to steal" (275).

59. See Lawrence H. Houtchens, "Charles Dickens and International Copyright," *American Literature* 13 (March 1941), 20–21.

60. Harriet Martineau to R[ichard] H[engist] Horne, 4 June 1844, *The Collected Letters of Harriet Martineau*, ed. Deborah Anna Logan (London: Pickering and Chatto, 2007), II, 311.

61. Mary Howitt to Anna Harrison, 18 March 1839 and [1845], Howitt Papers 1/1/120, 1/1/170, and 1/1/180, Manuscripts and Special Collections, The University of Nottingham Library.

62. Elizabeth Gaskell to Elizabeth Holland, late 1841, in *The Letters of Mrs. Gaskell*, ed. J.A.V. Chapple and Arthur Pollard (Manchester: Manchester University Press, 1966), no. 15, p. 44.

63. Harriet Martineau to Mrs. Somerville, 1 November [1836], in *Collected Letters*, I, 317. A subsequent letter to Joanna Baillie, written late in 1836, *Collected Letters*, I, 330, confirms that Somerville, Aikin, and Mitford had signed, but that Edgeworth and Baillie had not yet done so.

64. Martineau to Somerville, 1 November [1836], in *Collected Letters*, I, 317.

65. Quoted in Seville, *Literary Copyright Reform*, 176n1. This letter is not in-cluded in the *Collected Letters*, though another written on the same day to Lady Maria Graham Calcott, author of travel books and children's literature, suggests that Martineau was canvassing all possible women authors.

66. Harriet Martineau to Lord Brougham, [3 November 1836] and 5 November [1836], and Harriet Martineau to William Cullen Bryant, 8 November 1836, in *Collected Letters*, I, 318–19, 320–21. A letter of 8 November 1836 to her friend Maria Weston Chapman, in *Collected Letters*, I, 321, also includes a copy of the petition and a request to "help us get up a similar one from American authors. Rouse all Boston and New York."

67. Harriet Martineau to the Honourable Henry Clay, M.C., Lexington, Kentucky, 15 May 1837, in *Collected Letters*, I, 347.

68. Seville, *Literary Copyright Reform*, 182n16. Seville observes, "Impressive as Talfourd's list is [with thirty-four signatures], Harriet Martineau collected fifty-six signatures from British authors for the petition on international copyright" (*Literary Copyright Reform* 182n17).

69. Colón, *The Professional Ideal in the Victorian Novel*, 13–14. Colón distin-guishes between two aspects of the emergent profession of letters, its "materiality"

and its "ideality," arguing that the "ideal of service" is as important for understanding Victorian authorship as are the material aspects of authors' work (16–21).

70. Lewes, "Condition of Authors," 285, 295.

71. Ibid., 295.

72. Leary, *"Fraser's Magazine* and the Literary Life," 113–14.

73. "Preface to the First Edition," "The Lay of the Last Minstrel," in *Complete Poetical Works of Sir Walter Scott,* 4.

74. Lewes, "Condition of Authors," 285. Lewes's anxiety can be explained biographically. In the 1840s Lewes had undergone a financially rocky decade as he tried his hand at novel writing, drama writing, and acting. In *G. H. Lewes: A Life* (Oxford: Clarendon Press, 1991), 70, Rosemary Ashton reports that his income in 1847 "would have been only £247 had not Chapman and Hall, the publishers of his first novel *Ranthorpe* (1847), given him another £100." Anonymously, Lewes may have written in "Condition of Authors" that an author "will be very unlucky or very 'impracticable,' if he do not earn an income which will support him and his family,—an income varying from a thousand down to two-hundred a year" (288), but privately, he had difficulty moving up from the bottom rung, for the competition in the literary marketplace proved stiff. Yet Lewes's anxiety also stems from an intractable problem that authors recognized but could not resolve: the lack of entrance requirements to the literary field. As the anonymous author of "The Trade of Journalism" in *Saint Pauls: A Monthly Magazine* 1 (December 1867), 309, observed: "It is emphatically one of those trades . . . which require no capital and are all profit. A ream of paper, a box of pens, a bottle of ink, a table, and a chair, are all the stock-in-trade required." As a modern sociologist has dismissively added, "contemporary writers do not control entry to or expulsion from their profession. Thus, they do not meet even a watered-down definition of professionalism"; see Tuchman and Fortin, *Edging Women Out,* 35.

75. See Thrall, *Rebellious Fraser's,* 111–12, for *Fraser's* treatment of aristocratic lady novelists.

76. [G. H. Lewes], "Recent Novels: English and French," *Fraser's Magazine* 36 (December 1847), reprinted in Rosemary Ashton, ed., *Versatile Victorian: Selected Writings of George Henry Lewes* (London: Bristol Classical Press, 1992), 82. This review includes Lewes's first discussion of *Jane Eyre.*

77. Quoted in Elizabeth Gaskell, *The Life of Charlotte Brontë,* ed. Linda H. Peterson (London: Pickering and Chatto, 2006), in *The Works of Elizabeth Gaskell,* ed. Joanne Shattock, VIII, 219.

78. Ibid., 220.

79. The first quotation comes from Lewes's review, "Currer Bell's Shirley," *Edinburgh Review* 91 (January 1850), 155; the second is Ashton's in *Versatile Victorian,* 18.

80. Vivian [G. H. Lewes], "A Flight of Authoresses," *The Leader* (15 June 1850), 284.

81. Lewes, "Condition of Authors," 294.

82. Ibid. Cf. note 70.

83. Julie Codell, *The Victorian Artist: Artists' Life Writing in Britain, 1870–1910* (Cambridge: Cambridge University Press, 2003), 174–75.

84. Mary Jean Corbett, "Bourgeois Subjectivity and Theatrical Personality in the Late Victorian Theatre," in *Representing Femininity: Middle-Class Subjectivity in Victorian and Edwardian Women's Autobiographies* (New York: Oxford University Press, 1992), 130–49.

85. See, e.g., [J. W. Kaye], *"Pendennis*—The Literary Profession," *North British Review* 13 (August 1850), 335–72, which summarizes the charges against *Pendennis* and defends Thackeray against them. Pettitt discusses this debate in "The Indignities of Literature," esp. 149–71.

86. Besant, *Pen and Book*, 299. Besant ironically adds that "later on, when that intellect got the management of George Eliot's novels, it proved extremely practical."

87. Lewes alludes to *The Dispatches of Field Marshal the Duke of Wellington, during his various campaigns in India, Denmark, Portugal, Spain, the Low Countries, and France; compiled from official and authentic documents, by Colonel Gurwood*, which had just been published in eight volumes (London: Parker, Furnivall, and Parker, 1844–47). Gurwood received a civil list pension in 1846.

88. The first phrase is Thackeray's, the second Colby's, both in Robert A. Colby, "Authorship and the Book Trade," in *Victorian Periodicals and Victorian Society*, ed. J. Don Vann and Rosemary T. Van Arsdell (Toronto: University of Toronto Press, 1994), 147.

89. Jerdan, *Autobiography*, I, 39.

90. Ibid. This argument—in favor of maintaining the early nineteenth-century model of authorship as a supplement to a learned profession—is what Lewes rejects, and their disagreement is about more than annual income. Although Jerdan initially emphasizes financial reward as the defining feature of a profession, he is equally concerned with social recognition and non-monetary honors. Jerdan's salary during his editorship of the *Sun* in the 1810s and 1820s was over £500 per year (well above Lewes's requisite £300); he earned additional income by contributing to provincial papers and publishing his own books with John Murray. Even so, for Jerdan money is not the main criterion for professional status. The friends of his youth who had gone to the bar had attained high office in their maturity—David Pollock as Chief Justice of Bombay, his brother Frederick as Lord Chief Baron of Her Majesty's Exchequer, and Thomas Wilde as Lord High Chancellor of England. In contrast, Jerdan found himself without financial security *or* social status in old age. He was, in fact, writing the installments of his *Autobiography* to earn his bread and keep himself from the workhouse or debtor's prison.

91. Burton J. Bledstein, *The Culture of Professionalism: The Middle Class and the Development of Higher Education in America* (New York: W. W. Norton, 1976), ix–xi, 4–5.

92. "Reviews: *The Autobiography of William Jerdan*," *Literary Gazette* no. 1843 (15 May 1852), 411–12.

93. "The Profession of Literature," *Westminster Review* 58 o.s. (October 1852), 514. This review is anonymous, included in an issue with essays by G. H. Lewes, Harriet Martineau, and J. S. Mill. Jerdan rebutted "critical contemporaries" in the second volume of his *Autobiography*, claiming that they had "entirely mistaken" his intention: "It has been held that my narrative, as far as it has gone (the sequel being unknown), tends to the disparagement of the literary class or 'profession,' and has

consequently not only provoked the animadversions of members of that class or 'profession,' but [also] the *ruse* of carrying the war into the supposed enemy's quarters, and charging me with ingratitude where I ought to have been exceedingly thankful for the success accorded to me." Jerdan argues that his account was "hardly amenable to the inapplicable law of a personal and individual test" (II, 2); rather, his memoir demonstrates that even "the most cultivated and distinguished literary men" are not "adequately requited, in comparison with far less gifted individuals in intellectual and other walks of life," including "bishops, and judges, and eminent physicians" (II, 39). As evidence, he cites cases ranging from Walter Scott and Thomas Moore at the high end of "genius" to J. C. Loudon, Samuel Maunder, and John Britton at the low end of industrious labor. All provided service to the nation (one of Lewes's criteria for professionalism); only Scott received a baronetcy (one of Jerdan's marks of success); almost all died poor or with little to show for a life of labor (financial security being a criterion for both Lewes and Jerdan). Jerdan thus concludes: "Since I was connected with the press, now nearly half a century, I have read, and I have written, many obituaries of deceased authors in every line of literature; and the conclusion—the epitaph might be stereotyped—has always been, 'He died in poverty, and left his family in distress.'"

94. In "The Profession of Literature," 525, the anonymous reviewer chastises Jerdan for "mistak[ing] the nature of the profession to which he belongs" and measuring success in financial and social terms: "But literature presents none of these temptations in prospect; it has no offices to give away, no sinecures, no pluralities, no snug retreats from work and poverty; . . . the appeal lies direct from the author to the public, and distinction must be won and carved out by merit alone."

95. For a review of volume II, see *Literary Gazette* no. 1857 (21 August 1852), 635–37. The anonymous "The Profession of Literature," 507–31, reviews vols. I and II of Jerdan's *Autobiography*.

96. Kaye, *"Pendennis,"* 370. In *Uneven Developments*, Poovey quotes this review, along with the anonymous "The Profession of Literature," cited above, to argue that a "laissez-faire image of writing" dominated the mid-Victorian literary field. In my view, her account flattens the field and makes authorial opinions more uniform than in fact they were. As the writings of both Lewes and Jerdan reveal, many authors wanted not laissez-faire, but government support of literature and the arts.

97. Besant documents Martineau's intelligent advice and support in his history of this failed society in "The First Society of British Authors," 271–307, and quotes in full her letter of 25 April 1845. His essay mentions male writers whose aid was sought but who responded with self-serving, platitudinous, or ignorant letters.

98. Caroline Norton, *A Plain Letter to the Lord Chancellor on the Infant Custody Bill* (London: James Ridgway, 1839), 8. In this passage Norton repeats an observation made by Lord Brougham in support of the bill.

99. Caroline Norton, *English Laws for Women in the Nineteenth Century* (London: Privately printed, 1854), 164. For Norton, women's inability to control earnings was a fundamental flaw in English law, but it signaled a larger problem in women's rights that needed redress: "in the law which permits the most indecent and atrocious libel against her, without a chance of legal defence,—in the law which countenances and upholds far worse than cheating at cards, and renders null and

void a contract signed by a magistrate, because that contract was made with his wife,—in the law which gives a woman's earnings even by literary copyright, to her husband,—in the whole framework, in short, of those laws by which her existence is merged in the existence of another, (let what will be the circumstances of her case); and by which Justice in fact divests herself of all control and responsibility in the matter—England sees nothing worthy of remark." For a discussion of Norton and the Married Women's Property Act, see Lee Holcombe, *Wives and Property: Reform of the Married Women's Property Law in Nineteenth-Century England* (Toronto: University of Toronto Press, 1983).

100. Christine Battersby, *Gender and Genius: Toward a Feminist Aesthetic* (London: Women's Press, 1989), quoted in Susan P. Casteras, "From 'Safe Havens' to 'A Wide Sea of Notoriety,' " in *A Struggle for Fame: Victorian Women Artists and Authors*, by Susan P. Casteras and Linda H. Peterson (New Haven: Yale Center for British Art, 1994), 11.

101. Mrs. [Anna] Jameson, *Sisters of Charity, Catholic and Protestant* and *The Communion of Labour* (Boston: Ticknor and Fields, 1857), 25.

102. Ibid., 26.

103. Ibid.

104. Ibid., 27.

105. Ibid., 29.

106. Ellen Jordan, " 'Women's Work in the World': The Birth of a Discourse, London, 1857," *Nineteenth-Century Feminisms* 1 (Fall/Winter 1999), 24–25.

107. In *Independent Women: Work and Community for Single Women, 1850–1920* (Chicago: University of Chicago Press, 1985), Martha Vicinus traces this strand of thinking in women's advances in education, social work, and medicine. As her subtitle indicates, Vicinus limits her study to single women, and dates the movement for women's public work from the 1850s when it appeared in full force. For women writers, the movement begins earlier and includes—indeed, almost necessitates—the participation of married women.

108. [Margaret Oliphant], "Two Ladies," *Blackwood's Edinburgh Magazine* 125 (1879), 206–7.

109. Ibid., 220.

110. Barbara Leigh Smith, *Women and Work* (London: Bosworth and Harrison, 1857), 6.

111. Ibid., 7, 15.

112. Ibid., 10, 16–17.

113. "XXXIII.—What Can Educated Women Do?" the *English Woman's Journal* 4 (December 1859), 217–27. On p. 218 the writer cites Jameson's lecture as she introduces "our chief social institutions under these four heads:—Sanitary, Educational, Reformatory, and Penal." See also "XLIII.—What Can Educated Women Do? Part II," the *English Woman's Journal* 4 (1 January 1859), 289–98, which advances arguments like those in Leigh Smith's *Women and Work*, on the necessity of women's labor, and an article by Bessie Rayner Parkes that preceded these, "XXII.—The Market for Educated Female Labor," the *English Woman's Journal* 4 (1 November 1859), 145–52.

114. Quoted phrases are taken from the petition on behalf of the Married Women's Property Bill, included in an anonymously published article by Caroline

Frances Cornwallis, "The Property of Married Women," *Westminster Review* 66 (October 1856), 336–38.

115. Bessie Rayner Parkes, *Essays on Woman's Work* (London: Alexander Strahan, 1865), 106.

116. Ibid., 107.

117. See Besant, "First Society of British Authors," 285–88.

118. Bonham-Carter, *Authors by Profession*, I, 119.

119. W. Martin Conway, "The Society of Authors," *The Nineteenth Century* 38 (December 1895), 978.

120. Quoted in Bonham-Carter, *Authors by Profession*, I, 130.

121. Rothblatt, *Tradition and Change*, 184.

122. After the *Men of Letters* series was launched, it added major poets: Chaucer, Byron, and Pope in 1880, Gray in 1882, and Cowper in 1885. But its emphasis lay on prose writers, including lesser figures like Bentley (1882) and major essayists like Bacon (1884).

123. [Thornton Leigh Hunt], "A Man of Letters of the Last Generation," *Cornhill Magazine* 1 (January 1860), 85. This article was an obituary review of Leigh Hunt, the writer's father.

124. See Collini, *Public Moralists*.

125. In *Edging Women Out*, 173, Tuchman and Fortin state that initially "the Society of Authors excluded women from membership," citing an unpublished ms. by G. H. Thring, "History of the Society of Authors" (British Museum Library Add. 56868 and 56869). But Bonham-Carter's more extensive history of the society suggests otherwise, and I could find no point in Thring's ms. that suggests a conscious exclusion of women.

126. On women's insistence that they participate in leadership of the Society of Authors, see Molly Youngkin, "Henrietta Stannard, Marie Corelli, and Annesley Kenealy," in *Kindred Hands: Letters on Writing by British and American Women Authors, 1865–1935*, ed. Jennifer Cognard-Black and Elizabeth Macleod Walls (Iowa City: University of Iowa Press, 2006), 147–50. Youngkin reproduces letters to S. Squire Sprigge, the society's secretary, and George Herbert Thring, his successor, that demonstrate these women's insistence on full inclusion in the society.

127. Besant, *Pen and Book*, 56. Earl A. Knies points out, in "Sir Walter Besant and the 'Shrieking Sisterhood,'" *Victorian Literature and Culture* 21 (1993), 211–32, that Besant was "partial to the feminine type known as the 'womanly woman,'" but that he consistently supported the right of intellectual women to enter the professions and of women writers to receive decent payment for their work (211, 229).

128. Lewes, "Condition of Authors," 285, 295.

129. Besant, *Pen and Book*, 56–59. In this inclusiveness Besant differs from Arnold Bennett, whose *Journalism for Women: A Practical Guide* (London: John Lane, Bodley Head, 1898) opens the profession of journalism to women but chastises them for their failures, ranging from unbusinessmanlike and unreliable conduct to transgressions of the rules of grammar. A more optimistic view appears in Wilhelmina Wimble's "Incomes for Ladies: Journalism," *Lady's Realm* 2 (1898), 467–68.

130. Bourdieu, *Field of Cultural Production*, 47–48.

131. In *Pen and Book*, 318–20, Besant discusses the roles of the printer, typewriter, and agent, as well as the author, publisher, and bookseller—a version of the

"communications circuit" later outlined in Robert Darnton's "What Is the History of Books?"

132. Walter Besant, "The Maintenance of Literary Property," in *The Grievances between Authors & Publishers* (London: Field and Tuer, 1887), 14–17.

133. See "Appendix—Prospectus of the Society of Authors," *Pen and Book*, 320–39.

134. Besant, *Pen and Book*, 6.

135. Ibid., 23–24.

136. Ibid., 29–30.

137. Ibid., 14. Yet Besant also complained in "Literature as a Career," an article first published in the New York *Forum* and later included in *Essays and Historiettes*, that Tennyson was the *only* such instance of high social honor (320) and that, at the 50th Jubilee of Queen Victoria, "there was not invited one single man or woman of letters, as such" (317).

138. Besant, *Pen and Book*, 39.

139. *The Bookseller*, 5 June 1884, quoted in Bonham-Carter, *Authors by Profession*, I, 123.

140. *The World*, 12 March 1884, quoted in Bonham-Carter, *Authors by Profession*, I, 122–23. More balanced notices occurred in the *Saturday Review* 64 (3 December 1887), 772–73, which begins with the observation: "*Il y a serpent et serpent*—there are publishers and publishers."

141. T. Werner Laurie, "Author, Agent, and Publisher, by one of 'The Trade,'" *The Nineteenth Century* 38 (November 1895), 850. Laurie dismisses the professionalism of the organization by pointing out flaws in one of its booklets by Hall Caine, *Cost of Production*, which fails to understand and account for the cost of paper, advertisements, and other material aspects of publication.

142. Walter Besant, "The Literary Agent," *The Nineteenth Century* 38 (December 1895), 895.

143. Bonham-Carter, *Authors by Profession*, I, 119–65; Colby, "Authorship and the Book Trade," 143–61.

144. [C. S. Oakley], "On Commencing Author," *Quarterly Review* 186 (1897), 90. An early essay by Robert Louis Stevenson, "The Morality of the Profession of Letters," *Fortnightly Review* 29 (April 1881), 513–20, similarly objects to the current "point of view . . . calculated to surprise high-minded men, and bring a general contempt on books and reading"; Stevenson argues that only two reasons justify the choice of the literary life: "the first is the inbred taste in the chooser; the second some high utility in the industry selected" (514).

145. Oakley, "On Commencing Author," 90.

146. Ibid., 90–91.

147. [Mowbray Morris], "The Profession of Letters," *Macmillan's Magazine* 56 (November 1887), 302–10. Mowbray adopts the common military metaphor but makes it "the noble army of Letters" (308).

148. Bourdieu, *Field of Cultural Production*, 40.

149. Bourdieu's penchant for thinking in binaries tends to reduce the literary culture of Flaubert's day into oppositional camps: e.g., when he describes Flaubert's representation of the literary field as "organized around the opposition between pure art, associated with pure love, and bourgeois art, under its two forms, mercenary art

that can be called major, represented by the bourgeois theatre and associated with the figure of Mme Dambreuse and minor mercenary art, represented by vaudeville, cabaret, or the serial novel, evoked by Rosanette" (*The Rules of Art: Genesis and Structure of the Literary Field* [Cambridge: Polity Press, 1996], 24). Tuchman and Fortin's *Edging Women Out*, written just after the publication of Bourdieu's *Distinction: A Social Critique of the Judgment of Taste* in 1984, suffers from a similar problem. My point is that the literary field in Britain differs from that in France and cannot so readily be reduced to these binaries before the twentieth century (and perhaps not even then).

150. Besant, *Pen and Book*, 24–25.

151. Bourdieu, *Field of Cultural Production*, 125.

152. Oakley, "On Commencing Author," 90.

153. Ibid., 94, 95–96, 99, 105. In Bourdieu's terms, one might say that both Besant and Oakley offer modes of resistance to market forces and "the subordinate position of cultural producers in relation to the controllers of production and diffusion media" (*Field of Cultural Production*, 125). For my purposes, the key point is that they imagine a *both/and* not an *either/or* relation to the market.

154. Oakley, "On Commencing Author," 99.

155. Besant, "Maintenance of Literary Property," 14–15.

156. Besant, *Pen and Book*, 3.

157. Ibid., 4, 15.

158. Bonham-Carter, *Authors by Profession*, I, 46, 63; John Sutherland, *Victorian Fiction: Writers, Publishers, Readers* (New York: St. Martin's Press, 1995), 80.

159. Saunders, *The Profession of English Letters*, 178; Bonham-Carter, *Authors by Profession*, I, 153; Gordon Haight, *George Eliot: A Biography* (Oxford: Oxford University Press, 1968), 370.

160. I am here using terms that appear throughout Bourdieu's work but are summarized by Susan Emanuel, trans., *Rules of Art*, 351n33.

161. Morris, "Profession of Letters," 303.

162. "The Trade of Author," *Fortnightly Review*, n.s., 45 (February 1889), 263, 266.

163. Bourdieu, *Field of Cultural Production*, 42–43.

164. One exception was Arnold Bennett in *Journalism for Women*.

165. Tuchman and Fortin, *Edging Women Out*, 87.

166. Onslow, *Women of the Press in Nineteenth-Century Britain*; see esp. her chapter "The Fifth Estate," 36–60.

167. Emily Crawford, "Journalism as a Profession for Women," *Contemporary Review* 64 (1893), 362.

168. Angela V. John, *Unequal Opportunities: Women's Employment in England, 1800–1918* (Oxford: Basil Blackwell, 1986), as cited in Tuchman and Fortin, *Edging Women Out*, 14.

169. Crawford, "Journalism as a Profession for Women," 366.

170. Meredith, "Mrs. Meynell's Two Books of Essays," 770.

171. Morris, "Profession of Letters," 308.

172. Ibid.

173. [Mowbray Morris], "The Profession of Letters (A Postscript)," *Macmillan's Magazine* 56 (December 1887), 456. Morris also ranks "The Solitary Reaper" over

"The Blessed Damozel," Gibbon over Carlyle, and the philosopher Berkeley over Mill.

174. Peter D. MacDonald, in *British Literary Culture and Publishing Practice, 1880–1914* (Cambridge: Cambridge University Press, 1995), traces examples of such positioning in the work of Joseph Conrad, Arnold Bennett, and Arthur Conan Doyle.

175. Norley Chester, "How I didn't become an Author," *Temple Bar* 120 (August 1900), 565–72.

176. After the turn of the century, the *Men of Letters* issued volumes on George Eliot by Leslie Stephen (1902), Fanny Burney by Austin Dobson (1903), and Maria Edgeworth by Emily Lawless (1904).

CHAPTER 2

Inventing the Woman of Letters

1. [Joseph Conder], review of *Illustrations of Political Economy* by Harriet Martineau, *Eclectic Review* 8 (1832), 44–72; rpt. in Deborah Anna Logan, ed., *Illustrations of Political Economy: Selected Tales* (Petersborough, Ontario: Broadview Press, 2004), 413.

2. Harriet Martineau, *Autobiography* (London: Smith, Elder, 1877), I, 119–20.

3. Darnton, "What Is the History of Books?" 67–68.

4. Martineau uses the phrases "professional son" and "citizen of the world" in a letter to her mother, 8 July 1833, included in the *Memorials* (ed. Chapman) volume of her *Autobiography*, III, 91. The designation "Mrs. Barbauld's daughter" comes from Shelagh Hunter's *Harriet Martineau: The Poetics of Moralism* (Aldershot: Scolar Press, 1995), ch. 2, 59–103, which concentrates on Martineau's place within a women's didactic tradition.

5. Darnton, "What Is the History of Books?" 67.

6. Martineau, *Autobiography*, I, 140. Martineau misdates the publication, saying, "I think it must have been in 1821" (I, 117), but if the article appeared immediately after submission in "the forthcoming number," then the year was 1822. See "Female Writers on Practical Divinity," *Monthly Repository* 17 (November 1822), 593–96, and (December 1822), 746–50. These articles are signed "Discipulus."

7. [Harriet Martineau], "Female Writers on Practical Divinity," 593.

8. Ibid., 748, 750.

9. [Harriet Martineau], "On Female Education," *Monthly Repository* 18 (February 1823), 81.

10. In a letter from Harriet to her brother James, 3 October 1822, later transcribed by him and now in the archives of Manchester College, Oxford, the topic of her first article is projected as "English Female Dramatic Authors," "embracing Hannah More, Mrs. Barbauld, Miss Talbott, Elizabeth Smith, and continuing in subsequent papers, if this is accepted, with writers on education." Perhaps at this initial stage of literary endeavor, Martineau imagined writing plays as well as devotional literature.

11. [Harriet Martineau], *Devotional Exercises: Consisting of Reflections and Prayers, for the Use of Young Persons, to which is added A Treatise on the Lord's Supper* (London: Rowland Hunter, 1823) was self-financed, with Martineau paying a Norwich bookseller for the printing of its sheets, some binding, and some advertising

and in return receiving profits in cash and books on account. She had a similar arrangement with Rowland Hunter, a London bookseller, though all three editions (1823, 1824, 1832) were printed in Norwich.

12. Erickson, *The Economy of Literary Form*, 72.

13. See Richard Garnett, *The Life of W. J. Fox: Public Teacher & Social Reformer, 1786–1864* (London: Bodley Head, 1910), 94–134; Francis E. Mineka, *The Dissidence of Dissent: The Monthly Repository, 1806–1838, Under the Editorship of Robert Aspland, W. J. Fox, R. H. Horne, & Leigh Hunt* (Chapel Hill: University of North Carolina Press, 1944).

14. Lewes, "Condition of Authors," 285–95.

15. Ibid., 285. According to Lewes, "able literary men in England mak[e] incomes *averaging* 300£ a-year" (286), and "the real cause we attribute to be the excellence and abundance of periodical literature" (288).

16. See the "Biographical Notice of Ellis and Acton Bell," published in a new edition of *Wuthering Heights and Agnes Grey* that Charlotte Brontë edited (London: Smith, Elder, 1850).

17. Martineau, *Autobiography*, III, 91. I have discussed this ambivalent treatment of gender in *Traditions of Victorian Women's Autobiography: The Poetics and Politics of Life Writing* (Charlottesville: University Press of Virginia, 1999), 54–79. See also Valerie Pichanick, *Harriet Martineau: The Woman and Her Work, 1802–76* (Ann Arbor: University of Michigan Press, 1980), 92–99.

18. See Harriet Martineau, "The Hanwell Lunatic Asylum," in *Miscellanies* (Boston: Hilliard, Gray, and Company, 1836), I, 230–47; "Prison Discipline," in *Miscellanies*, II, 281–95; and "West India Slavery," in *Miscellanies*, II, 375–86. The essays in this collection represent Martineau's best periodical writing from the *Monthly Repository* from 1827 to 1832, the exception being the essay on Scott, which appeared in *Tait's Edinburgh Magazine* in 1832.

19. Martineau, *Miscellanies*, vol. II, includes four sections: Philosophical Essays, Moral Essays, Parables, and Poetry.

20. Martineau, *Devotional Exercises*, 121. In the second edition, the treatise on the Lord's Supper was dropped, a new essay added, and the whole retitled *Devotional Exercises: Consisting of Reflections and Prayers, for the Use of Young Persons, to which is added a Guide to the Study of the Scriptures* (London: Rowland Hunter, 1824). A third edition, bearing Martineau's name, was published in 1832 (London: Rowland Hill and Charles Fox, 1832).

21. These archives have been microfilmed as *Women, Emancipation and Literature: The Papers of Harriet Martineau* (Wiltshire: Adam Matthew Publications, 1991), reel 10. They include Martineau's financial records, as well as business letters relating to her publications.

22. *Papers of Harriet Martineau*, reel 10. The first correspondence from S. Wilkins is addressed to her brother Henry, one statement lists James Martineau as the recipient, but the rest, including all accounts from Rowland Hunter, went to Harriet herself. Wilkins handled the printing of the first two editions; the third edition lists Rowland Hunter and Charles Fox as publishers but includes the imprint of "Bacon and Kinnebrook, Printers, Norwich."

23. *Papers of Harriet Martineau*, reel 10. My calculations derive from the records she retained from S. Wilkins and Rowland Hunter but do not include the local

bookseller's charges for advertisements in regional newspapers, nor the books Martineau occasionally took in lieu of cash payment from him, but these more or less cancel each other out. Her "books and facts," copied by John Chapman and now in the Birmingham University archive, lists £50 as her profit from *Devotional Exercises*; however, as the early entries on the list seem to be drawn up from memory, it is possible that Martineau underestimated her profits.

24. Harriet Martineau to Thomas and Helen Martineau, 3 January 1824, in *Collected Letters*, I, 11. The original is BANC MSS 92/7542, Bancroft Library, University of California–Berkeley. My thanks to Alexis Easley for drawing my attention to this letter.

25. Martineau recorded her publications and profits, along with an annotated list titled "books and facts"; see *Papers of Harriet Martineau*, reel 10.

26. See *Papers of Harriet Martineau*, reel 10.

27. Harriet Martineau to Richard H. Horne, 5 June [1844], in *Collected Letters*, II, 311.

28. William Roberts, *Memoirs of the Life of Mrs. Hannah More*, 4 vols. (London: R. B. Seeley and W. Burnside, 1834), and Henry Thompson, *The Life of Hannah More* (London, 1838; Philadelphia: E. L. Cary and A. Hart, 1838) emphasize More's service to God and humanity.

29. Martineau to Horne, 5 June [1844], in *Collected Letters*, I, 311.

30. This generalization holds true for the 1820s; once Martineau recognized the possibilities of didactic narrative in the *Illustrations of Political Economy* and made her name as a political writer, she used both books and periodicals to promulgate her views.

31. Lewes, "Condition of Authors," 295.

32. Pichanick, *Harriet Martineau*, 203–4, notes that Martineau ceased to write for *Household Words* when her "ideological differences" on women, religion, and political economy brought her into conflict with Dickens's editorial views.

33. "The Profession of Literature," *Westminster Review* 58 o.s. (October 1852), 518–19.

34. The *Wellesley Index* does not identify the author of this review, and given Martineau's list of work for the *Westminster Review* in her *Autobiography* (II, 415–17), it may be fanciful to suggest that she wrote it. Yet the references to cotton-spinning, glass-blowing, and iron-smelting reflect topics she understood through the manufacturing career of her brother Robert and on which she wrote in the early 1850s for *Household Words* (see *Autobiography*, II, 385–89, including footnotes).

35. Harold Perkin, "Professionalism, Property, and English Society since 1880," *The Stenton Lecture 1980* (Reading: University of Reading, 1981), 8.

36. Martineau, *Miscellanies*, I, 272–88. Martineau argues that "every member of society who studies and reflects at all [must] inform himself of its leading principles" (276), given how relevant they are to government, philanthropy, and everyday life.

37. The essays on Scott open the first volume, thus receiving a prominent position.

38. William Wordsworth, *Poetical Works*, ed. Thomas Hutchinson, rev. Ernest de Selincourt (Oxford: Oxford University Press, 1969), *The Prelude*, Bk. XIV, ll. 444–47.

39. See Charlotte Brontë's preface to a new edition of *Wuthering Heights* and *Agnes Grey*.

40. "Obituary," *Daily News*, 29 June 1876, rpt. in *Memorials*, ed. Chapman, III, 469–70.

41. Harriet Martineau, "The Characteristics of the Genius of Scott," in *Miscellanies*, I, 14.

42. Ibid., I, 16.

43. Martineau reprinted "Literary Lionism" in the *Autobiography*, I, 271–97. As Alexis Easley notes of this essay: "For Martineau, the author's role was to reflect and shape the discourses circulating within her culture as a whole, rather than actively to express ideas that originate within the authorial persona"; see "Authorship, Gender and Power in Victorian Culture: Harriet Martineau and the Periodical Press," in *Nineteenth-Century Media and the Construction of Identities*, ed. Laurel Brake, Bill Bell, and David Finkelstein (London: Palgrave, 2000), 162.

44. Martineau, *Miscellanies*, I, 1.

45. Ibid., I, 6–7, 10.

46. Ibid., I, 12–14.

47. Ibid., I, 3.

48. Isaac Disraeli, *The Literary Character; or, the History of Men of Genius*, ed. B[enjamin] Disraeli (1795; rpt., London: Frederick Warne, 1840).

49. Martineau, *Miscellanies*, I, 2.

50. Perkin, *The Rise of Professional Society*, 399.

51. Martineau, *Miscellanies*, I, 24–26.

52. Ibid., I, 51.

53. Ibid., I, 28.

54. Martineau, *Autobiography*, I, 143, 249.

55. Janice Carlisle, *John Stuart Mill and the Writing of Character* (Athens: University of Georgia Press, 1991), 242.

56. Harriet Martineau to Lord Brougham, 10 October 1832, in *Harriet Martineau: Selected Letters*, ed. Valerie Sanders (Oxford: Clarendon, 1990), 32.

57. See James Martineau's transcriptions of Harriet's letters of 9 July, 17 July, and 18 August 1829, The Library, Manchester College, Oxford.

58. See *Autobiography*, I, 138–39, for Martineau's reading in 1827 of Jane Marcet's *Conversations on Political Economy in which the Elements of the Science are Familiarly Explained* (London: Longman, 1816). Marcet's "conversations" take the form of a dialogue between a schoolgirl named Caroline and her instructress, Mrs. B.

59. For "governess to the nation," see Hunter, *Harriet Martineau*, 38–58.

60. The private memorandum, dated June 1829, was originally published in the *Memorials*, ed. Chapman, III, 32–34. It appears as appendix B in the *Autobiography of Harriet Martineau*, ed. Peterson, 654–56.

61. See Harriet Martineau to James Martineau, 26 January 1830, The Library, Manchester College, Oxford, and Harriet to her mother, 22 January 1830, included in *Memorials*, ed. Chapman, III, 43–45.

62. Mary Martha Sherwood was the daughter of Dr. George Butt, rector of Stanford and chaplain to George III; after she married Henry Sherwood and went to India with him, she fell under the influence of Henry Martyn, the great Evangelical missionary, and began a life of good works, Bible study, and didactic

writing—including *The Indian Pilgrim* (a rewriting of *The Pilgrim's Progress*), *Little Henry and his Bearer*, and over three hundred tracts for Houlston. Her sister, Lucy Lyttleton Cameron, was another prize horse in the Houlston stable, best known for *The History of Margaret Whyte* (1798) and *The Two Lambs* (1821). According to Victor E. Neuberg in *The Penny Histories: A Study of Chapbooks for Young Readers over Two Centuries* (New York: Harcourt, Brace and World, 1968), 71–75, George Mogridge was "the most prolific writer of such little books," consciously modeling his edifying tales on the chapbooks he had read in his youth; under the pseudonyms "Peter Parley," "Ephraim Holding," and "Old Humphrey," he wrote series for the Religious Tract Society and for Houlston's "Juvenile Tracts."

63. Houlston's tracts conform to the description of chapbooks given by Neuberg, 6. Most are duodecimos, but Neuberg also describes "little 32mo books, with covers and pictures, costing a farthing each" (74).

64. E.g., the tract *A Drive in the Coach* is bound with seven other didactic tales from publishers in Glasgow, Edinburgh, and London; it bears the bookplate "Ex Libris, John Ruskin, Brantwood," and the annotations in pencil suggest that the tracts were given to him by his father in the early 1820s.

65. Mrs. Sherwood, *A Drive in the Coach through the Streets of London: A Story Founded on Fact* (Wellington, Salop: F. Houlston and Son, 1822), 6–7. I do not mean to suggest that all Houlston tales depict material commodities and conspicuous consumption, rather that whatever their subject, they evaluate human action within a biblical framework, without recourse to other theories or "laws." This at least holds true for the one hundred tracts collected in the British Library's "Houlston's Series of Tracts."

66. Susan Pedersen, "Hannah More Meets Simple Simon: Tracts, Chapbooks, and Popular Culture in Late Eighteenth-Century England," *Journal of British Studies* 25 (1986), 88–89.

67. [Harriet Martineau], *Christmas Day; or, The Friends* (Wellington, Salop: Houlston and Son, 1826), 67–68.

68. [Harriet Martineau], *The Friends; A Continuation of Christmas Day* (Wellington, Salop: Houlston and Son, 1826), 68, 70.

69. In her *Autobiography*, Martineau interprets human development, including her own, in Comtean terms as progressing from a "religious" through a "metaphysical" to a "scientific" (or "positive") stage.

70. Pedersen, "Hannah More Meets Simple Simon," 88.

71. Martineau recognized that the mode of didactic dialogue, common in textbooks and the catechism, was less effective than eyewitness narrative. When she proposed her series on political economy to Charles Fox, she refused to alter her "method of exemplification" and "issue my Political Economy in didactic form," as James Mill recommended (*Autobiography*, I, 169).

72. Greg Myers, "Science for Women and Children: The Dialogue of Popular Science in the Nineteenth Century," in *Nature Transfigured: Science and Literature, 1700–1900*, ed. John Christie and Sally Shuttleworth (Manchester: Manchester University Press, 1989), 181.

73. [Harriet Martineau], *The Turn-Out; or, Patience is the Best Policy* (Wellington, Salop: Houlston, 1829), 83. Martineau's use of a woman's critical perspective in these tracts and the later *Illustrations of Political Economy* suggests a modification

of Deirdre David's argument in *Intellectual Women and Victorian Patriarchy* (Ithaca: Cornell University Press, 1987) that her role was essentially one of "auxiliary usefulness" (32) in support of Victorian patriarchy; rather, we might see Martineau as inserting a critical feminist commentary into an otherwise masculine narrative or patriarchal discourse.

74. In 1829 Martineau was still a devoted advocate of Unitarianism and most likely would have seen a "providence" in the workings of the laws of nature, including those of political economy; yet this tale is virtually devoid of religious sentiment and anticipates the break she would make with Unitarianism in the 1840s and the embrace of "Baconian science" she would champion.

75. Martineau learned from writers other than More and those in the Houlston tract series. She was, as Shelagh Hunter demonstrates, "Mrs. Barbauld's daughter," and probably knew the *Evening Sketches* (1792–95) that Barbauld coauthored with her brother Charles Aikin. Martineau also knew Maria Edgeworth's tales of Irish economic woes and by 1827 was familiar with (though not always positively influenced by) Jane Marcet's *Conversations on Political Economy* (1816).

76. The story of this "safe and salutary reading" was first told by William Roberts in *Memoirs of the Life of Mrs. Hannah More*, 4 vols. (London: R. B. Seeley and W. Burnside, 1834), and by Henry Thompson, *The Life of Hannah More* (London, 1838; Philadelphia: E. L. Cary and A. Hart, 1838). These or similar accounts would have been known to Martineau, and they represent the political attitudes against which she reacted. Important modern histories of the *Cheap Repository Tracts* include Ford K. Brown, *Fathers of the Victorians* (Cambridge: Cambridge University Press, 1961); Pedersen, "Hannah More Meets Simple Simon," 84–113; Gary Kelly, "Revolution, Reaction, and the Expropriation of Popular Culture: Hannah More's *Cheap Repository*," in *Man and Nature: Proceedings for the Canadian Society for Eighteenth-Century Studies*, ed. Kenneth W. Graham and Neal Johnson (Edmonton: Academic Printing and Publishing, 1987), 147–59; Anne Mellor, *Mothers of the Nation: Women's Political Writing in England, 1780–1830* (Bloomington: Indiana University Press, 2000); Mona Scheuermann, *In Praise of Poverty: Hannah More Counters Thomas Paine and the Radical Threat* (Lexington: University of Kentucky Press, 2002); and Anne Stott, *Hannah More, The First Victorian* (Oxford: Oxford University Press, 2003).

77. Roberts, *Memoirs*, II, 425.

78. As Pedersen notes in "Hannah More Meets Simple Simon," 86, "Repository [tales] such as 'The Riot' and 'The Loyal Sailor; Or, No Mutineering' expressly forbade both crowd action and political revolt"; another repository ballad, "Turn the Carpet," was, according to More herself, intended "to vindicate the justice of God in the apparently unequal distribution of good in this world, by pointing to another." The latter quotation comes from a 1795 letter written by More to her sister, included in Roberts, *Memoirs*, I, 433.

79. For a discussion of More's influence, see Logan's introduction to *Illustrations of Political Economy*, esp. 27–34, and Linda H. Peterson, "From French Revolution to English Reform: Hannah More, Harriet Martineau, and the 'Little Book,'" *Nineteenth Century Literature* 60 (2006), 409–50.

80. See her letter of 26 March 1856, rpt. in *Memorials*, ed. Chapman, III, 293, in which she clarifies misstatements in the press about her family.

81. In organizing the *Illustrations of Political Economy*, Martineau followed the arrangement of James Mill's *Elements of Political Economy* (London: Baldwin, Craddock, and Joy, 1821): Production, Distribution, Exchange, and Consumption. See ch. 4 in Claudia Orazem, *Political Economy and Fiction in the Early Works of Harriet Martineau* (New York: Peter Lang, 1999), for a discussion of the structure of the series.

82. Mineka, *Dissidence of Dissent*, 227. Kathryn Gleadle discusses their agenda in similar terms in *Early Feminists: Radical Unitarians and the Emergence of the Women's Rights Movement, 1831–1851* (Houndsmill, Basingstoke: Macmillan, 1995), 45–54.

83. Mineka, *Dissidence of Dissent*, 172, 187, echoes the views of the nineteenth-century radical Francis Place.

84. *Monthly Repository*, n.s., 2 (September 1828), 656. Martineau refers to this "spirited advertisement" in her *Autobiography*, I, 106.

85. In a letter of 23 November 1831 to her brother James, she notes, "If, as he expects, Mr. Fox (being on the council of the National Political Union) goes as a prisoner to the Tower, he will devolve his editorship of the Monthly Repository on Harriet 'till he is acquitted or hanged' "; see James's transcription, The Library, Manchester College, Oxford.

86. Donald Winch, *Riches and Poverty: An Intellectual History of Political Economy in Britain, 1750–1834* (Cambridge: Cambridge University Press, 1996), 284. Of the philosophic radicals, the best-known figure associated with the *Monthly Repository* was John Stuart Mill, who began writing for Fox in 1831. As Mineka points out in *Dissidence of Dissent*, 101, as early as 1811, the magazine took a quotation from Jeremy Bentham as its title-page motto.

87. [W. J. Fox], "On the State and Prospects of the Country at the Close of the Year 1831," *Monthly Repository*, n.s., 6 (January 1832), 1–11; [Harriet Martineau], "On the Duty of Studying Political Economy," *Monthly Repository*, n.s., 6 (January 1832), 24–34; rpt. in *Miscellanies*, I, 272–88.

88. Ricardo was a friend of Robert Aspland, the first editor of the *Monthly Repository*; Malthus, educated at the Dissenting Academy at Warrington, had ties to London Unitarians; see Mineka, *Dissidence of Dissent*, 109, and Winch, *Riches and Poverty*, 254–56. Martineau, who deeply admired Priestley and memorialized him in *Briery Creek*, may have known of Cooper as editor of Priestley's memoirs.

89. Martineau, "On the Duty of Studying Political Economy," *Miscellanies*, I, 276–77.

90. Ibid., I, 274–75.

91. Gleadle, *Early Feminists*, 51. Even so, this was a significant advance on the position of Marcet who, in *Conversations on Political Economy* (1816), used political economy to justify the wealth of the landowning and manufacturing classes and feared sharing its principles with the working classes. On Marcet's audience, see Hilda Hollis, "The Rhetoric of Jane Marcet's Popularizing Political Economy," *Nineteenth-Century Contexts* 24 (2002), 379–96.

92. Noel W. Thompson, *The People's Science: The Popular Political Economy of Exploitation and Crisis, 1816–1834* (Cambridge: Cambridge University Press, 1984), 8. The first chapter, "Changing Attitudes to Political Economy in the Working-Class Press, 1816–1834," traces the shift from outright dismissal and vilification of political economists to an acknowledgment that their theories needed to be taken

seriously and successfully countered with an "anti-capitalist and socialist political economy" (35).

93. "To Parson Malthus: On the Rights of the Poor," *Cobbett's Weekly Political Register* 34, no. 33 (8 May 1819), 1020.

94. Marcet, *Conversations*, 158.

95. Quoted in Gleadle, *Early Feminists*, 47; see also 33–36 for the intellectual legacy of this circle.

96. Harriet Martineau, *A History of the Thirty Years' Peace,* A.D. *1816–1846* (London: George Bell and Sons, 1877), II, 408. The work was originally published by Charles Knight in 1849–50.

97. Martineau, *History of the Peace*, II, 426.

98. Ibid., II, 435.

99. Harriet Martineau, *Life in the Wilds, Illustrations of Political Economy* (London: Charles Fox, 1834), I, 31.

100. Martineau, *History of the Peace*, II, 416.

101. Martineau, *Miscellanies*, I, 53.

102. Ibid., I, 45, 53.

103. Martineau, *Life in the Wilds*, I, 6.

104. Martineau, *History of the Peace*, II, 444.

105. *Book of the Poets: The Modern Poets of the Nineteenth Century* (London: Scott, Webster and Geary, 1842), 13. An image of Wordsworth presides over the title page.

106. Ibid., 20–28.

107. Martineau, *History of the Peace*, II, 493–96. In her 1855 *Autobiography*, II, 297–99, she further complained of the "poverty and perverseness" of Whig ideas in the 1840s, calling the working classes "by far the wiser party of the two."

108. These topics are treated in *The Loom and the Lugger, Sowers not Reapers, Vanderput and Snoek, Life in the Wilds, Demerara, A Manchester Strike, Cousin Marshall, Weal and Woe in of Garveloch, The Tenth Haycock,* and *The Farrers of Budge Row,* respectively.

109. A misstep Martineau made in this regard was succumbing to Lord Brougham's plea that she write tales illustrating the new poor law for the Society for the Diffusion of Useful Knowledge, considered to be a Whig propaganda organ. As Richard Garnett, the Victorian biographer of W. J. Fox, observes, this publishing venue produced a consequent "suspicion under which she lay of abated Radicalism," of which Fox warned her and which she told Fox she meant to disprove (*The Life of W. J. Fox,* 87).

110. Martineau, *Collected Letters*, II, 311.

111. "Miss Martineau's Illustrations of Political Economy," *Tait's Edinburgh Magazine* (August 1832); rpt. in Logan, ed., *Illustrations of Political Economy,* 416.

112. William Maginn quotes this passage in "On National Economy: Review of Miss Martineau's 'Cousin Marshall,' " *Fraser's Magazine for Town and Country* 6 (November 1832), 403–13, citing "On Political Economy," *Westminster Review* 17 (July 1832), 1; quoted in Logan, ed., *Illustrations of Political Economy,* 420.

113. [Conder], review of *Illustrations of Political Economy,* 44–72; quoted in Logan, ed., *Illustrations of Political Economy,* 413.

114. [Maginn], "On National Economy," 403; quoted in Logan, ed., *Illustrations of Political Economy,* 420.

115. [William Maginn], "No. 42.—Miss Harriet Martineau," *Fraser's Magazine* 8 (November 1833), 576.

116. [George Poulett Scrope], review of *Illustrations of Political Economy*, *Quarterly Review* 49 (April 1833), 136.

117. Ross, *Contours of Masculine Desire*, 203.

118. *Memorials*, ed. Chapman, III, 91.

119. Harriet Martineau to "Madam," 25 May 1833, in *Selected Letters*, ed. Sanders, 40.

120. Harriet Martineau to Thomas and Jane Carlyle, 26 April [1840], in *Selected Letters*, ed. Sanders, 56.

121. Carlyle, *On Heroes, Hero-Worship, and the Heroic in History*.

122. Ibid., 179.

123. Ibid., 178.

124. Ibid., 165, 168.

CHAPTER 3

Working Collaboratively

1. Mary Howitt to Anna Harrison, February 1833, Ht 1/1/88, Manuscripts and Special Collections, The University of Nottingham. Quotations from Mary Howitt's letters to her sister Anna are held in this important archive and used with permission.

2. Elizabeth Barrett wrote to her friend Mary Russell Mitford on 2 December 1842, "Surely some of her [Mary Howitt's] ballads are beautiful, suggestive of a power which does not explain itself, I admit, in her longer efforts, . . . but still to be recognized as a form of poetry, in themselves." When Howitt published a collection of ballads in 1847, Barrett Browning, then in Italy, eagerly inquired, "Tell me of Mary Howitt's new collection of ballads. Are they good?" See letters of 2 December 1842 and 8 February 1847, in *The Letters of Elizabeth Barrett Browning to Mary Russell Mitford, 1846–1854*, ed. Meredith B. Raymond and Mary Rose Sullivan (Winfield, KS: Wedgestone Press, 1983), II, 109; III, 203. For Mary Howitt's Victorian reputation, see Carl Woodring, *Victorian Samplers: William and Mary Howitt* (Lawrence: University of Kansas Press, 1954), preface and chs. 2 and 4.

3. [Margaret Oliphant], "The Old Saloon," *Blackwood's Edinburgh Magazine* 146 (November 1889), 712–13.

4. Karen Karbiener, "Scribbling Woman into History: Reconsidering a Forgotten British Poetess from an American Perspective," *The Wordsworth Circle* 32 (Winter 2001), 49. In ranking Howitt second, after Felicia Hemans, Karbiener is discussing the American audience, but until Elizabeth Barrett's rise in the 1840s, the response would have been similar in England.

5. See Brian E. Maidment, "Magazines of Popular Progress and the Artisans," *Victorian Periodicals Review* 17 (Fall 1984), 82–94, and " 'Works in unbroken succession': The Literary Career of Mary Howitt," in *Popular Victorian Women Writers*, ed. Kay Boardman and Shirley Jones (Manchester: Manchester University Press, 2004), 22–45.

6. My understanding of these emerging professional spaces and practices derives from conversations with art historian Will Vaughan; see also Deborah Cherry,

Beyond the Frame: Feminism and Visual Culture, Britain, 1850–1900 (London: Routledge, 2000).

7. Mary Howitt, "Some Reminiscences of My Life," *Good Words* 26 (1885), 661. These reminiscences were revised, edited, and posthumously published by Howitt's daughter as *Mary Howitt: An Autobiography*, edited by her daughter Margaret Howitt, 2 vols. (London: Ibister, 1889).

8. Howitt, *Autobiography*, I, 24. *The Kaleidoscope; or, Literary and Scientific Mirror* was a weekly paper, considered Britain's first cheap miscellany, which was produced between 1818 and 1831 by the Liverpool publisher Egerton Smith with William and Mary as regular contributors.

9. Mary Howitt to Anna Harrison, 15 November 1822, Ht 1/1/10. In the 1820s the Howitts still used the Quaker practice of naming months by numbers—e.g., 11 mo. 15th 1822—a practice Mary dropped by 1827. I have used traditional dates.

10. Mary Howitt to Anna Harrison, 17 February [1834], Ht 1/1/92.

11. Mary Howitt to Anna Harrison, 26 February 1834, Ht 1/1/93.

12. Mary Howitt to Anna Harrison, 29 September 1834, Ht 1/1/95.

13. Mary Howitt, *Ballads and Other Poems*, new ed. (New York: George Putnam, 1848), 54–64.

14. Howitt gives these details in her *Autobiography*, I, 154, 173, 180, 197. Portions of the *Autobiography* were earlier published as "Some Reminiscences of My Life" and "Reminiscences of My Later Life" in *Good Words*, vols. 25–26 (1885–86).

15. In *Victorian Samplers* Woodring provides several examples of one member of the pair supplying material under the other's name—e.g., that William wrote two of Mary's *Tales in Prose for Boys and Girls* and translated segments of Frederika Bremer's novels, for which Mary had the contract.

16. Mary Howitt, *Ballads and Other Poems* (London: Longman, Brown, Green and Longmans, 1847).

17. Quoted in her *Autobiography*, I, 237. There are no illustrations in the first edition of Mary Howitt's *The Seven Temptations* (London: Richard Bentley, 1834).

18. Howitt, *Autobiography*, I, 279–80. The signature "Anna Mary" is visible in only two of the illustrations for "Marien's Pilgrimage," those for parts I and VIII. Anna Mary also illustrated "A Life's Sorrow" in the same volume; see Mary Howitt, *Hymns and Fire-side Verses* (London: Darton and Clark, 1839). The illustration for *The Boy's Country-Book* is not the tailpiece but the first drawing of ch. XVI in William Howitt's *The Boy's Country-Book: Being the Real Life of a Country Boy, Written by Himself*, 3rd ed. (London: Longman, Brown, Green, and Longmans, 1847), 248, originally published in 1839.

19. Mary Howitt to Anna Harrison, February 1833, Ht 1/1/88.

20. Mary Howitt to Anna Harrison, undated letter, probably 1834, Ht 1/1/98.

21. Letter dated St. Anna's Day, 1870, quoted in Howitt, *Autobiography*, II, 181.

22. Mary Howitt, preface to *The Children's Year*, with four plates from original designs by Anna Mary Howitt (Philadelphia: Lea and Blanchard, 1848), v. Mary comments that her column in *Howitt's Journal*, "The Child's Corner," was inspired by and written for her children.

23. Mary Jean Corbett writes about this model in her chapter "Literary Domesticity and Women Writers' Subjectivities," in *Representing Femininity: Middle-Class Subjectivity in Victorian and Edwardian Women's Autobiographies* (New York:

Oxford University Press, 1992), 83–106. Whereas Corbett sees Howitt as "subordinat[ing] her writing to her woman's role" (88–89), I see Howitt's model as collaborative and familial, based on her family's Dissenting culture and on her practical knowledge of the mores of professional artists. My different sense derives in part from treating the 1885–86 version of Howitt's life story, "Some Reminiscences of My Life" in *Good Words*, as the primary autobiographical text; these "Reminiscences" read more like a professional memoir, less like a family history.

24. Mrs. [Anna] Jameson, *Sisters of Charity, Catholic and Protestant* and *The Communion of Labour*, 26–27. More so than Howitt's, Jameson's conception of work is highly gendered: "The man governs, sustains, and defends the family; the woman cherishes, regulates, and purifies it; but though distinct, the relative work is inseparable,—sometimes exchanged, sometimes shared."

25. Cherry, *Beyond the Frame*, 20.

26. Mary Howitt to Anna Harrison, 12 November 1827, Ht 1/1/39.

27. Mary Howitt to Anna Harrison, 18 March 1839, Ht 1/1/120.

28. Holly Laird, *Women Coauthors* (Urbana: University of Illinois Press, 2000), 40, 48; see also Bette London, *Writing Double: Women's Literary Relationships* (Ithaca: Cornell University Press, 1999), which focuses on the history of writing practices and examines the complexity of the professional-amateur binary. For alternative approaches to collaboration that focus on its enabling (or disabling) metaphors, see Andrea Lunsford and Lisa Ede's emphasis on "conversation" in *Singular Texts/Plural Authors* (Carbondale: Southern Illinois University Press, 1990); Wayne Koestenbaum's notion of "penetration" in *Double Talk: The Erotics of Male Collaboration* (New York: Routledge, 1989); and Susan Leonardi and Rebecca Pope's discussion of current feminist metaphors in "Screaming Divas: Collaboration as Feminist Practice," *Tulsa Studies in Women's Literature* 13 (1994), 259–70.

29. Oliphant, "Old Saloon," 712–13.

30. Mary Howitt to Anna Harrison, 7 January [1844], Ht 1/1/147.

31. Corbett, *Representing Femininity*, 88–89.

32. Amice Lee, *Laurels and Rosemary: The Life of William and Mary Howitt* (London: Oxford University Press, 1955), xi.

33. Wordsworth, *The Prelude*, Bk. IV, ll. 308–38; Elizabeth Barrett Browning, *Aurora Leigh*, ed. Kerry McSweeney (Oxford: Oxford University Press, 1993), Bk. II, ll. 10–12.

34. David Macbeth Moir, *Sketches of the Poetical Literature . . . in Six Lectures* (London, 1851), 272.

35. William and Mary Howitt, *The Forest Minstrel, and Other Poems* (London: Baldwin, Cradock, and Joy, 1823).

36. William and Mary Howitt, *The Desolation of Eyam: The Emigrant, A Tale of the American Woods and Other Poems* (London: Wightman and Cramp, 1827); see Mary Howitt to Anna Harrison, 13 December 1826, Ht 1/1/37.

37. Neither of the Howitts' biographers, Amice Lee or Carl Woodring, offers information about the financial details of these early poetic ventures, and Mary's letters to Anna Harrison do not refer to profits or losses. The half-profits contract for *The Seven Temptations* signed with Colburn and Bentley appears in the Bentley Papers, 46612, f. 68, in the British Library. William had earlier sold copyright of *The Book of the Seasons* to Colburn and Bentley for "75 guineas for the first edition

of 1250 copies, 25 guineas for the second edition" (4661, f. 135)—a contract suggesting that the publishers expected to make a profit on this volume (as they in fact did).

38. Mary Howitt to Anna Harrison, 26 February 1834, Ht 1/1/93.

39. Lee Erickson, "The Market," in *A Companion to Victorian Poetry*, ed. Richard Cronin, Alison Chapman, and Antony H. Harrison (Oxford: Blackwell, 2002), 345–46; see also his chapter, "The Poets' Corner: The Impact of Technological Changes in Printing on English Poetry," in *The Economy of Literary Form*.

40. Erickson, *The Economy of Literary Form*, 28–29.

41. Ibid., 49–69.

42. Paula R. Feldman, "The Poet and the Profits: Felicia Hemans and the Literary Marketplace," in *Women's Poetry: Late Romantic to Late Victorian*, ed. Isobel Armstrong and Virginia Blain (London: Macmillan, 1999), 71–101.

43. Mary Howitt to Anna Harrison, November 1826, Ht 1/1/36.

44. Paula R. Feldman, introduction to *The Keepsake for 1829*, ed. Paula R. Feldman (Petersborough, Ontario: Broadview Press, 2006), 22–23.

45. Feldman cites these figures, 18, 20–21, for the 1829 *Keepsake*.

46. Mary Howitt to Anna Harrison, 31 December 1824 and November 1826, Ht 1/1/22 and 1/1/36. Richard D. Altick cites this sales figure in *The English Common Reader: A Social History of the Mass Reading Public, 1800–1900* (Chicago: University of Chicago Press, 1957), 362; Erickson, "The Market," 345, cites figures for *The Literary Souvenir* of 6,000 for 1825 and 8,000–9,000 for 1829.

47. Mary Howitt to Anna Harrison, 22 February 1829, Ht 1/1/47.

48. Mary Howitt to Anna Harrison, November 1826, Ht 1/1/36.

49. Mary Howitt, preface to *Ballads and Other Poems*, vii. In the preface Howitt notes that most of her ballads were written in the 1830s, "ten or fifteen years ago" (viii).

50. "Far-Off Visions" appeared in *The Forget-Me-Not* of 1833, "Tibbie Inglis" in *The Forget-Me-Not* of 1834, "The Dream of Peticus" in *The Literary Souvenir* of 1828, "The Faery Oath" in *The Literary Souvenir* of 1830, and "Marian Lee" in *The Literary Souvenir* of 1833. Robert Southey recommended a similar strategy to Ebenezer Elliott, the "Corn-Laws" poet: "Feel your way before you with the public, as Montgomery did. He sent his verses to the newspapers; and when they were copied from one to another it was a sure sign they had succeeded. He then communicated them, as they were copied from the papers, to the Poetical Register; the Reviews selected them for praise; and thus, when he published them in collected form, he did nothing more than claim, in his own character, the praise which had been bestowed upon him under a fictitious name"; quoted in Erickson, *The Economy of Literary Form*, 153.

51. Woodring, *Victorian Samplers*, 22. Woodring cites Howitt's comment about *Fisher's Drawing Room Scrap-book*—"I was not proud of the work" (p. 30, quoting Howitt, *Autobiography*, II, 22)—to sum up Howitt's work on the annuals, but this comment applies only to the effects of editing an annual in its decline and the necessity of writing nearly a poem a day to meet the publisher's deadline. In writing for annuals in the 1820s and early 1830s, Mary Howitt typically contributed at most a poem or two.

52. Howitt, preface to *Ballads and Other Poems*, vii–viii.

53. Mary Howitt, "The Poor Scholar," in *The Seven Temptations, The Poetical Works of Mary Howitt* (Philadelphia: Crissy and Markley, 1849), 3. This poem, the shortest of the seven, is the only one reprinted in later collections of her work.

54. Review of *The Seven Temptations: A Dramatic Heptalogy, The Literary Gazette*, no. 891 (15 February 1834), 118. Howitt ascribes the review to William Jerdan, the editor, but it could have been written by another staff writer, including Laetitia Landon.

55. Woodring, *Victorian Samplers*, 32.

56. "The Annuals of 1830," unsigned print, Lewis Walpole Library Collection, 1830.1.1.1, Yale University Library.

57. See Maidment, "Literary Career of Mary Howitt," 35, 42n32, for a discussion of this poem and Mary Howitt's counterpart, "The Lost One."

58. It is arguable that Howitt's most lasting contribution as a woman of letters emerged from her translations of Hans Christian Andersen and Frederika Bremer and her contributions to *The Literature and Romance of Northern Europe* (London: Colburn and Company, 1852), coauthored with William. As Woodring documents in *Victorian Samplers*, 167ff., this seminal work was used by Longfellow in his translations of Norse poetry and by Edmund Gosse who, in Woodring's view, is often given credit for introducing Scandinavian literature to England that the Howitts had, in fact, pioneered twenty-five years earlier.

59. Mary Howitt to Anna Harrison, November[?] 1844, Ht 1/1/153.

60. Mary Howitt, *The Children's Year* (London: Longman, Brown, Green, and Longmans, 1847), 9.

61. Ibid., 53.

62. In her survey of Victorian children's literature, "The Publishing of Children's Books in Victoria's Day," in *Book Selling and Book Buying: Aspects of the Nineteenth-Century British and North American Book Trade*, ed. Richard G. Landon (Chicago: American Library Association, 1978), 17–33, Judith St. John notes a reaction in the 1840s against the heavy didacticism of earlier decades, often referred to as "anti–Peter Parleyism." Howitt's emphasis on seeing events from the child's point of view is part of this reaction, but the book is nonetheless didactic in its motivation.

63. Howitt, "Reminiscences of My Later Life," *Good Words* 27 (1886), 57.

64. Howitt, *Children's Year*, 9, 179.

65. Benedict Anderson, *Imagined Communities: Reflections on the Origins and Spread of Nationalism*, rev. ed. (London: Verso, 1991), 5–6.

66. For Mary's induction of her daughter into the life of a professional writer and artist, see my "Mother-Daughter Productions: Mary Howitt and Anna Mary Howitt in *Howitt's Journal, Household Words*, and Other Mid-Victorian Publications," *Victorian Periodicals Review* 31 (1998), 31–54. Bette London discusses apprenticeship as collaboration in *Writing Double*, esp. 33–62. Although she objects (rightly) to this model for understanding the juvenilia of the Brontës, I believe that it applies to many mid-Victorian literary and artistic families like the Howitts, who viewed their work as a family business. Their approach to writing as professional work undermines a common modern view of collaboration as amateur production; quite the contrary, an apprenticeship model requires that such literary and artistic collaborations be treated as (pre)professional.

67. Quoted in Lee, *Laurels and Rosemary*, 164.

68. Lee, *Laurels and Rosemary*, 186. Edward La Trobe Bateman, Anna Mary's fiancé, was a friend of the pre-Raphaelites.

69. Mary Howitt to Anna Harrison, 1845, Ht 1/1/170.

70. Mary Howitt to Anna Harrison, early 1847, Ht 1/1/192. Howitt seems to have been influenced by the discussion of literature as a profession in contemporary periodicals, as she also begins in this period to refer to her work as "literary property."

71. See, e.g., Casteras's research on the illustrations of Florence and Adelaide Claxton in "From 'Safe Havens' to 'A Wide Sea of Notoriety,'" 24–30.

72. "The Child's Corner," *Howitt's Journal* 1 (1847), 303. In 1847 the Howitts were editing two journals: the *People's Journal* and *Howitt's Journal*. The details of this editorial work remain unclear, despite the sleuthing of Carl Woodring for *Victorian Samplers*, 115–43. The *People's Journal* began publication in 1846 under the editorship of John Saunders, and both it and *Howitt's Journal* were published in 1847. Volume VI of the former (1848) shows the title page as *The People's Journal into which is incorporated Howitt's Journal*, thus suggesting that the two journals merged midway through 1848. However, Mary states that her husband was involved as early as 1846 in the *People's Journal* as "one of the editors and part-proprietor of a new cheap weekly publication, *The People's Journal*" (Howitt, *Autobiography*, II, 39)—a statement Woodring corroborates, adding that William struggled with Saunders over the editorship of this magazine.

73. Cherry, *Beyond the Frame*, 26, citing Lee, *Laurels and Rosemary*, 185.

74. See Christopher Wood, *Dictionary of Victorian Painters*, 2nd ed. (Woodbridge, Suffolk: Antique Collectors' Club, 1978), s.v. "Absolon"; Rodney K. Engen, *Dictionary of Victorian Wood Engravers* (Cambridge: Chadwick-Healey, 1985), s.v. "Measom."

75. "The Child's Corner," *Howitt's Journal* 1 (1847), 304–5.

76. Howitt, *Autobiography*, I, 284–85; see Casteras, "From 'Safe Havens' to 'A Wide Sea of Notoriety,'" 24–30.

77. Howitt, *Children's Year*, v. The publication date of the original British edition is 1847; the preface is dated October 1847.

78. These phrases appear on the title pages of the first British editions of *The Children's Year* (London: Longman, Brown, Green, and Longmans, 1847) and *Our Cousins in Ohio* (London: Darton and Co., 1849). Most subsequent editions do not include John Absolon's name.

79. The illustration appears in *Our Cousins in Ohio*, opposite 89. The tale itself omits Dr. Jack's death, focusing instead on the children's gift of apples to the sick man and their surprise when, on a later visit, they learn that he has died and they have missed his funeral.

80. Howitt, *Autobiography*, II, 56, 63–64.

81. Ibid., II, 58–59, 63.

82. "Bits of Life in Munich" appeared in *Household Words* in these issues: 32 (2 November 1850), 133–37; 41 (4 January 1851), 358–59; 43 (18 January 1851), 395–97; 49 (1 March 1851), 535–40; 53 (29 March 1851), 9–13; 54 (5 April 1851), 43–46; 61 (24 May 1851), 209–11; and 64 (14 June 1851), 261–64. These articles correspond roughly to the following chapters in *An Art-Student in Munich* (London: Longman, Brown, Green, and Longmans, 1853): I, v, xiv, xvii, xix, xxi, and II, i, ii.

83. Included in *An Art-Student*, I, xvii, 172–73, and II, ii, 21–22.

84. The articles appear in the *Athenaeum* 23 (30 November 1850), 1251–52; 24 (11 January 1851), 56–57; 24 (1 February 1851), 143–44; and 24 (12 April 1851), 406. They are signed "H." and correspond to the following chapters of *An Art Student*: I, xv, 157–61; I, ix, 107–13; I, xxiii, 233–38; and I, xxii, 223–26. There is one other unsigned paragraph published in 25 (18 October 1851), 1097, under "Fine-Art Gossip," which is a description of the new Basilica at Munich.

85. "Bits of Life in Munich," *Household Words* 32 (2 November 1850), 133.

86. Howitt, *Autobiography*, II, 63–64.

87. Ibid., II, 89, 90.

88. Anna Mary Howitt, *A School of Life* (Boston: Ticknor and Fields, 1855). The dedication reads: "To my beloved brother Alfred, these collected papers, which, in their original form, were read by him in the wilds of Australia, are affectionately inscribed."

89. The characters cannot, of course, simply be equated with the real-life originals in that Howitt exchanges details of their lives and work, as if what mattered was not individual histories but collective experiences.

90. From a letter to her husband, William, written in 1852 while he traveled in Australia with their sons; quoted in Howitt, *Autobiography*, II, 90.

91. A.M.H., *The Sisters in Art, Illustrated Exhibitor and Magazine of Art* 2 (1852), 319.

92. Recorded by Anna Mary in *An Art-Student in Munich*, 45.

93. *Sisters in Art* 2 (1852), 334.

94. Ibid., 362.

95. Joanne Shattock, ed., *The Oxford Guide to British Women Writers* (Oxford: Oxford University Press, 1993), s.v. "Bessie Parkes."

96. Anna Mary Watts, *Pioneers of the Spiritual Reformation: Life and Works of Dr. Justinus Kerner* and *William Howitt and His Work for Spiritualism* (London: Psychological Press Association, 1883), 269–71.

97. In 1875 Anna Mary and her husband published *Aurora: A Volume of Verse* (London: Henry S. King, 1875), in which the poems alternately carry the signatures "A. A." (Alaric Alfred) and "A. M." (Anna Mary). Following London's suggestion in *Writing Double* that mediumship represents a form of collaboration, we might see Anna Mary's interest in spiritualism not as a retreat but as a fuller immersion into collaborative practice.

98. Mary Howitt, "Some Reminiscences of My Life," *Good Words* 26 (1885), 383–90, 423–29, 494–502, 565–73, 660–67, and "Reminiscences of My Later Life," *Good Words* 27 (1886), 52–59, 172–79, 330–37, 394–402, 592–601. According to a letter in the Briggs collection (Bg 22), Manuscripts and Special Collections, The University of Nottingham Library, Howitt was asked to expand the "Reminiscences" into an autobiography; her daughter Margaret, writing to Eliza Oldham ["Lizzy"] on 13 July 1888 after her mother's death, requests the loan of any letters that Eliza or her family might have preserved.

99. *Mary Howitt: An Autobiography*. The preface, written by Margaret, explains that her mother had written segments of her childhood experience at earlier dates (1843, 1868), largely at the request of her children, and that the death of her husband, William, in 1879 initiated another period of auto/biographical reflection.

100. For discussions of the possibility that Mill's *Autobiography* was a coauthored text, see Jonathan Loesberg, *Fictions of Consciousness: Mill, Newman, and the Reading of Victorian Prose* (New Brunswick, NJ: Rutgers University Press, 1986); Jack Stillinger, "Who Wrote Mill's *Autobiography?*" *Victorian Studies* 27 (1983), 7–23, and *Multiple Authorship and the Myth of Romantic Genius* (Oxford: Oxford University Press, 1991); Janice Carlisle, *John Stuart Mill and the Writing of Character* (Athens: University of Georgia Press, 1991); and Laird, *Women Coauthors*. For the composition of Elizabeth Davis's autobiography, see the introduction to *The Autobiography of Elizabeth Davis* by its modern editor, Deirdre Beddoe (Cardiff: Honno, 1987), who discusses the editorial decisions that Jane Williams made in transcribing Davis's oral testimony (xiii–xv).

101. [Oliphant], "Two Ladies," 206–24. For further discussion of this class and its memoirs, see Linda H. Peterson, "Margaret Oliphant's *Autobiography* as Professional Artist's Life," *Women's Writing* 6 (1999), 261–78.

102. Howitt, "Reminiscences," 26 (1885), 383. When Margaret revised the text for book publication, she made the narrative chronological and, in so doing, diminished the rhetorical power of this opening.

103. Cherry, *Beyond the Frame*, 187–89.

104. Opposite the title page of *An Art-Student in Munich* is this quotation from Ruskin: "There is that to be seen in every street and lane of every city, that to be felt and found in every human heart and countenance, that to be loved in every roadside weed and moss-grown wall, which, in the hands of faithful men, may convey emotions of glory and sublimity continual and exalted."

105. Quoted in Cherry, *Beyond the Frame*, 187.

106. Pamela Gerrish Nunn, *Victorian Women Artists* (London: Women's Press, 1987), 56; see also 67n75.

107. Margaret Howitt to Bessie Rayner Parkes Belloc, 13 January 1918, GCPP Parkes 7/33, Girton College Library; quoted with permission of the Mistress and Fellows of Girton College, Cambridge.

108. Howitt, *Autobiography*, I, xi.

109. Howitt, *Homes and Haunts of the Most Eminent British Poets*. Although the title page bears William's name, both husband and wife contributed to the research and writing; Anna Mary provided many illustrations.

110. Whether Anna Mary concurred in her mother's auto/biographical interpretation, we cannot know. During her trip to Switzerland Anna Mary developed diphtheria and died on 23 July 1884, before the "Reminiscences" or the *Autobiography* appeared in print.

CHAPTER 4
Parallel Currents

1. [Elizabeth Rigby], *Quarterly Review* 84 (December 1848), 153–85; the letter is included in *The Letters of Charlotte Brontë*, ed. Margaret Smith (Oxford: Clarendon Press, 1995, 2000, 2004), II, 242–45. Cited hereafter as *Brontë Letters*.

2. See Juliet Barker, *The Brontës* (New York: St. Martin's, 1994), 605–7, for an account of this preface.

3. Elaine Showalter, *A Literature of Their Own: British Women Novelists from Brontë to Lessing* (Princeton: Princeton University Press, 1977), 106; the quotation comes from Margaret Oliphant's anonymous review, "Modern Novelists—Great and Small," *Blackwood's Edinburgh Magazine* 77 (1855), 568.

4. Elizabeth Gaskell to George Smith, 31 May [1855], *The Letters of Mrs. Gaskell*, ed. J. A. V. Chapple and Arthur Pollard (Manchester: Manchester University Press, 1966), no. 241, p. 345. Cited hereafter as *Gaskell Letters*.

5. Patrick Brontë to Elizabeth Gaskell, 16 June 1855, Christie Library, Manchester University, quoted in Angus Easson, *Elizabeth Gaskell* (London: Routledge and Kegan Paul, 1979), 134.

6. Alexander Dyce, *Specimens of British Poetesses* (London: T. Rodd, 1825); Mrs. [Anne Katherine] Elwood, *Memoirs of the Literary Ladies of England*, 2 vols. (London: Henry Colburn, 1843).

7. Elwood, *Memoirs of Literary Ladies*, I, v–vi.

8. When Elwood collected the memoirs, she was a young author with one published book, *Narrative of a Journey Overland from England to India etc., 1825–8* (London, 1830). According to the *DNB*, she was "unable to find any published biography of literary females, [and] decided to write her own."

9. Emma Roberts, "Memoir of L.E.L.," in *The Zenana and Minor Poems of L.E.L.* (London: Fisher, 1839).

10. Laman Blanchard, *Life and Literary Remains of L.E.L.*, 2 vols. (London: Henry Colburn, 1841).

11. Henry F. Chorley, *Memorials of Mrs. Hemans, with Illustrations of her Literary Character from her Private Correspondence*, 2 vols. (London: Saunders and Otley, 1836); *Memoir of the Life and Writings of Mrs. Hemans*, by her sister (Edinburgh: William Blackwood and Sons, 1840), 1.

12. Laetitia Elizabeth Landon, "A History of the Lyre," in *Selected Writings*, ed. Jerome McGann and Daniel Riess (Toronto: Broadview Press, 1997), 127, ll. 430–45.

13. Geraldine Jewsbury, *The Half Sisters*, ed. Joanne Wilkes (Oxford: Oxford World's Classics, 1994), ch. 27, 390–91.

14. Gaskell, *Life of Charlotte Brontë*, in *Works*, ed. Shattock, VIII, 223. This statement appears in vol. II, ch. 2 of the *Life*, where Gaskell notes, "I put into words what Charlotte Brontë put into action" (224). All citations are to this edition of the *Life*, with vol. and ch. references included for the convenience of readers using other editions.

15. These judgments come from the *Atlas* (23 October 1847) and the *Christian Remembrancer* (April 1848), respectively; rpt. in Miriam Allott, ed., *The Brontës: The Critical Heritage* (London: Routledge and Kegan Paul, 1974), 67, 89.

16. [Rigby], quoted in Allott, *The Brontës*, 109.

17. Ellen Nussey to A. B. Nicholls, 6 June 1855, *Brontë Letters*, I, 27.

18. Margaret Smith speculates that the article was written by Frank Smedley, a novelist and former editor of *Sharpe's* (see *Brontë Letters*, I, 27n1); he was perhaps an acquaintance of Catherine Winkworth, from whom he may have heard tales about Currer Bell initially deriving from the letter that Gaskell wrote to Winkworth on 25 August 1850, after first meeting Brontë at the Kay-Shuttleworths. For a thorough discussion of Gaskell's role in this unfortunate transmission, see Linda K. Hughes

and Michael Lund, *Victorian Publishing and Mrs. Gaskell's Work* (Charlottesville: University Press of Virginia, 1999), 124–40.

19. All phrases but the penultimate come from "A Few Words about 'Jane Eyre,'" *Sharpe's London Magazine*, n.s., 6 (June 1855), 339–42. The hurtful expression, "who had long forfeited the society of her sex," is Elizabeth Rigby's in the unsigned *Quarterly Review* article cited above, which the reviewer for *Sharpe's* elsewhere paraphrases.

20. Elizabeth Gaskell to Ellen Nussey, 6 September 1855, in *Brontë Letters*, III, 376. This letter includes a key conception of Brontë as "the *friend*, the *daughter*, the *sister*, the *wife*."

21. Virtually every critic who has written on the *Life* addresses the concept of "duty"; the most important discussions include those by Easson, Hughes and Lund, Arthur Pollard, *Mrs. Gaskell: Novelist and Biographer* (Manchester: Manchester University Press, 1965), and Deirdre d'Albertis, " 'Bookmaking Out of the Remains of the Dead': Elizabeth Gaskell's *The Life of Charlotte Brontë*," *Victorian Studies* 39 (1995), 1–32. The letters to Ellen Nussey and Mary Taylor raise this issue repeatedly, and thus are points of origin for Gaskell and all subsequent biographers.

22. *Life*, I, vii, 79, quoting Charlotte Brontë to Ellen Nussey, 18 October 1832, in *Brontë Letters*, I, 118–19.

23. Rosemarie Bodenheimer, *The Real Life of Mary Ann Evans: George Eliot, Her Letters and Fiction* (Ithaca: Cornell University Press, 1994), 33.

24. Gaskell often had her daughters (and sometimes her husband) copy letters into the manuscript, which she would then edit and combine. As Easson comments, "Gaskell is generally careful and accurate in reproduction and in indicating how the letters are handled. That she edits and omits was part of her authorial policy, made explicit in the work itself"; see his "Note on the Text," in *The Life of Charlotte Brontë*, by Elizabeth Gaskell, ed. Angus Easson (Oxford: World's Classics, 1996), xxviii.

25. Robert Southey to Charlotte Brontë, 12 March 1837, and Brontë to Southey, 16 March 1837, in *Brontë Letters*, I, 165–67, 167–68.

26. Nussey uses this phrase in her "Reminiscences of Charlotte Brontë," *Scribner's Monthly*, May 1871, p. 18; rpt. in *Brontë Letters*, I, 589–610.

27. Elizabeth Gaskell to George Smith, 19 August 1856, *Gaskell Letters*, no. 303, p. 404.

28. Harriet Martineau, "Charlotte Brontë ('Currer Bell')," *Biographical Sketches* (London: Macmillan, 1869), 46.

29. See Barker, *The Brontës*, 669–71, for an account of this proposal, including Patrick Brontë's sense that an engagement with a deferral of marriage for five years while Taylor went to India would be a good arrangement.

30. Barker, *The Brontës*, 343–45.

31. See Marnie Jones, "George Smith's Influence on the *Life of Charlotte Brontë*," *Brontë Society Transactions* 18 (1984), 279–85.

32. Elizabeth Gaskell to Ellen Nussey, 9 July 1856, *Gaskell Letters*, 393–96.

33. Mary Taylor to Mrs. Gaskell, 18 January 1856, in *Mary Taylor, Friend of Charlotte Brontë: Letters from New Zealand and Elsewhere*, ed. Joan Stevens (Auckland: Auckland University Press, 1972), appendix B, 161–62.

34. Gaskell initially copied this passage into vol. I, ch. 13; see *Life*, ed. Peterson, in *Works*, ed. Shattock, textual note 175a, p. 497.

35. Lucasta Miller, *The Brontë Myth* (London: Jonathan Cape, 2001), 2. Miller points out that this myth is at odds with the "positive myth of female self-creation" embodied in Brontë's autobiographical heroines Jane Eyre and Lucy Snow.

36. Hughes and Lund, *Victorian Publishing and Mrs. Gaskell's Work*, 125. On the interweaving of the biographer's self with her subject, see Gabriele Helms, "The Coincidence of Biography and Autobiography: Elizabeth Gaskell's *The Life of Charlotte Brontë*," *Biography: An Interdisciplinary Quarterly* 18 (1995), 339–59.

37. Elizabeth Gaskell to Eliza Fox, [c. February 1850], *Gaskell Letters*, no. 68, p. 106.

38. Ibid., 107.

39. Mrs. [Anna] Jameson, *Sisters of Charity, Catholic and Protestant* and *The Communion of Labour*, 25.

40. Colón, *The Professional Ideal in the Victorian Novel*, 13–16. Colón discusses *My Lady Ludlow*, but her terms aptly apply to Gaskell's earlier work.

41. Jenny Uglow, *Elizabeth Gaskell: A Habit of Stories* (London: Faber and Faber, 1993), 117.

42. "Sketches among the Poor, No. 1," *Blackwood's Edinburgh Magazine* 41 (January 1837), 48–50; rpt. in *Journalism, Early Fiction and Personal Writings*, ed. Joanne Shattock, in *Works*, ed. Shattock, I, 33–36.

43. Elizabeth Gaskell to Mary Howitt, [18 August 1838], *Gaskell Letters*, no. 12, p. 33.

44. See Shattock, *Journalism, Early Fiction and Personal Writings*, in *Works*, ed. Shattock, I, 31, for a discussion of these early attempts at authorship. The judgment of this early prose comes from Elizabeth Gaskell to John Blackwood, 9 March [1859], *Gaskell Letters*, no. 417, p. 533.

45. William Howitt, *The Rural Life of England*, 2 vols. (London: Longman, Orme, Brown, Green, and Longmans, 1838) and *Visits to Remarkable Places: Old Halls, Battle Fields, and Scenes Illustrative of Striking Passages in English History and Poetry*, 2 vols. (London: Longman, Brown, Green and Longmans, 1840), both of which Mary contributed to. Gaskell may also have had in mind Mary Howitt's novel *Wood Leighton* (London: Richard Bentley, 1836) for its "charming descriptions of natural scenery."

46. Elizabeth Gaskell to William and Mary Howitt, [May 1838], *Gaskell Letters*, no. 8, 14–15.

47. Howitt, *Visits to Remarkable Places*, 135–39; rpt. in *Works*, ed. Shattock, I, 39–41.

48. Howitt, *The Rural Life of England*, 2nd ed. (London: Longman, Brown, Green, and Longmans, 1840), 589–90; rpt. in *Works*, ed. Shattock, I, 45–46.

49. *Mary Howitt: An Autobiography*, II, 28.

50. In her biography, Uglow cites a letter by Mary Howitt, suggesting that "Libbie Marsh" was one of "many manuscripts which lie in a certain desk drawer, & may have lain there for years" (*Elizabeth Gaskell*, 173).

51. Cotton Mather Mills [Elizabeth Gaskell], "Life in Manchester: Libbie Marsh's Three Eras," *Howitt's Journal of Literature and Progress* 1 (1847), 310–13, 334–36, 345–47, rpt. in *Works*, ed. Shattock, I, 49–69.

52. "Libbie Marsh, Era III, Michaelmas," in *Works*, ed. Shattock, I, 69.

53. Elizabeth Gaskell to Eliza Fox, c. February 1850, *Gaskell Letters*, no. 68, p. 107.

54. Easley, *First-Person Anonymous*, 81, 98.

55. William Gaskell did, however, edit and proofread his wife's compositions, as we can detect from the manuscript of *The Life of Charlotte Brontë*, where he alters words and even inserts a Haworth incident he witnessed.

56. William Gaskell published the occasional sermon and, with George Rickword, a volume of exemplary biographies, *Warwickshire Leaders, Social and Political* (London: E. R. Alexander and Sons, n.d.).

57. "William and Mary Howitt's Address to their Friends and Readers," *Howitt's Journal* 1 (1847), 1. Gaskell published "The Sexton's Hero" in *Howitt's Journal* 2 (1847), 149–52, and "Christmas Storms and Sunshine" in 3 (1848), 4–7, both under her pseudonym Cotton Mather Mills. *Howitt's Journal* ceased publication with volume 3.

58. Elizabeth Gaskell to Lady Kay-Shuttleworth, 7 April [1853], *Gaskell Letters*, no. 154, p. 228.

59. Easley, *First-Person Anonymous*, 97.

60. Easson, *Elizabeth Gaskell*, 109.

61. *Life*, II, 2, p. 233.

62. For Howitt's conception of authorship, see ch. 3 as well as Linda H. Peterson, "The Auto/biographies of Mary Howitt and Her Family," *Prose Studies* 26 (2003), 176–95. For an overview, see Mermin, *Godiva's Ride*, 18, who argues, "women were anxious to redefine their art as womanly service: selfless in intent, self-effacing in execution, enhancing rather than replacing womanly responsibility, and if possible attributable to the impetus of a man."

63. Elizabeth Barrett Browning, *Aurora Leigh*, ed. Kerry McSweeney (Oxford: Oxford University Press, 1993), Bk. IX, ll. 645–49.

64. Elizabeth Gaskell to Eliza Fox, c. February 1850, *Gaskell Letters*, no. 68, p. 107.

65. Elizabeth Gaskell to unknown, 25 September ?1862, *Gaskell Letters*, no. 515, p. 695.

66. Elizabeth Gaskell to George Smith, ?25 July 1856, *Gaskell Letters*, no. 297, p. 398.

67. Disraeli, *The Literary Character*. From 1791 to 1834 Isaac Disraeli also issued six volumes of *Curiosities of Literature*, biographical anecdotes about (male) authors that gave evidence of their unique character.

68. J. G. Lockhart, *Memoirs of the Life of Sir Walter Scott, Bart.* (Philadelphia: Carey, Lea, and Blanchard, 1838), I, 16, 63–64, 67.

69. Chorley, *Memorials of Mrs. Hemans*, I, 11–12, 31, 39.

70. Ibid., I, 6–7.

71. Elizabeth Gaskell to George Smith, ?25 July 1856, *Gaskell Letters*, no. 297, p. 398.

72. Elizabeth Gaskell to Charlotte Froude, c. 25 August 1850, *Gaskell Letters*, no. 78, p. 128.

73. D'Albertis, " 'Bookmaking Out of the Remains of the Dead,' " 12–13; see also Donald D. Stone, *The Romantic Impulse in Victorian Fiction* (Cambridge, MA: Harvard University Press, 1980).

74. Preface to the second edition of *Jane Eyre* (1848); rpt. *Jane Eyre*, ed. Richard J. Dunn (New York: Norton, 2001), 2.

75. See, e.g., Charlotte Brontë to Messrs. Smith and Elder, 15 July and 24 August 1847, *Brontë Letters*, I, 533, 537 (quoted in II, ii, 210).

76. Charlotte Brontë to G. H. Lewes, 6 November 1847, *Brontë Letters*, I, 559–60. The phrase is Brontë's.

77. Charlotte Brontë to G. H. Lewes, 19 January 1850, *Brontë Letters*, II, 332–33.

78. Quoted in Allott, *The Brontës*, 161–62.

79. In *Versatile Victorian*, Rosemary Ashton accounts for this lapse by suggesting that Lewes was preoccupied with his wife Agnes's condition—"six months pregnant with her first child by Thornton Hunt" (18).

80. See, e.g., "Currer Bell" to G. H. Lewes after the appearance of the *Edinburgh Review* article: "I can be on guard against my enemies, but God deliver me from my friends!" (*Life*, II, v, 272), and the subsequent letter of 19 January 1850, also signed "Currer Bell" (*Life*, II, v, 272).

81. Parkes, *Essays on Women's Work*, 6.

82. The amount of payment is omitted from Charlotte Brontë to George Smith, 10 December 1847, *Brontë Letters*, I, 570, quoted in *Life*, II, ii, 215; see also Brontë to Smith, 6 December 1852, in *Brontë Letters*, III, 88, quoted in *Life*, II, xi, 340, which omits financial dealings; for a letter about publishers, see Mrs. Gaskell to John Forster, 3 May 1853, included in *Brontë Letters*, III, 159.

83. Most notably, Smith cut and edited the account of his first encounter with Anne and Charlotte Brontë, who had traveled to his office at 65 Cornhill to prove that Acton, Currer, and Ellis Bell were distinct persons and thus to disprove Newby's claim that all novels by the Bells were authored by the same pen. See the textual notes for vol. II, ch. 2, in Gaskell, *Life*, ed. Peterson, in *Works*, ed. Shattock, VIII, 501–3.

84. See Elizabeth Gaskell to George Smith, 2 October [1856], in *Gaskell Letters*, no. 314, p. 418: "Do you mind the law of libel.—I have three people I want to libel—Lady Scott (that bad woman who corrupted Branwell Brontë) Mr Newby, & Lady Eastlake, the {two} first \& last/ not to be named by name, the mean publisher to be gibbeted."

85. On the substitutes women found for the normal literary affiliations of male authors, see Joanne Shattock, "Victorian Women as Writers and Readers of (Auto)biography," in *Mortal Pages, Literary Lives: Studies in Nineteenth-Century Autobiography*, ed. Vincent Newey and Philip Shaw (Aldershot, Hants: Scolar Press, 1996), 140–52.

86. Gaskell's professionalism has been variously treated by scholars. In *First-Person Anonymous*, 103–12, Easley sees the *Life*—and its treatment of the "abused woman author"—as pivotal in the coalescing of Gaskell's literary professionalism. Shattock argues that "Gaskell was an astute judge of the literary marketplace, one who was not overly concerned about the status of the periodicals in which her work was published, but who regarded the press as a key element in her writing life" (*Works*, I, xxxvi). My sense is that Gaskell's literary professionalism developed during her first decade of public writing (1847–57) but that she downplayed the professional element in Brontë's career for strategic reasons, emphasizing instead the genius of her subject.

87. Bock, "Authorship, the Brontës, and *Fraser's Magazine.*"

88. For the business negotiations over a new edition of *Wuthering Heights* and *Agnes Grey*, see Charlotte Brontë to W. S. Williams, 10 September, 13 September, and 20 September 1850, in *Brontë Letters*, II, 464–66, 473–74; and Charlotte Brontë to George Smith, 18 September, 31 October, and 3 December 1850, in *Brontë Letters*, II, 470–73, 491–95, 522–24.

89. See Pierre Bourdieu, "The Field of Instances of Reproduction and Consecration," in *Field of Cultural Production*, ed. Johnson, 120–25.

90. Harriet Martineau to Lord Brougham, 10 October 1832, *Selected Letters*, ed. Sanders, 32, and *Autobiography*, I, 268.

91. See Charlotte Brontë to Messrs Smith, Elder and Co., 12 September 1847, in *Brontë Letters*, I, 539–40, 541n8; Charlotte Brontë to George Smith, 17 February 1848, in *Brontë Letters*, II, 28–29, 29n2; and Charlotte Brontë to W. S. Williams, 20 April 1848, II, 51–52, 52n1.

92. Showalter, *Literature of Their Own*, 106; Miller, *Brontë Myth*, 2.

93. Samuel Smiles, *Self Help, with Illustrations of Character and Conduct* (London: John Murray, 1859).

CHAPTER 5

Challenging Brontëan Myths of Authorship

1. In *The Oxford Guide to Women Authors*, s.v. "Riddell," Joanne Shattock gives 1856 as the date of emigration and 1857 as the date of first publication. In "Charlotte Riddell's *A Struggle for Fame*: The Field of Women's Literary Production," *Colby Library Quarterly* 36 (2000), 118, Margaret Kelleher gives 1855 and 1856, respectively, as does Charlotte Mitchell in the new *Dictionary of National Biography*, s.v. "Riddell [née Cowan], Charlotte Eliza Lawson (1832–1906)." S. M. Ellis, who knew Riddell personally and had access to some of her letters, states that *Zuriel's Grandchild*, her first novel, was "published about 1855 by T. C. Newby," but notes that Riddell herself retained no copy of this novel and went "at a time of financial anxiety" to Newby's office in pursuit of a copy; see *Wilkie Collins, Le Fanu, and Others* (New York: Richard R. Smith, 1931), 280, 323. It is difficult to establish the exact dates of Riddell's life and career because, as Shattock notes, Riddell's "first two books disappeared without a trace"—but even this may not be true because copies of *The Moors and the Fens* (London: Smith, Elder, 1858), published under the pseudonym F. G. Trafford, exist in the British Library and at the Harry Ransom Research Center at The University of Texas.

2. Patricia Srebrnik, "Mrs. Riddell and the Reviewers: A Case Study in Victorian Popular Fiction," *Women's Studies* 23 (1994), 69–84. Srebrnik quotes Edmund Gosse's review, "The Tyranny of the Novel," *National Review* 19 (April 1892), 574–75, to advance her second claim. In fact, Riddell's choice of subject was praised in the 1880s when, in a review of *A Struggle for Fame*, the *Spectator* began by noting that her novels avoided "the love-and-twaddle business" and didn't "run in the same groove as every other novel . . . published within the last twenty years"; see "The Struggle for Fame," *Spectator* 56 (6 October 1883), 1285.

3. Kelleher, "Charlotte Riddell's *A Struggle for Fame*," 117–18, paraphrasing Bourdieu's *Field of Cultural Production*.

4. All citations are to Mrs. J. H. Riddell, *A Struggle for Fame*, 3 vols. (London: Richard Bentley and Son, 1883); hereafter cited in the text by volume and page. There is no modern edition of this novel.

5. Mrs. J. H. Riddell, "Literature as a Profession," *Illustrated Review* 2 (July 1874), 6–7.

6. *Choice of a Business for Girls: Artistic and Intellectual Employments*, Tract 3 in *Tracts for Parents and Daughters* (London: Emily Faithfull, Victoria Press, 1864); Parkes, *Essays on Woman's Work*; Lewes, "Condition of Authors," 285–95; "The Trade of Journalism," *St. Paul's Magazine* 1 (December 1867), 306–18; Crawford, "Journalism as a Profession for Women," 362–71; E. A. Bennett, *Journalism for Women: A Practical Guide* (London: John Lane, Bodley Head, 1898). Even earlier, a short pamphlet, *The Search for a Publisher; or, Counsels for the Young Author*, had been published by the London firm of Alfred W. Bennett in 1855, the year Riddell chooses for the conversation between Glen and Mr. Vassett; it was reviewed by Geraldine Jewsbury in the *Athenaeum* on 21 July 1855 (see Monica Correa Frycksted, *Geraldine Jewsbury's Athenaeum Reviews: A Mirror of Mid-Victorian Attitudes to Fiction* [Uppsala: Almqvist and Wiksell, 1986], 96).

7. The novel *Paul Ferroll* (1855) was written by "V," Mrs. Caroline Archer.

8. Disraeli, *The Literary Character*; Elwood, *Memoirs of Literary Ladies*; Jane Williams, *The Literary Women of England*, 2 vols. (London: Saunders and Otley, 1861).

9. Hughes and Lund, *Victorian Publishing and Mrs. Gaskell's Work*, 139 and passim.

10. Joanne Shattock, "Victorian Women as Writers and Readers of (Auto)biography," in *Mortal Pages, Literary Lives: Studies in Nineteenth-Century Autobiography*, ed. Vincent Newey and Philip Shaw (Aldershot: Scolar Press, 1996), 161–62.

11. Wordsworth, *The Prelude*, Bk. IV; Barrett Browning, *Aurora Leigh*, Bk. II; Charlotte Elizabeth Tonna, *Personal Recollections* (London: Seeleys, 1854), 134–37.

12. Riddell's account was given in an interview with Helen C. Black for the *Lady's Pictorial*, republished in *Notable Women Authors of the Day* (Glasgow: David Bryce, 1893), 15.

13. Gaskell, *Life*, ed. Peterson, vol. VIII of *Works*, ed. Shattock, II, ii, 217. Citations will be to this scholarly edition and include volume and chapter for the sake of readers using different editions of the *Life*.

14. Gaskell, *Life*, II, ii, 210.

15. Glen's disheartening trudge may echo Harriet Martineau's similar experience, recounted in her *Autobiography*, I, 164–78, of taking her prospectus for the *Illustrations of Political Economy* from publisher to publisher.

16. *Saturday Review*, 4 April 1857, p. 313; quoted by Hughes and Lund, *Victorian Publishing and Mrs. Gaskell's Work*, 144.

17. Gaskell, *Life*, I, ii, 27.

18. Tuchman and Fortin, *Edging Women Out*, 82.

19. In fact, Riddell's *kunstlerroman* predates Macmillan's purchase (which occurred in 1898), and her predicament may not have been as dire as that of other women authors, including Mary Cholmondeley (see chapter 7). By the late 1880s, Riddell had shifted publishers to Ward and Downey, and in the 1890s she shifted

again to F. V. White; even in 1900, Macmillan was issuing new editions of her best work for Richard Bentley, including *George Geith*, *Susan Drummond*, and *Berna Boyle*.

20. John Sutherland, ed., *The Longman Companion to Victorian Fiction* (Harlow, Essex: Longman, 1988), 620.

21. See Kelleher, "Charlotte Riddell's *A Struggle for Fame*," 121, who also suggests the Irish-born novelist and publisher Edmund Downey, with whom Riddell worked, for some of Kelly's traits.

22. See "Sala Sets the Ball Rolling," in Peter Newbolt, *William Tinsley: "Speculative Publisher"* (Aldershot: Ashgate, 2001), 53–65. Sala collected his journalistic sketches, "The Key of the Street," into a volume published by the Tinsleys, just as Kelly takes his "Street Sketches" to Felton and Laplash.

23. John Carey, *Thackeray: Prodigal Genius* (London: Faber and Faber, 1977), 15, 19.

24. Ibid., 20.

25. *DNB*, s.v. "Edmund Yates," 1203. Young "Grub Street" in *The Virginians* was considered Thackeray's rebuttal.

26. Charles Dickens, *David Copperfield*, ed. Jerome H. Buckley (1849–50; New York: W. W. Norton, 1990), 439, 528. This amount—£300—was typically cited as an annual income that made authorship a middle-class profession; see Lewes, "Condition of Authors," 285–95.

27. Poovey, *Uneven Developments*, 106.

28. Coventry Patmore, "The Social Position of Women," *North British Review* 14 (1851), 281. Patmore later retracted this statement for the work of Alice Meynell (see chapter 6).

29. *St. James's Magazine* did not include reviews, and there is no evidence from the letters, interviews, and obituaries about Riddell to suggest that she ever took up this aspect of professional literary work. She wrote columns of topical interest for the *Illustrated Review* during the 1870s, including "Literature as a Profession," cited above.

30. See Elisabeth Jay, *Margaret Oliphant: A Fiction to Herself, A Literary Life* (Oxford: Clarendon Press, 1995), 4–5, for the argument that George Eliot's career was exceptional rather than paradigmatic in the history of women's writing.

31. Riddell to Victoria Matthews, dated 1886 and quoted in Ellis, *Wilkie Collins, Le Fanu, and Others*, 302–4. Ellis's biographical study includes extracts from a cache of letters given him by Miss Matthews and a bibliographical list of Riddell's works supplied in part by Montague Summers.

32. Riddell to Victoria Matthews, quoted in Ellis, *Wilkie Collins, Le Fanu, and Others*, 302–4.

33. [C. S. Oakley], "On Commencing Author," *Quarterly Review* 186 (1897), 90.

34. Arthur Waugh, "The New Era in Letters," *National Review* 21 (1893), 510–17, quoting p. 512.

35. Ellis, *Wilkie Collins, Le Fanu, and Others*, 277–78.

36. William Tinsley, *Random Recollections of an Old Publisher* (London: Simpkin, Marshall, Hamilton, Kent and Company, 1900), 86. Riddell narrates a version of this episode in *A Struggle for Fame*, III, v.

37. See Newbolt, 70, and *The Autobiography of Mrs. Oliphant*, ed. Mrs. Harry Coghill (1899; rpt. Chicago: University of Chicago Press, 1988), 125.

38. See *Woolf Uncat.* 4, Harry Ransom Research Center, The University of Texas. The twelve novels include *Too Much Alone, The Rich Husband, George Geith, Maxwell Drewitt, Far Above Rubies, A Life's Assize, The World in the Church, City and Suburb, Phemie Keller, The Race for Wealth, Austin Friars,* and *My First Love, My Last Love*—that is, all of the major novels Riddell published with Skeet or Tinsley between 1860 and 1871.

39. See "Lady Novelists—A Chat with Mrs. J. H. Riddell," *Pall Mall Gazette,* 18 February 1890, and "Mrs. Riddell," in Black's *Notable Women Authors,* originally in the *Lady's Pictorial.*

40. Leo Braudy, *The Frenzy of Renown: Fame and Its History* (New York: Oxford University Press, 1986), 425.

41. Gaskell, *Life,* II, i, 201.

42. Ellis, *Wilkie Collins, Le Fanu, and Others,* 289.

43. Ibid., 298.

44. *Autobiography of Margaret Oliphant,* ed. Jay, 10, 15.

45. Harry Furniss, *Some Victorian Women: Good, Bad, and Indifferent* (London: Bodley Head, 1923), 44.

CHAPTER 6
Transforming the Poet

1. Beverly Seaton, *The Language of Flowers: A History* (Charlottesville: University Press of Virginia, 1995), 168–69.

2. Song of Songs 2:12 (KJV): "The flowers appear on the earth; the time of the singing of birds has come, and the voice of the turtle is heard in our land." It is tempting to think that Meynell knew the fourth sonnet of Christina Rossetti's *Monna Innominata* in manuscript, particularly the lines "I loved you first: but afterwards your love / Outsoaring mine, sang such a loftier song / As drowned the friendly cooings of my dove." She could not have read them in print, as Rossetti's sonnet sequence was published six years after Meynell's *Preludes.*

3. Anne Kimball Tuell, *Mrs. Meynell and Her Literary Generation* (New York: E. P. Dutton, 1925), 31. As Meynell's first biographer, Tuell met and interviewed Meynell in the early 1920s and had access to personal views, letters, and early published work, even though she was restrained by Meynell's wishes about what might be published.

4. Jeremy Siepman, "Frédéric Chopin: The Preludes, Op. 28," for London compact disc, D 102410. Mrs. Thompson, née Christina Weller, was a concert pianist who gave up her career, much to her parents' regret, on her marriage to Thomas James Thompson. Both daughters received extensive musical training.

5. A. C. Thompson, *Preludes* (London: Henry S. King, 1875); copy in Meynell library, Greatham, West Sussex. This comment was penciled in by Alice Meynell at a later date, but it is impossible to know when. I thank Oliver Hawkins, Meynell's literary executor, for his help with this identification and others in the Greatham library.

6. Meredith, "Mrs. Meynell's Two Books of Essays," 770; Joanne Shattock, *The Oxford Guide to British Women Writers* (Oxford: Oxford University Press, 1993), s.v. "Meynell."

7. Quoted in June Badeni, *The Slender Tree: A Life of Alice Meynell* (Padstow, Cornwall: Tabb House, 1981), 52.

8. Viola Meynell, *Alice Meynell: A Memoir* (London: Jonathan Cape, 1929), 54.

9. Quoted in Badeni, *The Slender Tree*, 72.

10. The phrase is Tuell's in *Mrs. Meynell and Her Generation*, 13.

11. Meynell, "James Russell Lowell," in *The Rhythm of Life and Other Essays* (London: Elkin Matthews and John Lane, 1893), 68–69. The original quotation applies this excellence to successful American writers, but as Meynell applies ripeness to all true contributions to letters, I extend it to her own work here.

12. Badeni, *The Slender Tree*, 61.

13. Ibid., 65.

14. See ibid., 69–71, for a summary of this work, as well as Meaghan Clarke, *Critical Voices: Women and Art Criticism in Britain, 1880–1905* (Aldershot, Hants: Ashgate, 2005), 45–80, for an account of Meynell's early career as an art reviewer.

15. *Some Modern Artists and their Work*, ed. Wilfrid Meynell (London: Cassells, 1883); *The Modern School of Art*, ed. Wilfrid Meynell (London: Cassells, 1886–88); and *London Impressions: Etchings and Pictures in Photogravure by William Hyde and Essays by Alice Meynell* (London: Archibald Constable, 1898). Alice also produced several introductions to volumes of the *Red Letter Library of Poets* (1902–11).

16. Quoted in Badeni, *The Slender Tree*, 88; see also p. 94.

17. Quoted in ibid., 94.

18. According to family tradition, Wilfrid considered himself an enabler of poets, including Francis Thompson and his wife, Alice. Their son Francis Meynell describes his father as "a writer in his own right, but always willing to be her impresario rather than his own" (introduction to *Essays*, by Alice Meynell [London: Newman Bookshop, 1847; rpt. Westport, CT: Greenwood Press, 1970], xvii); their granddaughter Elizabeth Hawkins repeated this characterization in April 2007, when I visited the Meynell library at Greatham.

19. John Oldcastle, *Journals and Journalism: with a Guide for Literary Beginners* (London: Field and Tuer, 1880). This guidebook initially sold at 3s 6d, but soon was issued in a one-shilling edition.

20. On Wilfrid Meynell's participation in the Society of Authors, see Bonham-Carter, *Authors by Profession*, I, 119–20, as well as Nigel Cross, *The Common Writer*, 228–30. Cross speculates that Meynell's the *Pen* furnished the model for Alfred Yule's *Letters* in George Gissing's *New Grub Street* (1891), based on the evidence that *The Pen* carried an advertisement for Gissing's novel, *Workers in the Dawn*; but Wilfrid was quite unlike Yule in personality and in professional success.

21. Badeni, *The Slender Tree*, 141.

22. See Clarke, *Critical Voices*, 45–53, who discusses Meynell's support of women artists through her articles and exhibition reviews; her arguments on behalf of women's admission to life study classes and membership in the Royal Academy; and her innovative criticism on the Newlyn School. Information on the *Magazine of Art* and the *Art Journal* derives from the "Dictionary of the Periodical Press," in *Journals and Journalism*, ed. Meynell, and from the *Oxford Dictionary of National Biography* online.

23. As examples, see Alice Meynell, "Our Living Artists: William Quiller Orchardson, R.A.," *Magazine of Art* 4 (1881), 276–81; Alice Thompson, "A Bundle of

Rue: George Cruikshank," *Magazine of Art* 3 (1880), 169–74; John Oldcastle, "Story of an Artist's Struggle," *Magazine of Art* 4 (1881), 250–52, 501–4; and Mrs. Meynell, "George Mason: A Biographical Sketch," *Art Journal* 45 (1883), 43–45, 108–11, 185–88. Alice Meynell also contributed a biographical sketch of Laura (Epps) Alma-Tadema in the same issue of the *Art Journal* 45 (1883), 345–47, though she generally does not take up women's issues in these mini-biographies.

24. Alice Meynell, "Henri Regnault," *Magazine of Art* 4 (1881), 69.

25. Meynell, "Our Living Artists," 276.

26. Quoting the preface to *Journals and Journalism*, 3.

27. Additionally, Alice Meynell's chapter on Herbert von Herkomer appears in *The Modern School of Art*, ed. Wilfrid Meynell (London: Cassells, 1886–88).

28. Tuell, *Mrs. Meynell and Her Literary Generation*, 90.

29. Ibid.

30. Ibid., 13.

31. See Ana Parejo Vadillo, "Alice Meynell: An Impressionist in Kensington," in *Women Poets and Urban Aestheticism: Passengers of Modernity* (Houndsmill, Basingstoke: Palgrave Macmillan, 2005), 78–116, for a discussion of Meynell's use of her Kensington houses, the last at Palace Court designed and owned by the Meynells, to advance her career, as well as Vadillo's "New Woman Poets and the Culture of the Salon at the *Fin de Siècle*," *Women: A Cultural Review* 10 (1999), 22–34.

32. Katherine Tynan, *Memories* (London: Eveleigh Nash and Grayson, 1924), 41.

33. Quoted in Elizabeth L. Vogt, "Honours of Mortality: The Career, Reputation and Achievement of Alice Meynell as a Journalistic Essayist" (Ph.D. diss., University of Kansas, 1989), 119.

34. See, e.g., Talia Shaffer, "The Angel in Hyde Park," in *Forgotten Female Aesthetes* (Charlottesville: University of Virginia Press, 2000), 166. In my reading, the "angel-in-the-house" persona begins after this early phase of Meynell's career, particularly after Coventry Patmore champions her prose in his 1896 essay in the *Fortnightly Review*, 13 June 1896.

35. Alice Oldcastle [Alice Meynell], "Mrs. Jameson: A Biographical Sketch," *Magazine of Art* 2 (1879), 123–25. The article does not mention Jameson's dress but reviews the recent biography by Jameson's niece, Gerardine Macpherson, *Memoirs of the Life of Anna Jameson* (London: Longmans, Green, 1878).

36. Fanny Kemble's description, quoted in Macpherson's *Memoirs*, 44–45. Kemble says that Jameson had "hands and arms [that] might have been those of Madame de Warens," the elegant mistress of Jean Jacques Rousseau, and the frontispiece to the *Memoirs* shows Jameson in a pose with an elegant hand uplifted to heaven (or perhaps to her face). Less admiringly, John Ruskin quoted Sophia Russell, Baroness de Clifford, in a letter to his father: "She's an authoress. I'm certain of it. She's the very type of a great class"; see John Ruskin to John James Ruskin, [28 September 1845], in *Ruskin in Italy: Letters of his Parents, 1845*, ed. Harold I. Shapiro (Oxford: Clarendon Press, 1972), no. 136.

37. Quoted by Derek Patmore in *The Life and Times of Coventry Patmore* (London: Constable, 1949), 218.

38. Henley's modern biographer, writing under the pseudonym John Connell, states that in 1880 he briefly edited "an obscure, short-lived periodical called the *Pen*, which was published from 22 Tavistock Street"—possibly the successor of

the Meynells' *Pen: A Journal of Literature*; see *W. E. Henley* (London: Constable, 1949), 92.

39. L[eslie] Cope Cornford, *William Ernest Henley* (London: Constable and Company, 1913), 66.

40. Derek Patmore, *Life and Times of Coventry Patmore*, 232.

41. According to Tuell, *Mrs. Meynell and Her Literary Generation*, 265, the essay on James Russell Lowell was never published in the *Scots Observer* or any other periodical—a conclusion my research confirms—but the essay was clearly written in the mode of the "Modern Men" column. Its importance to Meynell's thinking about the profession of letters emerges in her assessment of Lowell's achievement.

42. See W. E. Henley to Charles Whibley, 15 January 1888, Gordon Ray Papers, Pierpont Morgan Library, MA 4500 H: "We pay (monthly) a guinea a column all round." I thank Linda Hughes for providing me with this citation. See also Connell, who states that Henley "paid [his contributors] fair rates, and that "when retrenchment set in" and his chief backer Fitzroy Bell "demanded cut rates for contributors," "Henley fought him doggedly" (*W. E. Henley*, 147). Interestingly, in a letter to her mother, Christiana Thompson, 24 March [n.d.], Meynell library, Greatham, Meynell says that the *Observer* pays "moderately, but steadily."

43. W. H. Henley, "The Tory Press and the Tory Party," *National Review* 21 (May 1893), 371; the second phrase comes from Tuell, quoting "a reminiscent sympathizer" (*Mrs. Meynell and Her Literary Generation*, 81).

44. Henley notoriously dedicated a collection of critical essays, *Views and Reviews* (London: Nutt, 1890), "To the *Men* of the 'Scots Observer,' " dismissing the magazine's eminent women writers as window-dressing and naming "Mrs. Graham Tomson, Mrs. Meynell, Miss May Kendall, and 'E. Nesbit' " as "a few dainty window curtains—all the women are good for"; quoted in McDonald, *British Literary Culture and Publishing Practice*, 37. See McDonald's excellent discussion on Henley's promotion of "men of letters" in the *Scots Observer* and *National Review*, 32–53, as well as Linda K. Hughes's reassessment of Henley as an "imperialist aesthete and progressive misogynist"—terms that capture the "violent contradictions in Henley's career" (81)—in "W. E. Henley's *Scots Observer* and *Fin-de-Siècle* Books," in *Bound for the 1890s: Essays on Writing and Publishing in Honor of James G. Nelson*, ed. Jonathan Allison (High Wycombe: Rivendale Press, 2006), 65–86.

45. Meynell, "Decivilised," in *The Rhythm of Life and Other Essays* (London: Elkin Matthews and John Lane, 1893), 7; the essay originally appeared in the *National Observer* 5 (24 January 1891), 250–51. "New-Worldliness" appeared in the *National Observer* 9 (25 March 1893), 466, after the publication of *The Rhythm of Life*.

46. Alice Meynell to Christiana Thompson, 24 March [n.d.], Meynell library, Greatham.

47. See her letter to John Lane, 15 December 1898, John Lane Company Archives, Box 32, Folder 4, Harry Ransom Research Center, The University of Texas. Meynell inquires about the timing of the seventh edition, stating, "I wish to dedicate the book retrospectively to Mr. Henley."

48. "New-Worldliness" appeared on 25 March 1893, after her volume *The Rhythm of Life* was published. Henley's periodical ceased publication later that year.

49. Henley had the admirable quality of leaving his authors alone and not overediting or mutilating their work to "fit" his magazine. Tuell notes that Meynell

removed passages from the "Unit of the World" that were "a direct multitudinous assault upon the personal and unfortunate Oscar [Wilde]" and speculates that Henley may have "contributed to the text his editorial heightening" (*Mrs. Meynell and Her Literary Generation*, 87). There is no evidence, however, that Henley did so, and Meynell also chose not to reprint "New-Worldliness," another provocative (and dismissive) essay—a choice that suggests her decision to collect essays that were classic, not controversial.

50. Meynell, "The Rhythm of Life," in *The Rhythm of Life*, 1–2.

51. Quoted in "Opinions of the Press" for *The Rhythm of Life*, in *The Children*, 2nd ed. (London: John Lane, 1902), 98.

52. Schaffer, *Forgotten Female Aesthetes*, 168, 172. Such revelation became more common in later work, especially the columns Meynell wrote about children and childhood for the *Pall Mall Gazette* in 1894, the *Album* in 1895, and the American *Delineator* in 1898.

53. "Of Repentance," in *Montaigne: Selected Essays*, ed. Blanchard Bates (New York: Modern Library, 1949), 286.

54. Meynell, "The Rhythm of Life," in *The Rhythm of Life*, 4.

55. Tuell, *Mrs. Meynell and Her Literary Generation*, 78–79; Viola Meynell, *Alice Meynell*, 73.

56. Patmore, "Mrs. Meynell," 762, 763; see his "Distinction," 826–34, for his initial judgment.

57. Badeni notes, quoting a letter from Meynell to her husband, that Lane later thought a slight delay in issuing the poems would cause "a general demand in the notices 'What about the poems?' " (*The Slender Tree*, 88), but early reviews suggest that both volumes were released together or, at least, very near.

58. Lane's partner Elkin Matthews also saw himself as the Edward Moxon of his era. According to "About Mr. Elkin Matthews," an article in the *St. James's Budget* (Literary Supplement) 29 (1894), 26, the young bookseller, an admitted expert on "ancient tomes of many periods," "began not only to deal but to publish," intent on realizing his long-cherished ambition "to become the Edward Moxon of his time"; quoted in James G. Nelson, *Elkin Matthews: Publisher to Yeats, Joyce, Pound* (Madison: University of Wisconsin Press, 1989), 5.

59. Bourdieu, *Field of Cultural Production*, 46–52.

60. See Meynell's letters of 11 August 1898, 8 March 1899, 25 February 1900, and 3 September 1901, John Lane Company Archives, Box 32, Folder 4, Harry Ransom Research Center, The University of Texas, all of which ask for the half-yearly accounts.

61. J. W. Lambert and Michael Ratcliffe, on whose centennial history, *The Bodley Head, 1887–1987* (London: The Bodley Head, 1987), I have relied, notes that the press was "financially insecure, and decidedly under-capitalised" (104), that designers like C. H. Shannon and Charles Ricketts often had to write dunning letters to get paid (73), and that royalties "might be anything up to two years late" (119). Nonetheless, and improbable as it may sound, Lane is credited with "introducing the publishing principle that *all* authors should *always* get a royalty" (51).

62. Richard Le Gallienne, *Retrospective Reviews: A Literary Log* (London: John Lane, Bodley Head, 1896), I, 205, 206, 207. The review was published in December 1892.

63. Badeni, *The Slender Tree*, 100; Connell, *W. E. Henley*, 140–41, 250–52.

64. Badeni, *The Slender Tree*, 100–101.

65. Derek Patmore, *Life and Times of Coventry Patmore*, 233.

66. Viola Meynell, *Alice Meynell*, 99.

67. In *Alice Meynell, 1847–1922: Catalogue of the Centenary Exhibition of Books, Manuscripts, Letters and Portraits* (London: The National Book League, 1947), 9, Francis Meynell quotes an undated letter in which his mother writes to Patmore, "By my cheque, I think that they pay me £3 a column."

68. Only a few account books remain in the Meynell library at Greatham. The 1898 book (a tall, narrow book measuring 4" × 13") records payments in one direction, ideas for essays and stories in the other. The 1921–22 account book records royalties and commissions in one direction, with expenses for dress in the other; it comments for 1922: "good year."

69. Badeni, *The Slender Tree*, 142, quotes a letter from Alice to Wilfrid citing these figures. Her royalties from the Bodley Head for the entire year were probably higher, as she lists profits from July to December only.

70. Even so, Meynell's income from writing essays and poetry in the late 1890s probably did not exceed £500 per year—considerably less than a popular novelist earned; her income also included royalties and payments for commissioned collections, introductions to volumes, and other such editorial work.

71. Bourdieu, *Field of Cultural Production*, 47–48.

72. Patmore, "Mrs. Meynell," 763.

73. Meynell, *The Rhythm of Life*, 81, 96, 98, 2.

74. Viola Meynell, *Alice Meynell*, 54.

75. Alice Oldcastle, "Mrs. Jameson: A Biographical Sketch," *Magazine of Art* 2 (1879), 123–25; "Mary Wollstonecraft," *Spectator*, 22 February 1879, 245–46. The review of Martineau's *Autobiography* appeared in a journal called *Yorick* and was preserved by Wilfrid Meynell in a scrapbook of his wife's early writings (see P. M. Fraser, ed., *The Wares of Autolycus: Selected Literary Essays of Alice Meynell* [London: Oxford University Press, 1965], xii, n. 1). Meynell also wrote reviews of Margaret Oliphant's *Makers of Florence* and George Eliot's *Daniel Deronda* in 1876.

76. Alice Oldcastle, "Mrs. Jameson," 123.

77. Meynell, "James Russell Lowell," in *The Rhythm of Life*, 68.

78. Ibid., 69.

79. *Preludes*, 1–2. Citations will be to this edition; significant variants in the *Poems of Alice Meynell*, complete ed. (London: Oxford University Press, 1940), will be noted. Many poems in the original *Preludes* included epigraphs not reprinted in later editions.

80. *In Memoriam*, section 77; "Anactoria," ll. 204–5, 210, 214.

81. Meynell, "Innocence and Experience," in *The Rhythm of Life*, 98.

82. Alice Meynell, "Some Thoughts of a Reader of Tennyson," in *Hearts of Controversy* (London: Burns and Oates, 1917), 3–4.

83. See Bloom, *Anxiety of Influence*.

84. Meynell, "James Russell Lowell," in *The Rhythm of Life*, 71.

85. Ibid., 17.

86. Meynell, *Preludes*, 20.

87. Patmore, "Mrs. Meynell," 763.

88. Antony Harrison, *Victorian Poets and Romantic Poets: Intertextuality and Ideology* (Charlottesville: University Press of Virginia, 1990), 2.

89. Meynell, *Preludes*, 70.

90. Le Gallienne, *Retrospective Reviews*, I, 204. Le Gallienne's praise undermines Meynell somewhat when he adds that this is "the same transfiguration of the unit by the absolute as Tennyson's vision of the 'Flower in the crannied wall' "—a comparison that makes Meynell's poem secondary to Tennyson's.

91. Susan E. Lorsch, *Where Nature Ends: Literary Responses to the Designification of Landscape* (London: Associated University Presses, 1983), 51; [Anna Mary Howitt Watts], "The Repose of the Fair Maid Patience," in *Aurora: A Volume of Verse* (London: Henry S. King and Company, 1875), 18.

92. Meynell, "The Rhythm of Life," in *The Rhythm of Life*, 4.

93. Meredith, "Mrs. Meynell's Two Books of Essays," 768. Meredith refers to all Meynell's essays on things of daily life—"cheap daily things"—but his observation is particularly apt for her essays on ordinary things of nature.

94. These phrases come from Meynell, "Some Thoughts of a Reader of Tennyson," in *Hearts of Controversy*, 4.

95. Ibid., 17–18.

96. Alice Meynell, *Last Poems* (London: Burns and Oates, 1923), published posthumously.

97. Shelley J. Crisp, "Meynell's 'The Return to Nature: Histories of Modern Poetry,' " *Explicator* 50:1 (Fall 1991), 28.

98. Angela Leighton, *Victorian Women Poets: Writing against the Heart* (Charlottesville: University Press of Virginia, 1992; Yopie Prins, *Victorian Sappho* (Princeton: Princeton University Press, 1999). As her title suggests, Leighton sees all Victorian women poets as in some way resisting this tradition; in her treatment of Meynell, she focuses not on *Preludes* but on later poems about motherhood that "issue a quiet challenge to the still-standing icon of the sublime Madonna" (265).

99. Quoted in Badeni, *The Slender Tree*, 29, from ms. diary at Greatham.

100. Quoted in the notes to *The Poems of Alice Meynell*, complete ed., 211. According to the notes, "Renouncement" was first printed in Hall Caine's *Sonnets of Three Centuries* (1882).

101. Badeni reads "Parted" and "After a Parting" biographically, as "inspired by the separation from her Jesuit friend" (*The Slender Tree*, 40).

102. See also the sonnet "To the Reader Who Should Love Me," published in *Poems* (1940) from a ms. dated 1869.

103. See Mary Robinson, *Sappho and Phaon* (1796; London: Minerva Press, 1815); Laetitia Landon, *A History of the Lyre* (1828) in *Letitia Elizabeth Landon: Selected Writings*, ed. Jerome McGann and Daniel Riess (Peterborough, Canada: Broadview Press, 1997), 115–27; and Christina Rossetti, "Sappho" (1846) in *Poems and Prose*, ed. Jan Marsh (London: Everyman, 1994), 9.

104. Other poems in *Preludes* extend the Sapphic mode but align themselves with contemporary European male poets. Taking its epigraph from Victor Hugo, *"Alors je te plaindrai, pauvre âme"* ("Well, I pity you, poor soul"), "In Autumn" reflects on the "dead delights" of "That tuneful Spring," and the sad knowledge that "his heart has beat to bright / Sweet loves gone by." "A Tryst that Failed" cites Alfred de Musset: *"Ce pauvre temps passé"* ("That sorry time gone by"). These

epigraphs seem unnecessary in that neither Hugo's nor de Musset's verse is relevant to the poems—except in the sense that Hugo's poetry was deeply meaningful to Meynell personally, as she explains in her essay "Poetry and Childhood" (see *Alice Meynell: Prose and Poetry*, ed. V. Sackville-West [London: Jonathan Cape, 1947], 137–41). Meynell removed the epigraphs from later published volumes.

105. This reading is convincingly pursued by Badeni, *The Slender Tree*, 40–41, 48–50, using Meynell's diaries as well as poetry.

106. Le Gallienne, *Retrospective Reviews*, I, 205. In " 'The Fair Light Mystery of Images': Alice Meynell's Metaphysical Turn," *Victorian Literature and Culture* 34 (2006), 663–84, Tracy Seeley notes, "the diminutive 'little,' the patronizing 'poetess,' and the praise for deep-heartedness, all suggest that when critics read Meynell, they found what they were looking for and overlooked the rest" (664).

107. Leighton, *Victorian Women Poets*, 259, 265.

108. In " 'The Fair Light Mystery of Images,' " 673, Seeley suggests that Meynell entered a new phase in the mid-1890s when she discovered seventeenth-century metaphysical poetry and began to "employ such metaphysical elements as the sensuality of the divine and the erotics of inspiration." While this influence is apparent in religious poems such as "Veni, Creator" and "The Moon to the Sun," it is less apparent in her poems of motherhood, which I argue show the influence of her *PMG* journalism on children and childhood.

109. Alice Meynell, *The Children* (London: John Lane, Bodley Head, 1896), 11, 12, 21.

110. See the excerpt from a review in the *Pall Mall Gazette*, quoted in "Opinions of the Press," in Alice Meynell, *Later Poems* (London: John Lane, Bodley Head, 1901), [41].

111. See "Illness," 107–9; "Authorship," 77; and "Real Childhood," 130, in *The Children*.

112. A direct link is unlikely, given the limited circulation of the Howitts' periodical, but the didactic use of natural history continued well into Meynell's era, and it was against this practice that Meynell reacted.

113. Meynell, *Later Poems*, 18.

114. Leighton, *Victorian Women Poets*, 261.

115. The first phrase comes from Meynell's introduction to *Prometheus Bound and Other Poems*, by Elizabeth Barrett Browning (London: Ward, Lock and Bowden, 1896), rpt. in *The Wares of Autolycus: Selected Literary Essays of Alice Meynell*, ed. P. M. Fraser (London: Oxford University Press, 1965), 161. The second and third phrases are Elizabeth Barrett Browning's in *Aurora Leigh*, Bk. IX, 348–49 and Bk. V, 164.

116. Meynell, *Later Poems*, 20–21.

117. Leighton, *Victorian Women Poets*, 265.

118. Oscar Wilde, *De Profundis*, ed. Robert Ross (New York: G. P. Putnam's Sons, 1905), 33; see also Wilde's comments in "English Poetesses," *The Queen* (1888); rpt. in *The Uncollected Oscar Wilde*, ed. John Wyse Jackson (London: Fourth Estate, 1991), 59–66.

119. Cited in "Opinions of the Press" in *Later Poems*, 41.

120. Meredith, "Mrs. Meynell's Two Books of Essays," 769–70.

121. Cited in "Opinions of the Press" as "Mr. George Meredith, in *The National Review*," in *Later Poems*, 41.

122. Meredith, "Mrs. Meynell's Two Books of Essays," 765.

123. Ibid., 766.

124. In a letter of 8 March 1899 (John Lane Company Archives, Box 32, Folder 4, Harry Ransom Research Center, The University of Texas), Meynell recommends two quotations to advertise *The Spirit of Place*, and in a letter dated 5 July 1907 (Meynell library, Greatham), Lane responds to Meynell's complaint of inadequate advertisements of her books, pointing out that she has not published with him in six years and stressing the preferential treatments she receives on royalties of 20–25 percent, in comparison with the "next woman essayist after herself who takes no royalties on the first 500, & 10% thereafter."

125. Coventry Patmore, "Alicia's Silence," quoted in Viola Meynell, *Alice Meynell*, 116–17.

126. Coventry Patmore, "Alicia," quoted in Viola Meynell, *Alice Meynell*, 117. In "Patmore's Law, Meynell's Rhythm" (*The Fin-de-Siècle Poem: English Literary Culture and the 1890s*, ed. Joseph Bristow [Athens: Ohio University Press, 2005]), Yopie Prins has brilliantly read the dainty "feet" as Patmore's praise of Meynell's metrical achievement, its "deft manipulation of subtle intervals according to his own prosodic theory" (264); even so, the public effect was likely to have been a feminization and diminution of her professional status.

127. Francis Thompson, "Her Portrait," quoted in Badeni, *The Slender Tree*, 112.

128. See Schaffer, *Forgotten Female Aesthetes*, esp. 162–74, "Biography and Hagiography: Becoming the Angel in the House." Although I use Schaffer's apt formulation, I disagree that it pertains to Meynell's entire career; rather, I suggest that it is a post-1895 reconstruction of Meynell's public persona.

129. Meynell, *Later Poems*, 9. This volume reproduces the privately printed *Other Poems* (1896), which also begins with "The Shepherdess."

130. Leighton, *Victorian Women Poets*, 263–64.

131. Sharon Smulders, "Looking 'Past Wordsworth and the Rest': Pretexts for Revision in Alice Meynell's 'The Shepherdess,'" *Victorian Poetry* 38 (2000), 35–48. Smulders adopts the concept of reinscription from Harrison, *Victorian Poets and Romantic Poets*, 2.

132. Seeley, "'The Fair Light Mystery of Images,'" 675.

133. According to her son, Alice Meynell may not have intended "The Shepherdess" to apply to her own poetry but to that of her friend and fellow poet Agnes Tobin. In "A.T. and A.M.," in *Agnes Tobin* (San Francisco: Grabhorn Press, 1958), xvi, Francis Meynell observes, "It is an odd thing that verses as personal as a portrait should have been given by generations of readers a generalized significance beyond the poet's intention." His view cannot be adopted without caution, however, because many of the poems in *Other Poems* draw on the same metaphor of the poet as shepherd(ess) of thoughts, safely bringing them into the fold.

134. Alice Meynell, "A Woman of Masculine Understanding," 11 October 1895; rpt. in *Wares of Autolycus*, ed. Fraser, 8–12.

135. According to Lambert and Ratliffe, *The Bodley Head*, 105, William Watson and Wilfrid Meynell, on behalf of his wife, Alice, wrote that unless Wilde's books were withdrawn, they would withdraw their books. J. Lewis May gives a different account in *John Lane and the Nineties* (London: John Lane, Bodley Head, 1936), 80; in his version, when the scandal broke, Lane was in America and cabled his office,

"lea[ving] the decision in the hands of competent members of his staff, with Mr. William Watson and Mr. Wilfrid Meynell as advisers."

136. For a discussion of John Lane's reaction to the Wilde scandal, see Lambert and Ratliffe, *The Bodley Head*, 105–8, and Victorian Web, http://victorianweb.org/decadence/yellowbook.html.

137. Similarly, "A Poet's Wife," which figures the poet and his thoughts as husband and wife in an embrace, chooses a legitimate erotic relationship to characterize the creative act.

138. Notably, Meynell proposed three titles for the volume that became *Later Poems* (London: John Lane, Bodley Head, 1901): *Other Poems, The Fold and other Lyrics,* and *The Lady Poverty and other Poems*—the last two of which stress the religious element of her 1890s verse; see Alice Meynell to John Lane, 7 August 1900, John Lane Company Archives, Box 32, Folder 4, Harry Ransom Research Center, The University of Texas.

139. In 1847 Meynell's children edited a centenary volume, *Alice Meynell: Prose and Poetry* (London: Jonathan Cape, 1847), and chose not to include "The Shepherdess" in the selection of verse.

140. The phrase appears in Meynell's essay on Arabella Stuart (*Poetry and Prose,* 182) and is quoted by Smulders, "Looking 'Past Wordsworth and the Rest,'" 36, to denote Meynell's case in a recuperative article on "The Shepherdess."

CHAPTER 7
The Woman of Letters and the New Woman

1. Tuchman and Fortin, *Edging Women Out,* passim.

2. Talia Schaffer, *The Forgotten Female Aesthetes* (Charlottesville: University Press of Virginia, 2000), 6. Schaffer also discusses the valorization of "decadence" in literary histories as an emphasis that excludes women writers.

3. Lyn Pykett, *The "Improper" Feminine: The Women's Sensation Novel and the New Woman* (London: Routledge, 1992), 3.

4. Showalter, *Literature of Their Own,* 182–215; Coventry Patmore, "Distinction," *Fortnightly Review,* n.s., 47 (June 1890), 826.

5. According to Elizabeth MacLeod Walls, "'In pursuit of us of the Nineties': Letter-Writing as Material Activism for New Women Writers in the Modernist Marketplace": "As the nineteenth century waned, these authors' narratives lost their audience; their former cachet as didactic prognosticators of women's awakening had been eclipsed by radical suffrage in the culture and inward-looking modernist fiction in the marketplace. New Woman novelists continued to publish, but with little success" (paper presented at the North American Victorian Studies Association [NAVSA] conference, 2007). I thank Professor Walls for sharing her paper with me.

6. Penny Boumelha, "The Woman of Genius and the Woman of Grub Street: Figures of the Female Writer in British *Fin-de-Siècle* Fiction," *English Literature in Transition* 40 (1997), 164–80.

7. Lyn Pykett, "Portraits of the Artist as a Young Woman: Representations of the Female Artist in the New Woman Fiction of the 1890s," in *Victorian Women Writers and the Woman Question,* ed. Nicola Diane Thompson (Cambridge:

Cambridge University Press, 1999), 137, quoting (in the first phrase) Ella Hepworth Dixon's memoir, *As I Knew Them: Sketches of People I Have Met on the Way* (London: Hutchinson, 1930), 136. Pykett further notes a disjunction between the fictional representations and magazine interviews in which New Woman writers typically presented themselves as models of professional work, commitment, and success, fulfilling the requirements of domesticity while producing high-quality fiction, poetry, or essays.

8. Boumelha, "The Woman of Genius and the Woman of Grub Street," 177.

9. Vineta Colby, " 'Devoted Amateur': Mary Cholmondeley and *Red Pottage*," *Essays in Criticism* 20 (1970), 213–28.

10. Entry from Mary Cholmondeley's diary, 16 May 1877, quoted in Percy Lubbock, *Mary Cholmondeley: A Sketch from Memory* (London: Jonathan Cape, 1928), 74. Some biographies—e.g., Wikipedia, http://en.wikipedia.org/wiki/Mary_Cholmondeley—state that this work was published as a book, but there is no record of publication in archives that hold Cholmondeley's papers or in the British Library catalogue.

11. We know that "Geoffrey's Wife," published under the initials L. R., is Cholmondeley's, given its later inclusion in *Moth and Rust* (1902). I have speculated that the earlier story is also hers, given its use of the pseudonym "Lee Russ" and her journal notation that she sold her first story in 1882, the year of its publication in *The Graphic's* Summer Number.

12. Colby, " 'Devoted Amateur': Mary Cholmondeley," 222.

13. *Waterloo Directory of English Newspapers and Periodicals, 1800–1900*, s.v. "Temple Bar," p. 4610.

14. Cholmondeley uses this term in a letter to Henry Newbolt, 15 October 1901, Wolff 1213b, Harry Ransom Research Center, The University of Texas.

15. See Ann Heilmann, " 'New Woman' Fiction and *Fin de Siècle* Feminism," *Women's Writing* 3 (1996), 197–216, for a discussion of key features.

16. Lubbock, *Mary Cholmondeley*, 24.

17. Diary entry post-1900, quoted in ibid., 92.

18. Heilmann, " 'New Woman' Fiction," 205.

19. Grant Allen, *The Woman Who Did*, ed. Sarah Wintle (Oxford: Oxford University Press, 1995), 42–43. Cholmondeley had also used this quotation prior to the publication of *The Woman Who Did* in *Diana Tempest* (1893) to describe Colonel Tempest's bitter regret at a dishonorable deed of his youth.

20. Mary Cholmondeley, *Diana Tempest* (London: Richard Bentley, 1893), I, 18. The epigraph appears in chapter 4. An inquiry to Cholmondeley about the epigraph produced a response that she thought it derived from a sermon by John Hamilton Thom, but an editor of *Harper's Magazine* traced it to Dean Frederic Farrar's "Selling the Birthright," a sermon in his collection *Everyday Christian Life* (1888).

21. George Bentley to Mary Cholmondeley, 17 August 1886, quoted in Lubbock, *Mary Cholmondeley*, 83.

22. See contract for "Deceivers Ever" (original title of *Sir Charles Danvers*), 14 June 1888, in Bentley Add Ms 46623 f. 1, British Library. It specifies the sale of copyright for £50, plus "£20 if 550 copies are sold in Library Edition, £20 if 650 copies are sold, and addl. £20 for each addl. 100 copies."

23. See contract for "Nemesis" (original title of *Diana Tempest*), 2 September 1892, in Bentley Add Ms. 46624, f. 228, British Library. The novel went into a fifth edition by 1895, according to a letter from Mary Cholmondeley to James Payn, 3 January 1895, Wolff 1212b, Harry Ransom Research Center, The University of Texas. The profits on subsequent cheap editions and on American sales are not recorded in the Bentley archives.

24. Tuchman and Fortin, *Edging Women Out*, passim.

25. Mary Cholmondeley to Mssrs. Macmillan, 29 January 1899, Macmillans Archive 55262, f. 53, British Library.

26. Mary Cholmondeley to Mr. Macmillan, 2 July 1900, Macmillans Archive 55262, f. 162, British Library.

27. Mary Cholmondeley to Rhoda Broughton, 20 May 1919, Delves Broughton Collection, Bundle C, MF 79/1/2/17, Chester County Archives, Chester, UK. This and other letters between Cholmondeley and Broughton are published in Linda Peterson, "Mary Cholmondeley (1859–1925) and Rhoda Broughton (1840–1920)," in *Kindred Hands*, 107–19.

28. Lubbock, *Mary Cholmondeley*, 87.

29. Ibid., 90. In this journal entry Cholmondeley admits that she enjoys her celebrity: "How amused and elated I was at the time—how I enjoyed my popularity! That such a wave of success should have reached *me* was and is still a constant source of astonishment to me" (89–90).

30. Lubbock, *Mary Cholmondeley*, 91.

31. Mary Cholmondeley, *Red Pottage* (1899; London: Penguin-Virago, 1985), 29, 30. Further citations to this novel will be included in the text.

32. Boumelha, "The Woman of Genius and the Woman of Grub Street," 168–72, discusses the theories of Galton, Lombroso, and Ellis, noting the common belief that genius, in men or women, represents abnormality—that is, "a congenital deviation from the norm" (170).

33. Diane M. Chambers, "Triangular Desire and the Sororal Bond: The 'Deceased Wife's Sister Bill,'" *Mosaic* 29 (1996), 24.

34. Ella Hepworth Dixon, *The Story of a Modern Woman*, ed. Kate Flint (1894; London: Merlin Press, 1990), 34. This statement is quoted by Heilmann, " 'New Woman' Fiction," 206, who notes, "Unlike male writers, female writers could found their identity as New Women and, often, politically active feminists on the autobiographical experience of a 'sisterhood of women', an idea which in their works took on a distinctly programmatic tone."

35. Dixon, *The Story of a Modern Woman*, 107. These episodes appear in chapter 10, "In Grub Street."

36. George Paston [Emily Morse Symonds], *A Writer of Books*, ed. Margaret D. Stetz (1898; Chicago: Academy Chicago Publishers, 1999), 79, 81.

37. The phrase "devoted amateur" was first used by Lubbock, *Mary Cholmondeley*, 47, who intended a contrast with the "professional author" who regularly and routinely turns out copy; it was then adopted by Colby in her title, " 'Devoted Amateur': Mary Cholmondeley and *Red Pottage*," to indicate a writer dedicated to her art but unconcerned about professional details (a characterization that I believe misrepresents Cholmondeley's career).

38. For examples of Cholmondeley's concern for fair payment, see her letters to Rhoda Broughton, published in *Kindred Hands*, 107–19.

39. Heilmann, " 'New Woman' Fiction," 201, discusses the "images [New Women] constructed" in these terms.

40. Lubbock, *Mary Cholmondeley*, 46.

41. Ibid., 48–49.

42. Boumelha, "The Woman of Genius and the Woman of Grub Street," 177.

43. Pierre Bourdieu, "Flaubert and the French Literary Field," in *Field of Cultural Production*, ed. Johnson, 145–211; quotation from 174.

44. Mary Cholmondeley, *Moth and Rust, Together with Geoffrey's Wife and The Pitfall* (London: John Murray, 1902), 53–56.

45. "Novels of the Week," the *Spectator* (28 October 1899), 612–13.

46. Arnold Bennett, "Miss Mary Cholmondeley," *The Academy* 57 (9 December 1899), 689.

47. Ibid.

48. "Women in the Day's News," *Harper's Bazaar*, 7 April 1900, p. 301; see also "Autobiography and Fiction—Mary Cholmondeley's Stories and Her Life," *Munsey's Magazine* 23 (August 1900), 109–10.

49. Carol Huebscher Rhoades, "Mary Cholmondeley," *Nineteenth-Century British Women Writers: A Bio-Bibliographical Critical Sourcebook*, ed. Abigail Burnham (Westport, CT: Greenwood Press, 2000), 110.

50. In *British Women Fiction Writers of the 1890s* (New York: Twayne Publishers, 1996), 6, Carolyn Christensen Nelson mentions Sarah Grand, George Egerton, Vernon Lee, and Menie Muriel Dowie as examples of women writers who followed up their best-sellers by placing shorter, often lesser work in popular magazines.

51. I speculate that it is "In the Small Hours," *Lady's Realm* 23 (December 1907), 129–33, that Cholmondeley refers to as "under contract to an English periodical" in a letter to Henry Newbolt, 15 October 1901, Wolff 1213b, Harry Ransom Research Center, The University of Texas.

52. Ibid.

53. See Mary Cholmondeley to Henry Newbolt, 12 February and 26 March 1901, Wolff 1219, 1216c, Harry Ransom Research Center, The University of Texas. She also told Newbolt that she received £50 for American rights to a story of 4,000 words and that £10 per 1,000 words was a typical American payment.

54. The letters of 12 February 1901 and 26 March 1901 to Newbolt, cited above, make it clear that he has asked for essays and commentary. In addition to "An Art in its Infancy," Cholmondeley offered a chapter omitted from *Red Pottage* because it "did not advance the story": "a conversation between the Bishop and Hester Gresley." This offer was not accepted by Newbolt, but Cholmondeley seems to have placed the article, titled "Vicarious Charities: A Dialogue," in *Cornhill Magazine* 100 (1909), 34–43; see Jane Crisp, *Mary Cholmondeley, 1859–1925: A Bibliography*, Victorian Fiction Research Guides VI (St. Lucia: University of Queensland, n.d.), 36.

55. Mary Cholmondeley, "Votes for Men: A Dialogue," *Cornhill Magazine* 100 (1909), 747–55; *Harper's Bazaar* 44 (January 1910), 10–12. See Crisp, *Mary Cholmondeley*, 35–36, for a list of periodical publications, not all of which have been located, especially later works and American reprints.

56. Cholmondeley, "Votes for Men," 751. In this satire Queen Eugenia objects to the tactics of the "brawling brotherhood" (instead of the "shrieking sisterhood") and reaches the conclusion that "Those who have the upper hand cannot be just to those who are in their power" (755).

57. Rhoades, "Mary Cholmondeley," 110.

58. Kate Flint, *Dictionary of National Biography*, rev. ed. (Oxford: Oxford University Press, n.d.), s.v. "Mary Cholmondeley."

59. Elaine Showalter, introduction to *Red Pottage* (New York: Penguin-Virago, 1985), xiii.

60. Bennett, "Miss Mary Cholmondeley," 689.

61. Meredith, "Mrs. Meynell's Two Books of Essays," 769–70.

62. By the time Cholmondeley began her career, Eliot's pronouncements had been collected in such volumes as *The Wit and Wisdom of George Eliot* (Boston: Roberts Brothers, 1878). Cholmondeley admired the epigraphs and discursive passages in Eliot's novels and imitated them in her novels.

63. Mary Cholmondeley to Mr. [Henry] Newbolt, 7 November 1901, Wolff 1213c, Harry Ransom Research Center, The University of Texas.

64. Mary Cholmondeley to Lord Aberdeen [Marquess of Aberdeen], 21 October 1906, Wolff 1215a, Harry Ransom Research Center, The University of Texas. The letter also expresses a sense of relief and pleasure that Lord Aberdeen had enjoyed reading *Prisoners*.

65. The first three arguments are advanced, respectively, by Showalter in *Literature of Their Own*, 182–215; Patricia Stubbs, *Women and Fiction: Feminism and the Novel, 1880–1920* (Brighton: Harvester, 1979); and Ann Ardis, *New Women, New Novels* (New Brunswick, NJ: Rutgers University Press, 1990), 10–28. The final point about modernists subsuming the successful experiments of fin-de-siècle writers, including New Woman, appears in several critical studies, including Sally Ledger's *The New Woman: Fiction and Feminism at the Fin de Siècle* (Manchester: Manchester University Press, 1997).

66. Osbert Burdett, *The Beardsley Period: An Essay in Perspective* (London: John Lane, Bodley Head, 1925), 256.

67. Teresa Magnum discusses Sarah Grand's deployment of publicity in *The Lady's Realm* and other venues in *Married, Middlebrow, and Militant: Sarah Grand and the New Woman Novel* (Ann Arbor: University of Michigan Press, 1998).

68. Bennett, "Miss Mary Cholmondeley," 689; "Autobiography and Fiction— Mary Cholmondeley's Stories and Her Life," *Munsey's Magazine* 23 (August 1900), 109–10. Cholmondeley had, in fact, spent many childhood and adolescent days in London with her fashionable aunt, Mrs. Legard, but she was not her "ward."

69. See Badeni, *A Slender Tree*, 100–101.

70. See, for example, Meynell's letter to Coventry Patmore: "I cannot send you *Sylvia's Journal* with an interview with me. It is too ghastly. It makes me talk frightful grammar and say things I could never have said" (Badeni, *The Slender Tree*, 100). She also apologized to William E. Henley for a misquotation in which she tells an interviewer that the *National Observer* takes anything she cares to write: "It sounded so insolent that I wrote to Henley to disclaim it" (100).

71. Mary Cholmondeley, preface to *The Lowest Rung, together with The Hand on the Latch, St. Luke's Summer and The Understudy* (London: John Murray, 1908), 9.

72. Ibid., 10, 13.

73. Ibid., 18.

74. Ibid., 11.

75. Ibid., 14–16. *Aunt Anne* told the story of a woman of sixty-eight who falls in love with a young married man of twenty-seven; see Joanne Shattock, *The Oxford Guide to British Women Writers* (Oxford: Oxford University Press, 1993), s.v. "(Sophia) Lucy Clifford," 106.

76. In this tactic Cholmondeley continues a practice of Victorian women writers discussed by Helen Elizabeth Howells in *Facing the Page: A Study of the Prefaces of Nineteenth-Century British Women Writers* (Greensboro: University of North Carolina Press, 2001).

77. Mary Cholmondeley, "Introduction: In Praise of a Suffolk Cottage," *The Romance of His Life and Other Romances* (London: John Murray, 1921), 11.

78. Ibid., 12.

79. Showalter, *Literature of Their Own*, 215.

80. See Mary Cholmondeley to Rhoda Broughton, 18 February and 5 December 1919, in *Kindred Hands*, 116, 118.

Index

Index

Radcliff, Ann: 4
Radford, Dollie: 198
Reade, Charles: 50
Regnault, Henri: 176
Reviews and reviewers: 9, 39–40, 42–43,
    53–58, 62–66, 70–71, 90–92, 99, 104, 123,
    125, 135–36, 152, 158–62, 173–77, 182–84,
    201–202, 217–18, 220
Rhoades, Carol: 218
Ricardo, David: 84, 94, 247n88
Ricketts, Charles: 182, 269n61
Riddell, Charlotte: 8, 58, 151–70; as critic of
    Brontëan myths: 164–70; as magazine
    editor: 152–53; as novelist: 151–53; as tragic
    figure: 167–70
Rigby, Elizabeth (Lady Eastlake): 131,
    134, 137
Ritchie, Anne Thackeray: 162
Roberts, Emma: 33, 133
Roberts, William: 82
Robinson, Mary: 197
Rogers, Samuel: 37
Ross, Marlon: 26, 30, 91, 231n36
Rossetti, Christina: 98, 197, 198, 227n23
Rossetti, Dante Gabriel: 50, 98, 122, 195, 198
Rothblatt, Sheldon: 50
Ruskin, John: 123–24, 128–29, 147, 192,
    256n104, 267n36

Saint Pauls: 234n74
Sala, George Augustus: 158–59, 264n22
Sargeant, John Singer: 178–79
Saturday Review: 156, 174, 180, 184
Saunders and Otley: 61
Schaffer, Talia: 181, 204, 207–8, 273n128
Schellenberg, Betty A.: 4, 19, 225n1, 227n24
Scots Observer (later National Observer): 8, 58,
    176, 178–82, 185, 190, 193, 201, 219, 268n41,
    268n44, 278n70
Scott, Sarah: 4
Scott, Walter: 3, 13, 34, 36, 38, 42, 50, 56–57,
    71–75, 87, 89, 100, 107, 136, 143, 226n13
Scott, William Bell: 116
Scribner's Monthly: 220
Scrope, George Poulett: 91
Seeley, Tracy: 204, 272nn106, 108
Séverine, Madame de: 58

Seville, Catherine: 2, 35, 233n68
Sharpe's London Magazine: 134
Shattock, Joanne: 123, 155, 173, 261n86, 262n1
Shelley, Mary: 33, 227n20, 232n45
Shelley, Percy: 69, 73, 89, 181, 182
Sheridan, Richard: 4
Sherwood, Mary Martha: 76–77, 80–81,
    244n62
Showalter, Elaine: 131, 149, 207–8, 218–19,
    233, 278n65
Siddal, Lizzie: 121
Sisters in Art: 7, 121–125, 217
Skeet, Charles (publisher): 158, 161, 164
Smiles, Samuel: 43, 149
Smith, Adam: 84–85, 94
Smith, Barbara Leigh: See Bodichon,
    Barbara Leigh Smith.
Smith, Charlotte: 4
Smith, Elder (publisher): 39, 61, 65, 132, 138,
    145, 147–48, 156, 161
Smith, Elizabeth: 64
Smith, George: 131, 132, 137–38, 142, 144–45,
    147–50
Smith, Margaret: 147–48, 257n18
Smulders, Sharon: 204, 273n131, 274n140
Society of Authors: 5, 49–53, 152–53, 162–63,
    175, 238nn125–26
Society of British Authors: 41, 44, 49, 123,
    236n97
Southey, Robert: 13, 14, 35–36, 89, 136, 252n50
Spectator: 174, 186, 216–17, 262n2
St. James's Magazine: 152, 158, 161, 264n29
St. John, Judith: 253n62
Staël, Madame de (Anne-Louise-Germaine
    Necker): 133
Stannard, Henrietta (John Strange
    Winter): 50
Staves, Susan: 227n18
Stetz, Margaret: 276n36
Stevenson, Robert Louis: 178, 180, 239n144
Stowe, Harriet Beecher: 58
Strebrnik, Patricia: 152, 157, 262n1
Strickland, Agnes and Elizabeth: 98
Stubbs, Patricia: 278n54
Sturgis, Howard: 210
Sully, James: 201–2
Sutherland, John: 240n158, 264n20

288